THE ORIGINS OF
GREEK RELIGION

Also available or forthcoming as IGNIBUS Paperbacks

Clio's Cosmetics, T.P. Wiseman
Euripides the Rationalist, A.W. Verrall (Introduction by P. Burian)
The Authoress of the Odyssey, S. Butler (Introduction by T. Whitmarsh)
Aeschylus' Supplices: *The Play and the Trilogy*, A.F. Garvie
Rome and the Unification of Italy, A. Keaveney

THE ORIGINS OF GREEK RELIGION

B.C. Dietrich

An IGNIBUS Paperback
BRISTOL PHOENIX PRESS

Cover illustration: based on a terracotta figurine
from the shrine at Karphi in Crete, *ca* 1100 BCE

First published in 1974 by Walter de Gruyter & Co. Berlin
Reprinted 2004 by
Bristol Phoenix Press
PO Box 2142
BRISTOL
BS99 7TS

© 1. Auflage 1973, by Walter de Gruyter GmbH & Co. KG, Berlin.

All rights reserved. No part of this publication
may be reproduced, stored in a retrieval system, or
transmitted, in any form or by any means, electronic,
mechanical, photocopying, recording or otherwise,
without prior permission of the publisher.

A catalogue record for this book is available
from the British Library.

ISBN 1-904675-31-X

BRISTOL PHOENIX PRESS
Reed Hall • Streatham Drive
Exeter • EX4 4QR • UK
uep@exeterpress.co.uk • www.exeterpress.co.uk

Printed in England by Booksprint

Πολλὰ δ' ἂν καὶ ἄλλα τις ἀποδείξειε τὸ παλαιὸν Ἑλληνικὸν ὁμοιότροπα τῷ νῦν βαρβαρικῷ διαιτώμενον.

Thucydides, I, 6.

CONTENTS

PREFACE IX
ABBREVIATIONS ....
I. BEGINNINGS IN THE EAST 1– 68
II. SOME OLDER TRADITIONS IN MINOAN CRETE .. 69–127
III. A MYCENAEAN GODDESS OF NATURE 128–190
IV. THE PROBLEM OF CONTINUITY IN THE DARK AGE 191–289
    Append. I: MINOAN PEAK CULTS IN CRETAN THOUGHT 290–307
    Append. II: APOLLO AT DELPHI 308–309
    Append. III: GREEK MYTHOLOGY IN THE MYCENAEAN AGE 310–314
BIBLIOGRAPHY 315–321
INDICES 321–345

PREFACE

In writing about the origins of Greek religion I have tried to fill a gap which is evident in many histories of the subject. Much has been said about the nobility of the classical Greek gods and their cults, but, with few exceptions, it is possible to detect in such accounts a certain reluctance to accept that Greek religion owed much to prehistoric and foreign sources. Of course, the picture of Bronze Age Greece, Crete and the Aegean in general is not complete and caution is advisable in dealing with the occasionally fragmentary evidence. This is unfortunate but should not be regarded as an insurmountable barrier to a careful attempt at placing classical Greek religion in its proper context, that is, linking it with what had gone before. A good deal of our information about the Greek Bronze Age is, and probably always will be, uncertain and open to a variety of interpretations. There is accordingly no place for any claims for a definitive history of the period but this does not mean that we should refuse to work with the many rich areas of evidence that have become available from recent archaeological and linguistic discoveries.

Religion has always been the most conservative force which binds together a society through political vicissitudes and times of natural disaster. Many aspects of classical Greek religion, many rites, cultic practices, many festivals and gods suggest the survival of inherited traditions, the continuation of divine figures and beliefs through centuries of diverse fortunes. We should then be gravely at fault, if we were to ignore what is known of the antecedents of fifth century thought. In fact a good number of cult localities, and divinities associated with them, endured across the void of the Dark Age, that is the period immediately following the end of the Bronze Age. The remarkable feature of the Bronze and Dark Age periods is the continuous steady growth of evidence which therefore inevitably outruns any publication. It is hoped, however, that new discoveries will tend to fill gaps in this book and further illuminate some obscure areas rather than contradict my conclusions.

Without doubt the study of the Minoan and Mycenaean civilizations is central to an assessment of developing Greek religion, if we are to avoid the common fallacy that the collapse of the Bronze Age world and the ensuing Dark Age marked the watershed of Greek culture. Admittedly the Minoan evidence is almost exclusively of an archaeological nature, a picture-book without words, while many of the Mycenaean texts are still beset by severe problems. If, in a seemingly growing chorus of protest, I do extensively use the Linear B texts in my endeavour to establish cultural links between the classical and prehistoric worlds, I do so with my eyes open to the dangers of misinterpretation but with firm belief in the soundness of the decipherment. Also these tablets, archaeology and myth apart, constitute a valuable, and occasionally our only, source for proving the survival of, amongst other things, divine and human nomenclature.

The second edition of Nilsson's great work on *Minoan-Mycenaean Religion and its Survival in Greek Religion* appeared in 1950, and the discoveries of the past twenty years, while in no way diminishing the value of the book, have made some changes and additions necessary. His chapter on prehistoric Indo-European migration in the mainland of Greece particularly is now out of date. Our knowledge of such popular movements has increased enough to make no longer tenable any assumptions of large scale *en bloc* migrations of people within a narrowly defined time limit. Whenever the first Greek-speaking people may have arrived on the mainland, it seems certain that they did not come in neatly spaced waves of entire new racial groups supplanting and obliterating existing local cultures. One penalty of our increasing, but still incomplete, knowledge in this field is, of course, the growing complexity of the problem of Indo-European arrival, and in a way we are now worse off than we were at the time of more convenient comprehensive theories. But perhaps the most significant advance in knowledge during the last two decades concerns a fuller understanding of Greece's debt to the East: cultural ties, which existed between the Greek mainland and Asia in the Neolithic period, were never entirely severed during the Bronze Age. Also the theocratic structure of the Minoan and Mycenaean city had much in common with comparable Oriental set-ups, in such a way, however, that the relationship was probably one of interdependence rather than slavish imitation by the West of Near Eastern practices. All these factors had an obvious impact on the religion of the Bronze Age, so that we may learn about the inadequately documented beliefs of Crete and Mycenaean Greece from the full Oriental literature and are in a position to explain some religious features which endured and were ultimately inherited by the classical Greeks. There were many strands linking Greece with Eastern centres like Anatolia, Syria, Mesopotamia and Egypt: we may be unsure of the direct route of transmission, if indeed there was only one, but can no longer dispute the fact that such borrowing occurred over a large time span.

These points of contact I have explored in the first chapter which, however, attempts to show not only Greek dependence on the East but especially the extent to which such borrowed material was remoulded and given an individual, peculiarly Greek, flavour. The second chapter is devoted to an examination of some Neolithic Anatolian cult observances which, in my opinion, help to throw light on Minoan cult (particularly cave cult) and cultic objects. In this discussion I am deeply indebted to the brilliant work of J. Mellaart at centres like Çatal Hüyük and Haçilar which, despite the chronological gap, may well have served as models of Cretan practice. The Minoan evidence suggests that a good many of such early religious beliefs were transferred to the palace during the Middle Minoan period. The interplay of Minoan and Mycenaean culture then forms the subject of the third chapter which also deals with the gradual evolution of individual deities and their particular functions. The fourth, and longest, chapter attempts to bridge the gap of the Dark Age. The problems involved in this ill-documented period are legion and familiar to all Greek historians. This was no doubt a time of poverty and hardship on the mainland; but the absence of tangible evidence is no proof of a true historical and political lacuna. More important still: our lack of sources for the Dark Age does not entitle us to assume a complete break between Bronze Age and Archaic Greece, as if historical Greek culture had risen like a phoenix from the ashes or had begun only in the course of the eighth and seventh centuries. Such a conclusion would, in my opinion, be most unreasonable and leave unexplained so much of surviving tradition in the classical age. The difficult question, how, in a scattered post-Mycenaean society, any aspect of earlier culture could have endured, is best answered by the tenacious survival of particular cult localities where essentially the same gods were revered by succeeding generations of worshippers whose basic tribal structure, of which there remains some indication in the Mycenaean documents, weathered the storms of the ending Bronze Age and continued into Archaic times. It is surprising, too, how few of the early Greek monumental remains, art and architectural forms can be considered as revolutionary in the sense that they had no antecedents in previous ages. Some relevant problems, arising from the main discussion in the text, are dealt with in separate appendices on Minoan peak cult and on Apollo at Delphi. The third appendix attempts to vindicate Nilsson's view, which he presented in the 1932 Sather Classical Lectures, that the most important Greek myths were formulated during the Mycenaean Age. This position has been sharply attacked in recent years, notably by L. Banti, and it seemed timely to examine anew whether Nilsson's conclusions of four decades ago need to be fundamentally reassessed.

This book was conceived in the course of teaching Greek religion to university students and born after years of effort devoted to illustrating that the development of this religion was a slow and continuous process. Far from wishing to belittle the achievment of the classical Greek genius, I trust, if anything, to have added to its lustre by showing the early beginnings from which arose the splendid religious institutions of the fifth century. The study of prehistoric religion in Greece and the Aegean involves a variety of disciplines in some of which, like Near Eastern language and literature, I have had to rely on the conclusions of experts in the field. It will also be obvious that I have heavily drawn from archaeological as well as linguistic research and reports. To bring these various strands together into one more or less continuous whole is not an easy task, and I ask the reader's pardon if, in a fairly vast subject, I have concentrated on some salient points in my account without attempting to fill in all the details where this seemed impossible. I apologize, too, if at times I appear to have been more dogmatic than the limited evidence allows. In my approach to the subject I have tried to follow Nilsson's model, for he has been, as it were, my spiritual guide and to his memory I wish to dedicate this book.

I could not hope to thank adequately all my colleagues who have helped me through discussion, correspondence and critically reading drafts of the manuscript. All these have often and freely given me their expert advice and saved me from numerous embarrassing errors. I owe a particular debt of gratitude to V. R. d'A. Desborough, M. S. F. Hood, R. F. Willetts, P. Warren, H. Herter, W. Burkert and Lord William Taylour who have done a very great deal to contribute to what merit the text may possess. I am also deeply grateful for the generous hospitality and kind support afforded me by the British School of Archaeology at Athens and by the London Institute of Classical Studies which I have come to regard as a home from home. Finally I should like to thank the Walter DeGruyter Verlag for their interest, assistance, and extremely careful preparation of the manuscript for press. Of course, mistakes which remain in the text are entirely due to my own oversight. I regret the occasional variation in the spelling of Greek proper names and toponyms. It seems that absolute consistency in these matters proved an impossible goal.

Two important books on the archaeology of the Greek Dark Age by Dr. A. M. Snodgrass and Mr. V. Desborough appeared too late to be taken into account by the present study. My conclusions would have remained unaltered, I think, but there is fresh evidence and there are many valuable discussions which should have been included in the pages of this book.

Grahamstown, 1972

ABBREVIATIONS

Periodicals

A. C.	=	Acta Classica
Aeg. N. E.	=	Aegean and Near East (1956)
A. J. A.	=	American Journal of Archaeology
A. kl. A.	=	Anzeiger der klassischen Altertumswissenschaft
A. M.	=	Mitteilungen des deutschen archaeologischen Instituts, Athenische Abteilung.
Ant.	=	Antiquity
Ant. Ab.	=	Antike und Abendland
Ant. Cl.	=	L'Antiquité Classique
Anz.	=	Archaeologischer Anzeiger
Anz. Öst.	=	Anzeiger der Österreichischen Akademie der Wissenschaften
A. Or.	=	Archiv Orientalni
Arch.	=	Archaeology
Arch. Hom.	=	Archaiologia Homerica (1964)
ARW	=	Archiv für Religionswissenschaft
A. S.	=	Journal of Anatolian Studies
A. S. I.	=	Annuario della Scuola Archeologica di Atene
ASozEth	=	Archiv für Soziologie und Ethik, Griechisches für neugriechische Gesellschafts- und Geistesgeschichte
Ath.	=	Athenaeum
B. C. H.	=	Bulletin de Correspondence Hellénique
BICS	=	Bulletin of the Institute of Classical Studies
B. J. R.	=	Bulletin of the John Rylands Library
Boll. d'Arte	=	Bolletino d'Arte del Ministero della Pubblica Instruzione
B. S. A.	=	Annual of the British School of Archaeology at Athens
B. soc. L.	=	Bulletin Societé de Lettres de Lund
Bull. Met. Mus.	=	Bulletin of the Metropolitan Museum of Art
C. H. M.	=	Cahier d'Histoire Mondiale
C. J.	=	Classical Journal
Cl. Med.	=	Classica et Mediaevalia
C. Ph.	=	Classical Philology
C. R.	=	Classical Review
Deltion	=	Archaiologikon Deltion

ABBREVIATIONS

Eph. Arch.	= Archaiologike Ephemeris
Epig.	= Epigraphica
Er.	= Eranos
Ergon	= to Ergon tes Archaiologikes Hetaireias
Et. C.	= Études Crétoises
G.	= Glotta
Gn.	= Gnomon
G. R.	= Greece and Rome
Gym	= Gymnasium
H.	= Historia
He	= Hermes
Hell.	= Hellenika
Hesp.	= Hesperia
H. T. R.	= Harvard Theological Review
H. Z.	= Historische Zeitschrift
I. L. N.	= Illustrated London News
Ind. F.	= Indogermanische Forschungen
Jahrb.	= Jahrbuch des deutschen archaeologischen Instituts
J. C. S.	= Journal of Cuneiform Studies
J. H. S.	= Journal of Hellenic Studies
J. N. E. S.	= Journal of Near Eastern Studies
J. W. C. I.	= Journal of the Warburg and Courtauld Institutes
K.	= Kadmos
K. Ch.	= Kretika Chronika
Kl. F.	= Kleinasiatische Forschungen
L.	= Lustrum
M.	= Minos
Mem. L.	= Memorie dei Lincei
M. H.	= Museum Helvetikum
M. H. K.	= Mitteilungen über Höhlen- und Karstforschungen, Berlin 1928
Mnem.	= Mnemosyne
Mon. Ant.	= Monumenti antichi pubblicati per cara della Reale Academia dei Lincei
MusIt	= Museo Italiano di Antichità Classica
N.	= Numen
Öst. Jahr.	= Jahreshefte des Österreichischen archäologischen Instituts
Öst. M.	= Österreichische Mitteilungen
Op. Ath.	= Acta Instituti Atheniensis Regni Sueciae: Opuscula Atheniensia

PCPS	= Proceedings of the Cambridge Philological Society
P. d. P.	= La Parola del Passato
Phil.	= Philologus
Praktika	= Praktika tes en Athenais Archaiologikes Hetaireias
Préh.	= Préhistoire
ProcPS	= Proceedings of the Prehistoric Society
R. A.	= Revue Archéologique
R. Et. A.	= Revue des Études Anciennes
R. F.	= Rivista di Filologia
R. M.	= Rheinisches Museum für Philologie
R. Phil.	= Revue de Philologie
R. R.	= The Review of Religion
S.	= Saeculum
Sitzb.	= Sitzungsberichte der preußischen Akademie der Wissenschaften
St. G.	= Studium Generale
St. Urb.	= Studia Urbinati
Symb. Osl.	= Symbolae Osloenses
T. A. D.	= Turk Arkeologi Dergisi
T. A. P. A.	= Transactions of the American Philological Association
T. Ph. Soc.	= Transactions of the Philological Society
T. P. R.	= Town Planning Review
Z. Ass.	= Zeitschrift für Assyrologie

Publications

ANET	= Ancient Near Eastern Texts Relating to the Old Testament, J. B. Pritchard ed., second edition, Princeton 1955
VIIArcCon(I)	= Atti del VII Congresso Internazionale di Archeologia Classica I (1961)
Asine	= Asine: Results of the Swedish Excavations, Stockholm 1938
Auck. Cl. Ess.	= Auckland Classical Essays Presented to E. M. Blaiklock (B. F. Harris, ed), Auckland 1970
C. A. H.²	= Cambridge Ancient History, revised edition
VIIIConHRel.	= (Contributions to the General Theme of the VIII International Congress for the History of Religions, Rome April 1955), Essays presented to R. Pettazzoni, Leiden 1959
IConMyc.	= Atti e Memorie del 1° Congresso Internazionale di Micenologia (Sept.–Oct. 1967), Rome 1968
VIConPre.	= Atti del VI Congresso Internazionale delle Scienze Preistoriche e Protoistoriche, Rome 1962

ABBREVIATIONS XVII

XIConScHist	= *Rapports du XIe Congrès International des Sciences Historiques*, Stockholm 1960
IICrCon	= *Acta of 2nd International Cretan Congress*, Athens 1968
Délos primitive	= Gallet de Santerre, *Délos primitive et archaïque*
Ex. arch. D.	= *Exploration archéologique de Délos*
Gesch.	= Nilsson, *Geschichte der griechischen Religion*
L. M.	= Desborough, *The Last Mycenaeans and their Successors*
L. & Sc. J.	= Liddell & Scott, *Greek English Lexicon*, revised by H. Stuart-Jones, 1940
Min. H.	= *Minoica und Homer*, Berlin 1961
Minoica	= *Minoica, Festschrift J. Sundwall*, Berlin 1958
M. M. R.	= Nilsson, *Minoan-Mycenaean Religion*
P. M.	= A. Evans, *The Palace of Minos at Knossos*
Proc. Myc. St.	= *Proceedings of the Cambridge Colloquium on Mycenaean Studies*, Cambridge 1966
P.-W.	= A. Pauly, G. Wissowa and W. Kroll, *Realencyclopaedie der klassischen Altertumswissenschaft*
RGVV	= *Religionsgeschichtliche Versuche und Vorarbeiten*
RoscherML	= W. H. Roscher, *Ausführliches Lexikon der griechischen und römischen Mythologie*
StudsRob.	= *Studies presented to D. M. Robinson*, Washington 1951
Studs. Gold.	= *Studies H. Goldman*, New York 1956
Sub. St.	= Styrenius, *Submycenaean Studies*

I. BEGINNINGS IN THE EAST

One classical scholar wrote earlier this century that the Greeks were the most religious of all people[1]. This judgment probably did not intend to suggest that the Greeks spent more time than others in cultic ceremony, or that their worship was more devout. Neither claim could easily be justified. The truth of this remark lies rather in the fact that many of the finest products of Greek culture, like their architecture, sculpture and dramatic art, derived from religious practice which was at once deeply felt and singularly free from superstitious fear or narrow traditional ritual observance. It follows, therefore, that to understand the Greek genius it is necessary to appreciate as far as possible the religious beliefs that gave form to it.

The study of Greek religion which confines itself to the Classical and Hellenistic periods alone cannot bear fruit, for the Greeks, like other peoples, did not conceive their religious ideas in a vacuum. Greek religion was not suddenly devised in the sixth or fifth centuries B. C. as a perfect system which could satisfy the spiritual needs of all citizens. To think thus means to lose perspective: to be carried along uncertain routes on a wave of philhellenic emotion. Within the last hundred years or so the horizons of scholars have widened enough to admit more light on questions of religious origins and development. Even these new boundaries at times seem narrow for our purposes, and we must make certain that our work takes full account of fresh evidence as it continually appears from the fields of archaeology and philology. Nothing can be gained by a fond belief in the original power of the Greeks to create from nothing a system of divinity and ritual with its attendant mythology[2]. On the contrary, what gave Greek religion its strength was the ability not only to syncretise the beliefs of other peoples, but to shape such beliefs in fresh ways which resulted in the splendid form we find in the fifth century.

---

[1] U. v. Wilamowitz-Möllendorff, *D. Glaube d. Hellenen*³, Darmstadt 1959, I, e.g. 42 f.
[2] Cf. R. Pettazzoni, *Essays on the Hist. of Religions*, 69.

One must also bear in mind that any religion which hopes to capture popular imagination and endure for any length of time must make use of older and existing beliefs, such as had been acceptable to every worshipper for many generations. To a large extent Greek religion observed this rule, so that the picture of official belief and religious practice we find in the fifth century *polis* owed a number of facets to older traditions. If men's faith in public cult was fading at the period, we should seek the reasons for this decline partly in the influence of Homeric epic on the development of state religion, and partly in the fact that the aspects of the gods revered in this cult seemed to appeal only to a section of the city-state: the ruling classes. But this is another story which does not fall within the province of this chapter.

Where should a history of Greek religion begin? A reasonable point would seem to be the time when the Mycenaeans, who are generally admitted to be the ancestors of the Greeks, created their civilization on the mainland. They were an Indo-European people whose cults and gods, after fusion with earlier religious practices on the mainland, might have produced the chief aspects of Classical Greek religion. Continuity of Mycenaean into Greek culture and thought has still to be established, and this problem will occupy us in the third and fourth chapters of this book. But there are other more immediate problems to be considered concerning the origin and identity of these "first Greeks".

The two kinds of sources which could be expected to provide some information about such questions are archaeological and linguistic. It is disappointing therefore that experts in both fields are still a long way from agreeing on essential points of Early Bronze Age migration into Greece and on the dating of a possible or even probable cultural break. If cultural continuity, as we shall see, can be demonstrated beyond the end of the Bronze Age on archaeological grounds, the same continuity stretches backward in time perhaps as far as the Neolithic period. However, some archaeological features which become noticeable in Greece at the end of the Early Bronze Age, that is Early Helladic[3], and which mark the transition to Middle Helladic at about 1900 B.C. suggest that this could have been the crucial period of the Indo-European arrival on the mainland. Such features include the destruction of older settlements, like Eutresis in Central

---

[3] For discussions of Bronze Age chronology see e.g. W. C. Hayes, M. B. Rowton, F. H. Stubbings, "Chronology. Egypt; Western Asia; Aegean Bronze Age", *C. A. H.*[2], 1962, Lord W. Taylour, *The Mycenaeans*, ch. 2; F. Schachermeyr, *Die minoische Kultur des alten Kreta*, ch. 4; T. B. L. Webster, *From Mycenae to Homer*[2], xvf.

Greece[4], the foundation of new settlements, the expansion of cist-grave burials, and the "systematization of the megaron-type of houses"[5]. At the same time the so-called Grey Minyan Ware began to appear throughout Greece, and this distinctive type of pottery was naturally coupled with the arrival from the north of invading Indo-European tribes together with their culture and religion[6]. But no single item on this list is entirely novel, in the sense that it possessed no forerunners in previous periods, so that inevitably some doubt attaches to the theory of a mainland invasion by an Indo-European or any other race at the beginning of Middle Helladic. The evidence of the Minyan pottery especially has recently been questioned, because, far from being a foreign import, it could well have been developed in Central and Southern Greece[7]. In any case the diffusion of this ware in Greece at the time might be explained by the popularity of a new fashion, a technological innovation, which was locally devised[8].

It can be said, therefore, that there are no convincing archaeological grounds for supposing an invasion of Greece in Early Helladic III[9]. It is possible, of course, that migratory movements into this region left no recognizable archaeological traces; but this is a dangerous and unworkable argument. It seems best then to abandon the belief in a large scale incursion accompanied by a clear and sudden cultural break. Although the linguistic evidence points to the introduction of Indo-European languages during this

---

[4] Evidence in M. S. F. Hood, "Northern Penetration of Greece at the End of E. H. III". This paper, and some of the others cited in this context, was presented at the Colloquium on Bronze Age Migrations in the Aegean Region, held at the University of Sheffield from 23rd–26th March 1970. All these papers will be collectively published in the near future.

[5] S. Marinatos, "The First Mycenaeans in Greece", Sheff. Coll.

[6] See e.g. Schachermeyr, P.-W., XXII, 1489 ff.; *Griechische Geschichte*, Stuttgart 1960, 38 f.; *A. kl. A.* 19, 1, Vienna 1966; J. L. V. Caskey, "Greece and the Aegean Islands in the Middle Bronze Age", *C. A. H.*^{2}, 1966, with further references; Taylour, *Mycen.* 22 ff.; V. Ehrenberg, *From Solon to Socrates*, London 1968, 3; 377 n. 7, for some general histories of the period. A much later date for the arrival of Greek speakers (13th cent. BC) is suggested by Hood, *The Home of the Heroes*, 126.

[7] E.g. D. H. French, "Migrations and Minyan Pottery in Western Anatolia and the Aegean", Sheff. Coll.

[8] J. Bouzek, "Bronze Age Greece and the Balkans: problems of migrations", Sheff. Coll.

[9] This is not to exclude the possibility that more evidence may eventually come to light. Cf. the arrival (at the end of E. H. II) of "Anatolian" type pottery in Hagia Eirene on Keos, Lefkandi, Euboea, and some mainland regions, together perhaps with Eastern cultural elements, Caskey, "The Early Bronze Age at Ayia Irini in Keos", *Arch.* 23, 4 (1970) 432.

period, this was an infiltration rather than an invasion. The origin of such Indo-European elements is uncertain, but Anatolia remains a candidate; for there is cultural similarity between early Troy VI and Middle Helladic Greece[10]; it is possible that the "pre-Greek" -nth-, -ss- place names existed in Anatolia; and cultural contact between that part of the world and the Greek mainland is evident in archaeological finds from as early as Neolithic. Those who continue to accept the theory that the first Greeks arrived on the mainland at the beginning of Middle Helladic[11] will draw comfort also from the fact that this is the approximate date when the Hittites, another Indo-European group of people, came to Asia Minor, and a new population took possession of Troy[12].

In sum, the foregoing discussion illustrates the great difficulty of precise dating for this period. Migration on a large scale at the time becomes an unlikely theory, and it seems advisable to work on the assumption that Indo-European elements could have been present in Greece for much of Early Helladic. It has even been suggested that Indo-European languages were spoken in Greece before the beginning of the Bronze Age, indeed, one scholar asks why we should not "think of the Greeks as autochthonous, present in Greece perhaps since the late Pleistocene"[13]. Against such extreme views one should set the evidence of a clash between two non-identical religious strata represented on one hand by a kind of elemental nature cult centred on fertility and the recurring cycle of nature with a type of Mother Goddess as its focal point, and the Indo-European Weather-god on the other. Therefore, even although it is impossible, beyond the broadest outline, to rely on linguistic and archaeological evidence in order to discover a point of time when Greek religion began to envolve, we may believe the Early Bronze Age to have witnessed cultural changes whose effect survived into Classical times. But it is also important to recognize that such a development was a gradual coming into being, a syncretising of diverse elements, to give the appearance almost of an historical continuum which stretched backwards in time beyond the Bronze Age. Yet, Greek religion, largely the result of internal development occurring within its own borders, was

---

[10] J. G. Macqueen, "Geography and History in Western Asia Minor in the second millennium B. C.", *A. S.* 18 (1968) 184. See also n. 9.
[11] E.g. Marinatos, "The First Mycen. in Greece".
[12] G. S. Kirk, *The Songs of Homer*, 17.
[13] C. Renfrew, "Difficulties in General Correlation of Archaeological and Linguistic Strata in Greece", D. H. French, "Migration and Minyan Pottery in Western Anatolia and the Aegean", Sheff. Coll.

dependent, as well, on outside influence and ready to absorb new ideas particularly from more advanced cultures to the south and east of Greece. In other words, the history of the beginnings of Greek religion during the Bronze Age is in some measure an account of Greece's debt to Eastern thought.

There is some evidence for cultural contact between Greece and the East from as early as the Neolithic period. This will be considered presently. Through this kind of link the Greek mainland at the time quite probably shared with a wide Aegean area a common belief in the efficacy of vegetation cult associated with a fertile Mother Goddess. But above we mentioned a clash between such cultic practice and the worship of the Indo-European Weather-god who survived to become the supreme deity of the Classical Greek Olympian family. The name Zeus is an Indo-European word whose etymology probably means "Sky-God", like the Latin *deus*[14]. This figure of the Weather- or Sky-God the Greeks shared with other Indo-European peoples like the Indians, Illyrians, and Romans, and his function in the Bronze Age Minoan and mainland religious context suggests not only his early arrival on the Greek scene, but also the presence of an Indo-European element in what might possibly have been a common Aegean religious substrate. Needless to say, such a clean division between a common Aegean and Indo-European cult is an over-simplification of rather more complex religious processes whose separate stages are no longer apparent. But Zeus remains the one identifiable Indo-European contribution to Greek religion who may be connected with the Indo-European Mycenaean culture. Although, as has been noticed, their forefathers may have been in Greece during the Early Bronze Age already, the Mycenaeans as an apparently unified cultural and political force did not come into prominence until about 1600 B. C., that is, approximately at the end of Middle Helladic. Then the Mycenaean world embraced much of the Peloponnese to Pylos, it reached southward to Crete, and to Attica on the mainland, as well as to the Boeotian cities of Thebes and Orchomenus, and even as far north as southern Thessaly. Whatever previous acquaintance with the East the Mycenaeans enjoyed, they showed sufficient enterprise to explore a wide area of the eastern Mediterranean and the Near East. Archaeologists have found their distinctive pottery in Cyprus, Rhodes, in parts of northern Syria, and at Miletus in Asia Minor. Egyptian and Hittite records afford

---

[14] M. P. Nilsson, *Gesch.* I, 336; 390 f.; R. Pettazzoni, *La Religione nella Grecia antica* 15.

evidence of Archaean contact with those nations, while the Homeric story of the siege of Troy reveals Archaean activity in northern Anatolia.

If these Mycenaeans, or rather their ancestors, did in fact bring with them their own cults and in particular the figure of Father Zeus, then we should probably distinguish between an early period of contact in Early Helladic with indigenous beliefs shaped through Eastern influence, and another subsequent period extending roughly through Late Helladic when the Mycenaean world as a great political power was connected with the East by means of trade and settlement. A geographically close link with the East, especially with north-west Anatolian cultures, was the island of Crete[15] which came within the Mycenaean ambit no later than about 1450 B.C., this being the approximate date of, among other features, the Linear B tablets found at Knossos, the introduction of new pottery styles, and of a Mycenaean type of stone carving[16].

The great significance of the Mycenaean adventure ist that, together with linguistic unity, it may have spread and imposed some similar cultural and religious forms on the mainland and parts of Crete during most of the Late Bronze Age. In the field of religion, at least some of the uniform gods and cults were destined to survive the collapse of Mycenaean civilization and to continue into historical times, thereby demonstrating the strength of these early forms. These from the beginning probably contained Eastern elements, the fruit of the first contact already mentioned. However, to define any sort of proportion in such a mixture, beyond that outlined above, involves the knowledge both of the ultimate origin of the Indo-European Greeks and of the gods and cults which belonged only to them; and this knowledge we do not possess. All that one can hope to establish is that a meeting of differing religious concepts did actually occur in the Bronze Age and that Classical Greek religion eventually emerged from this process. But the main purpose of this discussion is to show that for much of the Bronze Age the principal and senior partner in any religious alliance on the mainland was the East, the source which produced some basic cultural material. The subject of Oriental influence on the Western Aegean is vast, its ramifications extending to art, architecture, and literature. These we can only touch on, but wish to concern ourselves with some aspects of religion which proved significant to its subsequent development. Such aspects include what

---

[15] On these Eastern links with Crete see now P. Warren, "Crete, 2300 B.C.–1400 B.C. Immigration and the Archaeological Evidence", Sheff. Coll.
[16] *Op. cit.*

has already been called a kind of religious substrate consisting in vegetation cult and the associated Mother Goddess, with both of which the Indo-Europeans, or the ancestors of the Greeks, came into contact in the Early Bronze Age, the introduction to the West, probably during the period of Mycenaean expansion in Late Helladic, of certain theogonical motifs and of associated myths, the idea of kingship in a theocratic society, and the relationship between gods and men.

Literary evidence for the Bronze Age is lacking in Greece. The Linear B tablets have only limited use for our purposes, for the names of gods which appear on them tell us little beyond the fact that they were known to the Mycenaeans in the fifteenth and fourteenth centuries. This is important in another context to be treated in later chapters, but can partly be gathered from our earliest Greek literary source: the Homeric *Iliad* and *Odyssey* which to some extent describe the Mycenaean society of this period. But these epics were recorded much later, in the Dark Age, probably before the sixth, but certainly not before the eighth century when the Greeks had devised their alphabet from Phoenician letters. Whatever the name of the poet or poets, who gave form to the *Iliad* and *Odyssey*, we are told that the actual writing down occurred at the end of a long oral tradition when epic language and metre had reached a high standard of perfection. After the disturbance on the Greek mainland, the minstrels who composed the original lays, in all likelihood, followed the migrations to Asia[17]. Thus their songs, though they dealt with events in the Mycenaean Age, contained numerous anachronisms like the practice of cremation[18] and reference to iron in a Bronze Age society[19]. Such points, and more, are instances of different historical levels of belief which can be found side by side in Homer, and which occasionally fuse or overlap. Nonetheless the *Iliad* and *Odyssey* constitute a helpful source of evidence for the careful researcher who can separate out memories of Eastern belief that might already have been alien and obscure to the poet. The most striking example in this connection is Homer's knowledge of a divine genealogical structure which ultimately derived from the East[20].

The Homeric poets were vigorously opposed to traditions which ran counter to the Mycenaean picture of the Olympian gods, so that we find

---

[17] Cf. e.g. Pettazzoni, *Relig.* 46 f.
[18] See esp. H. L. Lorimer, *Homer and the Monuments*, 103 ff.; *J. H. S.* 53 (1933) 161 ff.
[19] Pettazzoni, *Rel.* 44; Lorimer, *Homer* 117–21.
[20] See below n. 213.

scant mention of popular or chthonic elements like the Hesiodic figure of *Gaia* (Earth). Yet it is such elements which formed the religious substrate that left its mark not only on the indigenous Greek inhabitants but also on the people of Crete, and which was to a large extent assimilated in Mycenaean religious practice.

From at least the later periods of the Stone Age, ideas of fertility of vegetation and men were current in the settlements about and near the Aegean. This religious concept may have been universally shared by primitive cultures but more probably took its origin in the Near and Middle East, the birth place of the first human civilization, whence it radiated outward. The reason for the Eastern origin of organized communities lies in the fact that it was this part of the world which first saw the change from what scholars named the food-gathering stage of society – an unsettled, nomadic existence – to that of food-producing society[21]. The change involved the introduction of agriculture and with it the building of walled cities, inhabited by settled groups paying obeisance to a type of fertility Mother Goddess – in the widest sense – who played the predominant part in their religious life. In the East these developments, associated with the "Neolithic Revolution", began to appear as early as 9000 B. C.[22], and they precipitated the evolution of new skills within the community. The most important of these was to be the working of metal which gradually replaced stone implements and vessels before the end of Neolithic and led to the Early Bronze Age.

The majority of idols from shrines and sanctuaries representing the figure of a Mother Goddess are quite explicit in their significance. Emphasis is placed on the maternal functions of the women shown often to the point of grotesqueness. They were modelled with over developed breasts, reproductive organs; even the navel at times was out of proportion to the rest of the figure. Their arms, legs, and buttocks (steatopygic) were excessively large, and they are often seen holding or pressing their breasts. In the West the first examples of this type of Mother Goddess figurine have come to light in Thessaly, Macedonia, and Southern Greece, as well as Crete[23]. Five clay idols from a sanctuary at Macedonian Nea Nikomedeia[24] may be as early as the seventh millennium. These and, for example, vases in the shape

---

[21] Schachermeyr, *min. Kultur* 13 ff.
[22] J. Mellaart, *Earliest Civilizations of the Near East*, ch. I, II.
[23] The early history of the Cycladic islands is still obscure. Mr. Hood kindly informed me that amulets and possibly female idols have been found on Neolithic Saliagos.
[24] Mellaart, *Earl. Civ.* fig. 103; Hood, *Heroes* 21 f.

of the goddess, or the clay figurine from Lerna in the Peloponnese, are reminiscent of Anatolian shapes found in important sites like Hacilar[25]. While Cretan Neolithic idols of this type remained steatopygic throughout the period, mainland examples tended to lose their more exaggerated features towards the end of the Late Stone Age. But, whatever the artistic conventions at the time, the common dedication of such female figurines in sanctuaries throughout the Aegean, Anatolia, and other parts of the East suggests the universal cult of a Mother Goddess[26]. More difficult to maintain on the evidence, but nevertheless probable, is the continuation in some form of this Eastern inspired cult in the Aegean area during the Bronze Age not only on the Greek mainland but in the islands including Crete. The archaeological evidence is not exactly strong on this point. On the contrary the number of female idols found on the Greek mainland decreases during Early Helladic and, unlike the Cycladic examples, figurines become small, stubby, with beaked faces and striped dress. Against this apparent decline of visible evidence must be set the absence of other remains which might indicate a dramatic departure from inherited religious practice[27]. Such change seems unlikely in view of the continuing cultural similarity over a wide area, including the west and eastern Aegean area, from Neolithic into the Early Bronze Age.

Crete already had her own cultural contacts with the East from Late Neolithic to the beginning of the Early Bronze Age, that is, from the end of the fourth millennium until about 2800 B.C. Cretan links were mainly with Troy I and earlier north-west Anatolian cultures, and there is some archaeological evidence of immigration into the island in this period from west Anatolia[28]. Unfortunately, no proof exists as yet of direct contact in Neolithic between Crete and south-west Anatolia, with sites like Çatal Hüyük and Hacilar, but we shall see in the next chapter the surprising similarity of some Minoan and south-west Anatolian cultic practices, so that the presence in Early Minoan of the type of Mother Goddess worship, which penetrated the mainland, is not an unreasonable assumption.

It is to be remembered that the extant evidence from Neolithic and the Early Bronze Age leaves no more than a vague impression of religious practice in the period in which clear definition in different regions is out of the question. The obviously arbitrary title of Mother Goddess is used

[25] Mellaart, *op. cit.* 117.
[26] Cf. E. Vermeule, *Greece in the Bronze Age*, 21, with more examples of figurines.
[27] This is argued by Vermeule, *op. cit.* 44.
[28] P. Warren, "Crete, 2300 B.C.–1400 B.C.", Sheff. Coll.

to describe the main figure in that type of fertility cult which in basic significance, at least, was imported to the West and which formed the substratum of later Greek religion. In a recent study of Late Stone Age figurines the connection of such female idols with cult has been questioned[29].

While it seems overly critical to insist on the secular nature of all these figures, in view of the Anatolian and related Greek evidence from shrines and sanctuaries, there are valid objections to the picture of a single and universal goddess continuing into the third and second millennium as the sole object of worship in Crete and Greece. Simplistic histories therefore of an all-embracing Mother Goddess in the Early and especially Middle Bronze Age, together with a belief in a kind of monotheism in Minoan Crete, are no longer tenable[30]. Objections to this kind of theory have been voiced, fully discussed, and need not detain us here[31]. Cretan Bronze Age idols, for example, have no obvious cultural lineage leading back to Neolithic, and by the Middle Bronze Age we can distinguish between two main groups of figures, those found (a) in sanctuaries or shrines, and (b) in graves and tombs[32]. Within the first group one should also probably make the far from easy distinction between cult idols and votive figurines. Altogether the wealth and variety of Bronze Age finds in Crete and on the mainland make it sometimes virtually impossible to separate divine from secular figurines, especially regarding the idols from tombs where we may be dealing with gifts to the dead of no particular religious significance[33], or possibly with a kind of Egyptian *oushebti,* that is a mistress or helper of the dead in the underworld[34].

By the second millennium, and possibly earlier, religion in the Western Aegean had progressed beyond a universal goddess figure: other divine aspects had become isolated and received separate worship in different localities. For this reason alone it would remain an unconvincing exercise

---

[29] P. J. Ucko, *Anthropomorphic Figurines,* e.g. 415 ff.; 434 ff.

[30] E.g. G. Glotz, *La Civilisation Égéenne,* "La déesse" 281–290; Ch. Picard, *Les Religions Préhelléniques,* 56. Also unproven is the existence of matriarchal societies in Crete and in the East; see e.g. Schachermeyr, *min. Kult.* 14; 126–8. For an anthropologist's definition of matriarchy see A. E. Jensen, *St. G.* 3 (1950) 418–33.

[31] E.g. M. P. Nilsson, *M. M. R.,* 290 ff.

[32] Practically all Cycladic figurines contemporary with Early Minoan appear to come from tombs, Nilsson, *M.M.R.* 293; Hood, *Heroes* 43 f. Recently, however, marble idols have been uncovered on Keros by C. Doumas. I owe this information to Mr. Hood.

[33] Nilsson, *op. cit.* 307.

[34] E.g. Picard, *op. cit.* 49.

to trace the conventions of Cycladic, Minoan, and mainland idols of the period in the hope of identifying representations of an early Mother Goddess[35]. However, a general vegetation cult was never entirely buried in subsequent religious development but in some form continued as an undercurrent even in cults of Classical times. The nature of a fertile Mother Goddess was firmly imprinted on the figure of Demeter for example. Traces of this old cult survived in the celebrations observed at the Eleusinian sanctuaries[36], possibly at Delphi and other sites which endured beyond the end of the Bronze Age[37], and in myth as witness the crude Baubo episode in the Homeric Hymn to Demeter[38]. In fact mythological tradition, which was preserved through continuous memory and oral transmission, could be expected to fill some gaps left by the fragmentary or ambiguous archaeological evidence.

An essential feature of this vegetation cult was the *hieros gamos* (sacred marriage), the union of the Mother Goddess with a male figure in order to ensure human fertility and the fruitfulness of the fields. Examples of this central rite have survived in Neolithic representations of *symplegmata* from Çatal Hüyük and Hacilar in Anatolia, and from Thessalian Sesklo[39]. The male was usually a subsidiary figure, an associate or *paredros* of the goddess. In the Anatolian centres just mentioned he appears either as a child or young man, or as an older bearded god[40]. He may be both son and husband to the goddess, in a relationship which left its mark on subsequent legend. Famous Oriental examples of the *Magna Mater* and her satellite are Cybele and Attis, Ishtar and Tammuz, and Aphrodite and Adonis in Phoenicia[41]. In these pairs, and compare Isis the mother and lover of Osiris in Egyptian belief[42], the young god represented the annual birth, growth

---

[35] The literature on this subject is vast, cf. Nilsson, *M. M. R.* 293 n. 12. It is interesting, however, to compare the typically upraised arms of Minoan cult idols (St. Alexiou, *K. Ch.*, 179 ff.) with the similar gesture of goddess figures scratched or moulded on vases from the East (Schachermeyr, *min. Kult.* 144 fig. 69) or found in a sanctuary at Çatal Hüyük (Mellaart, *A. S.* 13 [1963] 61 and Pl. IX a).
[36] Cf. e.g. Picard, *op. cit.* 87; 111.
[37] Cf. the nude idol from the sacred precinct at Delphi, Nilsson, *M. M. R.* 305 f. and fig. 149.
[38] *Hom. Hymn Demeter* 192 ff.; cf. Apollodorus I, 5, 1.
[39] Schachermeyr, *min. Kultur* Pl. 43; Mellaart, *A. S.* 13 (1963) Pl. 21 (d).
[40] Mellaart, *Earl. Civ.* 92 f.; 106.
[41] Nilsson, *M. M. R.* 403; P. M. Witzel, *Tammuz-Liturgien* VII; XIX.
[42] S. Morenz, *Ägyptische Religion*, Stuttgart 1960, e.g. 281.

and death of nature herself[43]. His recurring fate gave rise to a vast *corpus* of mythology – related in its essentials – which can be found throughout the East from Syria to Anatolia[44]. This religious belief, too, may have travelled to Crete and Greece, but at any rate it was so deeply rooted in popular imagination that even Homer could not ignore it but spoke of the sacred union between Demeter and Jasion that occurred in Crete[45]. The *hieros gamos* of the Anthesteria, celebrated in Athens in Spring still in Classical times, was the focal point of the three-day festival[46].

Neither Crete nor Greece preserved any literary record of a goddess and her young consort[47]. The close cultural links, however, between Greece and Crete and the Eastern world suggest that similar ideas obtained on both sides of the Aegean. The archaeological evidence is thin. Neolithic and Early Bronze Age male figurines in Crete, on the mainland, and in the islands are extremely rare. One outstanding Neolithic example of an apparently male statuette fashioned in white marble has been recovered at Knossos[48]. The fact that some have turned up in the Cyclades, usually in tombs, seems to cast doubt on their divine status. A few of the island male figures represent musicians playing a harp or flute[49], and they may be entertainers rather than gods. Male figurines become more common in the Middle and Late Bronze Age both on the mainland and in Crete. They have been recovered from caves, like Petsofa and Psychro, which witnessed cult, and from peak and domestic sanctuaries. One Mycenaean idol of a nude man was found in a large votive deposit at Hagia Triada in Crete[50]. Slightly more impressive evidence comes from Cretan and Mycenaean rings which show a figure – presumably a Mother Goddess – together with a small, young (?), male figure who may be a god, or again, as Nilsson suggests, often

---

[43] See T. H. Gaster, *Thespis*², e.g. 280 and *passim*.

[44] See esp. Gaster, *op. cit.*

[45] *Od.* 5, 125 ff.

[46] L. Deubner, *Attische Feste*, Berlin 1956, 100.

[47] Schachermeyr, *min. Kult.* 150. It has been remarked that the young male consort of the goddess was a late arrival in Crete, and that it is now impossible to establish his original connection with Eastern belief. Nilsson, *Gesch.* I, 320, sees in the young Zeus a purely Cretan development in opposition to Evan's original proposal to derive the male companion from the East, see I, 324. But see Picard, *Rel. Préh.* 117 ff., who discusses Nilsson's view. The late appearance in Crete of a male figure beside the goddess is also emphasized by A. Severyns, *Grèce et Proche-Orient* 97; 147.

[48] Hood, *Heroes* figs. 8; 9.

[49] Hood, *op. cit.* figs. 29; 30.

[50] Nilsson, *M. M. R.* 307.

merely a votary[51]. The male figure may occasionally be seen descending from above, as on a gold ring from Knossos[52], or he may be engaged in a *sacra conversazione*[53] with the goddess, if we correctly interpret a scene on an electrum ring from Mycenae[54]. He may even appear armed, floating down from the sky, as on another gold ring from Knossos[55]. A similar armed and youthful male figure appears from the sky to the goddess sitting under a tree on a famous gold ring from Mycenae[56]. By themselves, of course, these scenes can be interpreted in a variety of ways, but one should not exclude the possibility that this male figure at times represented the youthful spirit of vegetation[57]. It is another question whether there existed, as between Adonis and Aphrodite, an equally sentimental bond between the two figures in the West[58].

Our monumental evidence from Crete and Greece on its own will not explain the significance of the male child or the goddess. This inadequate source will have to be supplemented, as was already suggested, by surviving memories of mythological traditions. Greek myth in some versions suffered contamination at the hands of Euhemerist writers who were particularly concerned with interpreting traditional tales to suit their own beliefs: that is they were anxious to preserve those myths which dealt with the birth or death of any deity. Nevertheless even such late syncretistic sources can reveal the original nucleus of the legend[59]. There exists a considerable body of mythology which knew of youthful male gods in some close relationship with vegetation or nature goddess types in Crete and on the Greek mainland. Such stories were old and pointed back at least to the Mycenaean period in Greece or even to the Middle Bronze Age. In some features these myths give evidence of an alliance of Greek and Minoan belief which was based on a common religious background of both cultures. The majority of such myths followed a common pattern: the male child generally was the offspring of the Mother Goddess, or an equivalent figure, and after birth

---

[51] *M. M. R.* 295.
[52] *J. H. S.* 21 (1901) 170 fig. 48; Nilsson, *M. M. R.* 256; 344 and fig. 123; *Gesch.* I, 299. Nilsson describes the female figure as a worshipper.
[53] *P. M.* III, 456.
[54] *J. H. S.* 21 (1901) fig. 51.
[55] *Ibid.* fig. 48; Nilsson, *Gesch.* I, 299; Schachermeyr, *min. Kult.* 151.
[56] Nilsson, *Gesch.* I, Pl. 17, 1. For a discussion of these figures see also Picard, *op. cit.* 111; H. Biesantz, *Kretisch-Mykenische Siegelbilder*, 85 f.
[57] Cf. Nilsson, *Gesch.* I, 299. Biesantz, *ibid.*, doubts the interpretation of all these rings.
[58] Cf., Picard, *ibid.*
[59] Nilsson, *M. M. R.* 544.

he was nurtured not by his mother, but by lesser deities of nature like nymphs, or even by an animal like the goat. The child himself was representative of the growth of vegetation, so that in many instances he was imagined as being born and dying annually.

Professor Nilsson[60] gives a full account of all these "Divine Children" whose functions and parentage were always the same. The youthful male figure was quite often given a transparent, or "speaking", name like Plutus or Erichthonius[61], and he was ubiquitous in the entire Mediterranean area[62]. His earliest cult, however, lay in the East, whence he was imported to the mainland of Greece, and to the Western Aegean in general. Greek mythology remembered several names of such youthful companions of the nature goddess: to the list belonged the young Zeus, Hyacinthus, Erichthonius, Plutus, and Dionysus. The most startling name in this group is that of Zeus, the Indo-European god who, as we saw, was introduced to Greece from outside and whose cult was at variance with indigenous religious practice. The memory of this clash survived in the figure of Zeus Kretagenes, the youthful male destined to be born and to die each year. This mortal Zeus was utterly unlike the Greek Weather-god, and his transformation later came to earn the Cretans much censure from poets like Callimachus[63].

Let us briefly consider the story of Zeus' birth which came to be added to Greek mythology and which was first told by Hesiod. Zeus was born in a Cretan cave[64] to Kronos and Rhea who concealed the child and gave to Kronos a stone wrapped in swaddling clothes which was swallowed by the god. Gaia received the child from Rhea and carried it to the Goat Mountain in Crete, while Kronos was forced to disgorge the stone together with Zeus' brothers and sisters. This stone subsequently was set up in Delphi as an object of worship. The features which this tale has in common with general folklore were pointed out by Nilsson[65]. They consist of the baby's not being brought up by its mother but by Mother Earth (Gaia), or an equi-

---

[60] *Op. cit.* ch. XVI; *Gesch.* I, 315 ff. See also A. W. Persson, *Religion of Greece in Prehistoric Times*, 136 ff..; Picard, *op. cit.* 136 with further references.

[61] See below. p. 18.

[62] Schachermeyr, *min. Kult.* 149.

[63] *Hymn Zeus* 8. Cf. the stirring lines of the Cretan Epimenides in his poem on Minos as recorded by St. Paul.

[64] Hesiod, *Theog.* 484; Callimachus, *Hymn Zeus* 6; Ant. Liberalis, *Metam.* 19, see P. Faure, *Fonctions des Cavernes Crétoises*, 110 and notes.

[65] For the conflicting traditions concerning Zeus' Cretan birth, youth, and death, see Nilsson, *M. M. R.* 534 ff.; *Gesch.* I, 319 ff.; P. Faure, *Minoica*, 133–48; *Fonct.* 96; 110; 122; R. W. Hutchinson, *Prehistoric Crete*, 201 ff.

valent goddess, and in the fact that the infant was suckled by an animal or by a lesser deity of nature like a nymph. In the present version the foster mother was Amaltheia – either a goat or a nymph[66]. But there is evidence of other animals, or nymphs, as foster parents of the babe from coins and mostly from Hellenistic authors[67]. Understandably numerous tales came into being of Zeus' birth and early life, tales which differed in some detail but agreed on the main features mentioned above[68].

The significance of all these myths, which have as their central point the birth and nurturing of Zeus, becomes clear from the participants in the drama. These were Gaia and a nymph or animal, and the attendants of the young god, that is the Kuretes who were said to dance about the cave where Zeus lay hidden, clash their shields and swords so that the baby's cries would not reach the ears of his father. Nilsson[69] convincingly shows that these Kuretes were in fact daemons of fertility whose cult began in Crete. Antoninus Liberalis[70] tells one strange and primitive version of this birth myth which, despite its many later accretions, shows that Zeus was thought to be born anew every year. According to this version Zeus was born in Crete in a cave which he shared with a swarm of bees[71] and which neither god nor man was allowed to enter. Once each year a fire was seen to flash from the cave when the blood of Zeus' birth flowed forth. This annually reborn god of vegetation also experienced the other parts of the vegetation cycle: holy marriage and annual death when he was thought to disappear from the earth. In these respects the young Zeus' fate did not essentially differ from those of for example the Babylonian Tammuz, the Egyptian Osiris, Adonis in Syria, and Attis in Asia Minor[72].

In Hagia Triada the temple of Zeus Velchanos was built over the ruins of the palace. Coins from nearby Phaistos[73] show Velchanos as a beardless, hence young, figure sitting among the branches of a tree with a cock in his lap. In all likelihood he is to be identified with the young Zeus Kretagenes. On a number of other coins Velchanos is depicted in bird form as an eagle

---

[66] Cf. L. Preller, *Griech. Mythologie*⁴, ed. Robert, 1887, I, 35 n. 4.
[67] Such evidence is collected by Nilsson, *M. M. R.* 539 f. with notes.
[68] See Faure, *Fonct.* 121 f.
[69] *Ibid.*
[70] 19.
[71] For the significance of bees see Nilsson, *M. M. R.* 542 f.
[72] See esp. Gaster, *Thespis* Part One. Cf. M. L. West, *Hesiod Theogony*, 291.
[73] *Catal. of Coins in B. M., Crete* XV, 10.

and in association with a goddess celebrating the rite of *hieros gamos*[74]. With this holy marriage of Velchanos we should compare the design on numerous coins of a bull seen carrying a goddess reminiscent of the Europa myth[75]. That this rite of Velchanos was wide-spread on the island of Crete becomes apparent from the varied provenance of these coins and from inscriptions from Gortyn and Lyttos, which make mention of the festival Velchania[76] that was probably celebrated in Knossos[77]. The myth of Zeus' death in Crete was told in many regions, although we learn of it only from late sources like Callimachus[78]. The different localities, like Knossos, Mt. Dikte, Mt. Ida and Mt. Jouktas, the supposed sites of his tomb, illustrate the diffusion of this belief in the young god's death[79].

These tales of his birth, life and death, in fragmentary form still survived in Greek mythology. They usually centred about Crete and quite explicitly point to the nature of the god as a symbolic representation of the growth and decay of vegetation. The extant versions of this type of myth are late, however, and therefore tinged with Greek thought which no longer recognized the old Aegean divine pair of a Mother Goddess and her *paredros* as we may see them on the Cretan and Mycenaean seals discussed above. It is thus impossible to make the monumental evidence agree with the surviving mythology in order to achieve a consistent picture of the history of the Cretan Zeus. The problems are obvious: Zeus in Greek myth was the child of Rhea whom one cannot easily equate with the Eastern Mother Goddess[80]. Rhea was never said to have a male companion, apart, of course, from her husband Kronos[80a]. The young Zeus in myth was in the care of Mother Earth, Gaia. But the goddess with whom he united in marriage as Velchanos has no name for us, and Greek mythology remains stubbornly silent about any connection between Zeus and a Great Goddess.

---

[74] E.g. A. B. Cook, *Zeus,* Cambridge 1914, I, figs. 397; 398.

[75] For the evidence see Nilsson, *M. M. R.* 551 and notes.

[76] Nilsson, *op. cit.* 550 n. 60.

[77] Nilsson also interprets the famous Hymn of Palaeokastro as pointing to a very old symbolic rite of Zeus' fertilization of nature, *op. cit.* 550. On this Hymn see now also West in *J. H. S.* 85 (1965) 149–59.

[78] Hutchinson, *Preh. Crete* 204, mentions that there is no classical reference to Zeus' death.

[79] See above n. 65.

[80] Cf. Nilsson, *M. M. R.* 536.

[80a] Prof. Burkert pointed out to me that in Orphic myth Zeus is said to have united with his mother (Pap. Derveni, *Deltion* 19 [1964] 17 ff. [col. 22]; *Ant. Ab.* 14 [1968] 101).

Despite such negative evidence the salient points in the history of the young male god, symbol of vegetation, remain valid and reasonably clear. In the case of the Greek and Cretan Zeus we are dealing with a concretion of two apparently diverse religious traditions. In Hesiod's story of Zeus' birth and subsequent fate, and in most of the later versions, folklore motifs and the figure of the Indo-European Weather-god – so unlike in nature to the Cretan young god – have to some extent combined with the Cretan, and quite generally the Aegean and Eastern, male companion of the Great Goddess. The mystery in this connection does not so much consist in the essential nature of the young and dying Zeus, as in the remarkable fact that this last figure, so universal in Aegean belief, was given the name of the imported god of weather. To date, there does not exist a convincing explanation of this identification of Zeus with the youthful vegetation figure[81]. Nilsson's proposal hat the young Cretan god came to be identified with Zeus by way of the youthful "Sons of Zeus" the Dioskuroi who, like Zeus, were worshipped as children-protectors of the Greek house, raises interesting points[82], but remains too problematical a solution. It is quite possible that the position of the young male in Cretan religion, who in our monumental evidence could possibly have also been represented in zoomorphic or even aniconic form, has hitherto been underestimated. His place, if not his functions, in Minoan cult might have been on a par with the Greek god of the sky, thus allowing an easy absorption by the latter[83]. Whatever the reason for the identification, the significance and origin of the young male figure remains evident and was never fully submerged in Greek myth. Zeus Kretagenes for the Greeks always remained the god who was born and died every year.

[81] A. Furumark, "Was there a Sacral Kingship in Minoan Crete?", in *The Sacral Kingship* 369, fixes the date of this identification at 1475 B. C. when the Greeks established themselves at Knossos.
[82] Nilsson, *M. M. R.* 541 ff. The Dioskuroi were protectors of the house and in particular the house-gods of the Spartan kings. Their sacred animal was the snake, a form in which they themselves could appear to take their share of the *panspermia* served to them. The question arises, to what extent could the Cretan snake and palace goddess be associated with the Great Goddess and her young *paredros* on Minoan seals? In other words, if these two goddesses were essentially the same figures, then the young sons of Zeus with their functions and attributes might well be parallel to the Cretan companion of the protecting and nature goddess.
[83] West, *J. H. S.* 85 (1965) 154 f., maintains that the Cretan vegetation spirit who – before Hesiod – came to be identified with the Greek Zeus nevertheless retained much of his original nature.

This Zeus was not the only memory of the young nature god and companion in Greek legend which tells of a similar old cult in Greek centres like Eleusis, Amyclae, Athens and others[84]. The names of these young gods generally are etymologically transparent like Erichthonius which is derived from ἐρι – "deep" and χθών "earth"[85]. Erichthonius was born by Earth and fostered by Athena[86]. A scene, familiar from vase painting, shows Ge holding out the young child to Athena[87]. This goddess found her way into the myth of this kind of vegetation cult through Athenian influence. Erechtheus (= Erichthonius) was an Athenian cult figure belonging to the oldest stratum of Athenian belief which went back to Mycenaean times. His old temple was built on the site of the Mycenaean palace on the Acropolis[88]. The scene of his birth is probably analogous to, and modelled on, the birth of Plutus (Wealth of Nature) at Eleusis during the Mysteries which may have been imported from Crete, but which certainly were practised in Mycenaean times[89]. At Eleusis the annual birth of the male child of nature must have formed the nucleus of the Mysteries from their inception[90]. The event is clearly depicted on a red-figure vase from Rhodes[91], where Ge is seen rising from the ground and holding out to a goddess a child seated on a cornucopia. The goddess most probably is Demeter, one of the two chief deities of the Eleusinian cult.

An interesting memory of a male god of vegetation is that of Hyacinthus at Amyclae, close to Sparta, and at other centres of the Doric world[92]. The remnants of his cult and festival, the Hyacinthia at Sparta[93], in myth became firmly attached to Apollo who absorbed his worship and made it his own. In fact the best known legend of Hyacinthus' fate was no more than an aetiological tale connecting the two figures. Hyacinthus was the

---

[84] for the following figures see Picard, *op. cit.* 136 f.; Nilsson, *M. M. R.* 557 ff.; Schachermeyr, *min. Kult.* 150; Nilsson, *Gesch.* I, 315 ff.
[85] Cf. Nilsson, *M. M. R.* 562.
[86] Homer, *Il.* 2, 547 f.
[87] Nilsson, *Gesch.* I, 317, for references.
[88] Nilsson, *M. M. R.* 563. In later versions Athena was said to receive him in her temple, cf. Nilsson, *Gesch.* I, 348.
[89] E.g. Nilsson, *M. M. R.* 468.
[90] The great age of the Plutus myth appears from the *hieros gamos* in Crete of his parents Demeter and Jasion, see above p. 12.
[91] For references see Nilsson, *M. M. R.* 559 and n. 89.
[92] E.g. at Tarentum, where according to Polybius 8, 30, Hyacinthus' tomb was shown.
[93] Nilsson, *Griechische Feste von religiöser Bedeutung mit Ausschluß der attischen*, Leipzig 1906, 129 ff.

favourite of Apollo who accidentally killed him with a throw of the discus. Hyacinthus' tomb was in the base of Apollo's throne at the old Mycenaean site Amyclae[94]. Hyacinthus shared his name with that of a flower: he was obviously a nature god like the Zeus Kretagenes who was born and died every year. A feature of particular interest regarding Hyacinthus is the fact that his name is non-Greek. Nilsson[95], who believes that the figure of the nature goddess and her divine child was of Minoan provenance, points to the pre-Greek element -nth- in this god's name[96].

It has already been noticed that the birthplace of this primitive vegetation religion, whose memory survived so tenaciously into classical times, was the East. Two points of considerable interest in this connection are (1) that the most probable specific area of origin was South-West Anatolia, particularly the Neolithic cultures of Çatal Hüyük, Hacilar, and Çan Hasan[97], and (2) the fact that, when the cult of the Mother Goddess was introduced to the West, Crete, the Aegean islands, and those areas of the Greek mainland in contact with this Eastern civilization formed part of a world largely uniform in religious matters. Evidence for this kind of religious *koine* derives from archaeological finds and to a lesser extent from linguistic studies. The Greek mainland at the end of Neolithic could quite generally be said to reflect Anatolian culture, but particular areas in touch with Anatolia at the time, apart from Crete in the south, are e.g. Sesklo and Dhimini in Thessaly[98]. Less certain members of this cultural unity are the settlements in the south of the mainland, but this doubt may be resolved by further archaeological discovery. A good case can be made out that the common religious forms in Anatolia and the Aegean at the time were the result of migrations which might have travelled westward in Neolithic and

---

[94] Nilsson, *Gesch.* I, 316.

[95] *M. M. R.* 556.

[96] Hyacinthus, he says, is a Cretan word. Hyacinthus most likely was worshipped in Crete (cf. the Amyklaion in Gortyn, which may have referred to a site of Hyacinthus', or similar, cult. See V. Ehrenberg, *From Solon to Socrates*, 382 n. 8; cf. below ch. 4 n. 182), but his name and, we suspect, his cult belonged to a wider circle extending across the "early Aegean world". Before Apollo usurped his name and cult, Hyacinthus, like Narcissus, may well have been representative of the typical male child of growing and dying nature, associated with a Great Goddess, cf. Vermeule, *Greece in Bronze Age* 63.

[97] Mellaart, *Earl Civ.* 77.

[98] On the various Neolithic periods in Thessaly and comparable pottery, implements etc. see Schachermeyr, *Das Aegaeische Neolithikum*, Lund 1964; Hood, *Heroes* 18; 25; Vermeule, *op. cit.* 9 ff.

perhaps the early period of the Bronze Age and been responsible for some degree of racial affinity between at least parts of the Greek mainland and Crete and Anatolia[99]. But it may be wrong to press this point, since so little is certain concerning the movements of peoples during this period. However, there survived in Classical Greek a number of common words and place names with suffixes in -ss- or -nth-[100] which belonged to a language, or group of related languages, spoken throughout Greece, and in large areas of Anatolia in Neolithic and the beginning of the Early Bronze Age[101].

It is of no great consequence for our purposes whether or not such a language, or languages, was Indo-European[102]. It is important that the linguistic *koine* probably originated in Anatolia, was distributed across the Aegean, and may have spread as far as the Balkans, Italy, and even Sicily[103], for it goes some way to explain the existence of communal religious practices in the areas under discussion. Such cult, basically dealing with fertility and including the worship of a Mother Goddess, was shared by our Aegean community at least during the first two periods of the Early Bronze Age. The Anatolian ties with Greece and Crete were especially close, and we shall have more to say about the occasionally striking resemblances between the S.W. Anatolian art (frescoes), cult figures (goddess types), and cult implements (bull horns, double axes) and those of Crete. Historically this close dependence on the superior, centuries old, Anatolian culture at the time gave the Aegean world a head start of some two-thousand years over the rest of Europe[104].

On the strength of the archaeological (Thessalian Neolithic and its Anatolian dependence) and linguistic evidence, Professor Schachermeyr constructed his theory of the "Vorderasiatische Kulturtrift", that is the

---

[99] Cf. Vermeule, *op. cit.* 13.
[100] Knossos, Parnassos, Olynthus, cf. Hyakinthos and Narkissos.
[101] E.g. Vermeule, *Gr. in B. A.* 60 ff.; J. Chadwick, "The Prehistory of the Greek Language", *C. A. H.*² (1963) 14; Hood, *Heroes* 26 f.; J.L. Caskey, "Greece and the Aegean Islands in the Middle Bronze Age", *C. A. H.*² (1966) 25; Schachermeyr, *min. Kult.* 15.
[102] Hinted at by Vermeule, *op. cit.* 63. Cf. Ph. H. J. Houwink ten Cate, "Anatolian Evidence for Relations with the West in the Bronze Age" Sheff. Coll. (1970); V. I. Georgiev, "L'Arrivée des Grecs: les données linguistiques", *ibid*.
[103] Cf. C. Renfrew, "Diff. in Gen. Correl. of Arch. and Ling. Strata in Gr." *ibid*.
[104] Cf. Schachermeyr, *min. Kult.* 16.

cultural movement from the Near East[105] according to which he traced the routes that connected East with West[106]. Although Schachermeyr's thesis has been questioned on a number of points, his main argument of Greek and Cretan religious unity at the time, and their dependence on Anatolian practice remains acceptable[107]. This picture of uniformity becomes disturbed, however, at the beginning of the Middle Bronze Age, and the archaeological evidence of the period suggests a considerable local diversification of inherited traditions. Crete, for example, went her own way and may have been out of touch with the mainland of Greece for some few centuries after 2000 B.C. Such a division was most likely attended by a certain measure of

[105] See Schachermeyr, "Die Vorderasiatische Kulturtrift", *S.* 5 (1953) 268–84; *Die ältesten Kulturen Griechenlands;* Cf. *min. Kult.* 13–25.

[106] The following will give a brief outline of Schachermeyr's arguments. From as early as the fifth and fourth millennia B. C. s.w. and central Anatolia witnessed a series of migratory movements which continued over several centuries. Such movements first came to the seaborder of the Anatolian peninsula, but in time crossed the Aegean and Mediterranean as far as Greece and Italy in the west, and the Danube in the north near to the Austrian border (see map in *min. Kult.* 16 f.). These migrations were one way and always followed one direction – westward (*min. Kult.* 17) – and, of course, took with them their culture (agriculture, vegetation religion), and their skills (the potter's art, the working of metal).
In this way the close ties between Çatal Hüyük, Hacilar, and Sesklo were established, the last of which acted as an intermediary station from which the Eastern import was spread across the Greek world. Crete, too, at that time was already in primary contact with the migrations from the East. Thessaly and Greece, however, as well as the island of Crete, proved to be the most fertile ground for Eastern culture which, in its continued north and westward migration, found little apart from roving bands of hunters or, beyond the Danube, met head-on with an autochthonous culture – the "Bandkeramischer Kreis" (on the influence on the south of "Bandkeramik" – ribbon ware – see also Lorimer, *Homer* 6) – where it could not prevail. On the other hand Crete was also subject to another, perhaps later, "Kulturtrift" which originated in Northern Africa and in Egypt (*min. Kult.* 16 f.). The latter country, like Sumeria, came into prominence after 3000 B. C. and thereafter provided the model for a number of architectural and religious features. Greece, ready to accept the Eastern import, was capable of parallel development with the Eastern civilization. The mainland therefore and Crete by the middle of the third millennium B. C. formed a part of a cultural community that bound Anatolia, Cilicia, together with Cyprus and the lands of the Aegean, into a "Kulturprovinz" which shared a common culture, religion and perhaps even language (apart from Schachermeyr see also K. Bittel, *Grundzüge der Vor- und Frühgeschichte Kleinasiens²*).

[107] Cf. Schachermeyr, *Aeg. Neolith.* 5; "Kann doch nun kein Zweifel mehr darüber bestehen, daß wir es in Griechenland mit einer Randprovinz der weit überlegenen Neolith- und Chalkolithkultur Anatoliens zu tun haben."

isolated development of cult. In Greece during these centuries the foundations were laid for the departmentalization of divine functions, the beginnings of which were already contained in the meeting of the Weather-god with a chthonic fertility religion. The various stages in this process are obscure, but the general result can be judged from the religious practices of the Late Bronze Age when the mainland and Crete were once more in close communication. Despite such evidence of separation in the Middle Bronze Age, both Crete and Greece continuously remained open to cultural impression from the East. Minoan activity in the young Middle Bronze Age, during the period of her naval greatness, was primarily in Syria and Egypt, but also extended across the Levantine seabord[108]. For example, Cretan wares were brought to Ras Shamra, the ancient Ugarit, as early as the beginning of the second millennium, and Ras Shamra texts grouped the island (*kptr*) together with Egypt as the "home of the arts"[109].

On the mainland this was a period of political development when the foundations of Mycenaean civilization were laid. A number of finds, however, from the preceding Shaft Grave era at Mycenae also establish unbroken contact with the East. About this time, or a little later (c. 1550 to 1450 B.C.) new people may have arrived in Greece from for example Syria or Egypt, if we are to believe the optimistic traditional chronologies which place the arrival of Cadmus the Phoenician at Thebes in the sixteenth century, and that of the Egyptian Danaus "before the flood"[110]. There is little certainty in this, however, despite some recent arguments in favour of Semitic settlements in Greece, and even Crete, during this period[111]. But these have found small or no support[112]. Conversely, however, Mycenaean trade with the East was continuous from the sixteenth and settlement from the fifteenth century. While the evidence for the existence of a Mycenaean kingdom (the much discussed Ahhiyawa) in western Anatolia, or anywhere else in the East for that matter, has now been questioned[113], and nothing clearly indicates actual Mycenaean settlement in Anatolia, "there does not seem to be any phase when Mycenaean pottery did not reach Western

---

[108] See the map in Schachermeyr, *min. Kult.* 79 fig. 32.
[109] J. Gray, *The Canaanites*, London 1964, 46.
[110] See e.g. Herod. 5, 58; Pausanias, 9, 5, 1.
[111] C. H. Gordon, e.g. "Eteocretan", *J. N. E. S.* 21 (1962) 211-14; M. C. Astour, *Hellenosemitica*, 109; 223 f.; 347.
[112] Cf. J. Boardman's review of Astour's book in *C. R.* 80 (1966) 86 ff.
[113] J. G. Macqueen, "Geography and History in Western Asia Minor", *A. S.* 18 (1968) 178 ff.; cf. J. Mellaart, "Anatolian Trade, Geography and Culture", *ibid.* 189.

Anatolia"[114]. Direct religious interchange therefore between Anatolia and Greece or Crete seems debatable in the second millennium on purely archaeological grounds, although Vermeule remarks on "certain areas of likeness" in Mycenaean Greece and Hittite Anatolia in the Late Bronze Age[115]. Better evidence on this subject derives from literary texts dealing with cosmogony and theogony, knowledge of which may have reached the West along a different route.

An important point of cultural exchange at the time was to be found on the north Syrian coast, in Ras Shamra, the ancient Canaanite city of Ugarit, which not only imported, and probably locally imitated, numerous Mycenaean works of art and pottery, but was exposed to Mycenaean influence through the fifteenth century settlements at Minet el Beida, harbour of Ras Shamra, and at Tell Abu Hawam. By the beginning of the Late Bronze Age Ras Shamra had become a truly international community of the civilized world. Here Mesopotamian merchants shopped for metals brought from Anatolia, the Taurus, and nearby Cyprus. Equally available was other merchandise from Egypt and the Aegean. Associated with commerce was a trade in, or rather assimilation of, culture including religion[116]. Canaanite Ugarit brought together cultural elements from Egypt, Mesopotamia, Crete, and Mycenae. Specifically Mycenaean contributions, for example, were the corbel-vaulted tombs at Minet el Beida[117]. The same type of tomb was incorporated in the great late thirteenth century palace in Ras Shamra[118], bearing witness to Mycenaean influence in this most important religious centre.

The significance of this kind of evidence is two-fold. Firstly the close communication of the Aegean world with the East at sites like Ras Shamra until the end of the Bronze Age provided the basis for some shared elements in art, literature, and especially religion, which help to explain a central feature of Minoan and Mycenaean society, namely the cult associated with a city's temple or palace, the divinity whose home it was thought to be, and the king, or priest-king, the human representative of the deity. Secondly it is to be remarked that, contrary to recent belief, the "Kulturtrift" which we noticed from East to West in the Neolithic and Early Bronze Age periods, if not reversed in the second millennium, in some respects became a two-way

---

[114] D. H. French, "Prehistoric Sites in Northwest Anatolia", *A. S.* 19 (1969) 73.
[115] *Op. cit.* 61.
[116] Cf. Gray, *Canaanites* 17.
[117] Gray, *op. cit.* figs. 6; 7.
[118] Gray, *op. cit.* 64.

affair[119]. This implies an independent development of inherited religious traditions in the West and the distinct possibility of religious export to the East during this period. Details of such export are unknown, but we have seen the example of the palace in Ugarit (c. 1200 B.C.) which incorporated Mycenaean-type tombs in its plan. It is as well therefore to guard against the impression of Cretan and mainland dependence on Eastern models in all departments of art and literature. It used to be thought that the Middle Minoan Cretan palaces derived from Eastern models, like the palace at Beycesultan, or Yarim Lim's palace at Alalakh in northern Syria[120]. Architectural resemblances, however, where they exist, are superficial and the Cretan palaces were not only locally designed[121], but, being as early as any palaces yet known in the Near East, may actually have influenced Eastern styles[122]. But in essence the parallel development of palace building in Crete and the East seems to have been the result of a similar cultural evolution[123], conditioned in part by the history of close contact at the time. As an illustration of this kind of interaction producing, or continuing, basically related social and religious elements, we may compare the 14th/13th century Mycenaean palaces. The great palaces of Mycenae, Pylos, and Tiryns borrowed architectural features from the Cretan Middle Bronze Age models. They were not identical, however, but possessed aspects, like the *megaron* and absence of central court, which were peculiar to themselves or possibly inherited from another source[124]. For all that, comparable features probably remained in the function of the palace as the central store house of the produce belonging to the palace deity which was administered by the king in an essentially theocratic society.

These are admittedly assumptions which in the West are based almost entirely on archaeological evidence. But this is supplemented by some

---

[119] Cf. J. D. Evans, "The archaeol. Evid. and its interpret.", Sheff. Colloqu.

[120] L. Woolley, *A Forgotten Kingdom, Results from the Excavation of Atchana and AlMina, in the Turkish Haty*, Baltimore 1953, 74 f.; C. F. A. Schaeffer, "Les fouill. d. Ras-Shamra-Ugarit", *Syria* 20 (1939) 292; "Reprise d. recherch. arch. à Ras-Shamra-Ugar.", *Syria* 25 (1946–8) 4 f. V. G. Childe, *The Dawn of European Civilization*², New York 1958, 26 f.; Astour, *Hellenosem.* 328; Hutchinson, *Preh. Crete* 166–9; 181; 213; 218; 219; 225; 311 f.

[121] F. Matz, "Minoan Civilization, Maturity and Zenith", *C. A. H.*² (1962) 9 f.; J. W. Graham, *The Palaces of Crete*, 229–33; cf. Hood, *Heroes* 55; Warren, "Crete, 2300 B. C.–1400 B. C.", Sheff. Colloqu.

[122] This is the opinion of Prof. Hrouda which he personally told me in Berlin.

[123] Cf. Schachermeyr, *min. Kult.* 118; 224.

[124] Hood, *Heroes* 119 f.

knowledge of the contemporary Near Eastern scene, and by the cautious use of literary documentation. The obvious dangers in close comparisons of religious belief appear from what has already been said about the measure of local autonomous development during the Middle Bronze Age, to which one may add the difficulty of interpreting the Cretan and Late Helladic Mycenaean monumental remains. Nevertheless comparable religious features existed in all the palaces, and some of these it may be possible to isolate. The value of this undertaking, despite its often unpleasantly theoretical result, consists in the ability to observe the transformation, or perhaps integration, of the basic forms of chthonic vegetation cult which we saw to be the central element of a type of religious *koine* at the beginning of the Bronze Age. In other words, both East and West started from common ground, while the uninterrupted two-way contact throughout the Bronze Age could only have been an aid to the continuation of basic religious forms which were adapted to the Bronze Age society centred on the palace with its king.

The process is easier to understand in the East, about which we are better informed, mainly because the integration of chthonic vegetation figures into a theocratic city system had been accomplished earlier there (in Mesopotamia). But most important of all, this development gave rise to a certain type of literary composition which in general outline was destined to set an accepted standard for much of the Near East (p. 48). Such a standard in religious matters was devised by Sumerian culture in the third millennium B.C., whence it spread across Mesopotamia as a unifying influence still a thousand years later. Sumerian religious concepts left their mark on Assyria, on the Hurrians (Upper Euphrates), and thence on the Hittites as far north as Bogazkeuy. We are mainly concerned with aspects of the theocratic city-state, centred on a temple or palace, and certain theogonic ideas which also impinged on the West. By the time Sumerian civilization rose into prominence at the end of the fourth millennium, Mesopotamia presented a largely unified picture composed of the Halaf culture in the north which, at the end of the Stone Age, had been superseded by, and combined with, the Ubaid culture from the south. This latter period was already capable of massive temple construction, like that discovered in level XIII at Tepe Gawra[125], to house divinities perhaps not too distantly related to Sumerian gods. The unique position enjoyed by Sumeria was due to the introduction

---

[125] Mellaart, *Earl Civ.* 131 f., fig. 108.

of a new form of temple architecture[126], and to the invention of a distinctive style of cylinder seals, both of which are traceable as far as Troy in the north, to Upper Egypt in the south, and to north-east Persia in the east. Furthermore in "Early Dynastic times, Istar temples at Mari on the Euphrates and at Assur on the Tigris were equipped with statues of Sumerian style, representing men in Sumerian dress"[127].

Aside from architecture it was, however, the Sumerian writing skill which moulded much of the East into a cultural unit[128], and which helped to spread common political and religious institutions, so that in fact Babylonian culture was always to retain a Sumerian flavour[129]. It is generally agreed that the cuneiform script was first developed into an effective writing tool by the Sumerians[130]. The date of this achievement is not clearly known but certainly came about before 3000 B.C., for a great number of Sumerian cuneiform tablets, which were discovered at Erech, were written late in the fourth millennium[131]. Although the second half of the third millennium already saw the introduction of the Semitic Akkadian script in Mesopotamia, Sumerian cuneiform for long was felt to be the official language of cult. In the second millennium the Babylonians took over with their language, used for ritual purposes, the Sumerian pantheon and religious organization, as well as their liturgies and incantations. The difficulties of adapting a non-Semitic language for expressing Babylonian, that is Semitic, speech are obvious to the modern decipherer who has to contend with different values given to individual signs. Also, by the second millennium, Sumerian was no longer thoroughly or widely understood, so that its continued use for religious purposes over wide areas of the Near East, even outside Mesopotamia, is evidence of the tenacious hold of Sumerian sacred traditions. An interesting instance of this spread and continuity is the fact

---

[126] Cf. for example the temple at Brak in Northern Syria which not only was built on the same plan as the Sumerian temple, but also contained similar cult objects, M. E. L. Mallowan, "Excavations at Brak and Chagar Bazar", *Iraq* 9, London 1947, cited by H. Frankfort, *The Birth of Civilization in the Near East*, 73.

[127] Frankfort, *op. cit.* 73, who cites W. Andrae, *Die archaischen Ischtar Tempel in Assur*, Leipzig 1922.

[128] Cf. S. N. Kramer, *History begins at Sumer*, 281; H. W. F. Saggs, *The Greatness that was Babylon*, 159 f.

[129] Saggs, *Babylon* 157.

[130] On this subject of writing see in particular A. K. Falkenstein, *Archaische Texte aus Uruk*, Leipzig 1936; Kramer, *Hist. begins at Sumer*, Appendix B; *Sumerian Mythology*, 16, and further modern literature in n. 17 on p. 109.

[131] Kramer, *Sum. Myth.* 16.

that Hittite scribes still compiled Sumerian "dictionary" tablets to cope with the difficulty of the archaic material[132].

The destruction (in 1595 B.C.) of the First Babylonian Dynasty by the Hittite king Mursilis I was followed by the new government in Babylon of the Semitic Cassites who, nevertheless, continued to use Akkadian as their official language. Akadian, too, was used in the El Amarna (c. 1400 B.C.) correspondence of Egyptian kings with the kings of the Hittites, Mitanni, Assyria, Babylonia, and the princes of Syria, Palestine etc., providing a useful survey, therefore, of the spread of Babylonian and ultimately Sumerian cultural influence. The disturbed political events of the second millennium had, paradoxically enough, both a disruptive and unifying effect on Mesopotamia. Indo-European and Semitic invasion by the Hittites, Cassites, Mitanni, and Hurrians obviously brought Mesopotamia into contact with new gods and cult. But the conquered gods rarely, if ever, were ousted: they joined another pantheon with the same ease with which Cyrus took over the neo-Babylonian gods when he sacked Babylon in 539 B.C. In this process, too, Mesopotamian religion proved to be the stronger partner, because, with the language, Sumero-Akkadian divine names were carried north into Anatolia[133] where, as we shall see, theogonic myth assumed a distinctive Mesopotamian flavour. We should then perhaps think less of a disruption than a *diaspora* of originally Sumerian religious thought. Political with religious unification in Mesopotamia came about in the First Babylonian Dynasty early in the millennium when Hammurabi (1728–1686 B.C.) brought together the many lesser city-states into the one Babylonian realm, imposed one language on business and administration, and probably adopted one pantheon composed of the numerous Sumerian city gods. The ancient head, however, of the Sumerian divine family, Anu, was now replaced by Marduk, chief god of Babylon, an event reflected in the myth of divine succession which was probably given its form at the time. At the end of the millennium, when the rising power of imperial Assyria founded the Second Dynasty of Isin (12th century), Marduk was taken to the new capital of Ashur where he was either deposed from his supreme position by the national god, Assur, or enjoyed equal honour beside him in the celebration of the New Year (Akitu) Festival. At any rate, Marduk and his Mesopotamian divine family was a disruptive influence in the national religion and cult of the Assyrians[134].

[132] See M. Vieyra, *Hittite Art*, London (Tiranti) 1953, 42.
[133] Cf. H. Otten, *Die Religionen des alten Kleinasien*, 97.
[134] Cf. Saggs, *Babylon* 85.

It would be surprising if such evidence of religious parallelism and even uniformity in the East during the second millennium did not find an echo in the West, particularly since the highly centralized civilization based on the palace in Crete and Mycenae at the time seems more closely related to Oriental practice than to the later Greek city-state. Comparisons, however, will be confined to general points of agreement regarding palace and temple administration, the formation of a pantheon from originally chthonic vegetation gods, and the position of priest-king. Obviously, it can never be suggested that Crete and Mycenae were replicas of Oriental institutions: this is impossible in view of what has already been said above. Even in the East, religious unity was in some respects superficial concerning the official state or city cults and did not include numerous aspects of purely localised practice and particularly magic ritual which never rose above the level of popular chthonic worship. Official cult was similar in Mesopotamia and beyond because of political events, a *corpus* of ritual texts, and the weight of ultimately Sumerian tradition.

The Sumerians were the first to organize into city-states in the period immediately following the Protoliterate (early third millennium). The centre of each state was the temple which, from humble beginnings, gradually developed into an elaborate complex of buildings – generally built about a central court – and comprising store rooms, chapels, priests' rooms etc. The temple was, of course, primarily the abode of the god who also owned the land attached to the temple both of which formed the nucleus of the city-state[135]. In other words, city-state and temple were synonymous terms for an organization in which the god represented an absolute ruler, while the human members of the community played the part of servants. One Sumerian myth, dealing with Enlil's separation of Heaven from Earth[136], makes this relationship quite explicit. After the separation, which according to the myth occurred at Nippur, the temple constituted the "Bond of Heaven and Earth". This society was clearly theocratic, but the gods who found themselves in this new role had probably all been chthonic fertility figures in the type of localised vegetation cult described above[137]. There is admittedly no conclusive evidence for this assumption. However, not unlike the formation of the official Olympian family of gods in Greece from largely localised vegetation figures, a similar evolution contemporary with the birth of the city-state is possible in Mesopotamia, if we consider

---

[135] Saggs, *Babyl.* 164; 165.
[136] *J. N. E. S.* 5 (1946) 136 f.
[137] Cf. Saggs, *Babyl.* 377.

two connected pieces of evidence which may illustrate this process. Dr. H. Lenzen remarked that Sumerian temples of the late Uruk (Jemdet Nasr) period, when the stepped temple tower (ziggurat) first appeared in Mesopotamian architecture, existed in pairs suggesting the common worship of the Mother Goddess and her youthful male associate[138]. The chief goddess of Uruk (Erech) throughout historic times was Innin[139], the Mother Goddess *par excellence* whose name in the Babylonian and Assyrian pantheon came to be Ishtar. Commonly associated with Innin (Ishtar), as the male vegetation god, was Tammuz (Sumerian Dumuzi, "True Son") who features on the Babylonian king-lists among the kings "before the Flood" and of the First Dynasty of Erech[140]. Myth and cult surrounding this divine pair were wide-spread in the East, as witness the many Tammuz liturgies[141], and tenaciously kept their hold on popular imagination: e.g. ritual weeping for the dying Tammuz was still practised in sixth century Israel (*Ezekiel* 8, 14). In Syria Tammuz was identified with Adonis, and the Ras Shamra texts illustrate the persistence of the Ishtar – Adonis (Tammuz) cult in popular belief not only in Syria and Canaan but over a much wider area[142]. It seems that the worship of the divine pair connected with the annual vegetation cycle may have formed part of the religious background in Mesopotamia until the official cult of the city-state relegated this fertility religion to the lower strata of popular belief.

Perhaps in the beginning each temple with its city-state belonged to one god. Thus Enlil, for example, was specially associated with Nippur, while Eridu was the chief centre of Ea's cult. During the third millennium already, however, one city could contain several temples of different deities, like Lagash which at the time of Gudea (c. 2060–2042 B.C.) had about twenty temples throughout its four city areas. This number nearly doubled in the period of the Third Dynasty of Ur. The large city of Babylon at the time of Nebuchadnezzar II possessed no less than fifty-eight temples. The Mesopotamian pantheon could, therefore, be said to have grown out of the development of individual city-states with common religious background. The exact process is no longer clear, nor can one do more than guess at the part played in this by rivalries and political friction between separate city-

---

[138] Cited by Saggs, *Babyl.* 25.
[139] This may not have been her name in the Uruk period although her functions remained the same.
[140] As the Shepherd or the Fisher, cf. S. H. Hooke, *Babylonian and Assyrian Religion*, 21.
[141] Collected by Witzel, *Tammuz-Liturgien*.
[142] On Tammuz see also Hooke, *op. cit.* 27 ff.; Saggs, *Babyl.* 377 ff.

states. However, the basic structure of the pantheon, which was to provide the general order for Babylonia and Assyria, had come into being by the middle of the third millennium when, perhaps in Erech, a standard list was drawn up. This, together with surviving Sumerian theogonic myth, suggests the result of reasoned theological thought[143] which imposed a strict order on the motley rule of gods with essentially similar background. This orderly structure continued through Mesopotamian history, although its pantheon grew in proportion to the *mise en scène* of new political powers whose own imports of gods were forthwith integrated in an expanding family. Apart from the Innin-Ishtar association touched on above, we may cite the Akkadian Shamash of Sippar introduced beside the older god Utu of Larsa who exercised equivalent functions. Enlil, originally chief god of Nippur, became the father of Ningirsu, god of Lagash[144]. Marduk of Babylonia found his place as son of Ea, or Enki, from Eridu, and so on.

Accordingly, two important features of the Mesopotamian pantheon are firstly the integration of the city-gods with their chthonic vegetation origin into a hierarchical family system[145], and secondly the fact that the divine "family" reflected the organization of the human society in the city[146]. Both features were destined to recur in the formation of the Greek Olympian family. We shall return to this point and the comparable divine homes in East and West.

At the peak of the Mesopotamian divine hierarchical order was the triad Anu, god of heaven, Enlil, god of earth, and Enki (Ea), god of the waters. Both Enlil and Anu appear at different times to have contended for the position of supreme god. One text describes Enlil as the son of Anu, while elsewhere Enlil is called the father of the gods. In the Epic of Creation Enlil plays the main part as destroyer of Tiamat, a role which was later taken over by the Babylonian and Assyrian national gods Marduk and Assur[147]. Anu's early position in the pantheon before the end of the third millennium is obscure, nor was he specially connected with one city but he

---

[143] See Kramer, *Hist. beg. at Sumer* 127 ff.
[144] Once Enlil became a more universal deity outside Nippur, his cult fell away, see Güterbock, *A. J. A.* (1948) 132. Perhaps a similar history explains Kronos' lack of worship in Greece.
[145] See also H. Schmökel, *Ur, Assur und Babylon*, 1955, 23; 39; cf. *Geschichte des alten Vorderasien* (Handb. d. Orientalistik II, 3), 1957, 36, where the author dates the arrangement of the gods in a family structure at c. 2500 B. C.
[146] Saggs, *Babyl.* 359.
[147] Cf. Saggs, *Babyl.* 331; Hooke, *Bab. Ass. Rel.* 14.

enjoyed important cults in e.g. Ur, Erech, Nippur, and Lagash. Associated with this triad was the Mother Goddess Ninhursag concerned with childbirth. The second triad in the early god-lists consisted of the sun-god Shamash (Sum. Utu), Sin (Nanna), moon-god, and Hadad, storm- or weather-god, with whom was associated Ishtar (Innin). Like Ishtar, Hadad in the second millennium rose to a position of supreme importance over much of the Near East: his cult was spread throughout Asia Minor, Mesopotamia, Syria, and Palestine. In the story of the divine dynastic succession the Weather-god generally represented the last stage. Lightning and thunder were his attributes, and we shall meet him under various names like Teshub among the Hittites, Baal in Canaan, or Resheph in Syria. He shared his attributes and features with the Hebrew Yahweh with whom he often came to be confused[148]. These two triads represent the most important figures on the official lists of gods. A good many other names include a group of chthonic deities at the end who never rose beyond their early functions as vegetation gods. Excluded from the lists, but important as primal elements in the myth of creation, are Tiamat, her consort Kingu, and Apsu.

According to myth, of course, kingship in heaven existed long before the human king. Innin was said to have bestowed the office on the Sumerian people as a gift from heaven. The Epic of Etana proclaims that, "At that time no tiara had been worn, ... Sceptre, headband, tiara and staff were deposited in heaven before Anu; there used to be no (royal) direction of her (the goddess') people; Kingship (then) came down from heaven..."[149]. The priest-king therefore was the god's representative within the city, and his subjects were the servants of the gods as well as the tenants of the city lands owned by the gods, to whom they were bound to pay their rents and services. The actual political administration of the Mesopotamian city-state was fairly complex and need not detain us[150] beyond the position of the king. He was directly chosen by the city-god. Hammurabi, for example, (early in the second millennium), still declared that he was "called" to his

---

[148] Hooke, *op. cit.* 19; cf. Saggs, *Babyl.* 335.
[149] Saggs, *Babyl.* 359; cf. Hooke, *op. cit.* 5 f.
[150] See Frankfort, *Birth of Civil.* 68 ff.; Saggs, *Babyl. passim* and full bibliography of detailed discussions on pp. 508 f.; H. Klengel, *Z. Ass.* N. F. 23 (1965) 223-36; A. J. Jawad, *The Advent of the Era of Townships in Northern Mesopotamia*, Leiden 1965. The third ed. of *C. A. H.* I, 1, with the chapter on "The Development of Cities from Al-Ubaid to the End of Uruk 5" by M. E. L. Mallowan has not yet come to hand.

kingship by Anu and Enlil, or Marduk[151]. In the Early Dynastic period the king's name was En ("lord"), and his home the god's temple where he functioned as chief priest in charge of temple possessions. Hence the "lord" and divine representative exercised supreme control over all religious matters in addition to his purely administrative and juridical duties within the city-state. In the Epic of Gilgamesh the hero, En of Erech, consults what might pass as a general assembly, but his despotic powers remain quite obvious to the reader. A division of power may have occurred, however, as early as the middle of the third millennium, when the texts mention the titles of other office holders in the state[152]. Also with the growth of the city-state the system of priestly administrators became increasingly complex[153]. The latter continued to be attached to the temple, while the king moved to his own palace, without, however, losing his position as representative of the gods or divine consort. It is important that throughout Babylonian and Assyrian history the king's connection with fertility ritual and the annual vegetation cycle remains evident: he continues to play his chief rôle in the Sacred Marriage[154] and to participate in the New Year Festival which served the same purpose of guaranteeing the fruitfulness of the lands.

[151] ANET 164; 165; 177. For a discussion of Th. Jacobson's and H. Frankfort's view (*The Intellectual Adventure of Ancient Man*, Chicago 1946), that already in Early Dynastic times the general assembly elected the king see Saggs, *Babyl.* 37.

[152] The citizen's assembly was normally governed by the *lugal* "king" to whom it acted as an advisory body in a structure which Astour (*Hellenosem.* 359 n. 3) compares with the Homeric *basileus* surrounded by his *boule* – council – and *agore* – general assembly. Extant sources suggest that the Mesopotamian city at times also had a priestly chief administrator of the god's temple, called *ensi* = "governor of the god", who was different from the king – *lugal* – (see C. J. Gadd, "The Cities of Babylon", *C. A. H.²*, 1962, 14) and rivalled the latter's power. This would mean that the offices of the political king and high priest could be divorced in one city. The exact significance of *ensi* and *lugal* is, however, no longer clear, and it seems possible that normally *lugal* and *ensi* were separate titles describing the same office of priest-king in different centres. The single ruler of Erech, for example, was called *ensi* – Frankfort, *Birth of Civ.* 69 n. 1. Perhaps again the title of *lugal* was a later invention, for the word does not appear in protoliterate texts – Frankfort, *ibid*. One may suppose that originally the functions of governor, and high priest, of a city were combined in the god's representative, the *ensi* – cf. Gadd, *op. cit.* 46. Saggs, *Babyl.* 345, suggests the following sequence of events. The *En* became *Ensi* on moving from the temple to a palace. Although he still played a part in the city's religious affairs, the actual temple administration was supervised by a priest. Subsequently when several city-states combined into one political unit the title *Ensi* changed to that of *lugal*, cf. pp. 38 f.; 168.

[153] See the lists in Saggs, *Babyl.* 345 ff.; Hooke, *Bab. Assyr. Rel.* 43 ff.

[154] See Saggs, *Babyl.* 37.

This raises the vital point whether the king was himself considered a god, or whether he remained the mortal representative of his god. In this respect the Mesopotamian concept of kingship diverged from that found in Hebrew religion where the Lord alone was felt to be king (*Samuel* 8, 7) and the institution of human kingship was a foreign import (*Deuteronomy* 17, 14), and from Egyptian practice according to which the king was always a god[155]. The uncertainty in the Mesopotamian situation is probably due to an inherent ambiguity in the priest-king's position which was at no time clearly defined. The Sumerian kings were "nourished by the trustworthy milk of Ninhursag (the Mother Goddess)"[156], a concept common to Near Eastern kingship and still reflected in the Ugaritic Epic of Keret whose son is one
> "Who sucks the milk of Atherat
> Who sucks the breasts of the Virgin Anat"[157].

During his life time, however, some important differences separated the king from his god with whom he might share food-offerings but never sacrifice. The king, in fact, made quite plain his humble station by building temples to the gods "for the king's own life". And yet some Mesopotamian

---

[155] The difference between Egyptian and Mesopotamian practice is striking: in the former the king was always a god, far removed from mortal men. His palace was less than, but nevertheless separate from, the temple. The Egyptian king never died, but continued his existence in his eternal dwelling, the pyramid, in his life-like form. In Mesopotamia, too, political conditions were far less stable than in the two kingdoms of the Nile. The city-states warred with one another and were subjected, but they added their gods to a growing family of divinities. Under Babylonian rule Marduk usurped the position of highest god, and he lived in his temple palace Esagila administered by a priest-king. "They raise high the head of Esagila", we read in the *Enuma Elish*, "equalling Apsu. Having built a stage tower (the ziggurat) as high as Apsu, they set up in it an abode for Marduk, Enlil, (and) Ea." (Speiser's transl. of Tabl. VI, 62–4). Webster, *Mycen. to Homer* 11, maintains that the Mycenaean king, too, was of divine rank unlike his Mesopotamian counterpart. In the same spirit P. Walcot, *Hesiod and the Near East*, 71, claims that the "Egyptian pattern of monarchy was reproduced by that of the Mycenaean world." Cf. *ibid.*, "Mycenaean kings were sacral kings in the full Egyptian sense." It is difficult to agree with him (pp. 72 f.) that *Od*. 19, 225–37 shows the Mycenaean king's power to act directly on nature and growth without the help of the gods. Hence, according to Walcot, Mycenaean, Hittite, and Egyptian kingship were related. Astour's objections to such proposals, *Hellen.* 359 n. 2, seem convincing. For a sceptical view of all kingship theories see A. N. Marlow, "Myth and Ritual in Early Greece", *B. J. R.* 43 (1960/1) 373–402.

[156] Cf. Kramer, *Hist. begins at Sum.* 147.

[157] Cf. the ivory panel from the royal bed in the palace of Ras Shamra on which twin youths are shown as suckling the breasts of the fertility goddess, Gray, *Canaan.* Pl. 9, and p. 107.

kings had their names written with the divine determinative, or possessed divine attributes like the horned cap which Naram-Sin is seen to be wearing on his *stele*. This ambiguity, part human part divine, may well be resolved by Frankfort's plausible suggestion that the Mesopotamian king only assumed divine status when as the representative of a god he shared the couch of a goddess in the ritual of the Sacred Marriage[158]. In other words, the priest-king's divinity was confined to his function as consort or *paredros* of a deity, and this harkened back to the beginning of Mesopotamian religion.

Perhaps at death, as has been supposed, the king was assimilated to the figure of the "dying" Tammuz[159] and thus achieved permanent divine rank, but more significant for our purpose is the likelihood of a real point of contact between the Mesopotamian king and divine consort and the Minoan – Mycenaean Wanax and his relationship to the figure of Potnia. The similarities between Babylonian, Assyrian, Syrian, Anatolian and Bronze Age Cretan and Mycenaean practice in this context seem to be more than fortuitous. Of course, the temporal gap separating the developments of the Sumerian, Babylonian city-state from the Minoan and indeed Mycenaean palaces of the Late Bronze Age is considerable. It should be remembered, however, that, according to Eastern texts, the Mesopotamian experience, far from unique, was shared by much of the Near East, and particularly by those cultures, including the areas of Hittite influence[160], which were in close contact with the West in the later second millennium. A similar evolution of a priestly hierarchy under the overlordship of a king can be observed in Canaanite Ugarit, for example, if we compare the epics of the two kings Keret and Danel with the administrative texts from Ras Shamra. Both sets date to about the fourteenth century but the royal legends, as suggested by a colophon to the Keret text, had been handed down (with elaborations) from the beginning of the second millennium and show an earlier stage of kingship. This was prior to the division of much of

---

[158] H. Frankfort, *Kingship and the Gods*, 297; cf. Saggs, *Babyl.* 360 f.; Hooke, *Bab. Assyr. Rel.* 25 f.

[159] Saggs, *Babyl.* 377.

[160] One text from the Bogazhkeuy tablets (in A. Götze, *J. C. S.* I [1947] 90 f.) seems to illustrate this common experience: "May Labarna, the king, be welcome to the gods. The land belongs to the Weather-god, the sky, earth (and) people belong to the Weather-god. He has made Labarna, the king, His administrator and has given him the entire land of Hatti. May Labarna now administer the entire land under his direction ("mit [seiner] Hand")."

the temple administration among a priestly hierarchy of twelve families which are described in the records from the chancellery of Ugarit[161]. By the thirteenth century the king of Ugarit lived in a splendid palace whose administration probably ran along inherited Mesopotamian lines, while its evident Mycenaean content we have already seen. The social structure of Ugarit can be learnt from literary texts, like the epics of Keret and Aqat, and from divine myth, because the arrangement of the Canaanite pantheon, too, reflects the human order within the city-state. Again the history of these myths and legends indicates a tradition in these beliefs which endured at least from the beginning of the second millennium until the Late Bronze Age[162].

The impact on the West of generally shared and continuing Oriental religious concepts, expressed in the structure of the pantheon and theocratic city administration, is evident from the monumental remains alone, although it can no longer be accurately measured. Particularly difficult is any sort of precise assessment of the undoubtedly individual features of Cretan and Mycenaean religion, and the extent to which the latter drew from Minoan precedent without the benefit of direct transmission from the East. The names of gods, for example, were not the same in Crete and in the East. Certainly the Greek pantheon absorbed a number of Minoan figures like Aphaea, Britomartis, Ariadne, or Dictynna. But the pattern of development ran along familiar lines, for in the West, too, the gods began as chthonic vegetation deities and grew into one hierarchical family. There seems to be an obvious parallel between the orderly arrangement of the Greek pantheon in which many lesser figures, inherited from other related cultures, became epithets of the great deities like Zeus, Artemis, Athena, and the process in Babylonian religious development, as witness, for example, a hymn, recited during the New Year Festival, which lists the fifty names of Marduk and describes the cults and attributes taken over from other gods[163]. More disturbing is the absence of any indication that the Cretan and Mycenaean palace, as the religious and administrative centre of the Middle and Late Bronze Age city, had replaced an earlier temple, or temples, as the original home of the chief deity. This may, of course, be due to accident of survival, which does not help us much, despite the recent startling discoveries of

---

[161] Cf. Gray, *Canaan*. 105; 109; 126 f.
[162] See also Gray, *op. cit.* 112.
[163] Hooke, *Bab. Assyr. Rel.* 25.

Bronze Age temples on *e.g.* Keos and in Mycenae[164]. The only two widely excavated Early Minoan settlements at Myrtos and Vasilike have revealed large single building complexes which possibly provided a model for the palaces[165]. These buildings may, or may not, have been temples: neither the remains nor the find of figurines can lead to certain conclusions about this or about the form of cult practised there, beyond the probability that it was concerned with a goddess of vegetation.

In the next chapter we shall see the evidence for the transference of a similar type of cult from earlier sanctuaries to the palace. In this way we get the impression of an integration of nature gods within the Cretan Middle Bronze Age "city" not unlike the Mesopotamian development, while admitting that in many respects Minoan religion was independent. We are, however, concerned with a general pattern of correspondence between East and West, so far as this may still be established, concerning the function of the palace, the position of the king, or priest-king, and the structure of the divine and human society. The temporal span of such correspondence should extend from the time of the palaces until the composition of Greek epic which, though recorded much later, may have begun in the Mycenaean Age. Apart from archaeological remains, we can draw from the Mycenaean Linear B records and Eastern survivals as well as borrowings in Greek epic literature.

The magazines and stores of the Cretan and Mycenaean palaces suggest their function as administrative and commercial centres. The analogy with Eastern practice and method is plain[166] and clearly borne out at Knossos, Pylos, and Mycenae by the detailed records which in form strikingly resemble those found in the palaces of Alalakh, Mari, and Ugarit[167]. The range of these documents is roughly the same in East and West and, together with the material remains, they draw a picture of a Mycenaean social structure "more akin to contemporary Near Eastern kingdoms than to the city-states of archaic and classical Greece"[168]. A significant part of this kinship

---

[164] On Keos see below p. 140. For an account of 13th century temples discovered at the site of the Citadel House in Mycenae see Lord William Taylour, "New Light on Mycenaean Religion", *Ant.* 44 (1970) 270 ff.
[165] Cf. Warren, "Crete 2300 B. C.–1400 B. C.", Sheff. Colloqu.
[166] Cf. Schachermeyr, *min. Kult.* 118; 222 ff.
[167] This was noticed already by M. Ventris–J. Chadwick, *Documents in Mycenaean Greek*, 106 f.; 113; 133, and has become generally accepted, see e.g. Webster's discussion in *Myc. to Hom.* 7 ff.
[168] Webster, *op. cit.* 23.

involves the central religious function of the palace beside its position as a commercial base. In Crete, as in the East, the entire building complex was pervaded by religious elements: the frescoes on the walls were connected with religious practice, so were, of course, the various rooms used as shrines, while the central courts, to judge from some frescoe scenes, witnessed the performance of large religious festivals[169]. An important Minoan religious symbol, albeit of uncertain significance, was the double axe. It was modelled in precious metal. It was carved, or painted, on the pillars, altars, pottery in shrines, on seals and elsewhere. The Minoan term for the axe was probably *labrys*, a word which may have once described the entire palace and whose etymology points to the East[170]. The find, therefore, of a stone-base for the double axe on the Mycenaean citadel serves as a valuable link between the mainland palace, Crete, and possibly the East[171].

The Mycenaean palace most likely continued as the central religious venue in the Late Bronze Age. This may be gathered from the presence within the building of shrines and sanctuaries. But, as in Crete, it was not the only place of worship which evidently could also be observed in the splendid temples recently uncovered by Lord W. Taylour[172]. Of interest to us is the probability that the Cretan and Mycenaean palace continued as the cult centre of the city-deity, or deities, in a special relationship with a king, or priest-king, along the lines we found in the East. The actual existence of priest-kings in Crete was first suggested by Evans[173], and has come to be generally accepted. This office continued in the Late Bronze Age mainland palaces. The king performed important religious and administrative, or political, functions in a central part of the palace, like the "Throne Room" at Knossos which in some respects is strikingly similar to the about two

---

[169] Cf. Webster, *op. cit.* 54.
[170] The Greek *labyrinthos* is apparently a distinct echo of *labrys* (e.g. C. Gallavotti, "Labyrinthos", *P. d. P.* 12 (1957) 171 ff. Cf. *ibid*., "Labyrinth derived from the Lycian laβra = "building of stone", "tomb".). But *labrys*, the axe and possibly the palace (*labyrinthos*), was a cultic word (cf. the Carian Zeus Labrandeus, "Zeus with the double axe(?)", Nilsson, *M. M. R.* 223. We note here Astour's claim, *Hellen.* 329 f., that the Cretan double-axe was borrowed from the Sumerians) which derived from Lycia or Caria, or, according to Plutarch (*quaest. graec.* 301 f. Cf. Lorimer, *Homer* 2), from neighbouring Lydia (see also below ch. 2 and notes), cultures which were perhaps part of the Lukka lands, that is provinces of the Hittite empire and therefore in close contact with Mesopotamian religion.
[171] Nilsson, *M. M. R.* 173; 331; *Gesch.* I, 276, Pl. III, 3; Webster, *op. cit.* 41.
[172] See n. 164 above.
[173] E.g. *P. M.* I, 224.

centuries younger *megaron* in the palace of Messenian Pylos[174]. The king has been identified with certain Minoan and Mycenaean artistic representations which are said to show him together with his special goddess or in the company of priests as part of the hierarchical system of palace administration[175]. Perhaps the most plausible examples of a priest-king from this somewhat uncertain source are the "Chieftain Vase" from Hagia Triada[176], the so-called "Priest-King Relief"[177], and a ring from Mycenae showing the king in front of a goddess[178].

The best known king of Knossos was Minos, and it has been suggested, mainly because of the contradictory later Greek tradition regarding this figure, that Minos was not an individual name but a dynastic title of the Cretan king and that, like Knossos and possibly *basileus* ("prince, king"), it belonged to our Aegean linguistic substratum being "common to Crete and to those regions in Asia where 'priest-kings' were a normal institution"[179]. This may well be true, at least in part, for we have similar evidence from the Linear B tablets of a descriptive title for the Mycenaean priest-king and his close relationship with the city-deity clear traces of which survived into Classical times. Nilsson was the first to see[180] that from the Mycenaean palaces subsequently developed the temples of public worship, for as the might of the Achaean kingship declined the palace site often became that of the temple, the locality of the god's home[181]. Thus we see Hera's temple constructed over the palace of Tirynth, and Athena's at the site of an old palace on the Athenian acropolis. The protective relationship

---

[174] For a discussion of Blegen's view that the Knossos throne-room was constructed in the thirteenth century by a Mycenaean ruler for primarily non-religious purposes (*A. J. A.* 57 [1953]; 60 [1956]) see H. Reusch, "Zum Problem des Thronraumes in Knossos" *Min H.*, 31 ff.

[175] E.g. Evans, *P. M.* I, 159; 224; 270 ff.; 447; II, 792 ff.; IV, 412 f.

[176] *P. M.* II, 790 ff.

[177] *P. M.* II, 253; 427; 774 ff. etc. Cf. R. F. Willetts, *Cretan Cults and Festivals*, 85.

[178] Nilsson, *Gesch.* I, Pl. XVII; *M. M. R.* 351 (describes the figs. as two mortals); A. W. Persson, *The Religion of Greece in Prehistoric Times*, No. 21 (describes the figs. as two divinities); J. Forsdyke, "Minos of Crete", *J. W. C. I.* 15 (1952) 19; Webster, *Myc. to Hom.* 53 and n. 7, who also cites a 14th century vase from Aradippo (Cyprus) showing "(a) a man with spear and rod approaching a seated goddess, (b) three men with spears approaching a seated goddess."

[179] Nilsson, *Homer and Mycenae*, 64 f.; Forsdyke "Minos of Crete" 17 ff.; Willetts, *Cret. Cults* 83; 89.

[180] *M. M. R.* 473. See also below (p. 227) and notes for objections to the theory that older cult sites determined the location of later temples.

[181] Cf. Webster, *Myc. to Hom.* 291.

between deity and king survived in Greek epic where Athena played the part of personal guardian of Heracles, or she helped Jason build the Argo. Like the kingship, the divine interest and assistance were hereditary: thus Athena defended not only Odysseus but also Telemachus his son. So, too, Diomede, in the *Iliad*, inherited Athena's guardianship from his father Tydeus.

But these are mere shadows of a strong Bronze Age tradition which Crete and Mycenae shared with the East. The king was close to his deity but he was not divine himself. This position is still discernible, albeit in vague and fragmentary form, from later Greek practice and literature concerning a pattern of periodic renewal of kingship (see below). There probably existed an ambivalence in the part divine and part mortal status of the Cretan and Mycenaean king similar to that noticed in the East[182] where it seems to have been confined to the king's deification after death and to the celebration of the *hieros gamos* between the youthful king and a goddess. A certain similarity can be established for the West from admittedly rather scattered sources. The most promising in this respect, the Linear B archives from Crete and Mycenae, also prove to be the most frustrating, for despite their close correspondence with Eastern methods of palace administration, they do not include any literary or juridical texts or letters. Whether or not such absence is accidental[183], it represents a most painful lacuna which rules out any close comparison with Eastern practice from this source alone[184], and greatly increases the difficulty of using contemporary Eastern legends and epics to illustrate Minoan and Mycenaean religious beliefs.

In the Linear B tablets the priest-king is called *wanax* ("Lord"); he seems to be at the head of a palace, or city, hierarchy, other important members of which are e.g. the *basileus* and the *lawagetas*[185]. Probable mention on the

---

[182] Cf. A. Furumark, "Was there a Sacral Kingship in Minoan Crete?", *The Sacral Kingship*, 370, "There is, consequently much evidence in favour of the view that in Minoan Crete there existed a sacral kingship of much the same nature as those of Oriental cultures. This type of kingship belongs to the pre-Greek civilization of Crete, but was taken over by the Greeks..."

[183] Webster, *Myc. to Hom.* 23 ff.

[184] Cf. L. A. Stella, *La Civiltà Micenea nei Documenti Contemporanei*, 193, "Cercare nei testi micenei echi di rapporti d'oltremare può sembrare impresa assurda."

[185] The subject of the probable distinction between *basileus* and *wanax* will be discussed in ch. 3 and 4 (e.g. p. 184 with n. 297 and p. 266 – on the *basileus'* position in mainland Bronze and Dark Age communities). At this point a few words about the problem will suffice. As in the case of the *lugal* and *ensi* – see above n. 152 – we encounter in Mycenae the problem of two no longer clearly defined titles for the king or priest-

tablets of complex lists of priests, and the frequent description in the Pylian archives of what might be divine slaves[186], generally fit in with the impression that the Bronze Age Minoan-Mycenaean city-state was theocratic in nature and owned by the city-deity. But this source material remains insufficient by itself. In Minoan-Mycenaean art divine protection of the king is symbolically expressed by surrounding the throne at Knossos and at Pylos with frescoes of the griffin in a borrowed Oriental motif[187]. The lion, similarly borrowed from the East, performs the same symbolic function, and we may compare the figures of the Lion Gate at Mycenae with the lions in front of the king's palace at Bogazhkeuy[188]. None of this is proof of the king's divinity, only of his closeness to divinity which, as we saw, partially survived into Classical times and which seems analogous to Eastern practice. Homeric terms like Zeus-born, Zeus-nurtured, applied to the king,

king: *basileus* and *anax(wanax)*, a word which frequently appears on Linear B tablets from Pylos and Knossos – J. Chadwick-L. Baumbach, "The Mycenaean Greek Vocabulary", *Glotta* 40 (1963) Heft 3/4 *q.v.* with modern references. Prof. Webster has proposed – *Myc. to Hom.* 11; 32; 143; 291 – that *Wanax*, the older of the two titles, referred to the King with divine status whose functions paralleled those of his Eastern counterparts (cf. above n. 152). Thus the griffins flanking the throne at Knossos, and the lions above the gate to Mycenae, represented the King's divine protection, like e.g. the lions carved in front of the King's palace at Bogazhkeuy. The *basileus*, on the other hand, according to Webster, signified a less important figure – king with a small "k" – who tended to exchange his royal offices for those of a priest. This development, Webster believes, occurred about the eleventh century B.C. when in Mycenaean thought the bond between the city's god and his mortal governor relaxed and fell apart, and in Athens "The goddess received her own dwelling", her temple, on the acropolis. An exciting echo of the former function and position of the king comes to us not from state practice but, as often, from popular cult, from the ancient festival of the Anthesteria. Here we discover a cheerful contamination of old and new. Not far below the layer of confusion, exemplified by the Greeks' appointing two deities – Dionysus and Hermes – for the three festive days, there yet remains the unity of a New Year type celebration like the Babylonian Nisan. The purpose of such celebrations was the renewal of the priest-king's power through communion with his god, as well as the granting of new life to nature by means of the *hieros gamos*.

[186] Collected and discussed by Stella, *Civilt. Micen.* 256 f.; 259 f. The comparison of a ritual anointing of the king's throne at Mari with a similar event in a Pylian "ritual calendar", is based on the disputed reading of *thornoekkheuterion*, p. 262.

[187] Webster, *Myc. to Hom.* 32; 39; 53; Furumark, *Sacr. Kingsh.* 370. Cf. the griffin in the palace at Megiddo (c. 1350–1150 B.C.) which is strikingly similar to those from Knossos, Gray, *Canaan.* Pl. 12; p. 227.

[188] O. R. Gurney, *The Hittites*, Pl. 8; Webster, *op. cit.* 32

strongly recall the divine rearing of Mesopotamian and Syrian kings[189], while there is some evidence from art that the Mycenaean king, too, was deified after death. The famous scene painted on the c. 14th century sarcophagus from Hagia Triada has often and convincingly been explained as depicting the cult, with offerings, of such a dead king[190], and the entire ritual may reflect Oriental practice in Mycenaean dress. Beyond this unique instance, which essentially still remains a "picture without text", we may think of vague memories of a similar belief enduring in Classical myth in stories like the translation of Menelaus and Rhadamanthys.

Again the concept of the sacred marriage of a god-like king with his deity survived perhaps into historical times in legend associated with the "Divine Child", or in the episode of Jasion and Demeter in Crete, and in religious festivals such as the ancient Anthesteria and Eleusinian Mysteries. In this kind of instance it is possible to detect the influence of Eastern ideas

[189] To what extent does the fact that the *wanax* possesses sacred land within the god-owned city lend him divine status, especially since the *lawagetas* and the *damos* apparently enjoyed similar privileges (cf. my "Prolegomena to the Study of Greek Cult Continuity", *A. C.* 11 (1968) 162 ff.)? *Temenos* signifies a tract of land which, according to Homer *Il.* 6, 194; 9, 578; 12, 310; 20, 184, may be owned by, or promised to as a reward for military services, outstanding heroes like Bellerophon, Meleager, Glaucus, and Aeneas. Originally, however, "The temenos is special land, otherwise only owned by gods and Kings, and implies divine status," Webster, *Myc. to Hom.* 106. Whether or not the Mycenaean king had divine status, he was certainly the representative of his deity, and as such administered the city's land owned by the god – the *temenos*. Now, *temenos* was one of a number of Semitic loan-words – Ventris-Chadwick, *Docs.* 135, had already listed five others – which derived from Akkadian *temmenu* (Ugaritic *tmn*?) – J. Aistleitner, *Wörterbuch der Ugaritischen Sprache*, herausgegeben von Otto Eisfeldt (Berichte d. Sächsischen Akademie d. d. Wissensch. zu Leipzig, Phil.-Hist. Kl., B. 106, Heft 3), Berlin 1963, No. 2773. *temmenu*, according to Astour, *Hellen.* 338, originally came from the Sumerian *temen* and means "temple-precinct" or "royal domain on public land", "sacral foundation of a temple", and may describe the temple itself, C. H. Gordon, *Before the Bible*, New York 1962, 53 n. 2. Thus *temenos* not only serves to illustrate the close religious ties between Crete, Mycenae, and eventually Sumeria, but allows us a welcome insight into the function of the palace in a theocratic city-state where the king's abode served the purpose of a temple – no less than the home of the god. For a list of other possible Semitic loan-words on Lin. B tablets see Astour, *Hellen.* 337 f.

[190] E.g. Evans, *P. M.* I, 447; Nilsson, *M. M. R.* 438, who believes this to be a Mycenaean rite with strong Egyptian elements; Webster, *Myc. to Hom.* 35; Furumark, *Sacr. Kingsh.* 370; Willetts, *Cret. Cults* 370. C. R. Long, *A. J. A.* 63 (1959) 59, believes the scene to represent the worship of the goddess who protected the king during his life time. For an entirely different interpretation of the painting (cult of Phoenix instituted by Europe) see H. van Effenterre, *B. C. H.* 85 (1961) 545.

concerning kingship and its association with a protective deity. The close relationship between the wanax and Potnia ("Lady, Mistress") seems quite clear from the records, and there is some evidence that the king in Bronze Age Crete and on the Greek mainland also may have played the part of the goddess' youthful male associate whose kingship had to be periodically renewed[191]. The Cretan Minos, for example, was "by a regal fiction" always young and closely bound to his goddess from whom he received his office of priest-king[192].

One can learn more about corresponding ideas of kingship from literary records which indeed exclusively derive from the East. How far are we entitled to trust recorded Eastern legends and epics of the second millennium as a competent source for contemporary concepts of gods and kingship in Crete and Mycenae? The previous discussion of cultural interchange provides arguments in favour of such use, but is not enough. Two other points offer more compelling evidence for our purposes. These concern the obvious Eastern impact on the manner and form of early Greek epic, and certain similarities with the East in the formation of the Greek pantheon whose beginnings lay in the Mycenaean Age.

Both points are related, but let us consider the second of these first. Some features of the Homeric Olympian family suggest an awareness of, and perhaps a conscious borrowing from, Oriental models. The most significant of these is the patently hierarchical structure of the pantheon[193] reflecting the human order in the city-state[194]. The gods, as befits a ruling class, lived a life of ease in abodes like those of men, except that their dwellings were fashioned of gold and brass by Hephaestus[195]. Willetts supposes[196] that a

---

[191] On this relationship see below e.g. 183 ff.

[192] Willetts, *Cret. Cults* 87; 91.

[193] See A. Jeremia, *Handbuch d. altorientalischen Geisteskultur*², Leipzig 1929, e.g. 171, cited by C. M. Edsman, "Zum sakralen Königtum in der Forschung", *The Sacral Kingship* 6 f.: "Als eines der wichtigsten Axiome der altorientalischen Lehre gilt, daß alles irdische Sein und Geschehen einem himmlischen Sein und Geschehen entspricht." Cf. p. 173, also cited by Edsman, *ibid.*, "Der irdische König erscheint seinerseits als Abbild des himmlischen Königs." For Mesopotamia cf. Gadd, "Cit. of Babyl." 46; Saggs, *Babyl.* 159; 160; for Ugarit see Gray, *Canaan.* 112.

[194] Nilsson, *Gesch.* I, 372 f.

[195] E.g. Homer, *Il.* 1, 608; 20, 12.

[196] *Cret. Cults.* 118. Cf. Nilsson's related view in *The Mycenaean Origin of Greek Mythology*, 221 ff. We cannot discuss these opinions at length, but it is worth mentioning that these Frazer Lectures were read in 1931, some fifteen years before Güterbock's work on the subject. An interesting observation comes from Astour, *Hellen.* 359, "The political way of life as described in the Homeric poems, presents a resemblance to the

newly evolved Mycenaean military kingship provided the pattern for the divine set-up, but the comparison with Mesopotamian practice lies closer to hand[197]. The extreme humanity of the Homeric gods found its parallel and possible source in the Sumerian pantheon whose anthropomorphism strongly contrasted with the hybrid forms and zoomorphism of Egyptian belief[198]. Their intense belief in the human form of their gods compelled the Mesopotamian artists to go to strange but not unequalled lengths in depicting the all-knowing, all-seeing divine powers. Thus gods were drawn with two heads, or two faces like the Roman *Janus Bifrons*. Marduk, like Assur, possessed two pairs of eyes and ears to exemplify their super-human powers in human shape. With this idea we might compare the many representations on Cretan seals of human ears and eyes floating in mid-air, emblems of the all-seeing, all-hearing, deity.

We will see in the last chapter that the Olympians were composed of diverse elements from different centres: protectors of cities, like Hera at Argos and Athena at Athens, were placed cheek by jowl with deities of localised cult, or originally chthonic divinities of nature[199]. Abdicating their narrow responsibilities within a particular community they were collected, perhaps first by the Homeric poets, and arrayed in a closely knit family. The legends of divine succession from father to son already suggest the ties of the assemblage of gods in East and West to have been those of a family. The Weather-god – *pater Zeus* in Homer – became the father of the family: he represented the strict *paterfamilias* who allotted to the other gods their

    Canaanite states of the second and first millennium to no less degree than the Mycenaean order."

[197] Cf. Frankfort, *Birth of Civ.* 52. For a recent study of the growth of the Mesopotamian city-state see A. J. Jawad, *Adv. Town. Mesop.*

[198] Animals we do find associated with gods in Homer, as witness the eagle of Zeus or the speaking epithets *glaukopis* and *boopis* of Athena and Hera. In Crete we see animals in association with gods on seals. In Mesopotamian art the eagle, lion, and serpent, too, are depicted, but these creatures do not necessarily hint at an earlier belief in zoomorphism: they merely serve as emblems of the deity to whom they are sacred. They are his defender, mount, or trusted companion which imparts to a particular god its qualities, that is, the strength of a lion, for example, the force of a bull, or perhaps even the fecundity of a cow. In the words of E. Dhorme, *Les Religions de Babylonie et d'Assyrie*, 18 f., "Far from allowing a god or goddess to descend to the rank of an animal, Mesopotamian art attempts to impart to animals human attitudes – *attitudes humaines* – which bring them near to man and permit them to associate with the religious life of men."

[199] For the similar function of nature gods in Mesopotamia see Frankfort, *Birth of Civ.* 58 f.

honours and functions. Thus Marduk in the Babylonian *Enuma Elish*, "After he had ordered all the instructions, To the Annunaki (normally a collective name for the nether-world gods, but here perhaps designating all the gods) of heaven and earth had allotted their portions[200]." In Hesiod Zeus distributed their honours to the gods[201]. Every member of the family has his clearly assigned place[202]. But Zeus' relationship with the other Olympians is still apparent: he was at the head of the family, father, for instance, of Athena, Artemis and Apollo, and brother of Poseidon, as well as of Hades in the underworld[203]. His consort Hera, again, was the mother of Hephaestus, and so on.

Some basic structural elements of the Greek pantheon, and the fact that it was modelled on the society of men, evidently corresponded with Eastern practice. It should then be possible to apply what we know of the function of the divine king to those of his human counterpart in the city, and not only in the East but, with due caution, to the Minoan and Mycenaean king. In Ugaritic legend Baal figures extremely large. His name may once have been associated with a particular locality but comes to signify simply "the lord". He is a youthful god, the brother and consort of the goddess Anath, and the most prominent portion of his myth is concerned with his kingship in the seasonal vegetation rites. That is, Baal represents the young male fertility figure whose renewal of kingship is celebrated in the Canaanite Autumnal New Year Festival in a rite which, as can be seen from the Ras Shamra texts, was the same in the Babylonian New Year Festival[204]. Baal's identity with Hadad shows a combination of male vegetational figures and Weather-god, the same in fact as the one we observed in the early history of Zeus. Furthermore Hadad had originally been worshipped in northern Syria by the Amorites as their Weather-god and supreme figure of their pantheon[205], which means that the ritual function of "the lord" Baal-Hadad was current not only in Canaan during the late second millennium, the date of the extant texts, but may reach back to the third or beginning of the second millennium[206] and link up, incidentally, with the Eastern religious

---

[200] Speiser's transl. of Tabl. VI, 45 f.
[201] *Theog.* 885, cf. v. 74. This idea becomes particularly clear in Aeschylus, *Prom. Vinct.* 230 ff.
[202] Cf. Ovid, *Met.* I, 171 ff., where position according to hierarchical rank is also set out.
[203] E.g. *Il.* 15, 189 ff.
[204] Gray, *Canaan.* 127 f.; 137.
[205] R. Dussaud, *Les Religions des Phéniciens*, 362.
[206] Hadad, associated with fertility cult, occurs in the Execration Texts from Saqqara (c. 19th century B. C.), cf. Gray, *Canaan.* 120.

koine including Mesopotamia, Assyria, Syria, and extending north to Anatolia.

Like the human king, Baal lived within an elaborate palace. This we gather from the poems about him and Anath, "He opens a casement in the house," we hear in one account, "a window within the palace. Baal opens rifts in the clouds. His holy voice convulses the earth, the mountains quake."[207]. But Baal was a god of mountain peaks[208], and his home was built on the summit of Mt. Saphon near Antioch in North Syria. This mountain was identified by Greek geographers with *Mons Casius* whither Zeus, according to Hesiod, pursued Typhon; but it is also identical with Mt. Hazzi, that is the home of the Hittite, and ultimately Hurrian, Weather-god Teshub which in the Kumarbi Epic was threatened by the monster Ullikummi. The peak of a mountain seems the natural abode of the Weather-god. Olympus, too, in Homer's mind occasionally appears more suitable to Zeus alone[209]. The idea, however, of a mountain peak as the home of all the gods seems to have been universal in the East and may have originated in Sumeria if it is correct to see in the Mesopotamian temple tower (ziggurat), like the famous structures at Ur and Babel, a symbolic representation of the divine abode[210]. Enlil's ziggurat at Nippur, for example, was called "House of the Mountain, Mountain of the Storm, Bond between Heaven and Earth"[211]. The Greek family of gods also dwelt on a mountain, Olympus. This name occurs more than once in Greece, in the Aegean (as at Lesbos), and in the East, at Mysia for instance. The word was pre-Greek, of Eastern provenance, and simply means "mountain". Olympus as a descriptive term for the abode of the gods may well have travelled to Greece *via* the Mycenaeans and Homer.

We spoke earlier of the impact on early Greek epic of Eastern literature. The most illuminating source in this respect is the texts of myths, epics and legends discovered at Ras Shamra (Ugarit) which, as we noticed, in their variety, including Hurrian documents, mirrored a good deal of commonly shared ideas regarding theogony and kingship and also provided an easy

---

[207] Ginsberg's transl. of *Poems about Baal and Anath* IIAB, vii, 25–7.
[208] Dussaud, *Rel. Phen.* 362.
[209] In two passages in the *Iliad* (13, 243; 16, 364) Zeus is imagined as inhabiting Olympus alone, whence he casts down on men a thunderbolt or a storm. Cf. Nilsson, *Mycen. Orig. Greek Myth.* 230.
[210] For a discussion of this vexing problem see Saggs, *Babyl.* 355 ff.
[211] Frankfort, *Birth of Civ.* 54. For parallels of the mountain of the gods see also Gaster, *Thespis* 183.

bridge to Crete and Mycenae in the West. Another important collection of similar literary texts comes to us from the Hittite capital Bogazhkeuy. The date of all these sources falls between 1400 and 1200 B.C., but the religious beliefs expressed in them are much earlier. The Hittite texts show a strong influence of Hurrian elements on state religion[212], so that through these intermediaries, as well as through the history of political contact with the south, we can assume the Hittites to have been familiar with, and absorbed, significant features of the structure of the pantheon and kingship that ultimately originated in Mesopotamia. Recent comparative studies of these texts have established some striking detailed and general similarities[213]. It seems that Homeric technique contains some important Oriental borrowings such as noun-epithet formulae, typical scenes, special formulae for opening and closing of speeches, poetic repetition, sending of messengers etc. On a wider level the comparable development and structure of the divine families in East and West resulted in some basic similarities in the epic function of the gods and their relationship to man. Thus the Homeric type of divine assembly occurs throughout Eastern epic and is convened for similar reasons. In Ugaritic and in Hittite epic the gods were like men but drawn on a larger scale: they displayed human emotions, the same passion for elaborate banquets and adornment as men. Again, the closeness of the city and its king to the gods in a theocratic society explains the easy, familiar, interchange between both human and divine levels. In the Ugaritic poem of Keret, for example, the king's wedding to the princess of Udum is attended by the gods. For the same reason the relationship between a hero and a god is comparable in Oriental and Homeric epic[214].

Such instances easily suggest the depth of Greek dependence in matters of style and composition, and more significantly in actual substance, on Oriental precedent. To be sure in no case does the West ever directly take over

[212] Gurney, *Hittites* 135; 140.
[213] See e.g. the following studies with further references: C. H. Gordon, *A. J. A.* 56 (1952) 93 f.; *M.* 3 (1955) 126; *Riv. Stud. Orient.* 24 (1955) 161; *Hebrew Union College Annual* 26 (1955); F. Dirlmeier, "Homerisches Epos und Orient", *R. M.* 98 (1955) 18–37; A. Lesky, "Hethitische Texte und griechischer Mythos", *Anz. Öst.* (1950) 137–159; "Zum hethitischen und griechischen Mythos", *Er.* 52 (1954) 8–17; "Griechischer Mythos und Vorderer Orient", *S.* 6 (1955) 35–52; A. Heubeck, "Mythologische Vorstellungen d. alten Orients im Archaischen Griechentum", *Gym.* 62 (1955) 508–525; T. B. L. Webster, *M.* 4 (1956) 104; *Myc. to Hom.* especially ch. 3; L. A. Stella, *Il Poema di Ulisse*; H. Haag, *Homer, Ugarit und das Alte Testament.*
[214] Cf. Webster, *Myc. to Hom.* 69. A hero enjoys a god's protection, he may appeal directly to a god or offend him etc.

Eastern myth or epic; the peculiarly Greek spirit always remains evident in the adaptation of foreign motifs. The Greeks, according to the author of the *Epinomis* (987 D), rendered more beautiful whatever they borrowed from the barbarians. In short, there are no exact parallels even in that type of literary composition which most plainly revealed Eastern influence, namely theogonic epic[215]. Such justified caution notwithstanding, it is important for our purpose to consider that patently Oriental motifs in Greek epic may have travelled West during the second millennium, in the Mycenaean Age, that is, the period when we have the strongest evidence of cultural interchange and of comparable religious concepts and institutions. If we can feel any certainty that there was in fact such early borrowing then the value of our Eastern texts as an illustration of contemporary society and religious beliefs will be enormously enhanced.

The case has been convincingly argued by Webster who analyses Eastern parallels to essential and original elements in the *Iliad* and *Odyssey*[216]. For example the tale of Odysseus' wanderings, told to Alcinous by the hero, has important features in common with Oriental poetry like the Gilgamesh Epic which has come down to us in versions containing original Sumerian mixed with Babylonian, Assyrian, Hurrian and Hittite elements. Again, the basic form of the *Iliad* may have been derived[217] from an earlier siege-poem, the Ugaritic Keret Epic[218]. If true, this seems another[219] plausible instance of early borrowing perhaps *via* Crete as an intermediary[220]. In every case the many changes as well as the brilliant and new Homeric treatment of Oriental ideas are obvious, and they also indicate the temporal gap separating the time of transmission and the actual date when the myths were finally recorded in their extant form[221].

[215] See especially Lesky, *S.* 6 (1955) 40; H. Erbse's review of E. Heitsch (ed.), *Hesiod*, Darmstadt 1966, in *A. kl. A.* 23 (1970) 26.
[216] *Myc. to Hom.* 67 ff. "The evidence for early borrowing can only be convincing if it can be shown ... that certain borrowings are so essential to the *Iliad* and *Odyssey* that they must have been very early if not original elements of the story ...".
[217] Webster, *op. cit.* 86 f.; Haag, *Homer, Ugar.* 59, speaks of the Ugaritic poem as the "Ur-Ilias".
[218] The hero is left by his wife and, obeying El's command given him in a dream, lays siege to the city Udm and sucessfully claims the king's daughter in marriage.
[219] For possible Egyptian parallels see Webster, *Myc. to Hom.* 87 f.
[220] Gordon, *M.* 3 (1955) 126 f.
[221] Heubeck, *Gym.* 62 (1955) 516 f., agrees that the Mycenaeans were familiar with Eastern myth and epic, but he argues that the memory of these stories could not have survived the illiterate Dark Age of Greece, so that Homeric and Hesiodic borrowing must have been late.

If we may believe with reasonable certainty that Eastern epic and myth were adopted by the Mycenaeans already, whether or not the latter possessed their own recorded versions, then it becomes possible to assume that basic social as well as religious practices which are reflected in the texts also obtained in the Mycenaean world. The actual route of transmission at the time from East to West is difficult to establish[222] but becomes less significant in the light of our knowledge (a) of Mycenaean contacts with important cultural diffusion centres like Ugarit and (b) that religious concepts, particularly concerning theogony and kingship, at the time were common coinage in the East. Like heroic epic, and the poem of Gilgamesh is a good case in point, legends about the origin of the gods, their dynastic struggles and kingship, as well as the structure of human kingship and its relation to the gods, ultimately began in Sumeria whence it spread by means of the Sumerian script, art, and political conquest in the manner outlined above. The impact of this *koine* on the West left a mark which in some form was destined to survive in Greek thought despite the collapse of the Mycenaean cities[223]. Therefore what we can learn from historical Greek sources regarding the survival of such theogonical and kingship concepts will give us some picture of a cultural debt which was incurred in Mycenaean times. The most illuminating Greek source for our purpose is, of course, Hesiod's *Theogony*[224]. The relevant Eastern texts are conveniently collected by J. B. Pritchard[225].

---

[222] Above n. 215. See also Barnett, *J. H. S.* 65 (1945) 101, who cites Forrer and Güterbock; Heubeck, *Gym.* (1955) 517 f.; Lesky, *Anz. Öst.* 87 (1950) 145; S. (1955) 50 ff.; *A History of Greek Literature*, transl. by J. Willis and C. de Heer, London 1966, 94 ff. See also A. Scharff – A. Mortgaat, *Aegypten und Vorderasien im Altertum*, 1950, who correctly maintain that "Die Brücke zwischen Churri und Griechen über Phoenikien ... dürfte eine von vielen sein" (p. 346). Cf. West, *Hesiod Theogony* 30. For further modern literature on this point see F. Lämmli, *Vom Chaos zum Kosmos*, II, 68 f. n. 243, and West, *op. cit.* 106 f.

[223] Webster, *Myc. to Hom.* 68; 78, traces the route of transmission in the East from Sumeria to Babylon, thence to Hurrian and Assyrian literature, from Hurrian to Hittite, Ugaritic, and Phoenician, and from Hittite, Ugaritic, and Phoenician to Mycenaean Greek.

[224] Hesiod's sources are now positively established and, in spite of isolated criticism (e.g. by R. Carpenter, *A. J. A.* [1958] 25–53), need no longer be confirmed by separate argument (For discussions of the material and parallel features between East and West see above n. 213 and e.g. Fr. Dornseiff's arguments collected in *Antike und Alter Orient*. U. Bianchi, *Dios Aisa*, Rome 1953, 146–91; H. Schwabl, "Weltschöpfung" in *P.-W.* Suppl. IX, esp. 1433–1513; West, *Hes. Theog.*, esp. 18–31; P. Walcot, *Hesiod*

The extant fragments of Sumerian mythology show us the basic features of this kind of literature, containing the creation of Heaven and Earth – a unity at first – and their separation, as well as the names of deities representing the elemental powers. The name and province of such deities became universal coinage in Asia Minor. Professor Kramer[226] renders for us the introduction of a Sumerian poem which had been translated into Akkadian as part of a standard liturgical text: "After Heaven had been moved away from Earth," it runs, "After Earth had been separated from Heaven, after the name of man had been fixed; after An had carried off Heaven, after Enlil had carried off Earth." This excerpt shows the separation of Earth from Heaven, either by peaceful means or not, prior to the creation of life on earth. In the poem, too, we meet the names of An, or Anu in its Semitic form, as the god of the sky, Enlil the god of the earth, Enki, Ea in the Babylonian form, as the god of water. In the beginning Earth and Sky – An-ki – formed a unity until separated by Enlil. Anu, Enlil, and Ea reappeared in Babylonian and Hurrian mythology as figures of signal importance in a pantheon which, however, for political reasons became more complex with the passage of time. Thus, for example, Enlil as leader of the gods in the Sumerian period was supplanted by Marduk, originally chief of the Babylonian pantheon during the first Babylonian Dynasty (beginning of second millennium)[227], while he in turn gave up his place to the Assyrian Assur. Yet Enlil never disappeared, nor did Anu, but the former in a word became a supernumerary in a divine dynasty of which we find the first continuous evidence in Babylon.

and the Near East; H. Herter, "Griechenland und Orient", *ASozEth.* 10 (1967/8) 4–60. For a further modern bibliography see West, *op. cit.* 106 f. H. Erbse, "Orientalisches und Griechisches in Hesiods Theogonie", *Phil.* 108 (1964) 2–28, is highly sceptical of any close parallels drawn between the theogonic material. Judgments, like those of Wilamowitz (*Der Glaube der Hellenen*³, II, 205 n. 2), are echoes from the past which did not benefit from the now available evidence (cf. Lesky, *Gym.* 67 [1960] 232, who speaks of the wrong attitude "grundsätzlicher Orient-Blindheit unserer Wissenschaft."), and this plainly shows that Hesiod worked with older traditions (Cf. also U. Hölscher, "Anaximander und die Anfänge der Philosophie", *He.* [1953] 406 ff.; West, *Hes. Theog.* 29 and n. 1; Herter, *ASozEth.* [1967/8] 54).

[225] *ANET.* See also H. G. Güterbock, *A. J. A.* 52 (1948) 123–34; "Song of Ullikummi", *J. C. S.* 5 (1951) 135 f.; 6 (1952) 8 f.; *Kumarbi*, Zürich/New York 1946; G. R. Driver, *Canaanite Myths and Legends.*

[226] *Sum. Myth.* 37.

[227] Above p. 30; cf. Güterbock, *A. J. A.* (1948) 132; West, *Hes. Theog.* 29, who believes *Enuma Elish* to be the oldest of the theogonic epics. Walcot's dates, *Hesiod and N. East* 37; 141, of the composition of the Babylonian tale are 1500–1200 B. C.

The general retention of the original divine system[228] in other Eastern myths, Indo-European and Semitic, the names of gods either assimilated in the new language or side by side with indigenous deities, caused some confusion as witness the variety of ideogrammes in, for instance, the Hittite texts. Here we meet with Alalash, Anush, Ellilush, and A'ash, the phonetic equivalent in Hittite to the Babylonian Ea. With this common ground, therefore, it is not surprising that from the various centres of Eastern culture there emerged creation and theogonic myths which observed a similar pattern. This we notice in the Hurrian story of Kumarbi from Bogazhkeuy, in the Akkadian *Enuma Elish*, and in the tale of Sanchuniathon, as recorded by Philo of Byblos. For the sake of convenience we shall give a brief description of the relevant portions of these creation myths, preceded by an outline of Hesiod's divine genealogy in the *Theogony*.

The primal elements in Hesiod[229] were first Chaos, then Gaia (Earth) and Eros. Chaos and Gaia spontaneously produced the first divine generation, including the abstract forces Erebos (Darkness), Nyx (Night) from Chaos, and Uranus (Sky), the Mountains and Pontos (Sea) from Gaia. The second generation, and we are concerned with the children of Uranus and Gaia, was composed of the offspring from Gaia and her children. Thus Uranus and Gaia produced the Titans one of whom was Kronos. Now Uranus, the Sky, became the first ruler of the world and, from hatred of his children, he consigned them to the underworld. Gaia as a consequence began to feel weighed down and crowded wherefore she fashioned the *drepanon* (*harpe* – sickle) of steel with which her son Kronos, rushing from ambush, emasculated Uranus on his way to embrace his wife.

Kronos, who assumed his father's rulership, married Rhea, one of the Titans, with whom, amongst others, he produced Zeus. Like Uranus, Kronos, fearful for his safety, swallowed all his children; but in place of Zeus Rhea gave him a stone in swaddling clothes. Zeus, the Weather-god, then formed the last step in the divine succession. After deposing his father and usurping the god's throne, Zeus maintained his power against a rebellious Kronos who was helped by his mother Gaia and the Titans. Ranged on the side of Zeus were the Cyclopes and Hekatoncheires (the hundred-handed Giants, both groups the off-spring of Uranus and Gaia) with whose assistance Zeus overcame Kronos and his army both of whom he confined in Tartarus. At

---

[228] The so-called "Former Gods", that is gods of past ages whom Ea addresses in a "remote place", Güterbock, *ibid*.

[229] See also particularly West's analysis, *Hesiod* 16 ff. For modern literature see Schwabl, "Weltschöpf." 1439.

the end of the contest with the Titans, the Titanomachy, which formed a natural conclusion to the succession of divine kingship, Hesiod adds the account of the birth from Gaia of the monster Typhon who threatened the Weather-god's rule, but was set alight by Zeus' thunderbolt and cast into the underworld.

The Babylonian *Enuma Elish* ("When on high")[230] knew as first elements Tiamat (the primeval salt water ocean) and her consort Apsu (the primeval sweet water ocean) from whom sprang the first gods like Anshar and Anu (Sky). The children became burdensome to their parents, so that Apsu planned to do away with them. However, he fell first himself, slain by a ruse of Ea (god of earth and water), son of Anu. Tiamat thereupon in revenge produced, like Gaia, eleven monsters (man-scorpion, man-fish etc.) who attacked Ea under the leadership of the most powerful creature, Kingu, whom Tiamat made equal to the gods. Neither Anu nor Ea could withstand the onslaught of Kingu and his army which seemed victorious until opposed by Ea's son Marduk. Marduk succeeded in overcoming Kingu, whereupon the former sent the winds into Tiamat's mouth, killed her and finally severed her body into two parts to form Heaven and Earth.

The story of the Phoenician creation legend is taken in the main from Philo's account in Eusebius[231] and supplemented by parts of the Ras Shamra tablets[232]. Basically it retained the same traditions which we observed in the other epics. At times, however, we find a certain dislocation of the natural succession of events, as when the emasculation of Uranus is said to have occurred only in the thirty-second year of El's (Kronos) rule, or an admixture of new elements with old stock, the best example of which perhaps is Athena's anachronistic rule of Attica during the reign of the Weather-god. Other elements, like Kronos' *harpe*, although present in the story, find only a vague motive in the context probably through a misunderstanding of their original true significance.

---

[230] For a good synopsis of the epic, together with a translation of the text – based on Pritchard, see above n. 225 – and glossary of divine names, see also E. A. Speiser, *Religions of the Ancient Near East* (The Library of Liberal Arts), New York 1955, 17–46; West, *Hesiod* 22 f.

[231] See above n. 224. Cf. below n. 245.

[232] In particular from the *Poems about Baal and Anath*, the text of which is also translated, with commentary, by H. L. Ginsberg in *Relig. of the Anc. N. East* (see n. 230). For a more detailed account of the story and for modern literature on the subject see Schwabl "Weltsch." 1487–9, on whose analysis this description is based. For excellent diagrams of Philo's divine genealogy, together with a full description of the deities of the Phoenician pantheon, see R. Dussaud, *Rel. Hitt. Hourr. Phén. Syr.*, 358 ff.

According to Philo, the first divine pair were Eliun (Hypsistos – the Highest) and his consort Beruth who lived near Byblos which was said to be the first city in Phoenicia. Eliun and Beruth produced the first generation consisting of Epigeios (Uranus – Sky) and Autochthon (Gaia – Earth). When Eliun was killed by wild animals Epigeios (Uranus) assumed the royal throne. Epigeios and Autochthon then gave birth to four children: El (Kronos), Baitylos, Dagon, the Corn-god, and Atlas[233]. Autochthon subsequently grew jealous of her mate who fathered more children on other consorts and separated herself from Epigeios. Epigeios retaliated by forcing his will on Autochthon and by planning to kill her offspring. Autochthon resisted with the help of Kronos who had fashioned for himself an iron spear and sickle (*harpe*). The latter displaced Epigeios and in turn, the third in succession, assumed the divine kingship. Kronos (El), however, was not the father of the Weather-god (Demarus), who sprang from the union of Dagon and one of Epigeios' paramours[234].

Epigeios subsequently devised various schemes against the life of his son. We need not mention these in detail, for, with one exception, they are not relevant to this study. This exception concerns the *baitylia*[235], sent against El. The *baitylia* Hesychius defined as "living stones" (λίθους ἐμψύχους), and they, therefore, directly recall the function of Ullikummi and the *omphalos* in the Hurrian and Hesiodic versions. None of Uranus' devices met with success and El (Kronos) continued as divine ruler.

Philo's account also contains mention of forces like Typhon and Pontos (Sea) hostile to the divine king. Such beings belonged to older traditions[236], but they differed from their model in that monsters comparable with Typhon[237] – the Babylonian Kingu, the Hurrian Ullikummi, and the

---

[233] Later Atlas was cast into the underworld by his brother El. On Homeric knowledge of Eastern creation myth in his description of Atlas in *Od.* I, see Webster, *Myc. to Homer* 84.

[234] It is interesting to note that Demarus in fact was Uranus' (Epigeios) child, and not that of Dagon, for when the latter married Uranus' concubine she was already pregnant. Demarus eventually became the father of Melqart (Heracles).

[235] Cf. the god Baitylos.

[236] Cf. the contest between the Ugaritic Baal and Yamm (Sea) in the *Poems about Baal and Anath* (see n. 232).

[237] The complex part played by the Sea in the creation myths falls outside the scope of this discussion. On the connection between water and the motif of the separation of Heaven and Earth see F. K. Numazawa, *Die Weltanfänge in der japanischen Mythologie*; W. Staudacher, *Die Trennung von Himmel und Erde*; Schwabl, "Weltsch." 1509 f. with numerous references to other modern literature. On the connection of Typhon and allied monsters with the sea see e.g. Güterbock, *A. J. A.* (1948) 131.

BEGINNINGS IN THE EAST 53

Hesiodic Typhon – were created to topple from power the last link in the divine generations: the Weather-god. In Philo's story it seems that Typhon and Pontos threatened Uranus, the Sky. It is Demarus, however, the Weather-god, whom Uranus charged to fight Pontos (Sea), and who at a second attempt vanquished his opponent with the help of Kusor, a master of incantations[238].

This description is followed by Uranus' emasculation at the hands of El (Kronos) in the thirty-second year of his reign. Uranus died – at the navel, or centre, of the earth – but was deified. El eventually yielded his power to the last generation, that of Demarus, the Weather-god, who henceforth ruled the world with his consort Astarte (Aphrodite) whom he had seized from Yamm (Sea). The manner of this succession does not, however, emerge clearly from Eusebius' rather sketchy transmission.

These brief accounts already indicate some common features which found their way to Greece, and which helped to shape some aspects of Greek religion. The story which served our purposes best in this context is the epic of Kumarbi recorded on the Bogazhkeuy tablets about 1400–1200 B.C., but going back in this version at least to the height of Hurrian culture in the fifteenth century B.C. if not farther[239]. This epic fell, so Güterbock remarks[240], into three parts, (1) the struggle for the kingship of heaven, (2) the song of Ullikummi, (3) the story of the Flood. The tale of the heavenly kingship spoke of four generations of gods: Alalu, Anu, Kumarbi and Weather-god. Each, the son of his predecessor[241], wrested the kingship from his father. A typical feature of this usurpation was that every deposed god was emasculated. Thus Kumarbi, in his struggle with Anu, bit off the parts of Anu. These he spat upon the earth which promptly gave birth, among others, to the Storm or Weather-god. Before the birth of the Weather-god,

---

[238] Cf. in this connection the part played by Ea the Wise in the Kumarbi myth, who advised the Weather-god in his fight against Ullikummi, with the magic charms used against Tiamat. For the common position of the Clever God in the Hurrican, Phoenician, and Greek versions see West, *Hesiod* 30.

[239] See above p. 46, and Güterbock, *A. J. A.* (1948) 123. "No later than the end of the thirteenth century B. C.", West, *Hesiod* 20. For the view that there is no relationship between the Greek theogony and the Kumarbi epic see Walcot, *Hes. and N. East* 1–26.

[240] *Kumarbi* 86 ff. For an excellent summary of all these and related theogonic myths see Schwabl, "Weltsch." 1433 ff. Cf. G. Steiner, *Der Sukzessionsmythos in Hesiods Theogonie und ihren orientalischen Parallelen*.

[241] Strictly speaking Teshub was the son of Anu, and Kumarbi could be said to have acted the part of a "foster-parent". Cf. the relationship between El and Demarus, West, *Hesiod* 27.

however, Kumarbi, who feared for his safety as ruling god, attempted to swallow the offspring of Anu's seed. As far as can be gathered from the fragmentary text at this point Kumarbi was given a diorite stone in place of the Weather-god. The stone, if our account is correct, was subsequently blessed by Ea, the god of water and wisdom, and set up as an object of worship for men. At the end of this part of the epic it seems that Kumarbi, too, was replaced by the Weather-god as supreme ruler. The song of Ullikummi dealt with Kumarbi's contest against the Storm-god. Once more the diorite stone played a vital part in the story, for Kumarbi begot on it a stone monster – Ullikummi, – which, placed on the shoulders of Upelluri an Atlas-like figure, grew to the abode of the gods and threatened the Storm-god whose Hurrian name was Teshub. On Ea's advice Teshub fetched the knife with which Heaven and Earth had been severed and with it cut Ullikummi from the shoulders of Upelluri thereby rendering the monster powerless.

These two parts of the epic, the story of the Flood apart, drew from Hurrian and ultimately Babylonian and other related legends, and they reveal a pattern whose main features found their way to Hesiod's *Theogony*. The connection was carefully analyzed by Güterbock[242] who even constructed a comparative table of dynastic succession in Babylonian, Hurrian-Hittite, Phoenician belief, and in Hesiod[243].

Obviously there are many points of detail where one version differs from another, and we cannot enter the maze of scholarship which has grown about the various divergent features[244]. Nor should the very real Greek original contribution be ignored, or the inevitable changes due to the temporal gap between the versions. But let us note that Hesiod stood at the end of a tradition which began with Sumero-Babylonian material, continued in Hurrian epic and in the Phoenician myth of succession[245]. Aside from minor

---

[242] *A. J. A.* (1948) 123–34; *Kumarbi* 86 ff.; *Arch.* 6 (1953); *C. H. M.* 2 (1954); *J. C. S.* 5 (1951) 135–61; 6 (1952) 8 ff.

[243] *Kumarbi* 115; Heubeck, *Gym.* 62 (1955) 518. Cf. Steiner, *Sukzess. Myth.*, who contrasts the four generations of the Phoenician and Hurrian epics with the three of the Babylonian and Hesiodic versions.

[244] See e.g. Steiner, *Sukzess. Myth.*; West, *Hesiod* 27 ff.

[245] The alphabetical Ras Shamra texts, discovered at Ugarit, have vindicated the antiquity of the Phoenician story recounted by Philo of Byblos, who claimed to have acquired his knowledge from the writing of a certain Sanchuniathon who lived "at the time of the Trojan War" (the main source is Eusebius, *Praep. Evangel.*, but the text is also given in e.g. Jacoby, *Fr. Gr. H.* III c No. 790), see Güterbock, *A. J. A.* (1948);

differences the basic motifs common to the Hurrian, Phoenician and Greek stories concern the parallel succession of gods in all instances: the Hurrian Alalu, Anu, Kumarbi, Teshub correspond with the Phoenician Eliun (Hypsistos), Uranus, El (Kronos), Demarus (Zeus), and the Greek (Oceanus)[246], Uranus, Kronos, Zeus. If we compare the second with the fourth generation we see the identical significance of all figures. Thus Uranus, like Anu, signifies "Heaven", while El, Kumarbi, and Kronos are shown to be identical by the "Doppelname" El-Kumarbi which has been found on a Hurrian tablet at Ras Shamra[247], and by Philo's equation: El-Kronos.

El and Kumarbi are further connected with Kronos through the story of the stone. Kumarbi's indigestible stone in the Greek version was *mutato nomine* repeated: in this case the actor was the *omphalos* (navel), honoured by Zeus and worshipped at Delphi. In the Phoenician account we hear of the βαιτύλια, λίθους ἐμψύχους which Uranus sent to El (Kronos)[248]. Another point: in all three cases the fourth generation was composed of Weathergods: Teshub, Demarus and Zeus. More difficult to explain is the likeness between the first links of the divine families. Eliun, Hypsistos of Byblos, eludes a clear definition: whether he came early or late to the Phoenician pantheon, his figure lacks colour. He is never more than "the father of El"[249]. Alalu and Anu derive from the Babylonian Alala and Anu in the *Enuma Elish*. There is some evidence to say that Alalu was connected with the concept of an "Urflut" (cf. Tiamat)[250], in which case he could well be compared with the Greek Oceanus, whose position as the "source of the gods" and the earliest link of the Greek divine succession is still remembered in Homer[251]. Thus the factor common to all, including the Babylonian

---

Kumarbi 111. For a history of the discovery see E. Jacob, *Ras Shamra et l'Ancien Testament*. See also West, *Hesiod* 24 ff.

[246] Only indicated in Homer, cf. below n. 251.

[247] Güterbock, *A. J. A.* (1948); *Kumarbi* 112.

[248] See Schwabl, "Weltsch." 1488.

[249] See Dussaud, *Rel. Hitt. Hourr.* 360. The Old Testament tried to identify him with El. "The first king is a nonentity", West, *Hesiod* 27.

[250] Schwabl, "Weltsch." 1487.

[251] *Il.* 14, 201; 302. Despite Herodotus (II, 53), Homer never composed a theogony. He was, however, fully aware of the Oriental system of divine dynastic progression. In *Iliad* 14 Oceanus is the father of the gods: Hypnos speaks of him as the primary force (14, 246). Hera, too, sets out to go to the bounds of the earth, to Oceanus the *genesis* of the gods, and to mother Tethys. Compare with this *Iliad* 5, 898, where we hear of Uranus as the father of the Titans, and again *Iliad* 4, 59, where Kronos' title of ἀγκυλομήτης (crooked in counsel) might well imply knowledge of the dread fate of his father

Enuma Elish, was a progression from the god of Heaven down to the Weather-god: Marduk, respectively Enlil, Teshub, Demarus, Zeus, except that Hesiod alone did not add a prior element before the Sky-god Anu or Uranus. The gods involved in these generations were forces of nature, and their fortunes represented cosmogonic concepts in mythological dress.

Such concepts were responsible for common features like the separation of Heaven and Earth, still apparent in Sumerian myth[252], and the struggle that usually accompanied the progression from generation to generation[253]. With the inclusion of these features in his *Theogony* Hesiod clearly betrays his dependence on Eastern mythology. His debt becomes all the more obvious by the fact that the struggles of succession, as well as the memory of the separation of Heaven and Earth, seem to lack motivation in his poem[254]. We do not, nor can we expect to, find uniformity of arrangement and description of these common motifs in the Babylonian, Hurrian, Phoenician and Greek epics. The separation myth alone, perhaps already implicit in the common emasculation motif, may be thought to happen at the beginning, or at the very end, of the epic[255].

Also the struggle between the cosmic forces may take varied forms. It may occur between the "Urprinzip" and the first gods, as in the *Enuma Elish* when Tiamat fashions the monster Kingu to destroy the gods. Or, as in the song of Ullikummi and in Hesiod's *Theogony*, the contest may be fought between the Weather-god and his displaced father and involve a monster Ullikummi, or Typhon respectively, which is sent against the Weather-god. Alternatively, as in the Phoenician creation story, other elements may be drawn into the fight[256]. In the Song of Ullikummi the struggle is between Kumarbi and the Weather-god. The monster Ullikummi grew on the shoulders of Upelluri until he reached heaven. Teshub caught sight of him from Mt. Hazzi and cut him from Upelluri's shoulder. At first glance the form taken by the contest between Kumarbi and Teshub is paralleled in Hesiod by that of Zeus' struggle with the Titans who had, of

---

Uranus. References in the *Iliad* to Zeus' struggle with the Titans (14, 201–4) the latter's confinement in Tartarus (8, 428–81), the fight with Typhoeus (2, 781 ff.), the god's revolt against Zeus (1, 397–401) etc., reveal Homeric knowledge of the Eastern dynastic struggle. For these and similar points see Heubeck, *Gym.* 62 (1955) 519.

[252] See n. 237.
[253] Cf. Schwabl, "Weltsch.", 1492.
[254] Cf. Dornseiff, *L'Ant. Class.* (1937) 253. But see below (pp. 58 f. and n. 274) for Hesiod's moral and ethical motivation of the divine succession.
[255] See below n. 279.
[256] See Schwabl, "Weltsch." 1488.

course, been sent by Kronos. However, there are many points of disagreement between both stories[257] which make it impossible to derive the Greek version directly from the Hurrian epic, although both tales belong to the same motif of the struggle between cosmogonic elements[258].

Closer to hand is the curious and unmotivated digression in the *Theogony* which deals with Typhon's threat to the rule of Zeus[259]. The correspondence between the figures Typhon and Ullikummi, and quite generally the Oriental monstrous creatures contesting the rule of the Weather-god, has frequently been noted[260]: the name Typhon[261] has been identified by Astour as Semitic[262], but, true or not, his rebellion against Zeus is closely parallel to that of Ullikummi against Teshub.

There are discrepancies between Hesiod's account of Typhon and the song of Ullikummi. Thus Typhon is said to be the offspring of Gaia[263] and not of Kronos, and he is imagined in monstrous shape with a hundred snakes growing from his shoulders[264]. But other Greek versions of this myth

[257] See Güterbock, *A. J. A.* (1948); *Kumarbi* 103. On these and similar divergencies see also Steiner, *Sukzess.*, and West, *Hesiod*.

[258] Cf. Schwabl, "Weltsch." 1452. Sumeria was most likely the source of theogonic myth which was transmitted to Babylonian epic and came to Greece already diversified by Hurrian and Semitic additions and alterations. Walcot, *Hesiod and N. E.* 1–26, discounts Hurrian influence on Hesiod, and he cites a Babylonian *Epic of Era* (composition c. 1050–750 B. C.) which, according to him (p. 51), in addition to *Enuma Elish*, influenced the Greek *Theogony*. This means that Babylonian tales of this type could not have reached Greece before the ninth century (Walcot, *op. cit.* 53). This history can only be partly true. Oriental influence on Greece was continuous, that is it began in the Bronze Age or earlier, but did not end with the collapse of the Mycenaean world.

[259] Hesiod, *Theog.* 820–80.

[260] For modern literature see J. Schmidt, "Typhoeus, Typhon" in *Roscher/M. L.*; W. Porzig, "Illuyankas und Typhon", *Kl. F.* 1 (1930) 379–86; Dornseiff, *Phil.* 89 (1934) 400; *Ant. Cl.* 6 (1937) 251; Güterbock, *Kumarbi* 103 ff. Cf. above n. 233. See also F. Vian, *Éléments Orientaux dans la Religion Grecque Antique*, Paris 1960, 17 ff., and for a detailed discussion of all these monsters see J. Fontenrose, *Python*, Berkeley 1959. For the structure of Hesiod's Typhon story see Schwabl, "Weltsch." 1452 f.; *He.* 90 (1962) 122 f., with further modern literature.

[261] Which also occurs in Philo's account beside the children of Kronos, Güterbock, *Kumarbi* 113.

[262] From West.-Sem. *Saphon* (the home of Baal), if Astour is right, *Hellenos.* 216 f. If true this would invalidate Vian's thesis, *Élém.* 17 ff., that Typhon was not of Oriental origin. West, *Hesiod* 392, believes that "this myth only came to Greece in the Hellenistic period."

[263] Hesiod, *Theog.* 821.

[264] *Ibid.* 825.

not only remarkably well preserve Typhon's Oriental background, but also satisfactorily establish the close relationship between the Hurrian and Greek accounts. In one instance[265] Typhon becomes the offspring of Kronos, while Pindar[266], Aeschylus[267], and Nonnus[268] localize his myth in Cilicia to the north of Syria. Consider, too, that Apollodorus[269] lets Zeus pursue Typhon to the *Mons Casius*, the classical name of Mt. Hazzi, where Teshub is said to have seen Ullikummi first[270].

Not all of Hesiod was borrowed, of course; the concept and function of Eros, for example, was the fruit of his own lucubration[271], while the account of the Five Ages has memories of popular tradition[273]. Far more important than isolated instances of original contributions to the age-old *corpus* of theogonic poetry are those parts of Hesiod's work in which the poet gives his own, peculiarly Greek, interpretation of old motifs. Hesiod's personal deeply rooted convictions of justice and fairness in the world imparted changed values to the purely temporal, or cyclic, dynastic progressions in heaven. The move from Uranus to Kronos to Zeus was achieved on moral

---

[265] Schol. on Homer, *Il.* 2, 783.
[266] *Pyth.* I, 17.
[267] *Prom. Vinct.* 357.
[268] *Dionys.* 1 and 2; the schol. in n. 265.
[269] *Bibl.* I, 39 ff.
[270] See above p. 45. For further comparative detail see Güterbock, *A. J. A.* (1948) 131; *Kumarbi* 103 ff. Porzig's comparison of the Typhon motif with features of the Illuyanka – snake – myth, *Kl. F.* 379–86, effectively shows that, contrary to Vian, *Élém.* 17 ff., and Schwabl, "Weltsch." 1453, Apollodorus was working with old sources. Cf. Güterbock, *Kumarbi* 104. On the dependence of the Typhon myth on the story of Illuyanka see now also Otten, *Rel. d. alt. Kleinasien* 115; and West, *Hesiod* 391 f.
[271] Perhaps here, too, we must suspect a memory of the Phoenician *Pothos* figure in the creation myth, see Dornseiff, *Ant. u. alt. Orient* 43; cf. Hölscher, *He.* 81 (1953) 396 f.
[273] For the story of the Five Age in the *Works & Days* see my *Death, Fate and the Gods*, App. VIII, 352–7. For probable Oriental links see also Heubeck, *Gym.* 62 (1955) 510 f. The concept of the Isle of the Blest may have been borrowed from Oriental and Egyptian tradition, see Nilsson, *M. M. R.* 629 f. It is interesting to note in this connection that the formulation of abstracts is not solely due to Hesiod, as is usually thought, but also derives from Babylonian and Phoenician practice. Thus, for example, the Hesiodic *Eunomia* and *Dike* are equivalent to the Akkadian *Kittu* and *Mesharu*, cf. Güterbock, *Kumarbi* 114 (see also West's discussion on abstract concepts in Hesiod, *Hesiod* 33 f.). The concept of a Golden Age of man can also be traced to Sumeria whence there has come to light a tablet belonging to a Sumerian epic poem describing the days when "There was no fear, no terror. Man had no rival." See Kramer, *Sum. Myth.* frontispiece and p. 107 n. 2. There may also be Babylonian parallels of this and the Silver Age, Astour, *Hellen.* 219 f.

grounds: in each case the father had sinned against his son and was bound to expiate his crime with the loss of his throne[274]. But these points are of greater relevance to literary appreciation than to an understanding of common origins. The elements most disturbing to later Greek thought, and excluded from their pantheon, were the two antecedents of Zeus: Uranus and Kronos, representing first the sky as primal element and secondly Kronos, a god of vegetation and the harvest, related to the Phoenician Dagon, as the divider of the Sky and Earth[275]. Zeus himself was the Indo-European name of the Weather-god superimposed on the Aegean male deity found in Greece and Crete who was destined to wrest the divine kingship from his father[276]. This Zeus we may perhaps identify with the Kretagenes, the god who, according to Hesiod[277], was born on the Goat Mountain[278].

All versions repeated three concepts with a bearing on later Greek development. The first concerned the separation of Heaven from Earth, the second the dynastic progression of either three or four generations, and the third the cruelty with which this progression was achieved. The first of these is of somewhat minor value to a comparative study between East and West, because, as a cosmogonic feature, it was too popular among primitive mythologies to be of much use to the student of Greek religion. Separation legends were prominent in many other cultures from New Zealand to Japan, similar enough in content to be classified together in the studies by Numazawa and Staudacher[279]. They were nonetheless an intrinsic portion

---

[274] This point is well brought out by Erbse, *Phil.* 108 (1964) 27.
[275] See below pp. 63 f.
[276] We may note in this connection an interesting thesis which in the main agrees with the theory advanced here, although in the former case the author perhaps assumes more than the evidence will bear. J. G. Macqueen, "Hattian Mythology and Hittite Monarchy", *A. S.* 9 (1959) 180, maintains that in both Anatolia and Greece the Indo-European invaders (Hittites and Achaeans) brought with them their Weather-god who in the East is imagined to marry an earlier Anatolian type Mother Goddess, and Hera in Greece. The only distinction, Macqueen asserts, between East and West in this respect was that the figure of the Anatolian goddess dominated the Weather-god, while Hera became secondary to Zeus.
[277] *Theog.* 484.
[278] Above p. 14, and see the interesting discussion of "The Birth of Zeus" by West, *Hesiod* 290–94.
[279] D. *Weltanf. in d. japan. Mythol.*; D. *Trenn. v. Himm. u. Erde*, cited by Bianchi, *Dios Aisa* 151 n. 1. Nonetheless even the Babylonian and Greek epics know of differences in detail that deserve to be noted. Thus in the *Enuma Elish* the separation takes place after the creation of the important gods and life on earth. Only then does Marduk sever Tiamat to form the two parts: Heaven and Earth. In Hesiod, however, and in

of our creation stories and can explain an otherwise puzzling feature of the divine succession. The dynastic progression was the central point of our epics: it consisted, as we noticed, of three or four links which stood for a primal element – except in Hesiod – followed by the god of Heaven, a general god of vegetation or corn, and the Weather-god. Perhaps Forrer and Güterbock[280] are correct in believing the Babylonians to have invented this system. Judging from the Mesopotamian religious tradition, however, we may, with Professor Hooke[281], suspect at least the germ of this idea to have been present in Sumerian myth. The close similarity of all the Oriental divine generations with their common features makes it appear as if we are dealing with a pattern, a pattern of kingship in fact, modelled, as it were, on that of a city-state in a theocratic society.

The pattern I have in mind is closely related to that shown to have existed in the East by Hooke[282], whose argument overruled Professor Frankfort's reservations[283]. The vital features of the kingship pattern consisted in the periodic renewal of the royal office, together with a complex ritual designed symbolically to celebrate the return of vegetation. This was normally done in one of two ways. Either the vegetation god re-emerged from hiding, like the Hittite god Telepinu[284], or he was annually reborn and each

---

the Kumarbi epic the separation is implied as happening in the beginning, so that we are closer here to the Sumerian story where at the beginning An carried off Heaven and Enlil carried off Earth. Further, the Kumarbi epic knows of a second, almost symbolic, act of separation when Teshub on Ea's command fetches "the copper knife with which they had parted Heaven and Earth", and with it cuts the monster Ullikummi from Upelluri's shoulders. We are no longer in a position to answer how much this duplication owes to outside influence, or how the closely connected story of the Flood fits into the structure, nor can we go into detail concerning the types of separation myths as established by Numazawa. On this point see Schwabl, "Weltsch." 1509 f.; cf. West, *Hesiod* 211–3, "The castration of Uranos".

[280] *Kumarbi* 106, where the reference to Forrer is given.

[281] *Bab. and Assyr. Rel.* 58. Cf. above n. 258 and West, *Hesiod* 22.

[282] In *Myth. Rit. and Kingsh.* 1–9.

[283] For references see Hooke, *ibid.* Cf. Frankfort, *Kingsh. and the Gods* 295; and n. 1 on p. 405.

[284] See the Myth of Telepinu. The different versions of the text from the Bogazhkeuy tablets is given by Gaster, *Thespis* 302–15. Cf. on this myth Gurney, *Hittites* 183 ff. Macqueen, *A. S.* 9 (1959) 174, believes that Telepinu was not a fertility god, because he did not die, but the Hattian Weather-god. Yet in the text (Gurney, *Hittites* 184) Telepinu is clearly stated to be the son of the Weather-god. For a view similar to that of Macqueen see Schwabl, "Weltsch." 1491, who draws the somewhat drastic conclusion that the similarity, or even identity, of Weather- and Vegetation-god explains why the Cretan *Kouros* could become identified with the Greek Zeus.

year celebrated a sacred marriage to refertilize nature. In Babylon the periodic renewal occurred during the New Year festival[285], the occasion on which the Creation Epic was solemnly recited. Now this periodic festival dealt both with the enthronization of Marduk (Bel), and with the reconsecration of the king who drew new strength for his divinely appointed office from a communion with his god. On each occasion Marduk, or Assur, or the equivalent god, relived his struggle for divine kingship. This struggle, one feels, was intimately connected with the contest of nature's elemental forces on the one hand, and the cyclical – that is growing and dying – form of human kingship on the other, whose representative could, as we have seen, on certain occassions enjoy divine status himself.

Much of this remains conjecture. Nonetheless the following is one example which not only suggests a cycle, but also reveals that the Oriental conception of kingship had a definite impact on Greek religion beyond Hesiod's acceptance of the outward mechanics of the genealogical system. In the Hurrian epic of Kumarbi Alalu reigned for nine years, was deposed by Anu who in turn after nine years yielded to Kumarbi. The number nine is important: it implies a definite temporal rhythm such as we find elsewhere in the office of kingship, namely in Crete as well as in Greece. In *Odyssey* 19, 179 Homer spoke of Minos who was king of Knossos for nine years – ἐννέωρος βασίλευε – and the bosom friend of Zeus. This reference we can interpret with the help of Plato, *Laws* 624 d, as meaning that Minos every nine years retired to the cave of Zeus where he renewed his kingship[286].

Connected with this periodic renewal is the famous story in Plutarch[287] of the tribute of seven youths and seven maidens sent to Knossos every nine years. Certain Delphic and Theban festivals, like the Daphnephoria, which recurred every nine years belonged to the same category. Compare with this another story of Plutarch, according to which the Spartan ephors every ninth year watched the night sky for signs of a shooting star which signified the end of the king's rule[288].

Such instances suggest the survival of the Oriental concept concerning a rhythmic cycle of kingship whose significance, however, was no longer perfectly understood in the West. In Hesiod's *Theogony* we find the Eastern

---

[285] For a good account of the ritual in the month Nisan, and the texts, see Hooke, *Bab. Assyr. Rel.* Append. pp. 101–23.
[286] Cf. Schwabl, "Weltsch." 1485 and n. Above p. 42.
[287] *Theseus* 15.
[288] *Agesilaus* 11. Cf. Willetts, *Cret. Cults* 94 f.

genealogical system stripped of its basic significance and subordinated to a theology which did not make due allowance to the original context of its sources, but was based on moral grounds[289]. Therefore the cruelty with which Kronos usurped supreme power from Uranus was senseless, because its original religious or mythological meaning had been ignored or forgotten. The savage manner in which Kronos deposed Uranus was similar to that found in the Kumarbi epic and originally[290], of course, carried the same significance as when Marduk cut Tiamat in half: "He split her like a shellfish into two parts: Half of her he set up and ceiled it as sky, pulled down the bar and posted guards[291]." In each instance the act referred to the separation of Heaven and Earth accomplished by a sword, copper knife, or sickle. The separation symbolically released fertility and life into the world. For example the emasculation of the Sky-god[292], which is an essential ingredient in the Greek and Hurrian myths, served to create some of the first vegetation powers like the river Tigris, chthonic beings like the Erinyes and the Melian Nymphs[293], and in the Kumarbi epic even the Storm-god himself.

It is possible to extract the general principle that underlay the common motif, namely the symbolic representation of the beginning of life in which the emasculation scene played an important part since it described the parting of the primal male and female elements and the first fertilization of Earth as a separate entity. Here Hesiod still betrayed his sources. Gaia, indeed, conceived her children from Uranus, but she was yet one with the Sky and felt confined by her children hidden within her; wherefore she prepared the *drepanon*, or *harpe*, with which Kronos performed his deed. Kronos, like the Phoenician El and the Hurrian Kumarbi, performed the function of the emasculation of the Sky. At one time Kronos was probably the god of corn[294], so that he seemed the natural agent to wield the *harpe* which released fertility on earth. The *harpe*, incidentally, was a suitable

---

[289] See n. 274.

[290] To what extent Hesiod still agreed with the original motivation of this succession – separation theme – is another matter which does not really affect our argument. On this point see Erbse, *Phil.* (1964) 6.

[291] Speiser's transl. of *Enuma Elish* Tabl. IV, 137–9.

[292] For the view that castration merely signified loss of sovereignty see J. G. Griffith, *The Conflict of Horus and Seth*, Liverpool 1960, 39 n. 1.

[293] Schwabl, "Weltsch." 1442 n. 2, correctly points out that the myth of the creation of the Melian Nymphs from the parts of Uranus conceals an old tradition concerning the origin of man.

[294] M. P. Nilsson, "The Sickle of Kronos", *B. S. A.* 46 (1959) 124.

implement for the god, because from pre-historic times it was used for the reaping of the harvest[295]. It is possible that the Greeks first thought of placing the common harvesting tool in Kronos' hands for this gruesome purpose[296], but more likely is the explanation that the *harpe* found its way into the Greek version on analogy with the instrument of separation in the Hurrian creation legend, and in the Babylonian *Enuma Elish*. The word *harpe* could be of Eastern, Semitic, origin[297], and its use for the emasculation of the Sky may well imply that a motive of fertilization of the earth is also contained in the story of the separation[298]. The connection between the *harpe* and the knife[299], or sword, with which the separation is achieved in the Kumarbi story and *Enuma Elish* is not obvious. Perhaps the Phoenician creation myth provides the link between East and West, for in this version Kronos' (El's) *harpe*, according to Schwabl, was derived from the Oriental sword[300].

How far may we compare the nature and function of Kronos, El, and Kumarbi? If Kronos, in fact, was a god of corn, it is interesting to note that his Phoenician equivalent El has at times been identified with Dagon, the god of corn (Zeus Arotrios, Siton), brought to Mesopotamia, and eventually to Syria, by the western Semites who founded the Dynasty of Akkad (third millennium B.C.). Dagon became El's brother in Philo's genealogical table[301]. Kumarbi fits our comparative scheme less easily; he is indeed often identified with Enlil, the Sumerian god of the Earth[302], but not in the

---

[295] *Ibid.* For a somewhat different view see West, *Hesiod* 217 f.

[296] Schwabl, "Weltsch." 1446, believes that the harvesting sickle and the Eastern "Sichelschwert" are one.

[297] See Barnett, *J. H. S.* (1945) 10; Staudacher, *Trenn. v. Himm. u. Erde* 69; Hölscher, *He.* (1953) 393 n. 1; Lämmli, *Chaos* II, 104 n. 389. Against Nilsson, *B. S. A.* (1951) 122, while Schwabl, "Weltsch." 1446, reaches a compromise.

[298] Cf. Schwabl, "Weltsch." 1445, who cites Lesky, *S.* (1955) 42.

[299] For a discussion, with literature, of this part of the text of the Ullikummi myth see Lämmli, *Chaos* II, 104 n. 389.

[300] Schwabl, "Weltsch." 1488. This derivation, however, seems to be disproved by West, *Hesiod* 218. As evidence of Oriental origin Lesky cites the picture of a god with sickle on an Assyrian relief in the British Museum, *S.* 6 (1955, 4 (Dornseiff, *Anz.* 48 [1933] 755 fig. 1). According to Dirlmeier, *R. M.* 98 (1955) 19, the tooth-edged (καρχαρόδους) sickle first appears in Greek art on an eighth century Boeotian *fibula*.

[301] See Dussaud, *Rel. des Hitt.* 364 f. While Dussaud denies the identification, he proposes that from the second millennium El supplanted Dagan.

[302] For references see Güterbock, *Kumarbi* 94 n. 14.

Kumarbi myth. One reference to Kumarbi's inflicting famine on the people[303] may not be judged sufficient for our purpose.

The basic features of the creation myths we studied reveal that we are dealing with what has been called a rhythmical pattern intimately joined with the birth and development of life and vegetation. Such a cyclical conception was utterly incompatible with the later Greek belief in the history and value of its gods who had to be permanent and immortal or else be denied admittance to the pantheon. Greek feeling was already lucidly reflected in Hesiod's theology, for there the divine genealogy was largely devoid of its Oriental significance. The central figure was Zeus, and it is from the point of Zeus' eternal, unalterable, rule that the earlier stages were considered. Uranus had no standing in the Greek family of gods. Kronos, when all is said and done, was a mythological figure in classical Greece, not a cultic one[304]. He was the god of the Golden Age. Apart from a statue beside Zeus and Hera[305] in Lebadeia, no image was dedicated to him. His only temple was that built by Peisistratus who took his model from Olympia.

Modern scholars have made much of the differences between the Oriental and Greek pantheon. The Eastern centralized despotism has been contrasted with the Mycenaean tribal city-state under the leadership of a military king. However, while it is impossible now to go into detail about the social structure of the Mesopotamian city of the fourth and third millennia[306], one should note that such distinctions rest on a misunderstanding of the society of a city-state, which during the Bronze Age reflected the divine structure on both sides of the Aegean. In fact, careful investigation of the development of the Mesopotamian and Greek city-states during the Bronze Age, and comparisons between the social features and structure of the pantheon in such cities on the Greek mainland and particularly in Syria, have revealed some striking similarities for the second and even first millennia

---

[303] *Keilschrifturkunden aus Bogazhkoey*, IV, 1, IV, 22 and 24, cited by Güterbock, *ibid*.
[304] Kronos cults seem to have been rare in Greece. Kumarbi enjoyed no cult in Hittite times – see Güterbock, *A. J. A.* (1948) 132 f. Kronos' original function as god of vegetation was seen above; but even if at some point he received cult in this capacity no trace of this survived into Classical times. Nor is there any clear evidence of Kronos – like the Ugaritic El – as King of the Gods. Such a theory was posited on the strength of a common etymology which derived χρόνος from κραίνω – Schwabl, "Weltsch." 1449, who also cites Pohlenz and Kretschmer.
[305] Pausanias, IX, 39, 4.
[306] See above n. 152; 197.

B.C.[307]. Our evidence for Mycenae is admittedly not as good as we might wish. But what has been said so far contains a fair quantum of proof that Mycenae borrowed certain features of the priest-king system together with the belief in a chief deity at the head of a theocratic society. Her creditor, both directly and indirectly, in large measure was the East. Perhaps the Homeric δημοβόρος βασιλεύς and his divine protection, as in the incident where Athena prevents Achilles from slaying Agamemnon in a fit of rage, may count as memories of the despotic king[308].

Zeus became the head of the Mycenaean pantheon. But the Mycenaeans also drew from other traditions: indeed a host of divinities – with speaking names in Greek (like Aphaea, Britomartis, Ariadne, Dictynna) – found their way to the mainland. Many of these, however, were absorbed by the more successful gods and goddesses, or, like Ariadne and Helen, they were given no significant place in the freshly evolving scheme. They passed into the shadowy realm of mythology. The surviving deities were above all the guardian figures of the palace and Mycenaean city, like Athena and Hera, who now joined a wider group of gods, eventually to be gathered into the Homeric family of Olympians. Their history and origin have been carefully traced by Nilsson[309], and recently summarized by Professor Guthrie in a separate fascicule of the *Cambridge Ancient History*[310]. From this history there emerges the notable fact that the Mycenaean pantheon consisted not only of Cretan borrowings, but also of gods – mostly powers of nature and wild life – who etymologically, or by reason of their functions, belonged to what we have named an Aegean substratum. In other words, they were revered under different names in both East and West. Such gods included Athena, Artemis, Poseidon – the husband of Earth – Apollo, and even Hermes. The family, we noticed, had important features in common with the Eastern pantheon, because, I venture to suggest, it was essentially born in the same manner under similar circumstances, and it served the same purpose in the same kind of city-state. However, Greek thought often found itself at variance with the Oriental religious attitude, and thus imposed

---

[307] See also Astour, *Hellen.* 359.
[308] *Il.* 1, 188 ff. F. Robert, *Homère*, Paris 1950, 7 f., interprets this passage as a poetic attempt at psychology.
[309] *Gesch.* I, 383 ff.
[310] W. K. C. Guthrie, "The Religion and Mythology of the Greeks", *C. A. H.²*, 1961, 45 ff.

changes on traditional material to cut itself spiritually adrift from the East, even until fresh bonds were forged by Alexander the Great[311].

The Greeks freed themselves from the old position of servitude and bondage to their gods, at the cost, one might add, of what we call moral purpose. Yet this was a small price to pay for the release from a rigid theocratic society in which each man was a servant of a god. When this release occurred we can no longer establish. We suspect, however, that it arose from the decay of the old priest-kingship which was concurrent with the dissolution, at the end of the second millennium, of the Mycenaean city-state. The process of liberation from divine servitude was complete at the time of the foundation of a new kind of *polis* that was held together not by tribal ties, but by the bonds of convenience. The acropolis of the new cities inherited the old pantheon: Zeus, Hera, Artemis and Athena still reigned supreme in a more or less harmonious family, but their relationship to the members of the city had altered. They had been progressively more humanized, partly under Mycenaean influence, and partly because in Homer the projection of the contemporary human on the divine society had become accomplished fact[312]. The boundary of man's influence, that is his mortality, remained the same in Homer and in the East[313]. Notice, for instance, the Homeric ring in the moving lines from the Babylonian version of the Gilgamesh Epic when the hero in his quest for Utanapishtim (the Mesopotamian Deukalion), and the plant of life, was upbraided by Siduri for aiming beyond his natural station: "Gilgamesh", she said, "Whither rovest thou? The life thou pursuest thou shalt not find. When the gods

---

[311] To appreciate these changes in detail we will have to consider Homeric religion and contrast it with some popular cults, the latter of which retaining memories of those parts of Mycenaean and pre-historic religion which the Homeric poets discarded as eventually unsuitable for the narrow circle of society for whom the lays were composed. Popular religion, and by that I mean cults like the Eleusinian Mysteries, will guide the researcher to Cretan and Eastern traditions imported into Greece, as well as mark out newly instituted practices, like hero-worship, which probably found its beginning in the Mycenaean Age. In short, everything pertaining to a belief in afterlife for man was, with the exception of some vague memories, excluded from epic. Such ideas could only subsequently develop and flourish under the influence of Orphism and philosophy.

[312] Although after the Dark Age the gulf between the actual divine and mortal sphere was destined to grow ever wider particularly through the agency of the lyric poets. Cf. Webster, *Myc. to Hom.* 291.

[313] Egypt again is an exception, and this is reflected, strangely enough, in the inconsistent tale of Elysium in the *Odyssey* (4, 563 ff.).

created mankind, death for mankind they set aside, life in their own hands retaining. Thou, Gilgamesh, let full be thy belly, make thou merry by day and by night."[314].

Mortality apart, man was entirely free. The gods in turn, provided they were paid their due in sacrifice and cult, did not make man account for his actions. Thus the Greeks, in drawing from another tradition, left no room for any force of moral arbitration. *Dike*, in anything approaching our modern sense of Justice, did not make her appearance in Homeric epic[315]. We are all familiar with the enlightened criticism such singular negligence called forth from the early philosophers, from men like Xenophanes. What may excite the imagination more, however, is the fact that in this Homeric conception of man's release from the old divine bondage lay the seed of the attitude of the subsequent classical *polis* to its gods, an attitude which allowed the untrammelled secular development of architecture, sculpture and drama, all of which had their beginnings in the religious life of man[316].

Human spiritual freedom was the unscaleable barrier separating the West from Eastern heritage, and nowhere was this divergence of beliefs better illustrated than in the altered concepts of fate. In Asia the religious calendar revolved about the New Year, the Nisan, or Akitu festivals, when men's destinies were fixed. Also throughout Akkadian and Ugaritic literature the possession of the tablets of destiny set apart the supreme figure of the pantheon like Marduk. Homer, however, rejected any idea of a complex fate as a tool of divine government. There was only one fate for man in the *Iliad* and *Odyssey*, and that was his mortality from which even Zeus could not deliver him, though the man be Sarpedon his own son.

Apparently there were areas of belief where East and West could never meet. Compared with the East, man in Homer had an easier life, less tied to ritual servitude or subject to religious fear. The only rules that bound

---

[314] Translated by Kramer from the old Babylonian version III, 1–7.
[315] To Homer and his audience the word conveyed no more than custom, usage, or order, among human affairs, as they were established by men for their own society. The concept of Dike as a divine power, manifest in every righteous act, began to be developed by Hesiod and Solon and found its full form in Aeschylean theology.
[316] Indeed, the gods did not remain as immoral as we see them in the *Iliad*. Their carefree abandon was curtailed by the piety of theologians like Aeschylus and Pindar. Even the poets of the *Odyssey* already felt the stirrings of a critical spirit which is reflected in the trust of Eumaeus in the gods' sense of fair play (14, 83 ff.), and, of course, in Zeus' speech in Book I (32 ff.), where he clearly attributes men's suffering to their own shameful lawlessness.

him were those devised by his fellow men, and these, we know, were kinder than the stern Eastern laws separating man from god. We need merely glance at a sacred Hittite text to hear that "The mind of the gods is the same as when a servant stands before his master... If the servant gives annoyance to his master; then one kills him, one mutilates his nose, his eyes, his ears... Then one disgraces him in public and one takes no account of him."[317] How alien would these sentiments have seemed to Homer's Zeus and Athena?

---

[317] Text in G. Furlani, *H. T. R.* 31 (1938) 4, 251–62.

II. SOME OLDER TRADITIONS IN MINOAN CRETE

"Out in the dark blue sea there lies a land called Crete, a rich and lovely land, washed by the waves on every side, densely peopled and boasting ninety cities. Each of the several races of the isle has its own language. First there are the Achaeans, then the genuine Cretans, proud of their native stock; next the Cydonians; the Dorians, with their three tribes; and finally the noble Pelasgians. One of the ninety towns is a great city called Knossos, and there, for nine years, King Minos ruled and enjoyed the friendship of almighty Zeus[1]." Odysseus' description of Crete shows not only that the Homeric poets had a fair acquaintance with the island, but especially the wonder and admiration with which they and their audience regarded Crete. To them Crete was a far off romantic island, the locale of Odysseus' lying adventure stories[2]: here Minos, the awful judge of the dead, had been king, here Daedalus had built the wondrous dancing ground for "fairtressed Ariadne"[3].

These and similar allusions in Homer strengthened the convictions of Heinrich Schliemann – Homer's most devout student – that the poet here, too, was describing more than legendary tradition. Illness, however, and frustrations[4] prevented him from achieving more than a little preparatory work; but one exploratory trench at Knossos alone produced such rich rewards that Schliemann spoke of uncovering the "Remnants of a civilization (in Crete), in comparison to which even the Trojan War is an event of yesterday." The main work of excavation and classification of finds at Knossos was left to the younger Arthur Evans who in time produced the great work on *The Palace of Minos at Knossos* in four volumes (and Index) the last of which appeared in 1936.

---

[1] Rieux's transl. of Homer, *Od*. 19, 172 ff.
[2] E.g. *Od*. 13, 256 ff.; 15, 291 ff.; 17, 522 ff.
[3] *Il*. 18, 591 f.
[4] See e.g. the last letters to Max Müller, *J. H. S.* 82 (1962) 104 f.

Since then, and in part contemporary with Evans' effort, archaeological work has been in progress throughout the island, but mainly in the north and south, in a truly international undertaking combining scholars from England, Germany, France, Italy, and Greece. Our knowledge of Cretan culture and history continues to grow every year with the increasing wealth of finds. A recent discovery, for example, was made at Kato Zakro where N. Platon in 1963 uncovered a palace dating to the L. M. period[5]. The religious historian's main interest, however, still lies in central Crete with its most important palaces and offerings, including sites from Herakleion to Amnisos and Mallia in the north, Mt. Ida, Jouktas, Lyttos in the centre, and Gortyn and Phaestos in the south, which borders on the fertile Mesara to the west.

The richest site remains Knossos, near the north coast between Herakleion and Amnisos. Knossos appears to have been the political and cultural centre of Crete throughout the Bronze Age. Here Evans excavated the island's largest and most impressive palace which he named the Palace of Minos after Homer's legendary king and judge of the dead. To Evans the Bronze Age Cretans became the Minoans, a title which they have since retained. In the course of his work at Knossos Evans noticed the almost regular levels of floors which seemed to point to a repetitive series of building and destruction reflecting the history of the island. The pottery found in the various levels helped, by means of comparative methods, to assign dates to the respective periods which Evans in this way classified in the chronological table of Early, Middle, and Late Minoan. The difficulty of this system rests in the fact that the Knossian historical periods, exemplified by the different levels, did not apply to all other Cretan centres, so that Evans' chronology, while convenient, may be said to simplify the course of Cretan events throughout the island.

Evans also came upon numerous examples of Cretan script of the two types which he named Linear A and B, the second of which has been deciphered as Mycenaean Greek, thus referring to a time not before the end of M.M. when Crete seemed to have been under Achaean domination[6]. Linear A, from the historian's point of view, is little more than worthless, because it remains undeciphered. The B script, therefore, together with the bulk of Cretan monumental evidence, forms the main portion of our tan-

---

[5] *J. H. S.* Archaeological Reports for 1963/4, 29.
[6] For a different view see J. T. Hooker, "Homer and L.M. Crete", *J. H. S.* 89 (1969) 60 ff. An L.M. III B stirrup jar with Linear B signs was discovered at Knossos in 1968, M. Popham, *K.* 8 (1969) 43 ff.

talizingly inadequate resources upon which to build an image of the culture of the Cretan Bronze Age community. The magnificent discoveries at Knossos confronted Evans with questions such as the kind of culture which obtained on the island of Crete, and the manner of religion practised by its inhabitants during the third and second millennium. What, indeed, were the origins of this people or their relationship with neighbouring states, particularly the peninsula of Greece?

Historically the Cretans appeared to move in a vacuum, as it were; what could be seen of their cultural and artistic achievements at the time not only was out of context, especially in relation to the classical Greek world, but also gave little evidence of a development over a particular period: it seemed to reflect a final stage of development. Evans' enthusiasm at the artistic perfection of Minoan remains not unreasonably convinced him of their vast superiority over what was left by the Mycenaean Greeks. It seemed to him that Greece in the Middle Bronze Age had been culturally and politically strongly influenced by the Minoans, because many of the finds on the mainland so obviously were Minoan in design and appearance, that they clearly either were imitations of Cretan work or indeed examples of Cretan workmanship wrought there or imported from the island.

Our knowledge of Crete has grown enough over the past thirty years to correct such first impressions. This work, however, has been, and still is, laborious and haunted by conjecture, for without understanding the early written texts our "evidence is purely archaeological, it has come down to us as a picturebook without a text."[7]. These pictures and the monumental remains must, of course, be interpreted on their own merits, and this has been done in great detail by scholars like M. P. Nilsson[8] whose discussions greatly illuminate much of the Minoan religious structure. In the absence, however, of written confirmation doubt inevitably attaches to any result which cannot be controlled by other independent evidence. Much can be done with the help of Mycenaean sources so closely related to Cretan art and, presumably, belief in the Late Bronze Age, as Professor Nilsson has conclusively shown. Again a number of Greek cult localities and practices, as well as a sizeable stock of Greek mythological material, which had their origin in Mycenaean times, contribute to our knowledge of Cretan affairs.

These aids suffice to paint a fairly broad and clear picture of the island's religion. However, from our discussion in the previous chapter it becomes

---

[7] Nilsson, *M. M. R.* 7.
[8] *Op. cit.*

apparent that we may now consider the extant Cretan material in a yet wider context which extends over much of the Aegean area; for Crete not only geographically but also culturally formed an integral portion of this. There are certain facts that place Crete in a group composed of members belonging to a larger community: chronologically the Bronze Age began for Crete at about the same time as for the rest of the Aegean peoples including e.g. the Cyclades and Asia Minor. The migratory movements which we noticed as occurring immediately preceding and during the Early Bronze Age in a westerly direction across the Aegean also involved the island of Crete which was further subject to contact with Egypt and Northern Africa[9].

In this way Crete became at this early time a part of a wider cultural group which, amongst others, shared – an important consideration for the study of Linear A – common linguistic features with the East[10], as well as aspects of religious cult. The palaces built on the island from M.M., that is from about 2000 B.C., give evidence of the high level of civilization attained by the Minoans. Unlike their later Mycenaean counterparts, such structures remained entirely unfortified. Evidently the inhabitants felt secure from outside attack. This millennium marked the best period of the Minoans when their fleet must have commanded mastery at least of part of the Aegean. Yet in part the design, purpose, and function of the Cretan palaces paralleled Eastern fashions[11]. The technique and style of frescoes seem to have been equally related, as were aspects of contemporary glyptic art[12]. The palaces, the bulk of the seal engravings and frescoes were part of the Cretan religious life; and the connection, of all these with the East helps to illustrate our thesis that Crete, at least at the beginning of her era of greatness, shared salient features of what we called an Aegean religious *koine*[13].

When we try to be more precise in fixing the Eastern provenance of Minoan thought, we are bound as far as possible to rely on our graph marking the prime areas of contact between East and West, where in fact the Cretans could have acquired their knowledge of the largely common religious beliefs: and the areas specially concerned in this quest were Syria and Anatolia. Supporting evidence for this thesis comes from ethnographic,

[9] See p. 20.
[10] See p. 20 and n. 103.
[11] Cf. p. 36 f. and notes.
[12] *Ibid*. Dr. Warren has privately told me of his different views on this point.
[13] See p. 20.

linguistic, researches, as well as from comparative archaeology on both sides of the Aegean. Unacceptable apparently is the proposal[14] that Phoenician, that is Western Semitic, colonies arrived in west and eastern Crete, during the second millennium B.C.

The Phoenician contribution, however, to Cretan religious life, with few exceptions like the Europa myth for example, at present remains vague. Much more fruitful in to-day's state of our knowledge is the astonishing correspondence, going back to Neolithic times, between certain features of Cretan and Anatolian culture particularly in the south-west portions of the latter. Schachermeyr's work on the remains of Neolithic and Bronze Age pottery in the Aegean area revealed to him the close ties between Greece and Crete and s.-w. Anatolia, especially at sites like Haçilar and Çatal Hüyük[17]. Professor John Evans, excavating the Neolithic levels at Knossos, discovered "that the first neolithic inhabitants there arrived with pottery and crops that can only be derived from western Anatolia[18]".

Western Anatolia is the scene of a great deal of work continuing to-day, of which the most exciting for us are the discoveries at Çatal Hüyük by James Mellaart. Here shrines, cultic symbols and figurines were uncovered which recall Cretan artifacts. This evidence we shall consider in greater detail in its context, although Mellaart's work is far from concluded, and much of what has been found does not easily agree with one particular interpretation. Our historical evidence, however, and the archaeological finds which are continually being brought to light compel us to look to the East for a better understanding of the mute pictorial Cretan remains; and it is the last source of information that gives the island her appropriate place in the Bronze Age Aegean community.

In the previous chapter we noticed that in religous practice Crete occasionally went her own way. Obvious differences concern the evident predominance of female deities as well as cult votaries: male deities appear to be rare and insignificant when compared with the number of goddess representations. Totally absent seem to be idols of gods associated with cult

---

[14] Astour, *Hellenosemitica* 347. The dates of Phoenician arrivals in the West remain uncertain. It is quite possible, so Prof. F. C. Fensham kindly informed me, that Astour's dates are too high. Cf. J. Boardman in his review of Astour's book in *C. R.* 16 (1966). Dr. Warren, again, expressed to me his disbelief in this theory. Faure, *B. C. H.* 89 (1965) 63, argues that Crete was colonized from the Peloponnese, the Cycladic and Dodecanese islands.

[17] Cf. p. 20 f.

[18] Cited from Mellaart, *A. S.* (1963) 78. Cf. *B. S. A.* 63 (1968) 271 ff.

and cult localities. Perhaps we should look for the male divine element in aniconic religious symbols like the double axe, or in other parts of the probable religious life of the island like the bull games. But there is little to be gained from hypotheses of this kind. Such problems in the Cretan context alone are insoluble, and we refrain from adding yet another conjecture to a field already replete with supposition. At times conjecture we must, but we shall try to work with known factors from other Aegean religions. Crete, we have said, belonged to a larger family and looked to the East for a number of fundamental religious concepts. In the beginning she shared in the religious *koine* we observed in the East. This is important, for it means that in their religious practices the peoples of the Bronze Age Aegean by and large had a common starting point, that is a shared heritage which was never entirely lost whatever the developments that occurred in Crete.

Much has been written since Evans about certain aspects of Cretan religion, and the most important work is still the second edition of Nilsson's work on "The Minoan and Mycenaean Religion and its Survival in Greek Religion." For sheer weight of exhaustive archaeological detail this study is fundamental to any analysis of the subject, as well as invaluable to a classification of cult localities and their divinities. Furthermore, in Part II of the book Nilsson discusses the most salient features of the relationship between Minoan-Mycenaean religion and Greek religion, such as "The Continuity of Cult and Cult Places", and the "Greek Goddesses of Minoan Origin". Nilsson still lacked the ability to read Linear B, he could not at the time make use of some of the Eastern archaeological evidence which led to the delineation of the "Kulturtrift". Nonetheless the picture of Cretan cult which emerged from his discussion is as clear as possible under the circumstances.

Equally clear, however, is the fact that this picture shows serious gaps: Minoan and Mycenaean material is still not readily separated, indeed there does not exist to-day a uniform history of Minoan religion alone for the simple reason that we do not know enough of the subject. The Bronze Age Cretans were an agricultural society, so that we can safely expect them, like their Aegean neighbours, to have observed certain common features of vegetation religion with its attendant ritual. In fact a number of Cretan seals and sealings give evidence of nature worship including in all likelihood a cult concerned with trees and celebrations in honour of a male deity symbolic of the growth and decay of vegetation. Such features fulfil our expectation in a Bronze Age society, like that of the Cretans, which conformed to the contemporary prevailing conditions that were discussed in the first chapter. We should rather be surprised if in this respect the Minoans differed from their neighbours. Therefore on the acceptable premise of common aspects of cult in the Aegean cultural community we may decipher some of the Minoan monumental evidence. It remains to be seen how dogmatic we can afford to be in the detailed interpretation of separate seals obviously depicting scenes from nature worship. In other words, no chronological sequence of events in the Cretan vegetation cycle will sound convincing if it is constructed from the pictorial design of seals alone without the help of written evidence. The risks of this procedure in any case are considerably enhanced by the fact that some of our Bronze Age rings may turn out to be forgeries.

Such a chronological sequence has been skilfully constructed by A. W. Persson[19]. In the absence, however, of corroborating evidence from a source other than the rings, Persson's discussions cannot be conclusive, but they remain vulnerable to the criticism that his material may equally persuasively be interpreted in other ways. We accept the fact that Cretan religion was based on nature worship: this merely signifies our admission that Crete, as a member of the larger Aegean cultural community, observed common aspects of cult practice which obtained throughout the area, from Greece to the Cyclades and Asia Minor. This factor enormously helps to evaluate several parts of Cretan religion by analogy with better documented centres, but by itself does not offer a uniform image of the island's religion, because we have no means of appreciating the extent to which the Minoans themselves developed inherited beliefs. In part perhaps Crete owed an independent evolution to a sense of security engendered by her protracted political isolation through centuries of peace which was ensured by her geographical position and the presence of a powerful fleet.

Some general forms of this nature religion were described in earlier pages to which we shall make reference when necessary. What we now hope to establish is the existence of a certain measure of cultural continuity uniting East with West, that is portions of Asia Minor with Crete, and the flourishing Crete of M.M. and L.M. with Greece. An example of the latter connection we already noticed in the figure of the "Divine Child" which survived in Greek belief and myth. But the question arises as to how we may benefit from the knowledge of the ties between East and West in the field of cultic practice, and particularly in that kind of cult which, both in Crete

---

[19] *The Religion of Greece in Prehistoric Times*; cf. K. D. White, "The Sacred Grove", G. R. 23 (1954) 112–27.

and in Anatolia, was first instituted in caves whence eventually it was transferred to other sites notably the domestic shrine. The cave, in both East and West, was the earliest locality of cult: there, it seems, was observed a ritual and religious worship which, basically concerned with nature religion, may have been diluted over the centuries, but which in essence persisted even when it came to be celebrated in different homes. Here, too, we are fortunate enough to have to hand new sources of information which, when exploited to the full, may also illuminate other important aspects of Minoan religion including the possible existence of a worship of the dead as well as the significance of the figure of the bull and its connection with a nature goddess.

Some archaeological finds of Cretan provenance point to the existence of a variety of cult localities "al fresco", which in certain instances consisted of altars in the open or in the courtyards of the palaces[20]. Larger separate cult-structures were the so-called temples, like the example at Gournia and Hagia Triada[21]. On a Cretan seal found in a Chamber Tomb, Mycenae, Sir Arthur Evans discovered a scene describing a cult about a sacred spring[22] such as probably existed at Mavro Spelio. These cult localities, however, were instituted relatively late: open and separate altars probably were not in use before M.M.[23], while no sacred chapel can be found to antedate L.M.[24]. Apart from such developments, we can distinguish in Crete three principal sites where cult was observed. Of these the oldest were the cave sanctuaries. The other two were the open peak sanctuaries on top of a mountain, and palace and domestic shrines. Temples there appear to have been none in Bronze Age Crete, and we may assume that other types of cult localities we encounter on the island derived from the three mentioned and particularly from the last – the domestic or palace cult. However, since Nilsson's detailed treatment of M.M. and L.M. Cretan domestic shrines and sanctuaries[25], additions to the subject will only serve a useful purpose if made in the light of fresh evidence. The goddess revered in such shrines was destined to play some considerable part in Mycenaean and Greek religion where she took her place as e.g. Athena. Accordingly,

---

[20] At Knossos, Mallia, Phaestus etc., Picard, *Rel. Preh.* 65 f.
[21] See especially N. Platon, *K. Ch.* 8 (1954) 428 ff.; *A. S. I.* 19/21 (1948) (1941/3) 28 ff.
[22] *P.M.* III, fig. 86, 137 ff.
[23] Cf. Picard, *op. cit.* 66.
[24] See Schachermeyr, *min. Kult. d. alt. K.* 159.
[25] *M. M. R.* 77 ff. Cf. the brief summaries in Hutchinson, *Preh. Cr.* 216 ff.; Schachermeyr, *op. cit.* 159 ff.

her Bronze Age history will be of some moment to the evaluation of the Greek religious scene. Our present concern is to consider that part of Cretan religion which can be interpreted anew with the assistance of recent Anatolian discoveries. For this reason a brief analysis of Cretan cave cult, sites, offerings etc. will serve as a firm basis of investigation and comparison.

Quite clearly the earliest sites were the caves where the evidence of some form of cult can at times be traced back to the Neolithic period. A factor of considerable interest is the knowledge that caves and rock shelters served the people of the Stone Age already as means of habitation. Here men not only spent their entire lives, but perhaps even offered worship and eventually were 'buried'. What divinities enjoyed cult in these caves obviously were felt either to live there together with the inhabitants, or at least appear in some form to their wards at regular intervals. The nature of such deities is, of course, unknown, but, especially with the arrival of agricultural cultivation, must have dealt with certain aspects of vegetation. Similar problems attach to any conclusions drawn from the many interments in caves. The first, and perhaps most important, question that arises in this connection is whether the proximity of the dead to the living[26] reflected a belief in after-life or at least in the power of the dead and their ability to influence the welfare of the living. This question will briefly recur later in this chapter; here we merely note the fact that caves continued to be used as burial places long after men had moved on to other forms of habitation, and that some caves give clear evidence of offerings made to the dead at least from E.M.

The most notable example of this practice may come from a cave northeast of Knossos, at Pyrgos where, beside many burials, there were found numerous objects of bronze like daggers, stone idols, obsidian flakes and more than 150 vases from E.M.[27]. Caves as burial locations from pre-historic times were so common indeed that later artificial tomb structures all derived from this model[28]. Another question concerns the possibility that, because of the use of caves as burial grounds, the gods revered on the same sites might well have been chthonic in nature[29]. Of further interest is the thought, although not really subject to proof, that a particular type of cult

---

[26] Willetts, *Cret. Cults and Fest.* 141, supposes that this form of burial "prompted the custom of burying the dead beneath the floor of the house, a custom which persisted in Greece to late Mycenaean times." Cf. Nilsson, *op. cit.* 53.
[27] Evans, *P.M.* I, 59; Xanthoudides, *Deltion* 4 (1918) 137; Nilsson, *op. cit.* 55.
[28] See e.g. F. Matz, *Kreta, Mykene, Troja* 37; 61; 121 ff.
[29] Cf. Matz, *op. cit.* 82.

observed in one or several of the Cretan caves was continued to historic times but in new localities, like the palace, to which the older practices had been transferred. These and similar questions will come up again in their context.

To begin with we shall consider a sampling of the many sites at present known with obvious traces of having been used for habitation and/or burial. Then we shall attempt to determine, as far as possible from the archaeological remains, if cult can be shown to have existed in some caves, whether such cult can be assumed to have been uniform in nature, how long in certain instances it may have continued, and if any deity can be isolated as the recipient of cult in such localities. Caves that are known to have been inhabited occasionally from Neolithic times extend over the length and breadth of the island[30]. In the west they include a cave on the peninsula of Diktynnaion where human remains were found together with Neolithic potsherds[31], and a cave at Hellenospelio[32]. One of the most interesting caves in Crete with remains suggesting the presence of cult from the Bronze Age to Roman times[33] is that at Amnisos which has been identified with Eileithyia's cave in Homer[34]. It has been fully explored by S. Marinatos[35] and by J. Hazzidakis[36], as well as by Faure who gives an account of its dimensions and contents[37].

Within the cave, which is about 60 m. long, the central position is held by a large stalagmite, surrounded by a low wall of stones not set in clay, and dating, according to Marinatos, to Minoan times. Throughout the cave there are scattered many sherds of all periods including Greek. The cult practised there may have been interrupted for a time during the classical Greek period, but was renewed in Roman and continued into Christian times, proof of which are the Roman and Christian lamps found there. In the plain of Lasithi another cave, with evidence of occupation and burial

---

[30] See e.g. the map at the back of P. Faure, *Fonctions*.
[31] Marinatos cited by Nilsson, *op. cit.* 67.
[32] P. Faure, "Grottes Crétoises", *B. C. H.* 80 (1956) 99.
[33] Few cult objects remain from archaic and classical times. Some vessels and a stone axe found in the cave suggest that the cult may have been instituted as early as the Neolithic period. But this is strongly contested by Faure, *Fonct.* 82 f., who does not believe Cretan cave cult could have come into being until later. According to him, the Stone Age objects were used for burial purposes. But see *B. C. H.* 96 (1972) 414.
[34] *Od.* 19, 188.
[35] *Praktika* (1929) 94; (1930) 91.
[36] *Parnassos* 10 (1886/7) 349.
[37] *Fonct.* 82 ff.

from Neolithic times, was found at Skaphidia, while not far distant Neolithic burials in rock shelters were discovered at Kastellos[38]. Other examples of habitation together often with interment in caves and rock shelters, from earliest times, come from a cave near Praesus with fragments of pottery from Neolithic to Geometric times[39], and one at Magasa near Palaikastro[40]. Caves that were used for burial extending over different periods of Cretan civilization can also be shown at Miamou, south of Hagia Deka, at Pyrgos, by the coast north-east of Knossos, at Gournia – where small rock shelters with graves from E.M.I. were uncovered – and a few miles east of Hierapetra[41].

Pyrgos we mentioned before as of special interest because of its large number of interments and the evidence of offerings to the dead. Another of these caves of great interest is the one at Miamou which has been explored by A. Taramelli[42] who discovered several layers with remains pointing to a long period of human habitation. The uppermost, and therefore most recent, layer was composed only of human bones and fragments of vases, which means that this cave had at one stage been abandoned as an habitation and subsequently was used exclusively for burial[43]. Probably the same separation between habitation and later use for burial occurred in another cave in the Lasithi plain at Meskine where burials were found from M.M. I[44]. In the same plain a cave at Trapeza contains evidence of having been inhabited from E.M. I, but used for burial from E.M. II probably until M.M. I[45]. Some caves, as we saw at Pyrgos, appear never to have served the living but were set aside for burial, a practice which persisted until the end of the Bronze Age. The dead commonly were placed in coffins or *larnakes*[46].

Whatever bearing on the existence of a cult of the dead this custom may have had, it is clear from these examples that in Cretan thought the significance of caves exceeded a simple utilitarian purpose of primitive dwellings to be abandoned as soon as men learnt to build their own abodes. Caves

---

[38] *B. S. A. 38* (1937/8) 4 f.; 9; 13.
[39] *B. S. A.* 8 (1901) 235. Faure, *op. cit.* 3, believes that burial and habitation were separate at Praesus.
[40] *B. S. A.* 9 (1902) 339; Nilsson, op. cit. 54.
[41] Sources and other examples in Nilsson, *op. cit.* 53 ff.
[42] *A. J. A.* I (1897) 287 ff.
[43] Cf. Faure, *Fonct.* 52 f.
[44] *B. S. A.* 38 (1937/8) 6 ff.
[45] *A. J. A.* 40 (1936) 371; *B. S. A.* 36 (1935/6) 31 ff.; 38 (1937/8) 14.
[46] Cf. Nilsson, *op. cit.* 56. For a full list of burial caves and the types of burial used see Faure, *Fonct.* 66 ff.

may not have been used as homes after E.M. I, but they did, most likely throughout the Minoan periods and into historical times, serve other, mainly religious, functions. One, we pointed out, was concerned with burial, others obviously dealt with wider aspects of the religious scene and continued in use, occasionally with some periods of interruption, for many centuries even in some instances down to Christian times. Caves in all likelihood were the earliest localities of some kind of worship. Such worship, however, was not a primitive step in a developing Cretan religion which came to find substitutes for these earlier forms. On the contrary, the special kind of religious observance found in the caves on the island never ceased to constitute an integral part of Cretan belief. Proof of this is contained not only in the prolonged cult continuity – whatever the changes in the original form – but also, and particularly, in the fact that a number of occasionally very important caves saw no cultic use before M.M. and later, that is at a time when worship already flourished in the palaces and their shrines.

Examples of such apparently late institutions of cult come from one of the most important sites of this nature in Crete, from Psychro near Lyttos. After some earlier preparatory work this cave – really a double cave – was excavated by the British School at Athens[47], which found a great many objects but none before M.M.[48]. Again, offerings found in another cave near Lyttos, at Phaneromeni, all belong to L.M. I[49]. Still later probably are the caves at Patso, sacred to Hermes Kranaios in historical times[50] and, on Mt. Ida, the so-called cave of Zeus which saw cult only from the Geometric period[51].

It is possible, of course, and likely that caves lent themselves to cult, because they had been the common shelter of man from the Stone Age, and, in Nilsson's words[52], "already at a rather early stage man has the idea of

---

[47] B.S.A. 6 (1899) 94.

[48] Dawkins, B.S.A. 19 (1912) 38, claims that almost all finds belonged to L.M., while Evans, P.M. I, 162, describes some votive figurines and weapons found there as still part of M.M.

[49] J.H.S. 57 (1937) 139; Nilsson, op. cit. 60.

[50] From an inscr. from Roman times, Inscr. Cret. II, IX, 1; Nilsson, op. cit. 67. Faure, Fonct. 12 n. 1, places the cave of Hermes Kranaios some 25 km. west of Mt. Ida.

[51] Faure, op. cit. 99 ff.

[52] Op. cit. 56. Cf. F. Matz, Kreta, Mykene, Troja 82; C. Zervos, L'art de la Crète néolithique et minoenne; 29; Willetts, Cret. Cults 141. For a different view see Sp. Marinatos, "Höhlenforschungen in Kreta", M.H.K., 4, 3 f. Faure, Fonct. 10 ff., firmly maintains that there is no evidence of cave cult in Crete or on the mainland as early as the Neolithic period. Stone Age remains from e.g. Psychro (op. cit. 11) and Pan's

providing his gods with habitations, and the human dwelling is always the prototype of the shrine of the gods." But, this last consideration apart, from very early times some idea of sanctity became attached to, or was felt to reside in, the cave as such. Otherwise, when they had acquired the skill of building their own more comfortable living quarters, the Minoans might be expected to have transferred their divinities as well. This could, indeed, have occurred in cases where a cult was moved to the domestic and palace shrines. In the main, however, the caves continued to retain their holy cults, so that we are bound to assume that such localities formed a natural residence for a particular kind of divinity or divinities who would not have felt equally at home in the new shrines.

The cave, by position or nature, was sacred in itself and did not acquire sanctity through human occupation. In fact the Kamares cave on Mt. Ida, famous for giving its name to a particular kind of Cretan pottery, and others, because of their inaccessible position, could not have been lived in by men at any time. The origin of this sanctity, and the sacred cave was not confined to Crete, can only be guessed at: one might suppose that the cave was the natural habitat of a nature spirit like the Nymphs who in Greek mythology haunted such abodes. But the rich finds of cultic remains, which suggest that caves were the scene of different types of ritual, seem to indicate that the Greek idea was no more than a memory of but a small part of more important and broader religious aspects. A quite general connection with nature seems certain, yet to define in detail the features of such a nature cult is extremely difficult especially in the light of some of the offerings found in particular caves where votive gifts differed enough to give the impression that cults were not the same in form on all sites.

Offerings varied from the burnt sacrifice of animals, as in the cave of Zeus on Mt. Ida where a deep layer was found with the remains of partially burnt animal bones, ox-skulls with horns still attached, to pottery, bronze weapons and implements, double axes of bronze and precious metal and statuettes of clay and bronze of both animals and humans. Cult implements include *rhyta* or libation vessels, libation tables and altars occasionally placed in a sacred precinct or *temenos* which at times was marked off by a low wall of stone. In a number of caves the prominent position of stalagmites or stalactites, as in that of Eileithyia at Amnisos, also suggests that

---

cave at Marathon (192) are merely signs of habitation. Faure's conclusions are determined by his view that habitation, burial and cult in caves always were kept separate (cf. *op. cit.* 79; 191).

they were objects of worship, especially in view of the fact that, as in the case of the stalactites in the lower grotto at Psychro, votive offerings were found stuck in their crevices. There appear to be no boundaries of time within which certain types of offering or implements occur; in other words, the date when a cult was instituted, either from E.M. or much later, seems to have had little bearing on the nature of the remains. Thus a cave below the summit of Mt. Jouktas, with evidence of a cult of long standing, has yielded to the explorer Taramelli[53] a rich harvest of pottery fragments and terracotta animals. The cave at Skoteino, near Knossos, which Evans calls the sacred cave of Knossos[54], contained remains dating from M.M. and consisting in bronze figures and one double axe. In the winding galleries of this cave there are a number of stalagmites about which worship probably occurred.

Another bronze statuette was found by Hazzidakis in a cave near Tylissos[55]. Human and animal figurines of terracotta or bronze were discovered in the Patso cave. These may well be late, because a number of the clay figures were painted in the last Minoan style. The same perhaps applies to the finds of a human head with special headdress and two pairs of horns of consecration. From the cave at Hagia Phaneromene evidence of L.M. I and later cult comes in the form of pottery, votive double axes – one of electrum[56] –, bronze knife blades, and bronze statuettes. The site of the cult was a chamber near the entrance of the cave where all these objects were found, together with three tables of offerings[57]. The cult here continued until Roman times, for, together with Geometric and Orientalizing pottery, Hellenistic and Roman ware was also found.

Very important to us, because of the rich archaeological yields, is the double cave at Psychro[58] which was frequented as a cult locality from M.M. or L.M. I to archaic times[59]. This cave has been fully explored[60] and a profusion of cult objects, as well as implements, brought to light which cannot be described in detail here[61]. The upper cave shows some traces of

---

[53] *Mon. Ant.* 9 (1898) 356; cf. A. B. Cook, *Zeus*, Cambridge 1914, I, 160.
[54] *Op. cit.* I, 163.
[55] *Et. C.* III, 75.
[56] Faure, *Fonct.* 160 and n. 1.
[57] *B. C. H.* 61 (1937) 475; *J. H. S.* 57 (1937) 139.
[58] See p. 80.
[59] No interruption in Geometric, Faure, *Fonct.* 12 n. 1; 151 ff.
[60] For description and refs. see Willetts, *op. cit.* 145; Faure, *Fonct.* 151 ff.
[61] See J. Boardman. *The Cretan Collection in Oxford.*

primitive pottery and burnt sacrifice antedating M.M.: they also prove earlier occupation which, however, was insignificant compared with the later periods mentioned. The main site of cult appears to have been within a bay along the sloping passage of the upper cave. A wall, of which only traces remain, marked off this bay from the passage, and another wall surrounded a *temenos* formed by the innermost recess of the bay. The floor of the *temenos* was composed of several layers, seven feet thick, which concealed pottery fragments, weapons, bronze knives and pins, and a human figurine, together with ashes of burnt offerings, deposited there mainly from M.M. Outside the *temenos*, in the bay, was a structure, about three feet high and built of squared stones fitted together without binding, which in all likelihood served as an altar. This altar was surrounded with the accoutrements of cult: libation tables, cups, fruit-stands etc., and ashes from burnt offerings.

The lower cave consisted of a downward sloping passage which ended in a pool of water containing numerous bronze statuettes, some engraved gems, as well as rings, pins and knife blades. Interesting are the stalactite (stalagmite) pillars in this cave, for some of their crevices had bronze objects stuck in them such as double axes, human figurines – those found in the upper cave mostly were of animals – and even a model chariot. Many other objects of daily use were found, including needles, hairpins, rings, knives and daggers, one of which had a handle ending in a human head. Some round dishes, from the Geometric period, one with a central boss, found there have been interpreted as shields[62]. Other items of note from the upper cave are small golden objects, and, mostly from the *temenos*, sherds of *rhyta* in the shape of oxen, together with jars decorated in relief with *bucrania* or double axes.

A probable clue to the nature of the cult practised there comes from a L.M. I bronze votive tablet found in the cave[63] and depicting on the right a worshipper, a tree in the centre, and on the left a pair of horns of consecration with a bough, which has a bird perched on the top, planted in the middle. The scene is fairly familiar from Minoan gems and shows, by its central position, the sacredness of the tree which was perhaps representative of a deity. The significance of the tree, again, appears from the second scene on the tablet where a bough of the tree is shown between the horns of consecration: the bird on top describes, as usually, the epiphany of a Minoan

---

[62] Cf. Nilsson, *op. cit.* 64; Boardman, *op. cit.* 49 ff.
[63] Boardman, *op. cit.* Nr. 217.

goddess, either as part of, or related to, the tree. The tree and, at the upper edge of the tablet, the sun and moon – perhaps symbols of the passing of the seasons – portray the concerns of a nature goddess, one or even several of whose aspects, we might suppose, were revered by her worshippers in the cave[64].

It lies close to hand to connect the significance of the tree with that of the stalagmitic (or stalactitic) pillars in the caves[65], in the sense that both possessed the identical religious import as central objects in what might have been a form of aniconic cult. This theory, which would account for the presence of the votive tablet in the Psychro cave beside the stalactites, is plausible in itself, but unfortunately not open to proof. More light, as we shall see, falls on the meaning of the stalagmite from Anatolian practices[66]. Furthermore, the presence of the weapons – shields, knives and daggers – is vexing, for such objects seem irrelevant to a cult of a nature goddess. Perhaps, then, this particular cave was the scene of more than one, not necessarily interrelated, cult? However, it is wise to reserve judgment in this respect, for even in classical Greece we have in Artemis an example of an armed goddess of nature and wild life.

With regard to weapons as cultic offerings, the most remarkable site is the cave at Arkalokhori, south-west of Lyttos, which was frequented throughout the Minoan periods. The cave is tripartite and the middle section was first explored by Hazzidakis[67], while Marinatos subsequently made a detailed examination of the entire cave[68]. The cult place, with perhaps an altar, was in the innermost recess of the cave. Around it was found a veritable treasure trove mainly of double axes and weapons of bronze or precious metal together with sundry statuettes mostly dating from M.M. III and L.M. I. Of interest, too, is an offering of a gold block, perhaps a "holy mountain". Pottery was remarkable for its absence. Cult there perhaps continued sporadically until the Protogeometric period, but suf-

---

[64] A more adventurous theory by Faure, *Fonct.* 157, makes this figure into a cosmic goddess who was sovereign of the heaven, earth and waters: the future Aphrodite Ourania.

[65] This theme was dear to Evans; see e.g. his *Mycenaean Tree and Pillar Cult*, and his Frazer Lecture on *The Earlier Religion of Greece in the Light of Cretan Discoveries*, 13.

[66] See below pp. 111 f.

[67] *B. S. A.* 19 (1912) 35 ff. Further refs. in Faure, *Fonct.* 160 n. 3.

[68] *Anz.* (1934) 251 ff.; (1935) 248 ff.; *Praktika* (1935) 212 ff.; cf. *K.* 1 (1962) 87 ff. 87 ff.

fered, or temporarily came to a stop, by the collapse of the roof in L.M. II. The nature of the offerings, which were almost entirely composed of weapons, seems to point to a special cult which may have differed from that occurring in other caves[69]. Picard[70] speaks of Arkalokhori as the cradle of a Warrior-god cult, the predecessor of the Indo-European Zeus; for, according to him, the nature of the offerings in this cave accords well with the legend of Zeus' childhood in Crete, when he was protected by the dances of the armed Korybantes and Kouretes. This interpretation which directly depends on S. Marinatos' identification of Arkalokhori with the legendary birth place of Zeus[71], must now be discarded as false, however, in the light of Faure's recent decisive argument. Arkalokhori can no longer compete with the *Idaion antron* as the site of Zeus' birth[72]. Votive objects like the double axe, knives and lances, were not confined to the Arkalokhori cave, although nowhere else have they been discovered in such profusion or to the exclusion of virtually every other kind of object. We should also remember that the double axe in the Near East (its probable home) and perhaps in Crete was not commonly associated with a male deity. What deity, then, received worship in this cave? Faure suggests a kind of prototype of Aphrodite Ourania[73]. But there is not a shred of evidence to support his proposal. We cannot say more than that the cult in this cave revolved about a deity of nature and wild life.

Exactly the same difficulty of interpretation exists in the Kamares cave, equally famous for its specialized cultic remains, near the southern summit of Mt. Ida. This site was explored by the British school in 1912[74]. Signs of

---

[69] Faure, *Fonct.* 162, suggests that the same goddess received cult in Psychro and Arkalokhori.

[70] *Op. cit.* 102.

[71] *Anz.* (1934) 254; *R. F.* (1934) 62, 549. *R. R.* 5 (1941) 132.

[72] Faure, *Fonct.* 99–136; 14 n. 4. Before Marinatos' discussion some scholars – e.g. Evans, *op. cit.* 625 and n. 2 – had identified the Psychro cave with Zeus' birthplace. Geographical considerations alone, however, made this impossible. Such identifications were prompted either by the wealth of finds, as at Psychro, or by their nature, as at Arkalokhori. The historical cave of Zeus was near the peak of Mt. Ida – Halbherr, "Scavi e trovamenti nell antro di Zeus sul Monte Ida", *Mus. It.* 2 (1888) 689 ff. –, but it shows no evidence of cult before the Geometric period, so that cult may at a comparatively late date have been transferred to this location – cf. Callimachus, *Hymn to Zeus* I, 6, who recorded the tradition of Zeus' birth on Mt. Ida.

[73] *Fonct.* 157.

[74] *B. S. A.* 19 (1912) 1 ff.

use date back to the Neolithic period, but the bulk of the finds (including the first examples of the beautiful Kamares ware) belonged to a cult and fell within the best Minoan artistic period of M.M. Other later remains continue down to L.M. III. The reason for supposing a special cult[75] to have obtained here rests on the fact that virtually all the finds made in this cave consisted of pottery and offerings of grain. Another feature of interest is the cave's inaccessible position high on the mountain – the entrance is blocked by snow for a large part of the year – which made it unsuitable for human habitation and reserved it for cultic use alone.

Faure names some forty-five caves in Crete which probably, or certainly, witnessed cult[76]. From this extremely conservative list only a few have been discussed above; but these are representative, and the finds in them allow some conclusions to be drawn which have a bearing not only on this particular type of cult but on certain aspects of Minoan religious forms in general which we shall pursue further.

Cave cult on the island was practised throughout all periods of Minoan history and beyond[77]. It was continuous, even if not always in the same cave[78], and held a position important enough to compete, if that is the right word, with other places of cult like that in the palace and domestic shrine. Up to the present it is impossible to assign to the caves a type of cult not found elsewhere in Crete, nor can we know – with one signal exception – the names, and more than the general nature of, the gods to whom a particular cult was sacred. This last reservation applies, of course, only to the Bronze Age, for names like Artemis, Demeter and Pan, in connection with cave cult[79] are not attested before classical times and usually much later. Nor can we yet learn anything from the tantalizingly illegible Linear A signs discovered in a few caves such as Psychro and Arkalokhori[80]. Zeus' cult in the *Idaion antron* does not antedate the Geometric and Orientalizing periods. We have already seen that his name covers the figure of an Aegean, and specifically Cretan, male figure of vegetation. The same history of

---

[75] "agraire et chtonien", Faure, *op. cit.* 181.
[76] *Op. cit.* 187 ff. See now *B. C. H.* 91 (1967) 114–150; 96 (1972) 402–415.
[77] This, I believe, is also implied by Faure, *op. cit.* 191.
[78] Faure feels very strongly that cult continuity cannot be proven for any one cave, see e.g. *op. cit.* 196. But if climatic, political, or any other, reasons temporarily put a stop to cult in one particular grotto, we are not entitled to draw the conclusion that this type of cult came to an end everywhere on the island.
[79] Faure, *op. cit.* 193.
[80] Faure, *op. cit.* 156; 162.

identifications of Zeus, and indeed other figures like Dionysus, with such youthful male gods can be told at other sites on the Greek mainland and in the East, wherever Zeus was said to have been born and nurtured[81]. Hermes is a yet stronger candidate for an early association with cave cult. On the mainland his connection with the cave on Mt. Cyllene in Arcadia may well have been prehistoric[82], but notices of Hermes' cult in the Melidoni and Patso (Hermes Kranaios) caves on Crete are Hellenistic and later[83]. Nothing said so far excludes the possibility that any or all of the deities mentioned had found a place in Minoan cave cult, but there is no proof of this, nor are we at present entitled to use the late written evidence to posit the existence of different gods and goddesses in the caves of Bronze Age Crete[84].

The cave of Eileithyia at Amnisos is in fact the only instance where we can connect an apparently Cretan divine name[85] with a particular cave[86]. We noticed that this was distinguished by a central cultic site marked out by a stalagmite which was surrounded by a low stone wall. The many sherds found in and about the sacred precinct belonged to vessels filled with offerings, notably oil and honey[87]. Eileithyia was a goddess of nature. Her particular functions are well known from the prominent position she held in cult later in Greece in many centres of the peninsula and on islands like Delos, Paros, Tenos and Naxos. She was a goddess of child birth and revered as such in all her cults[88] which also continued strong on the island of Crete in historic times: at Lato, she became the chief deity of the city[89]. Her function as goddess of birth brought her close to the great Greek goddess of wild life and nature Artemis who, as Lochia, was connected with

---

[81] See above and cf. Faure, *op. cit.* 121 f.

[82] *Hom. Hymn to Hermes* 1–9; 142; 227–34; cf. Faure, *op. cit.* 132 f.

[83] Faure, *op. cit.* 131 ff.; 136 ff. For attempts at explaining the Patso epithet see Nilsson, *M. M. R.* 72 f.; Willetts, *Cret. Cults* 289; Faure, *op. cit.* 137. For sources of Hellenistic and later Hermes cults in Crete see Willetts, *Cults* 287 ff.

[84] This is maintained by Faure, *op. cit.* 193.

[85] Faure, *Fonct.* 87, believes the goddess' name to be Greek.

[86] Faure, *op. cit.* 90 ff., assigns another cave recently discovered at Tsoutsouros to Eileithyia's cult.

[87] This is apparent from some Linear B tablets cited by J. Chadwick and L. Baumbach, "The Mycenaean Greek Vocabulary", *G.* 41 (1963) 188, and L. R. Palmer, *Mycenaeans and Minoans*, 120 f.

[88] Except at Paros where Eileithyia had a cult as goddess of healing, *IG* XII, 5, 185.

[89] Public inscriptions were set up in her temple. P. Deiters, *De Cretensium titulis publicis*, Diss. Bonn 1904, 27 ff., cited by Nilsson, *op. cit.* 519 n. 37. For the many votive terracotta figurines found in Lato and probably gifts to Eileithyia see P. Demargne, *B. C. H.* 53 (1929) 382 ff.

this aspect of nature cult and therefore at times absorbed the cult of the Cretan goddess and her name which then, especially in Boeotia, appeared as an epithet of Artemis. For our knowledge of Eileithyia's special function we are, of course, indebted to later Greek cult, especially that of Artemis. We may, however, suppose that birth, not only of humans but also, as in the case of Artemis, of animals, had always been the chief part of Eileithyia's sphere for which she received cult.

Thus, in the case of Eileithyia, cult continuity has been the fortunate circumstance which revealed the precise nature of the goddess who was worshipped in the cave at Amnisos during Minoan times[90]. The moment of birth, at which Eileithyia's assistance was invoked, forms a vital portion of a religion concerned with the recurring cycle of vegetation. The cave, moreover, by its very position was an ideal shrine for the worship of Mother Earth and her fruit. A cave, therefore, was the site of the birth and infant childhood of the Divine Child, the consort of the nature goddess in Crete[91]. We have already mentioned that Zeus subsequently came to be identified with this child[92]; and whatever particular cave might have witnessed the birth, the locality of the event is clear from Greek literary tradition preserved from Hesiod until Hellenistic times and later[93].

A remarkably uniform feature of Zeus' legend, as well as that of all divine children, speaks of the infant not as nurtured by his mother but by Mother Earth[94]. The child was, of course, symbolic of the birth and growth of vegetation, so that his cult would embrace the same event once every year, in spring[95]. The story of Zeus' birth in Greek tradition may help to throw some light on the military nature of the offerings in the Arkalokhori cave. The babe Zeus was hidden in a cave by his mother, and, in order that his cries might not be heard, the Kouretes, a band of armed figures, were said to dance about the entrance of the cave clashing their shields and

---

[90] Cult continuity in the Amnisos cave is denied by Faure, *op. cit.* 82; 89, who believes that finds from periods earlier than L.M. III, when at all present, belonged to funerary rites.

[91] Perhaps on some gems: e.g. the electrum ring from Mycenae, Evans, *P. M.* III, 463 f., fig. 324; cf. Picard, *op. cit.* 111; Schachermeyr, *op. cit.* 149 f.

[92] As Kretagenes, Velchanos. The young Velchanos was pictured on coins from Phaestos, *Cat. of Coins in B.M.*, *Crete*, XV, 10. On the startling "heterodoxy" of this belief in the annual birth and death of the Greek Zeus see above p. 14.

[93] See above p. 14; 15 and notes. Cf. Willetts, *Cults* 147; 239 f.; 250 f.

[94] See above p. 14.

[95] Cf. Antoninus' story – *Met.* 19 – of Zeus' annual birth in a Cretan cave, above pp. 16 f.

swords[96]. Now Nilsson has shown[97] that these Kouretes originally were figures of Cretan cult, and that in fact they were daemons of fertility[98]. The reason why arms came to be connected with vegetation deities or daemons need not concern us for the moment; we merely note that weapons played a part in certain aspects of nature cult, particularly those associated with the birth of the Divine Child. Therefore, the presence of the weapons among the votive offerings found in caves, and especially at Arkalokhori[99], need not surprise us.

In connection with Zeus' Cretan cave we may briefly mention another tradition of great antiquity which not only points to the cave as a site for vegetation cult but also hints at the part played by the cave in the concept of cyclical kingship discussed above[100]. King Minos of Knossos every nine years retired to Zeus' cave where he renewed his kingship[101]. Now Zeus replaced an originally Minoan deity in this function which, in all likelihood, was modelled on the Eastern pattern of cyclical kingship, again intimately connected with certain recurring vegetation rites. Plato's notice, therefore, supported in part by Homer's reference to Minos' nine years of royal office[102], connects an important occurrence in the religious life of the Near East with Crete. Naturally the cave as the locality for the renewal of kingship greatly strengthens the bond of this connection. There is no reason to suppose that Plato misunderstood his source when he made a cave the scene of the ritual. We shall consider below the wider implications of this Eastern practice in Crete. In this context it is enough to point to one particular aspect of Cretan cave cult, namely the concept of cyclic renewal[103] when the human king in some way was felt to commune with his deity.

The cave, which saw the birth and nurturing of the Divine Child as well as the renewal of Minoan kingship, was also the resting place of the dead.

---

[96] See above p. 15.
[97] *M. M. R.* 543 ff.
[98] Cf. above p. 15.
[99] Faure, *op. cit.* 161, compares the offerings from Arkalokhori with those found in the Psychro cave. He also points out the symbolic nature of the arms, that is they formed part of religious cult and could not have been put to practical use.
[100] P. 60.
[101] Plato, *Leg.* 624 d.
[102] *Od.* 19, 179. Cf. schol. *ad loc.*; Strabo, X, 4, 8; 19; XVI, 2, 38; Dion. Hal. II, 61; Diod. Sic. V, 78, 3.
[103] Cf. Faure, *Fonct.* 113. The nine year cycle is supposed to have "reconciled the course of nature with that of the social life represented by the king."

This last feature suggests the presence in the cave of a cult of the dead, or it is, as Matz supposes[104], evidence for the chthonic nature of the deities haunting the caves: it seems likely that both funeral cult and chthonic deities found a home in Cretan caves. The votive offerings found in burial caves, like that of Pyrgos, are proof that some significance was attached to the dead[105]. Again the divinity revered in these caves was concerned with many aspects of nature religion. As a deity of life and vegetation he, or she, was therefore intimately connected with the fruitful earth. Indeed there is no place more suitable than the cave for the abode of a chthonic figure: here Mother Earth nurtured the Divine Infant. The Minoans probably thought of caves and similar rifts in earth or rock as entrances to a lower world, and we may compare with this the equivalent Greek belief attached to sites like Colonus Hippius, the locality of the Semnae cult by the Aeropagus in Athens, and the Boeotian Tilphossion – all entrances to Hades[106].

The caves have yielded many specialized cult implements, and, apart from numerous figurines, votive offerings which were shared with other different cult sites, like domestic and palace shrines. We may well be dealing therefore with similar types of ritual in all these localities, as well as with gods whose nature, or perhaps functions, were the same. This point, of course, is of some moment to the religious historian, for we know from our dates of occupation that cave cult continued simultaneously with that practised in other shrines, which means that much can be learnt from the knowledge that gods revered in palace and cave might well have exercised similar functions. Implements found in caves and other shrines include libation tables (e.g. from Psychro), libation vessels or *rhyta*, a certain type of container of offerings named the *kernos* which, in Nilsson's words[107], was a "type of composite vessel which shows...smaller vessels fixed upon a base." The Minoan prototype of this *kernos* was found at Pyrgos[108], and many later examples come from tholos tombs[109], so that it can be said to have played a part in a cult concerned with the dead.

[104] *Kreta, Myk., Troja* 82.
[105] For a different view see K. Branigan, *The Foundations of Palatial Crete*, 154. We are not concerned with other evidence, outside caves, which might point to an established cult of the dead.
[106] See B. C. Dietrich, *Death, Fate and the Gods*, 111 f. and n. 1; cf. the couplet from Euripides, *Electra* 1270 f.
[107] *M. M. R.* 135.
[108] Reproduced in Nilsson, *Gesch.*, I, Pl. V, 2.
[109] E.g. Xanthoudides, "Cretan Kernoi", *B. S. A.* 12 (1905) 9 ff.

Typically Minoan objects with religious significance, which caves share with other cult sites, are the double axe (notably from the cave at Arkalokhori) and horns of consecration, sometimes with axes, or other objects, planted in their centre[110]. These horns are also depicted on the interesting bronze votive tablet from Psychro which was described above. Each of the three pairs of horns on the plaque shows a bough planted in the middle, and these perhaps, together with the rest of the design[111], refer to a cult concerned with a tree: a fully engraved tree forms the centre of the design, while the bird perched on the bough between the horns on the left represents the epiphany of a goddess.

This scene on the plaque gives evidence of a cult in which the tree played a dominant part. Such cult, of course, was not confined to the cave, but there are a great many Minoan seals which allude to it much more explicitly[112]. In the majority of instances the tree, usually in full leaf, appears to be enclosed in a sanctuary-like structure, although only the crown is shown above the structure and never the trunk[113]. Sometimes a goddess is depicted as sitting beneath the tree and receiving worshippers. The tree on the Psychro plaque is scratched onto the bronze in primitive manner, although the date of the tablet is probably late (L.M. I?)[114]. Quite clearly the tree, which is not surrounded by any structure, could hardly have been imagined in life-size form in the cave. Nor can we assume that this votive plaque found its way into the cave by chance. It follows, therefore, that the tree was symbolic of, or in some way represented, the divinity – a goddess as we gather from the gems – receiving cult within the cave as well as in other types of sanctuary.

[110] Cf. the painted pair of horns, with the base – probably of a double axe – only remaining in its centre, from Patso, repr. in Nilsson, *Gesch.* I, Pl. V, 7.

[111] Cf. a gem from the Idaean Cave – Nilsson, *Gesch.* I, Pl. VII, 4 – showing a woman blowing into a shell. Behind her, to the left, is a tree while the right part of the design is filled by an altar-like structure surmounted by horns of consecration, flanked by boughs, and with one single bough planted in the centre.

[112] For the sake of convenience examples are taken from the plates at the end of Persson, *Preh. Greece.* Reference to the provenance of individual gems will be found in the text – pp. 32 ff. Examples of trees, holding a central position in cult scenes, can be seen on 2; 3; 4 (Mycenae); 7; 10 (Mycenae); 12 (Mycenae); 15; 17; 20 (Kilia, Asia Minor?); 22 (Mycenae); 27; 29. The last, the so-called ring of Minos allegedly found near Knossos, truly has a remarkable design, but is probably a skilful forgery: Persson, *op. cit.* 101 ff.; Nilsson, *M. M. R.* 42 f.; *Gesch.* I, 282. Other examples of the tree in cult can be seen in Nilsson, *Gesch.* I, Pl. XIII; XVII.

[113] Cf. Nilsson, *Gesch.* I, 282.

[114] Cf. Willetts, *Cults* 145.

The nature of the finds in caves, then, does not in any way suggest the presence of a unique cult which was not in fact practised at other sites. In certain cases perhaps cults were transferred to, or rather duplicated in, shrines erected following the occupation of the caves. But the latter, in many instances, endured as holy sites beside other localities of cult throughout the Minoan periods and beyond. This sharing of cult, and its transference from the older caves, becomes obvious from the cultic use, for example, of stalagmites which, although by their very nature closely attached to the cave, were also found elsewhere[115]. Their religious import is clear[116], although for the moment we leave open the question whether such limestone concretions were forms of aniconic *numina*. Perhaps like the horns of consecration stalagmites etc. possessed divine qualities which could be imparted to objects placed near or about them. Apart from their location in caves, objects closely resembling stalagmites, in semi-iconic shape[117], were found in a shrine (a "bathroom" or "lustral chamber"[118]) in the so-called Little Palace which is a separate building some two-hundred and fifty yards north-west of the palace at Knossos. Such finds prove transference of cave cult to other locations which must have shared, or perhaps more likely continued, prominent features of the former[118a]. Evans at the time proposed that stalagmites served as representations of the *omphalos*, while certain naturally formed pillars from cave cult were baetylic types of the divinity[119]. Platon again maintained that such natural concretions gave rise to column and pillar cult[120], a view which is not far removed from Picard's interpretation of stalagmites as human or animal figures[121]. It is only now, however, that we are in a position to go beyond conjecture in explaining the signifi-

---

[115] Cf. Faure, *Fonct.* 191.

[116] See above e.g. p. 84.

[117] Reproduced in Nilsson, *Gesch.* I, Pl. III, 4.

[118] On this disputed question see now R. W. Hutchinson, *T. P. R.* 21 (1950) 209; Nilsson, "Bathrooms or Lustral Chambers"?, *A. J. A.* 65 (1961) 189; J. W. Graham, *The Palaces of Crete*, 99 ff.

[118a] Mr. S. Hood kindly pointed out to me that an "altar" and a concretion, which had evidently stood on it in the annexe of the tholos tomb, was excavated by the Germans at Apesokari during the war.

[119] *J. H. S.* 21 (1901) 99 ff.; *P. M.* I, 162.

[120] *Eph. Arch.* (1930) 160 ff.

[121] *Op. cit.* 58; cf. Nilsson, *Gesch.* I, 267. For criticism of Evans' and Platon's views see Faure, *Fonct.* 13 f. His argument that stalagmites etc. suggest different figures to different viewers does not take into account that in these instances we are dealing with aniconic cult.

cance of these configurations with the help of the recently discovered Anatolian evidence from Çatal Hüyük.

It is to be expected that the use of caves for human habitation, and for cultic purposes in the Neolithic period and later, was not confined to Crete. Matz speaks of such custom as spread throughout the Mediterranean area ("urmittelländisch")[122], while Faure prefers to believe in the parallel development of cave cult in Anatolia, Rhodes, Cyprus and the Aegean islands[123]. Recent archaeological work in the East tends to confirm the view not only that cult existed in caves throughout the Aegean but that it was similar in nature, and that some signal features of such cult crossed to the West from an originally Eastern home. There is to begin with a considerable body of evidence relating to cave cults and to caves as burial sites on the mainland of Greece from all periods, so that there can be no question of a cave cult's being instituted in the latter area in imitation of Cretan practice, despite the fact that a number of examples show remains which do not antedate the Mycenaean Age. This applies to the caves at Pharae in Achaea which yielded Mycenaean burial deposits[124]. However, the famous cave at Parnes, often named the cave of lamps – Lychnospelaion –, because many lamps were found there (Greek, Roman and Christian), was frequented from prehistoric times. In spite of some difficulties concerning the period and continuity of cult in this cave, which in classical times was sacred to Pan and the Nymphs[125], there is no doubt that this cave was frequented and used for cultic purposes from the earliest times.

Among the Aegean islands we note in this context the cave on Mt. Cynthus in Delos which may also have been occupied from prehistoric times[126]. From this early period in fact caves were used for occupation and burial in many parts of the world; and natural formations found within them served

---

[122] *Kr., Myk., Tr.* 82.
[123] *Fonct.* 193.
[124] *Eph. Arch.* (1919) 98 ff.
[125] E.g. the lowest archaeological level in this cave showed prehistoric mixed with Mycen. sherds. It also seems that at the end of the Mycenaean Age the roof collapsed, so that the cave was abandoned until after the Persian Wars when cult was revived and endured to Christian times. Cf. Nilsson, *M. M. R.* 67 f., where the relevant sources are cited.
[126] This is an artificial cave: slabs of stone were laid over a rock fissure and a wall was built before the entrance. A. Plassart, *Ex. arch. D.* 11, 228 ff.; 255. Nilsson, *M. M. R.* 68, says, in spite of the Minoan-type table of libations found there, that this cave was not constructed until the age of the Ptolemies.

artistic and cultic purposes as early as the Palaeolithic Period[127]. We are more concerned with the significance and origin of Aegean and particularly Minoan cult practices which occurred in caves and which, as we saw, in some instances were transferred to other shrines. The wide dispersion of cave cult shows that the Cretans were not unique in the religious use of these sites, but shared their belief with other peoples of the Mediterranean.

Recent archaeological work, which in many places is still in progress, has allowed us to link a number of features of Minoan religion – among them certain aspects of cave cult – with the Near East and with south-west Anatolia in particular. Professor J. Evans' discovery that the Neolithic inhabitants of Knossos had come from western Anatolia was mentioned above[128]. These people had brought with them from their Eastern home their special kind of pottery and grain, as well as, we must suppose, their religious ceremonial. Much of western Anatolian archaeology still remains unexplored, so that our knowledge of that part of the world, and its relation with the western Aegean, is severely limited. What evidence has come to light, however, in many respects already shows an astonishing resemblance between Anatolian and Minoan cult practice, and, because some of the Eastern cult objects are more explicit in their significance than the Minoan, we can learn from them some facts about Cretan belief. It will, accordingly, be necessary to examine in detail the work that is being done in that part of the world – and the site of Çatal Hüyük is the most important – and discuss the possible bearing the Eastern archaeological remains have on the Cretans scene.

The site of Çatal Hüyük lies in the Konya Plain of s.-w. Anatolia and was discovered in 1958. Actual digging there did not begin until 1961 under the guidance of James Mellaart, and the results so far of three campaigns have been published in three preliminary reports[129]. From these we gather that Çatal Hüyük was "the capital site of the Konya Plain", and that its remains give evidence of the high cultural level attained there[130]. At the time of publication of the third report in 1964 the excavators had not yet reached virgin soil, but they established some ten separate main levels[131] to

---

[127] Cf. P. Graziosi, *Palaeolithic Art*, London 1960.
[128] See p. 73.
[129] J. Mellaart, "Excavations at Çatal Hüyük", *A. S.* 12 (1962) 41–65; 13 (1963) 43–103; XIV (1964) 39–119.
[130] *A. S.* 12, 42; 46.
[131] *A. S.* 14, 40.

SOME OLDER TRADITIONS IN MINOAN CRETE 95

which eventually were assigned the dates ranging from 6500–5700 B. C.[132], which means that there was a temporal overlap between the last levels of Çatal Hüyük (II–O) and some earlier levels of Haçilar (IX–VI)[133].

To allow a quicker impression of earlier levels Mellaart carried on the digging in two areas: one from the top of the mound (area A), and the other on its western slope (area E)[134]. The sixth level revealed five separate shrines in various states of preservation, all forming an integral part of the city's "agglutinative" building complex. In the third campaign (1963), which saw more extensive excavations than the previous years, the areas A and E were linked up and three more shrines came to light in Level VI which, however, had to be subdivided into the earlier Level VI B and the later Level VI A[135]. This same campaign also revealed three more shrines. The subdivision of Level VI, it seems, has little bearing on the cult continuity of the different shrines, for, generally built in VI B, they endured to the end of VI A or were replaced. Below Level VI B eight shrines were found in Level VII[136], and perhaps six in the not yet fully explored Levels VIII–X[137].

All these shrines, wherever possible, have been reconstructed and fully described by Mellaart[138], and it will be enough to refer to them in the pages of his reports. Mellaart's examination already established that throughout the period represented by about ten levels – that is the space of one thousand years – the form of cult observed in these shrines varied little if at all, for, certainly from Levels VI–X – the levels from which we have the best shrines – the basic principles of architectural construction remained identical[139]. Also the continued use of a particular shrine over periods represented by more than one level, such as the first five shrines discovered from Level VI A and B, as well as, in many cases, the construction of a new shrine on the same sacred ground, where the old had stood[140], proves con-

---

[132] *A. S.* 14, 118.
[133] *Op. cit.* 116. These dates are obviously subject to change in the light of future discoveries, *op. cit.* 118.
[134] *A. S.* 13, 54.
[135] *A. S.* 14, 40; 41. For a comparison of the previous VI with the later VI A and B see Figs. 1 & 2.
[136] *A. S.* 14, 50.
[137] *Op. cit.* 70.
[138] *A. S.* 13, esp. 50 ff.; figs. 3 & 4; 61–78; figs. 8–18; *A. S.* 14, 40–73; figs. 4–10; 12–25.
[139] *A. S.* 73.
[140] *A. S.* 14, e.g. 40; 42; 45; 70; 73 for examples from Levels IV, VII, VIII, IX, X.

tinuity of cult[141]. Similarly, wallpaintings, reliefs, and the technique of figures cut into the plaster of the walls, were not confined to the shrines of any particular level but occurred throughout all the periods[142].

These points strongly argue that in all its Neolithic history Çatal Hüyük continued a certain type of cult which did not vary in its essentials. Therefore the date of a level to which a particular shrine belonged has comparatively little bearing on the significance of the cult paraphernalia found there[143]. A first glance at Mellaart's reconstructions of the Çatal Hüyük shrines reveals some surprising correspondences between these and certain features of Cretan Bronze Age religion. However, there is much that cannot be paralleled in Crete at any time, including some apparently unique architectural features of the Anatolian shrine, at least one of which was built with a clerestory raising the centre of the structure[144].

A good part of the cult "furniture" itself seems unique, such as the women's breasts modelled in plaster on the east walls of the First and Second Shrines of Level VI B[145], containing either the lower jaw of a wild boar[146], or the head of a vulture with beak projecting beyond the nipples[147]. Such breasts – whose obvious connection with fertility needs no comment –, if anything, call to mind the Ephesian Artemis rather than any Minoan goddess[148]. A great deal, too, of the wall painting in the different shrines, either decorative or of human skulls and bones, structures of reed and mat[149], paintings of kilims[150], or even of a town and volcano[151], appear alien to Cretan motifs. The vultures, again, which figure prominently in a number of paintings in the shrines at Çatal Hüyük – often together with

---

[141] There are also examples, however, where houses came to be built on former sites of shrines, so that Mellaart speaks of continuity of cult in Çatal Hüyük "not as absolute as in Mesopotamia", *A. S.* 14, 45.

[142] Certainly from Level VI to the earliest levels, *A. S.* 14, 45; 73.

[143] Cf. p. 98.

[144] The Second Shrine of Level VI B (EVI, 10), *A. S.* 13, 70 and fig. 14.

[145] EVI, 8; EVI, 10.

[146] EVI, 8; *A. S.* 13, 69.

[147] EVI, 10. *Op. cit.* 70.

[148] Cf. *A. S.* 13, 80. Mellaart may well be right in believing the vulture and boar to represent death, but the use of piglets as victims during the Greek Skirophoria and Thesmophoria is not a good example in this connection. Why only the heads and jaws of these animals? Perhaps they belonged to a cruel and primitive rite which failed to survive.

[149] *A. S.* 13, Pl. XXVI, a; b.

[150] *A. S.* 14, Pl. XI, b.

[151] *Op. cit.* Pl. VI, a. Cf. the "holy mountain" from the Arkalokhori cave, above p. 84.

headless corpses of men[152] – find no clear echo in Crete[153], although their significance as scavengers cleaning human bodies of flesh may well be obvious.

Equally unparalleled[154] in the West are the numerous "panels of hands" painted on the walls of houses and shrines in Çatal Hüyük[155]. They were done in black or red and occasionally with four fingers[156]. Their significance is mysterious[157]. Perhaps such hands were felt to suggest divine power and presence, like the separate human ears and eyes represented on Cretan seals[158]. But this interpretation, too, is not entirely satisfactory for at least one panel, in a house of Level VI (EVI, 15), shows fifty-seven hands of children.

These are some of the more striking divergencies between the places of cult at Çatal Hüyük and Crete; and they serve to sound a note of caution to the historian of comparative religion. To begin with, Mellaart's work on the Eastern site is by no means complete. The results of future campaigns

---

[152] E.g. *A. S.* 14, Pl. IX, a; b; Pl. XII, a; b; Pl. XIV, a; Fig. 20; 21; 22.

[153] Mellaart suggests – *A. S.* 13, 80 – that these birds were the forerunners of the Cretan griffins. But we simply do not know enough to confirm or refute his thesis. The griffin, like the sphinx, in Cretan art was very common in many scenes by no means always of a chthonic or funeral nature, see esp. Nilsson, *M. M. R.* 368 n. 96. The only certain fact known about these creatures is that they were imported to Crete from the East, *op. cit.* 255, probably from Syria, H. Frankfort, "Notes on the Cretan Griffin", *B. S. A.* 37 (1936/7) 106 ff. The griffin's position in Cretan belief is uncertain: the animal was frequently associated with a goddess, perhaps as Mistress of Animals. In all likelihood, the griffin, like the daemon, was an attendant of divinity rather than divine itself – cf. Dietrich, *Death, Fate* 16. Thus its function on the Hagia Triada sarcophagus – the head-end – drawing the goddess' car was parallel to that of the horses – at the foot-end – harnessed to a similar car (see F. Matz, *Göttererscheinung und Kultbild im Minoischen Kreta*, Pl. 12 & 13). Nowhere is there any clear proof that the griffin in Crete was involved in funeral cult. The ring of Nestor is a forgery, cf. Nilsson, *M. M. R.* 50. One should, therefore, more firmly than ever restate Picard's phrase, *op. cit.* 198, "on sera réservé sur le culte funéraire du griffon."

[154] One possible parallel is the hand modelled together with a scorpion, snake, and other animals, on a heart-shaped gold amulet from a tomb near Hagia Triada, Nilsson, *op. cit.* fig. 152.

[155] *A. S.* 13, Pl. XI, a, b; XVIII, b; *A. S.* 14, Pl. VI, a–c.

[156] *A. S.* 13, Pl. XII, a, c.

[157] Mellaart, *A. S.* 13, 81, notes that a similar sign of a four-fingered hand, placed sideways, occurs on a pot in a woman's grave at Haçilar, and he believes that the hand was an apotropaeic sign, or the signature of a person who participated in a cultic ceremony.

[158] Cf. above p. 43.

are bound to affect earlier interpretations of the archaeological material: corrections will have to be made and perhaps some theories discarded. What has been discovered thus far, most certainly belonged to a religion known in part to Crete by virtue of the cultural and ethnographic ties which bound the two centres. But, even if the earliest levels of Haçilar overlapped with the last of Çatal Hüyük, a space of three thousand years or more separated the latter Neolithic cultures from Bronze Age Crete. Inevitably the religious ideas which found their way into Crete from Anatolia not only came to be mixed or juxtaposed with practices from other areas like Egypt, for example, but they were also shaped in new, perhaps less barbarous, forms by the developing Cretan spirit and culture. Such, however, is the nature of our material which warns against the more obvious pitfalls of conjecture[159].

Yet there is another side to the coin: much of the religious belief which governed cult in the Late Neolithic and Early Bronze Age in the Aegean area had not only been introduced from the Near East, but was uniform in a number of basic concepts[160]. Furthermore one suspects that certain elemental features of cult in the Aegean communities, from the Near East to Crete and Greece, as tenaciously kept their hold on popular imagination as did the sacred cult locality itself which, in many instances, endured not only through the thousand years or more of Çatal Hüyük but also in some localities in Crete and Greece where cult can be shown to have continued on the same site at times into the Christian era[161]. Such extreme conservatism notwithstanding, the continued use of one type of locality for cult purposes does not always, of course, signify that the content of such cult remained unaltered. Therefore, particularly in view of the long gap of time involved, it is advisable to proceed carefully when comparing certain Anatolian with Bronze Age Cretan religious features.

There are, however, some correspondences between East and West which can be reasonably explained by the relationship of the two centres. As far as can be gathered from the remains and reconstruction at Çatal Hüyük, all the shrines there formed an integral part of the city's "agglutinative" building complex: although they obviously were places of worship and

---

[159] In addition to the chronological gap between East and West, one must also bear in mind that the migratory movements described above cannot yet be established with full certainty.

[160] Cf. p. 20; 72.

[161] Here again the most striking examples in this connection come from cave cult which suffered change and developed in form but endured on the same site. Cf. p. 78; 80; 136 f.; Nilsson, *M. M. R.* 58; 67. For a different view see Faure, *Fonct.* 196.

religious ceremonial, these shrines were in no way separate from the other domestic quarters. They further, either in part served as store rooms for produce or granaries, or were flanked by chambers or rooms for this purpose[162]. This functional use, which is an important reflection on the nature of the cult and deity revered there, the Çatal Hüyük shrines shared with the later palace sanctuaries or the palaces themselves not only in the East but also in Crete and Greece. There is no reason to doubt that the significance of this practice was the same in every instance: the deity, in or about whose shrine the produce was stored, had been responsible for its growth and owned it[163].

A remarkable feature of the Anatolian shrines consists in the important part played by animals: leopards, boars, heads of rams, which figured prominently moulded onto the walls. The most important animal in the shrines of all levels was the bull, obviously as vital to popular religious belief there as in Crete. A large figure of a bull was often modelled *in reserve* on the plastered wall, usually the north wall[164]. Very frequently walls were adorned with a single bull's head, or with a row of heads occasionally beside one or several heads of rams[165].

Of special interest for our purposes is the motif on the east wall of the First Shrine from Level VI[166]. The central panel of this wall, in the upper register, has a row of three painted bulls' heads separated by knobs and flanked in the right panel, at the same height, by the head of a ram. With this arrangement we may compare the scene on a Minoan gold signet ring found by Schliemann as part of a treasure south of the Shaft Grave Circle at Mycenae. The ring is reproduced by Bossert[167]. On it we see two registers of bull and goat heads, three each, attached side by side to a wall and separated by a row of knobs. As far as can be made out from the badly worn surface of the ring this scene is not unlike the Anatolian examples[168]. The similarity between the two representations is evident whatever we believe about the nature of the cult of which they were part[169].

---

[162] *A. S.* 13, 70 ff.
[163] Cf. above p. 24.
[164] In three separate levels: Shrines VI, 8; VII, 8; IX, 8, *A. S.* 13, 67; 14, 70.
[165] See e.g. the First Shrine in Level VI (EVI, 8), *A. S.* 13, figs. 8–13.
[166] EVI, 8, *A. S.* 13, fig. 12.
[167] *Alt Kreta*³, fig. 392 e.
[168] Persson, *Preh. Rel.* 76, describes these knots as rosettes.
[169] Compare the several crania in association with a goddess in a religious scene from a

The bull crania attached to the walls of many shrines obviously represented the whole animal which is occasionally found in the same shrine. These heads, therefore, together with another remarkable feature of the Anatolian shrine, at last solve the long disputed question of the origin and significance of the so-called Minoan horns of consecration. In Çatal Hüyük not only the head could stand for the whole bull, but also the horn cores, usually mounted in a rectangular, pillar-like, structure, or along the sides of a bench seven deep[170]. At times all three forms – the whole animal, the head, and the "bull pillar" – occurred together in one shrine[171]. The separate horns of the Anatolian shrines[172] were the ancestors of the Cretan horns of consecration which had been imported to the island direct from the East: in spite of the curious stereotyped shape they assumed in Cretan hands – a point that gave rise to much speculation concerning their significance[173] –, the association with the figure of the bull, as well as the important position they held in cult, is evident from the Anatolian finds[174].

The bull in Çatal Hüyük was quite clearly the object of worship: he could be represented merely by the head or the horn cores. It follows that wherever the horns might be found, in caves, as at Patso[175], in peak sanctuaries[176], in funeral cult, as on the Hagia Triada sarcophagus, in shrines, or elsewhere in the Minoan palace, they indicate the presence of the bull and the divine powers symbolised by that animal. This does not imply, of course, that horns were cult objects, for they occasionally served as ornamental motifs to Cretan artists, but they were more than receptacles or instruments used in the performance of religious rites[177]. The connection between the horns of consecration and the bull is ignored at one's own peril in any attempt to define the former's precise cultic function which depends,

famous Minoan ring found in the same treasure, Tsountas, *R. A.* (1900) Pl. VIII, 1. It has been suggested by Mellaart, *A. S.* 13, 79, that in Crete the goat replaced the ram in religious representations for reasons of ecology.

[170] E.g. Shrine AVI, 1. *A. S.* 13, fig. 4.
[171] E.g. EVI, 8, *A. S.* 13, fig. 9.
[172] They were also found in a shrine at Beycesultan, Seton-Lloyd – J. Mellaart, *Beycesultan* Fig. 16.
[173] See Nilsson, *M. M. R.* 183 ff.
[174] Cf. Schachermeyr, *Min. Kult. d. alt. Kreta* 157.
[175] Nilsson, *op. cit.* 167 and fig. 68.
[176] See e.g. the steatite *rhyton* from Kato Zakro, Archaeological Rep. for 1963/4, *J. H. S.* 84 (1964) fig. 39.
[177] This thesis was originally suggested by Sir A. Evans. Nilsson also supports it, *op. cit.* 183 f.

therefore, on a knowledge of the part played in Anatolian and Cretan religious belief by the bull. And even when due allowance is made for the temporal gap between the two cultures, we can expect to learn about the religious nature of the Cretan bull from the Eastern practice. To this we shall return below[178].

The remains of the Anatolian shrines under discussion emphasize the vital part played in religious belief by certain types of animals; a point which equally applied to Cretan cult, although, apart from the bull, ram (goat), stag, and leopard, the Cretan animals included in their ritual differ-

[178] The Cretan horns, aside from their now obvious relation to the bull, still present a number of problems, for in some aspects their cultic usage apparently differed from the Anatolian model. With one likely exception from Mochlos (E. M. – Evans, *P. M.* I, 57, fig. 16 C), most of the Cretan horns belong to L. M. II, III, with a few examples from M. M. II and III. Their shape has changed and seems at times to have only a tenuous connection with the original bull horns (an interesting theory has been proposed by S. Diamant & J. Rutter, according to which the Minoan horns of consecration derived from Eastern models which were used as "hearth furniture" and particularly "pot-stands", *A. S.* 19 [1969] 147–77). More important is the fact that in Crete the horns came to be associated with other objects, normally placed in their middle, of which there is as yet only a weak or no trace at all in Anatolian shrines. The most common object in this connection was the double axe: in Cretan religion a frequent and important part of the cultic paraphernalia both by itself and in association with the horns. Examples are too frequent and well known to require special mention. The origin and significance of the Cretan double axe is still obscure and need not detain us here (for the Near Eastern and Anatolian origin of this implement see Schachermeyr, *Min. Kult* 161 and refs.). So far it occurs only once in Çatal Hüyük in a wall painting from House AVI, 6 [*A. S.* 13, Pl. VIII (b)], in no wise obviously connected with the bull horns. Its butterfly shape, with the handle projecting in equal length from the axehead, was well known to the Chalcolithic Near East, as well as to Bronze Age Crete, as can be seen from a sealing from Phaestus (Schachermeyr, *op. cit.* fig. 86,; 87). The presence of the axe in Neolithic Anatolian wall painting adds strength to the well founded theory that this implement, too, had been imported to Crete from the East (cf. above p. 37. On this point see also H. G. Buchholz, *Zur Herkunft der kretischen Doppelaxt*), and perhaps originally from Anatolia. Beyond this we cannot go. In the painting at Çatal Hüyük the axe is shown beside other symbols which at present defy interpretation. These latter, in fact, tend to deepen the mystery surrounding the position of the double axe in Cretan cult where, for example, at times a sacred knot replaced the shaft of the axe in a symbolic arrangement which "became the proto-type for a decorative device of the later L.M. I ceramic style" (Evans, *P. M.* I 433 fig. 310 c–e). Neither the Anatolian example nor the instance of the Minoan axe in cultic use bear out Schachermeyr's thesis, *op. cit.* 161, that this implement was the symbol of power in a matriarchal Cretan society. It has recently been suggested that the double axe in Minoan Crete was closely connected with the tomb and death, I. Pini, *Beiträge zur Minoischen Gräberkunde*, Wiesbaden 1968, 65.

ed from the Eastern types. Neither snake nor lion occurred in Çatal Hüyük painting or plastic art. Instead of the dove or raven – well known to the Cretan – the former painted figures of the vulture which was so obviously thought to exercise a special function in burial or funeral cult. It is most likely that, beside the divergent geographical and climatic conditions, there were other reasons at play to explain the differences. Of greater value to our purposes is the fact that both in East and West these animals were felt either to possess divine powers themselves or, at any rate, they were closely associated with the deity revered in the shrine or cult locality where they occurred. This association between animal and deity – generally a goddess – was quite pronounced in Çatal Hüyük and may well have a bearing on a similar close relationship in Crete between the so-called Mistress of Animals and her animal; a point which will be discussed in greater detail later on.

A great many shrines at Çatal Hüyük showed the figure – sometimes to a height of ten feet and more[179] – of a goddess modelled in plaster usually against the west wall[180]. This goddess, sometimes represented twice or three times in the same shrine[181], marks the nature of the cult practised in these shrines as one concerned with fertility and birth in particular[182]. The goddess' arms are raised and bent at right angles at the elbows in a gesture familiar from Neolithic figures in the Aegean area, as well as from numerous Cretan statuettes and idols. This attitude of the arms has been convincingly explained as a "Segensgestus"[183]. The legs of the goddess are raised and in the position of giving birth, not unlike several Neolithic figures from the East[184]. She was obviously a Mother Goddess[185], also portrayed, with pro-

---

[179] EVI, 10, *A. S.* 13, 70 and fig. 14.

[180] This seems to be true mostly of the shrines of the Sixth Level, although in some cases the goddess was also found on e.g. the east or south wall. EVIB, 31 shows three figures: one on the west wall, another on the south wall, and the third on the east wall, of the shrine, *A. S.* 14, fig. 7 and 8.

[181] Cf. the previous note. It seems doubtful whether one may call the figure on the west wall of Shrine EVI, 14 an example of the "Twin Goddess", *A. S.* 13, 75 and fig. 18.

[182] *A. S.* 13, 79.

[183] See S. Alexiou, *K. Ch.* 12 (1958) 179 ff.

[184] See e.g. Schachermeyr, *op. cit.* fig. 69. Compare also the many remarkable Mycenaean figures of nude females shown sitting in a chair with arms raised and in a similar attitude. These were found at Delphi and in numerous tombs, Nilsson, *op. cit.* 305 f. and fig. 149, and incidentally recall the white (sitting?) female figure painted on the wall of a shrine from Level IV at Çatal Hüyük, *A. S.* 12 (1962) Pl. XIII, a, b.

[185] It is perhaps somewhat rash to reconstruct from the Anatolian shrines the "pantheon" of Çatal Hüyük "presided over by the mother goddess, her son, and husband – male

nounced female attributes, in a great many statuettes which were found in the same shrines. Birth, the act of giving birth, appears to have been her main concern: she was modelled on the walls in the attitude of labour. Once she was shown as pregnant[186], but several times as actually giving birth, graphically depicted in a clay figure from the shrine in Level VII[187].

Remarkable is her association, and even identification, with her special animals, the bull, ram and the leopard. Not only do these animals share the most prominent positions of the shrine with the goddess but she also gives birth to a ram[188], or to a bull[189]. She may either appear in animal form or perhaps be represented by one, as in the so-called Leopard Shrine (EVI, 44), where in all likelihood[190] the central motif had been the large panel of two leopards shown face to face on the north wall[191]. The platform in front of this panel still shows traces of grain offerings as well as statuettes of the standing goddess[192]. Some further support for the appearance of the goddess in animal shape comes from her curious animal (feline?) ears on some of her figures[193].

This close relationship with particular animals, apart from her function as goddess of birth, was a common part of a goddess of nature and life, a feature which we find again in the Cretan and Greek goddesses of popular belief, like Demeter and Artemis. She was a goddess of nature, and as such the Anatolian deity most probably governed all aspects of the constantly recurring cycle of birth, marriage and death[194]. There is, indeed, some evidence in Çatal Hüyük of the goddess' connection with death and,

spirits of fertility symbolized by large and small bulls – and her daughter (or daughters?), younger version(s) of the great goddess herself." Mellaart, *A. S.* 14, 47.

[186] Shrine VII, 23, *A. S.* 14, Pl. XIII, a, b.
[187] AII, 1, *A. S.* 13, Pl. XXIV, a–d; fig. 31; 32.
[188] EVI, 10, *A. S.* 14, fig. 9.
[189] EVI, 8; EVI, 14 (two bulls), *A. S.* 13, fig. 8, 18. Cf. VII, 1, *A. S.* 14, fig. 14.
[190] This shrine was badly destroyed by fire, *A. S.* 14, 42.
[191] *Ibid.* fig. 5.
[192] *Ibid.* 45; fig. 26.
[193] EVIB, 45; EVIB, 31; EVI, 10. Mellaart expresses some doubt about the presence and shape of these ears, *ibid.* 47. They could have been part of the goddess' hairstyle, *ibid.* 50, fig. 6; 7; 9.
[194] For the part this goddess probably played in a type of *hieros gamos* ceremony see the stone plaque of a *symplegma* from House EVI, 30, *A. S.* 13, Pl. XXI d and fig. 27. For a similar scene from Haçilar see Mellaart, *Excavations at Hacilar* (1971) where the goddess seems to be wearing a cloak, however. I owe this reference to Professor Burkert.

according to Mellaart, with the vulture, the bird of death[195]. Still more persuasive evidence comes from the fact that her shrine in Çatal Hüyük was not only the scene of birth but also of death and burial. The several murals with vultures attacking usually headless human corpses leave no doubt about the significance of such scenes[196].

The scenes of death and funeral cult appear generally to have been confined to, and about, the east wall of a shrine, that is directly opposite the wall given over to depicting the goddess in the act of giving birth. Mellaart remarks on this division[197] which, however, does have exceptions to the rule[198]. Nevertheless there is abundant evidence that the shrines at Çatal Hüyük[199] were used for burial grounds. The most usual way was for the human remains to be interred – in a secondary burial – below the east wall of a shrine[200]. The bones were often buried in random order, although at times an entire undisturbed skeleton was found[201]. One might reasonably expect that the scenes on the east wall, above the burial ground, dealt with the subject of death in such a way, however, that this event was merely considered one aspect – leading once more to birth and life – of the never ending cycle of nature religion. In this belief Çatal Hüyük could hardly have signally differed from other Stone and Bronze Age cultures practising the same beliefs; and the decorations on these walls should reflect features of cult which, even if not always certain in sense and interpretation, might well illuminate parts of the Cretan religious scene.

Some of the most interesting decorations come from the shrines of the Sixth Level. The First Shrine here (EVI, 8) had on its central panel, in the course of its four different phases, a row of three bulls' heads, two rows of women's breasts, each concealing the lower jaw of a wild boar, a series of hands, and wall painting depicting flowers, bees or butterflies, and probably chrysalises, over which was painted the design of a honeycomb[202]. The

[195] Mellaart (*A. S.* 13, 90) cites the statuette of an old squatting woman found in House EVI, 25 together with a finely carved animal – probably a vulture, Pl. XXII c, d; fig. 26. Cf. *A. S.* 14, 64.

[196] See e.g. the so-called Vulture Shrine VII, 8, *A. S.* 14, Pl. VII, b; VIII, b; IX, a, b; fig. 20. Cf. Pl. XII a, b; XIV, a; fig. 21; 22.

[197] *A. S.* 13, 79; 14, 47.

[198] Cf. for example the figure of a pregnant goddess on the east wall of Shrine VII, 23, *A. S.* 14, 66; Pl. XIII a, b.

[199] As indeed the private houses, certainly in Levels II–VII, *A. S.* 13, 95.

[200] *A. S.* 13, 79; 95.

[201] *Ibid.*

[202] *A. S.* 13, fig. 9–12; Pl. XI a, b; XII a–c, p. 67 ff.

connection between the breasts and birth and life is plain; no less clear is the significance of the boars' jaws within the breasts when compared with the pair of similar breasts on the east wall of the Second Shrine (EVI, 10) which were found to contain the beaks of vultures – the bird of death[203]. Both breast and jaw or griffin beak, in short, were indicative of birth and death. Their presence fully confirms the symbolic value the artists gave to their work; and they must obviously have a bearing on the meaning of the remaining wall decoration including the bulls' heads, the bees, chrysalises, honeycomb and so on.

Beside the pair of breasts on the east wall of the Second Shrine there recurs the bull's head attached to the wall above a deep niche painted in red and containing some bone tools. In front of this bull, sunk into a platform, was a hole in which were found some scattered human bones[204]. The Third Shrine (EVI, 14) merely had a bull's head fixed in the central panel of the east wall, while a niche, surmounted by a ram's head, formed the main decoration of the south wall[205]. The design of the niche and ram's head, side by side this time and flanked in the right panel by a bull's head, is found once more on the east wall of the Fourth Shrine[206] (EVI, 7). From these few shrines a definite pattern of decoration emerges, and this can be paralleled from shrines of other levels, in which the heads of the bull and ram, the very creatures to whom the goddess is seen to give birth, and a niche – usually painted red – predominate, together with paintings on the west walls featuring human hands, bees, or butterflies, honeycomb etc.

Burial in the shrine gave the worshipper at Çatal Hüyük the promise of life: this is not only symbolically shown by the women's breasts on the walls, below which the bones were discovered, but also by the nature of the burial itself, for the bones, as well as the niches, and a number of animal heads, were at times painted with red ochre[207]. This was a wide-spread and well-known practice of Stone and Bronze Age cultures to denote rebirth from death[208]. There is no doubt that the murals, the bull and ram crania, and the niche, played a vital role in this belief intimately connected with what must have been in essence a chthonic cult of vegetation and fertility.

The frequently recurring niche alone affords a clue to the original loca-

---

[203] *Ibid.* 70.
[204] *Ibid.* fig. 15; Pl. XIV a, b, p. 70.
[205] *Ibid.* fig. 17.
[206] *Ibid.* fig. 16.
[207] *Ibid.* 95.
[208] See Willetts, *Cults* 56 and refs.

tion of this type of cult, and it serves as a link, so to speak, with an important aspect of Minoan cult which also dated back to the Stone Age. The wall niche, in all likelihood, represented a cave[209]. Generally it is found on the east wall of the shrines below which the burials occurred; the wall, in fact, which was most closely associated with death in the cycle of nature. We saw that in Greek thought caves were entrances to the underworld. Such natural grottoes were avenues from below to the world of the living[210]. The same belief probably obtained in Crete concerning caves and natural fissures in the ground, and there is some evidence that this idea was transmitted to the West from Anatolia, or at least was shared by these Neolithic peoples[211].

The worshipper at Çatal Hüyük still associated the niche in his shrine, and other paraphernalia of the ritual, with a cult which at one time had been celebrated in a cave. Together with fully anthropomorphic statuettes of his goddess, he placed many lime-stone concretions and stalagmites or stalactites – occasionally partly fashioned to resemble human shape – in the shrine and below the "cave" in the wall, as in the Second Shrine of Level VI (EVI, 10). A number of similar natural formations have been recovered from caves in the Taurus Mountains to the south of Çatal Hüyük. The Turkish peasants call them *bebek* or "baby"[212], and they were clearly the ancestors of the stalagmitic objects found in many shrines and occasionally in a private house[213]. Shrines of other levels, too, contained such objects; following the 1963 campaign Mellaart could categorically state that "the discovery of cult statues is invariably accompanied by a collection of stalactites and concretions"[214]. The fertility cult, therefore, which was practised in the domestic shrines of Çatal Hüyük had at one time – perhaps in full, certainly in its essential parts – been transferred from a cave. Though the locality of the cult may have changed, its form did not relax its curious hold on the mind of the worshipper who, over many generations, retained

---

[209] Cf. Mellaart, *A. S.* 13, 79.

[210] See above p. 90 and n. 106.

[211] Mellaart, *ibid.* 79 and n. 25, aptly cites a Hattic text (from *A. S.* 9 [1959] 171 ff.) which speaks of the Weather-god Nerik (in central Anatolia) as disappearing (to the underworld) into a "hole". The motif is common, of course, and probably connected with the idea that the underworld can be entered from the mountains, cf. T. H. Gaster, *Thespis*², 197 f.

[212] *A. S.* 13, 82 n. 34.

[213] *Ibid.* Pl. XIX b–d; House EVI, 28, Pl. XIX a.

[214] *A. S.* 14, 73.

the aniconic stalagmite as an image of his goddess beside her figure developing to semi-iconic and eventually fully human and naturalistic shape[215].

From the finds at Çatal Hüyük there emerge two points of signal interest to the understanding of Cretan religion. The first concerns the probable transference of a cave cult, concerned with birth, death, and nature religion in general, to a domestic shrine, and the second consists in the fact that a number, if not all, of the cult statues evolved from the unfashioned limestone concretions, stalagmites and stalactites, found in caves. This can only mean that the stalagmites, which enjoyed a special position in religious worship, were in fact aniconic representations of a divinity. That is, far from being symbolic of a particular god or goddess, they, like the subsequent statue, functioned as true images of divinity. The many examples found in shrines and private dwellings make it possible to observe an evolution of these shapes from fully aniconic to semi-iconic and eventually anthropomorphic form. The Second Shrine at Çatal Hüyük alone has yielded examples of all stages which apparently developed from the original lime-stone concretions.

Such figures vary from the rough stalagmite with sculptured head[216], to a smoothed stone with superficially carved[217] or incised[218] features, to fully, though schematized, human statuettes[219] whose shape still betrays their origin. The same shrine also concealed fully developed statues of high artistic merit depicting single or more figures, or even figures associated with animals[220]. Of those representing deities at least some are male[221]. This picture of cult statues was strengthened and verified in the course of the 1963 campaign from discoveries in other shrines, such as the Boar's Head Shrine (VI B, 45), the Leopard Shrine (VI A, 44), and the Second Vulture Shrine (VII, 21) which, beside both the stalagmites and fully developed statuettes, had concretions with carved heads[222], as well as roughly moulded figures that still clearly show their origin[223].

[215] *A. S.* 13, 82. Mellaart, *ibid.*, suggests that the older aniconic or semi-iconic figures might have been examples of "ritual heirlooms".
[216] *A. S.* 13, Pl. XIX b.
[217] *Ibid.* Pl. XIX d.
[218] *Ibid.* Pl. XIX c.
[219] In black lime-stone, see *ibid.* fig. 19.
[220] See *ibid.* Pl. XX, XXI.
[221] E.g. *ibid.* Pl. XXI c.
[222] E.g. *A. S.* 14, fig. 28 a–c, from House VII, 24; Pl. XVII a.
[223] *Ibid.* e.g. fig. 26; 27; 30 a, b (pebble figurine in shape of stalactite with incised features on head from EVI, 10).

Here we have to hand some unequivocal material with a probable bearing on a few aspects of Cretan cave cult which not only enjoyed a wide dispersion but in certain instances endured throughout the history of that island. This is not to say that the Minoan cave cult as a whole was an import from Anatolia: this type of cult was too wide-spread, not only in the Aegean area but also in Europe from the Stone Age, to elect any one region or people as the first to have made use of a natural abode for themselves and their gods before they learnt the skill of building their own houses[224]. Nonetheless the rich Anatolian finds should throw some further light on the more thinly documented Cretan scene, particularly in view of the close ties between the two centres from Neolithic times. Thus the Anatolian cult, which in all likelihood had once been practised in the caves of the Taurus Mountains, had some features in common with what we know of Cretan practice. Indeed the finds from those Cretan caves where cult obtained were rich but hardly open to easy interpretation[225]. Cult statues or idols were rare but not entirely absent[226].

In spite of the eminent position of cave cult in Cretan belief, its precise nature remains a vexing problem, because of the variety of apparently unrelated offerings found there[227], the scarcity of what might be called "Kultbildnisse", and the fact that the cult extended over a vast period sometimes even – with occasional interruptions – enduring into Christian times. Cult content, therefore, was bound to change, become adapted or even attached to different deities. At times not only the deity but also the cult were relatively new, as in the case of the famous cave of Zeus on Mt. Ida where no cult occurred before the Geometric period[228]. The uncertainty of our evidence notwithstanding, it was already noticed that cave cult in Crete, too, was concerned with some basic aspects of nature religion, namely birth

---

[224] Cf. Nilsson, *M. M. R.* 53.
[225] See above pp. 81 ff.
[226] This is maintained by Picard, *Rel. Préh.* 58. J. Hazzidakis, for example, found a bronze statuette in a cave west of Tylissos, *Tylissos, Et. C.* III, p. 75, cited by Nilsson, *op. cit.* 58 n. 18. Perhaps the human bronze figurines from the Psychro cave belong here, too, as well as those from the cave at Patso, Nilsson, *ibid.* 63; 67 (but not on Mt. Ida, Faure, *Fonct.* 12 n. 1). Cf. the Neolithic clay idol recently discovered in Pan's cave at Marathon (*B. C. H.* [1959] 588) and some statuettes from a cave in Laconia, *B. C. H.* (1962) 724.
[227] Cf. the different nature of offerings in the shrines at Çatal Hüyük, ranging from bone tools to grain and weapons.
[228] Above p. 80.

and death[229]. The figure of Eileithyia at Amnisos is evidence of that, as is the legendary tradition concerned with the annual birth of the Divine Infant. The latter's curiously strong appeal to popular imagination is reflected both in the wide dispersion of the myth and in the basic features common to all versions which consisted in the babe's close association with Mother Earth or a Mother Goddess, and his nurture by an animal[230]. He is said to be born in a Cretan cave[231]; and, whatever his name, the stereotyped features of his myth mark him out as a part of Minoan and Aegean tradition of which one may well find a trace even in the Anatolian shrines of Çatal Hüyük. There is no extant archaeological evidence to show that one cave saw both the celebration of death and cult concerning rebirth[232]. But such a combination was more than likely, for funeral rites[233], like other religious ceremonies which occurred in a cave, belonged to the same chthonic divinities[234]. Traces of this kind of cult association we may also gather from later mythology describing the annual birth of Zeus in the same cave[235]. Furthermore, so far only vague evidence has come to light that the Mother Goddess in Çatal Hüyük had a youthful companion[236] whose precise cultic functions, of course, remain obscure at present. In the absence of contemporary written records this lack is no more than expected, and it is equally painfully felt in the West.

Under these circumstances firm analogies of religious practice between Anatolia and Crete are out of the question. However, we do possess enough knowledge, backed considerably by an appreciation of the cultural

---

[229] See p. 79; 88.
[230] A sacred cow, bitch, a swarm of bees, a cow, or most frequently the goat Amaltheia, see Nilsson, *Gesch.* I, 321; cf. L. Preller, *Griechische Mythologie*[4], ed. by Robert, 1887, I, 35 n. 4. Cf. above p. 15.
[231] See above p. 14; 85 and n. 72.
[232] Some caves, indeed, like that at Pyrgos, containing hundreds of interments (Evans, *P. of Min.* I, 59; Nilsson, *M. M. R.* 55; Willetts, *Cults* 142) appear in time to have been used exclusively for burial. Cf. above p. 77; 79.
[233] Even without the existence of an official cult of the dead, Faure *Fonct.* 76 ff.
[234] Burial and cult in caves are scrupulously separated by Faure, *Fonct.* 79; 191. Even in the Psychro cave, according to Faure, a long temporal gap divided its use for burial and cult. The position is ambiguous, however, for Faure, *op. cit.* 191, recognizes (1) that funerary rites and cultic practices in caves must have been instituted at the same time, and (2) that both practices were of a religious nature and related in that on all such occasions the dead and living were in some way felt to be brought in contact with a divinity who resided in the depth of the earth.
[235] See e.g. the version in Ant. Liberalis, *Met.* 19. Cf. Nilsson, *M. M. R.* 543.
[236] See Mellaart, *A. S.* 14, 90.

ties between East and West, to detect significant correspondences between a cult transferred from caves to a domestic shrine in Çatal Hüyük and Cretan cave cult, which, though it flourished throughout the island's history, also found a place in domestic shrines as in the Little Palace at Knossos. The latter has yielded up not only figures of horns of consecration and the goat but also lime-stone concretions, descendants of the stalagmite, with roughly shaped features not unlike the Anatolian manner[237]. In both localities the scene of the cult was intimately connected with a cave. The nature of the cult dealt with birth and death and was therefore in all likelihood symbolic of the annual growth and decay of vegetation. At the centre of this cult was a Great Goddess of nature particularly concerned with birth; a fact vividly portrayed in the shrines at Çatal Hüyük and explicit in Crete in the figure of Eileithyia at Amnisos. The Cretan goddess "of the cave" most likely was shown by the famous statuette – probably as late as L.M. III – of a woman and child found by Forsdyke in a tomb at Mavro Spelio ("Black Cave")[238], and similar, incidentally, to a group of a mother holding her child on a slate plaque from House EVI, 30 at Çatal Hüyük[239].

The Cretan goddess, in her cave, recurs – once with the young god – on a few Cretan seals[240]. This goddess of birth and nature in East and West was closely connected with certain animals. Indeed, our pictorial evidence suggests that goddess and animal may have been thought of as identical or at least interchangeable. In Çatal Hüyük the goddess gave birth to a bull or ram, animals which were also represented by their crania or simple horn cores (in the case of the bull) in the shrines, where once a pair of leopards (EVI, 44) may well have replaced the goddess (possibly in twin form). In

---

[237] See above p. 92.
[238] E. J. Forsdyke, "The Mavro Spelio Cemetery at Knossos", *B.S.A.* 28 (1926/7) 243 (Not to be confused with the Mavrospilio cave at Knossos, Faure, *Fonct.* 183). Evans, *P.M.* II, 556 f. fig. 327, calls the figure an example of the Minoan Mother Goddess. Nilsson, *op. cit.* 300; 304 f., contests this view on the grounds that the figure was late and probably influenced by similar Mycenaean statuettes. This point does not, however, detract from the significance of the goddess with child. On this point see also Picard, *op. cit.* 205.
[239] *A.S.* 14, fig. 27, Pl. XXI d.
[240] In a scene from an electrum ring from Mycenae, Evans, *P.M.* II fig. 324; and on a clay sealing from Knossos, reproduced in Schachermeyr, *Min. Kultur* fig. 72 d. Both scenes occurred in a cave which the artist represented by stalagmites or stalactites. A similar scene on a signet from Thisbe (Evans, *P.M.* III, fig. 328) is a forgery (Nilsson, *M.M.R.* 40 f.; *Gesch.* I, 284 n. 1).

Crete the same animals[241] played a vital role in the cult of this figure. The same ambivalence between anthropomorphic goddess and her animal, reflected in myth, obtained and must account for the goat's position as the foster mother suckling the babe, in a scene depicted once on a seal impression from Knossos[242]. The goat, shown within a cave on another sealing from Knossos[243], may perhaps have taken the goddess' place. Equally common to the Minoan cave sanctuary was the bull, that is generally the so-called horns of consecration which, at times together with numerous bull figurines, were found among the deposits, as for example in the cave of Hermes Kranaios at Patso[244], and which figured on the sealing from Knossos mentioned above[245]. This animals formed the central motif, too, on the bronze tablet (perhaps L. M. I) from the cave at Psychro[246].

The functional correspondence between the Anatolian lime-stone concretions and stalagmites, and those found in many Cretan caves where cult obtained is most valuable and seems quite unambigous. We noticed above[247] that the Anatolian stalagmites were actually cult idols. From them, stage by stage, developed the fully anthropomorphic idols, in such a way that the ancient concretions, which harboured divine powers from the earliest days of cult, never lost their efficacy but were preserved and revered beside the human statuettes. In Minoan cave cult, too, stalagmites were objects of worship. In fact, in many instances, they seemed to form its centre[248]. Our best examples again come from Eileithyia's cave at Amnisos and from the cave at Psychro[249]. The cultic importance attached to the stalagmite pillars in the lower cave at Psychro appears from the numerous bronze objects placed in their vertical crevices.

[241] Except that the goat, presumably for ecological reasons (see above n. 169), replaced the ram.
[242] Evans, *P. M.* III, fig. 326. Evans calls the animal a sheep. The boy sitting beneath the goat, especially when compared with similar groups, makes the nature of this scene obvious, although, as Nilsson remarks, *Gesch.* I, 321, the animal is not actually shown as suckling the infant.
[243] With stalagmites, reproduced in Matz, *Kreta, Myk., Troja* Pl. 54.
[244] Nilsson, *M. M. R.* 67; Faure, *Fonct.* 138. Cf. the bucrania and oxe-shaped *rhyta* discovered in the Psychro cave, above p. 83.
[245] See n. 240.
[246] See above p. 83; cf. Willetts, *Cults* 145 f.
[247] See above p. 106.
[248] This was not invariably true. At least Zeus' cave on Mt. Ida had neither stalagmites or stalactites. This cave, however, did not see cult before the Geometric period, cf. above p. 80. See also Faure's reservations on this point, *Fonct.* 14.
[249] Above p. 78; 82 f.

These examples have long suggested the sacred nature of such concretions[250] but their precise import could only be guessed at. Now their position in the Anatolian cult at Çatal Hüyük does clearly demonstrate that the stalagmite was no symbolic representation of divinity or divine power but an aniconic figure of the goddess who, in all likelihood, controlled growth and the cycle of birth and death. On this point we may now be more definite than was possible for Nilsson some fifteen years ago[251], whatever the changes that affected the cult in the passage of centuries before the historic age. Less easily rewarded, however, is the attempt to trace from Cretan remains a similar development beginning with the rough lime-stone concretions and culminating in the fully anthropomorphic figure. With one or two exceptions – like the semi-human concretions in the Little Palace[252] – there seems to be a gap between the crude and fully finished statuette in Crete. Poor preservation of sites and the depredations of plunderers through the ages only partly account for this hiatus.

The Cretan caves have yielded up a number of clay and bronze figurines of both animals and humans[253] but mostly belonging to M. M., L. M., and later. These, with few exceptions like the bronze statuette from Psychro[254], constituted votive figurines rather than cult idols[255]. Altogether the great majority of idols came from the Middle and Late Minoan periods, and they generally belonged to sites other than the cave[256]. What evidence is there, in fact, in favour of a similar evolution in Crete of the anthropomorphic divinity from aniconic and semi-iconic shape? By no means enough to warrant any dogmatic statement in this direction on the strength of the Anatolian development described above. The only figures which could be

---

[250] Nilsson, *M. M. R.* 74; 258. Picard, *op. cit.* 58, speaks of them as "images de la divinité secrète." For Evans' and Platon's views see above p. 92 and n. 121.

[251] *Op. cit.* e.g. 73.

[252] See above p. 92; 110.

[253] E.g. from Tylissos, see n. 226, from Psychro, Phaneromene, Zeus' cave on Mt. Ida, Patso, Kastellos and Khosto Nero on Mt. Jouktas (Faure, *Fonct.* 109; 138; 153 f.; 160; 175 f.). The Akrotiri finds are classical and Hellenistic (*Ibid.* 145).

[254] Above p. 83. Nilsson, *M. M. R.* 295, states his strong reservations here, too. Cf. the bronze statuette from Tylissos, above p. 82.

[255] We do not know, of course, whether cave cult in Anatolia existed concurrently with the domestic shrines at Çat. Hüy., and if so, whether such caves contained cult images beside the stalagmites and stalactites.

[256] Nilss., *M. M. R.* 295, divides them into three classes according to the sites where they were discovered: votive figs. from sanctuaries, from shrines (usually cult idols), and figs. from tombs. Cf. Willetts, *Cults* 58.

considered in this context are the semi-iconic – upper half human, lower half cylindrical, – idols, particularly from the Shrine of the Double Axes at Knossos[257]. Such idols were generally placed in domestic shrines and therefore did not occur before M. M.[258]. In spite of their pillar-like lower part, it is, of course, impossible to suggest that these cylindrical idols must necessarily be considered an intermediate stage between aniconic and iconic shape[258a]. They did, however, clearly belong to a religious tradition which greatly antedated M. M.[259], and they therefore illustrate the strong religious conservatism which, as in the East, often placed them beside fully developed idols.

Yet Crete apparently possessed no obvious examples of a transitional period: the crude and fully developed were side by side[260]. Thus, on the one hand, the roughly modelled concretions in the Little Palace intimate that the aniconic goddess had altered little when she came to be associated with domestic cult. Conversely the artists of the best and late Minoan periods conceived her in anthropomorphic form receiving cult in her cave sanctuary[261]. Perhaps the Cretans forbore to observe each stage of a laborious development of their plastic art, because as early as E. M. – the third millennium B. C. – they imported the goddess figure already in full anthropomorphic shape from Aegean islands like the Cyclades, from Egypt, and eventually perhaps from Anatolia[262]. Beyond this we cannot go, and it is as well to state here that our information is not enough to establish with any degree of certainty the extent to which this cave cult of a goddess of birth and the cycle of nature survived in its original form.

These few points just mentioned explain that a comparative study of Neolithic Anatolian and Minoan idols is not likely to advance our knowledge on the last issue, because with common beginnings, and these are

---

[257] Nilss., *M. M. R.* 80 ff. and fig. 14.
[258] Nilss., *M. M. R.* 316; 321.
[258a] In any case they are later than the representational figs. of M.M. III – L.M. I. This was kindly pointed out to me by Dr. P. Warren.
[259] Cf. Nilss., *M. M. R.* 80.
[260] Cf. Nilss., *M. M. R.*; Matz, *Göttererscheinung* e.g. 68.
[261] See the rings and sealings mentioned above n. 240.
[262] On the discussion of the Neolithic idols in Crete, their part in cult, and their origins, see Evans, *P. M.* I, 51 f.; Nilss., *M. M. R.* 289 ff.; Picard, *Rel. Préh.* 123 f., and the detailed study by P. J. Ucko, *Anthropom. Figurines*, who discusses the vast modern literature on the subject. Ucko does not take the Çat. Hüy. figs. into account (354) and denies contact between Haçilar and Crete "on the basis of the study of the figurines" (407).

worth noting, a Cretan goddess of nature found her own form at the peak of the island's culture. The discovery of the shrines at Çatal Hüyük is of more immediate service to that type of cult in Crete concerned with the natural cycle of birth and death. This cult was certainly observed in the cave sanctuary and it formed an important part of the Minoan religious scene, for it endured for many generations leaving its mark on historic Greek thought. We may also reasonably suppose that this cult found other sites of worship outside the cave; and it may well be that dominant figures in Minoan religion, like the bull and the so-called Mistress of Animals, had their first home here, or at least derived from cave cult.

The bull's important position in the Anatolian shrines is strong evidence firstly that in Crete, too, this animal was involved in cult, and that the latter could be represented either by the head or simply by the horn cores[263]. This has to be firmly established before investigating the significance of the bull's ubiquitous presence in the shrines of Çatal Hüyük and in the whole range of Cretan cult from the cave to the domestic shrine to the open area of the palace[264]. The shrines at Çatal Hüyük do not obviously show that the bull by itself was thought of as a god, so that there is no hope of further information from this source to resolve the discussion about the existence of a Minoan bull god. Such a figure has at times been identified with the Minotaur in Greek legend, or even with the sun[265]. More serious perhaps is the lack of any clear connection at Çatal Hüyük between the bull and the double axe[266], in view of the fact that in Crete the two are found so commonly together[267].

[263] This is doubted by Nilss., *M. M. R.* 232. Schachermeyr, *min. Kult.* 157, believes that the bull crania and horns, representing the whole animal, had already been brought to Crete separately during the Neolithic Age.

[264] Cf. the large pair near the south-entrance of the palace of Knossos, Evans, *P. M.* II, 160, fig. 81.

[265] The last theory probably owed its origin to A. B. Cook, *Zeus*, Cambridge 1914, I, 497 ff., but found some echoes in later works, including Persson, *Preh. Grk. Rel.* 132; Willetts, *Cults*, 111; W. K. C. Guthrie, *C. A. H.*² (1961) "Rel. and Myth. of the Greeks", 22; cf. L. Malten, *Jahrb.* 43 (1928) 90 ff. Nilsson, *M. M. R.* 231 f.; 373, briefly examines and rejects the evidence concerning a Cretan Bull-god. Cf. F. Matz, *K. Ch.* (1961/2) 215 ff.

[266] So far the double axe appears only once, in a wall painting in House AVI, 6, *A. S.* 13, Pl. VIII b, and not obviously connected with the bull.

[267] G. Glotz, *La Civilisation Égéenne*, 270, speaks of the axe as the fetish of the bull cult. Nilsson's explanation, *M. M. R.* e.g. 229, that the double axe merely entered cult by virtue of its use as an instrument of sacrifice loses force in view mainly of the frequent and curious combination in Minoan art of axe with the branch of the tree

SOME OLDER TRADITIONS IN MINOAN CRETE 115

Bull cult enjoyed great popularity in the Near East and in the West from Neolithic times[268]. The bull was important enough in Anatolia to lend his name to the Taurus and Antitaurus mountain ranges[269]. The nature of his cult – and this is well-known – was quite generally connected with vegetation and fertility. In Greek mythology, as Mellaart also points out[270], this connection was reflected by the association of river gods with the bull[271]. More particularly the bull was considered a chthonic animal, and as such was closely related with cave cult. In the Çatal Hüyük shrines the bull's head, fixed above or beside the niche in the east wall, suggested the animal's intimate association with the cave and the underworld, for the "cave", below which the bones of the dead were commonly buried, was also an entrance to the world below.

In Crete the same held true, for the bull was an important part of cave cult[272] where he had a function to fulfil in connection with the growth of vegetation[273], and, judging from the nature of cave cult, with death as well. Small wonder, then, that the bull occurs on the Hagia Triada sarcophagus in the scene depicting a rite in honour of the dead[274]; nor is it out of the way to see in the famous Cretan bull games not a "secular sport"[275], but a religious rite which in the words of one scholar formed a part of a *drame chthonien*[276]. Picard cites Greek parallels to support his view which appears to be verified by the chthonic nature of the animal in East and West. In fact, Mellaart's Anatolian discoveries give rise to the feeling that one is on the threshold of an accurate perception of the Minoan bull's cultic role. Quite

or even a "sacral knot" as handle. Some examples of such combinations are conveniently collected by Schachermeyr, *op. cit.* fig. 80; 88; 91 a–c. The word for axe (*labrys*) was Carian or Lydian, see above p. 37. For the wide-spread motif of the double axe in the Late Neolithic period, see especially Schachermeyr, *op. cit.* fig. 86, 1–3; cf. above n. 178.

[268] See esp. Malten's important work, cited above n. 265.
[269] *A. S.* 13, 79.
[270] *Ibid.*
[271] Poseidon's association with the bull, perhaps originally in Ionia, was due to the same reasons, cf. Nilsson, *Gesch.* I, 450; Schachermeyr, *Poseidon u. d. Entstehung des griech. Götterglaubens*, Munich 1950 e.g. 45 f.; 75.
[272] Cf. the many offerings (Bronze Age and later) of bull figurines etc. in e.g. the Psychro cave and at Patso, Boardman, *Cret. Coll.* 12 f.; 61 f.; 77.
[273] Cf. the tablet from Psychro, showing the horns of consecration together with branches of a tree, see above p. 83; n. 246.
[274] Matz, *Götterersch.* 403 f.
[275] Nilsson, *M. M. R.* 374.
[276] Picard, *op. cit.* 144.

true, to Cretans the bull was a sacrificial victim[277], and this fact could perhaps be used as an argument against the belief in the bull's sacred nature[278]. But he figured in rites connected with the dead[279], and until we understand the import of the sacrificial scenes – associated with such funerary rites[280] – we are obliged to reserve judgment on their significance in cult[281].

Consider, for example, the bull's near relationship with the goddess in the East: the goddess of birth, often his own mother. The bull in Çatal Hüyük was shown not only at the moment of birth but also as a chthonic animal connected with the dead. The cult there and, we believe, in the Cretan cave dealt with the natural cycle of life and death which in a particular form survived in Greek myth. What was the significance of the intimate connection between the goddess and her animal, particularly the bull? May we suggest that the bull, like the goddess' male escort, was born and died every year? There is at present no proof for our conjecture, but the bull's connection with the Divine Child survived strong in Greek tradition. This was the case with the youthful Zeus, mentioned above, who was identified with the Cretan Velchanos and figured on coins from Phaistos and Gortyn together with a bird and the bull[282]. The most striking example of the connection, or identification, of the bull with the male child and companion of a Great Goddess of nature was Dionysus, of course. Whatever his country of origin[283], to the Greeks he frequently appeared as

---

[277] See e.g. the sealstone in the Candia museum, reprod. by Nilsson, *M. M. R.* 230; fig. 113.
[278] Nilsson, *M. M. R.* e.g. 229 f.; 373 etc. But Prof. Burkert points out to me that a sacrificial victim is ἱερόν by definition.
[279] In addition to the scene on the Hagia Triada sarcophagus, see the figure of the bull, together with horns of consecration, on the *larnax* from Episkopi, Nilsson, *M. M. R.* 434, fig. 197.
[280] Nilsson, *M. M. R.* 434 f. In order to avoid unnecessary argument I do not use the word "cult" in connection with rites in honour of the dead. It seems, however, that the line drawn between the two by some modern scholars is rather thin, see e.g. Faure, *Fonct.* 76.
[281] Schachermeyr, *min. Kult.* 158, speaks of the bull's "ungezügelten und feindlichen Dämonenkraft" which was to be tamed by the sacrifice of the beast.
[282] Such coins are reproduced in Cook, *Zeus* I, 257 ff., fig. 391–400; II (1925), 946, fig. 838–41, with sources.
[283] Perhaps the East (Phrygia, cf. Nilsson, *Gesch.* I, 568). His cult in the West was of long standing, however, for the god was known to the Mycenaeans at Pylos, Chadwick & Baumbach, *G.* 41 (1963) 186, and may well have been worshipped by the Minoans, Matz, *Götterersch.* 67.

SOME OLDER TRADITIONS IN MINOAN CRETE 117

tauromorphic[284], and his history, preserved in Greek legend, was typically that of the male child and Mother Nature's companion who symbolised the growth and decay of vegetation[285].

The bull, thus, was a part of the Mother Goddess: her son, in a tradition which in all likelihood survived in Greek religion. His cult was primarily concerned with death, but also probably with birth, and occurred, for the reasons discussed above, in the cave, his cultic rather than natural home[286]. The vivid scenes of birth in the Anatolian shrines make it plain above all that there was thought to exist not merely an affinity between the goddess and her animal, but that they might have been identified in such a way that the animal, such as bull or leopard, might have represented, or given their shape to, her. This is a valuable point, and a hint of proof that the same relationship existed in the case of a particular and common aspect of the nature goddess in Crete and Greece whom Studniczka gave the Homeric title of *Potnia Theron*[287]. The bonds, though, which united goddess and animal were closer than those of a mistress and her servants[288].

The monstrous Mother Goddess from Shrine AII, 1, shown on her imperial throne in the act of giving birth, was not merely the mistress of the two feline creatures (leopards?) on whose heads she rests her hands and whose long tails curl up over her shoulders[289]: she was identified with her animals in the same way as the two related great goddesses of nature in Greek belief, namely Demeter and particularly Artemis[290], who at one time did receive worship in animal form[291]. The precise relationship between deity and animal in both East and West is still far from clear. One cannot

[284] In Thespiae: *IG* VII, 1787; B. C. H. 50 (1926) 393 and n. 4; Elis: Plutarch, *quaest. graec.* 36, 229 A. Cf. Athenaeus, XI, 476 A; Lycophron, V, 209; V, 1237 with schol.; Euripides, *Bacchae* 100; Sophocles, frg. 782 in Strabo XV, 687. Later images of the god commonly showed him with the horns of the bull: Plutarch, *Is. et Osir.* 364 F; Cornutus, *Theol.* XXX, 59 (Lang).
[285] Semele, his mother, signified Earth. This probable etymology was first proposed by Kretschmer, cited by Nilsson, *Griech. Feste*, 259; cf. *Gesch.* I, 568, „Diese Etymologie des Namens der Mutter des Dionysos ist sicher." Immediately after birth the young god was nurtured by Nymphs, Nilsson, *ibid.*
[286] This last point was suggested by Mellaart, *A. S.* 13, 79.
[287] F. Studniczka, *Kyrene*, 1890, 153 ff.
[288] The Cretan "Master of Animals", Nilsson, *Gesch.* I, 309, is analogous to the male figure (youthful or bearded) shown riding a leopard or bull in statuettes from Çatal Hüyük, *A. S.* 13, fig. 21; 22.
[289] *Ibid.* Pl. XXIV a–d; fig. 31; 32.
[290] See e.g. Nilsson, *Gesch.* I, 214.
[291] Nilsson, *Gesch.* I, 214.

yet safely claim identical functions for the so-called *Potnia Theron* and the Boeotian or Arcadian Demeter or Artemis Kallisto. Nonetheless the Anatolian evidence does support the reasonable hypothesis that at least one important aspect of a goddess of nature and vegetation in these cultures consisted in the intimate alliance with her animals, whether these might be the bull, lion, ram or goat, or even bird and snake. Whether the goddess and her animal were essentially one and the same figure, or if she was thought to be attended by a companion, are questions which at present remain unsolved. We have seen evidence to favour both beliefs. To this we may add, on the one hand, the numerous figurines and representations of half-animal half-human hybrids, like the statuette from the Patso cave of a bronze animal with a human head[292]. These mixtures, however, were generally classed among the Minoan daemons[293] who held an uncertain position in cult where they functioned as servants rather than deities in their own right[294].

More persuasive are the many examples of animals who embody the Minoan goddess and who are shown on her head or about her. She was thought to appear to her worshippers in animal form. The most common epiphany of the deity was in the shape of a bird[295]. But the goddess also appeared as a snake[296], and significantly in the form of a leopard, as she is modelled on one statuette from the eastern repository of the Central Palace Sanctuary at Knossos[297]. On the other hand, in many instances in Cretan art the goddess may have been accompanied by her animal[298]. In this way perhaps we should interpret the frequent so-called heraldic scenes on Cretan gems depicting a goddess[299] flanked by, or grasping, animals[300]. Two common

---

[292] *Mus. It.* 2 (1888), Pl. XIV, 8.
[293] Examples are collected and discussed by Nilsson, *M. M. R.* 374 and n. 16.
[294] Cf. Dietrich, *Death, Fate* 16 f. Nilsson, *Gesch.* I, 297, calls them "Geschöpfe eines von Fieber überhitzten Gehirns."
[295] Nilsson, *M. M. R.* 330 ff.; Matz, *Götterersch.* 397.
[296] Nilsson, *M. M. R.* e.g. 332; 340.
[297] Evans, *P. M.* I, 501 ff.; fig. 360 a, b; 362 a–d. Although the animal on the head of the goddess has the clear markings of a "spotted leopard", Evans sees in her a lioness. This statuette is smaller than the main figure of the shrine (fig. 359), but, contrary to Evans' opinion, represents a goddess by virtue of her headdress, cf. Nilsson, *M. M. R.* 86.
[298] Picard, *op. cit.* 112, in fact supposes that this, too, was the function of the birds shown together with the goddess.
[299] Occasionally a male figure: the *Potnios*.
[300] Nilsson, *M. M. R.* 357 ff. and figs. 168–74, and the famous seal of the "Mother of the Mountains" from Knossos, fig. 162.

motifs in this connection show the deity either standing beside her animal or riding it[301], similar, in fact, to a number of representations from Çatal Hüyük[302].

Such evidence in East and West makes it impossible to answer conclusively the exact function of the goddess' animal in cult. Perhaps the answer is that no clear distinction was felt to exist between deity and animal. The Anatolian scenes appear to suggest such an ambivalence of concept. Certainly, in spite of the temporal gap, they cast some light not only on the nature of the so-called Mistress of Animals but also on the type of cult from which she probably arose[303].

It remains to mention the honeycomb pattern, butterflies and chrysalises painted on the east wall of the First Shrine (first and second phase) in Level IV at Çatal Hüyük (EVI, 8)[304]. These designs raise two points of interest: firstly the apparent connection of the bee and butterfly. Two insects, whose life cycles extend from closed cell to bee and from chrysalis to fully grown butterfly, seem to be portrayed here[305]. The second point concerns the part these scenes played in the ritual or myth of the cult. The development from lifeless cell or chrysalis to the insect imaginatively depicts the interconnection between life and death, the birth of one from the other, so that we are not surprised to find the paintings on the east wall, that is

---

[301] See e.g. the sealings from the Temple Repositories at Knossos, Evans, *P. M.* I, fig. 363 a–c; Nilsson, *M. M. R.* figs. 163–65. The riding goddess appears on a lentoid gem from Chalkedon, found near Mycenae in Clytemnestra's tomb, Mylonas, *Anc. Mycenae*, 1957, 95, fig. 35; *B. C. H.* 81 (1957) 215, 34; on a glass plaque from Dendra – Midea, Persson, *Dendra* (1926) 65, 43, Pl. 25; cf. *Preh. Rel.* 133, fig. 24; and on sealings from Hagia Triada, *B. S. A.* 48 (1953) 86 n. 5, reprod. in Matz, *Götterersch.* fig. 22.

[302] *A. S.* 13, fig. 21; 22; 23; 24; Pl. XX c; XXI a, b; *A. S.* 14, Pl. XV c, d; fig. 29; 32.

[303] It may well be that the myth of Europa and the bull was born from this association of a Mother Goddess and her companion in the shape of a bull. Persson, *Preh. Rel.* 132 f., the association of Heaven and Sun or Moon apart, already saw the essential nature of the bull – Zeus in this legend; cf. Willetts, *Cults* 110 f. The concept of the riding goddess in Greek belief was not, however, confined to Europa, but recurs in the case of Aphrodite Ephippus and Epitragia, and deserves, together with the concept of the often youthful *Potnios*, a separate treatment. For the riding Aphrodite see Dietrich, *Death, Fate* 106 n. 3. Noteworthy in the representations of "Europa" (see above pp. 102 f. and n. 183) is the attitude of her arms, which was identified above as a "Segnungsgestus", although Matz, *op. cit.* 416, sees in it the sign of the goddess' epiphany.

[304] *A. S.* 13, Pl. XII a–c; IX b; fig. 11; 12.

[305] *Ibid.* 80.

that part of the shrine which was devoted to the symbolic portrayal of death and the underworld which we described above. In Minoan and Greek belief, too, the bee was associated with the cycle of life, and Mellaart cites some examples of this belief[306], of which the most striking is the ancient tale[307] of the nurture of the infant Zeus by bees in a Cretan cave[308].

An interesting parallel of the connection between bees and the annually born male infant, symbol of vegetation, comes from the myth of the Hittite god Telepinu who was thought to disappear each year to be found again by the bee[309]. Conversely honey and honey cakes were widely used as offerings in the cult of the dead in classical times, while the custom of burial in honey was wide-spread in prehistoric times in both East and West[310]. Further hints of the part played by the bee in this kind of belief can be found in the cults of Artemis of Ephesus and Demeter whose priestesses were sometimes bees[311]. Again the juxtaposition of life and death is suggested by the fine gold pendant from a tomb at Chrysolakkos, Mallia[312], showing two bees holding a honeycomb, as well as from the design of butterflies and probably chrysalises on the gold leaves discovered in the Shaft Graves at Mycenae[313]. The Anatolian finds, therefore, are exciting because they connect the bee and butterfly in a cult concerned with the dead, and because they may help

---

[306] *Ibid.*
[307] Although we have it recorded as late as Ant. Liberalis, *Met.* 19.
[308] Nilsson, *M. M. R.* 543; *Gesch.* I, 321.
[309] Cited by Picard, *op. cit.* 230. Perhaps the bee's connection with a belief in the annual birth and death of nature was responsible for the insect's part in the rediscovery of Trophonius' (The Feeder) oracular chasm at Lebadeia, Paus. IX, 1 ff., cf. Dietrich, *op. cit.* 349.
[310] Cf. the fate of Minos' son, Glaukos, who drowned in a jar of honey, Persson, *op. cit.* 12; 14 f. with refs.
[311] J. Harrison, *Prolegomena to the Study of Greek Religion*, 442, with other examples. The chorus in Euripides, *Hippol.* 563, compares Aphrodite with the bee when she gives death to Semele. A. B. Cook, "The Bee in Greek Mythology", *J. H. S.* 15 (1895) 1 ff., has fully treated this subject.
[312] Beautifully reproduced in Schachermeyr, *D. min. Kult.* Pl. 39 a.
[313] See Matz, *Kreta, Myk., Troja* Pl. 91. These small disks were sewn or stuck on the garments of the dead of both sexes (*op. cit.* 128). Add to these the six bees of gold foil used to adorn a burial gown, and found in 1962 by Marinatos in Peristeria near Pylos (cited by J. Zafiropulo, *Mead and Wine*, London 1966, n. 121). Zafiropulo enthusiastically identifies the *omphalos* and its design at Delphi with a beehive and honeycomb, and he believes that the tholos tombs in Greece owed their shape to the fact that "distinguished persons had themselves buried – as their god was buried – in beehive tombs etc.", *op. cit.* 40.

to reopen discussion – temporarily laid to rest by Nilsson – on the existence of such a cult and the part played in it by the butterfly and bee in Cretan and Mycenaean religion.

There is no evidence in Crete and Mycenae linking butterfly with bee, but this we may gather from the fact that in Greek and quite generally in Aegean belief both insects, like the snake, represented the dead or perhaps, as Picard and others believe, the soul of the dead[314]. Often, indeed, intentionally or not, the Minoan artist did not make himself clear when he fashioned or engraved on rings, disks or scales an insect whose species could puzzle the entomologist[315]. Perhaps the precise species was of less concern to the artist than the fact that the butterfly, bee, or similar creature, symbolised the rebirth from death, like Aristaeus' swarm of bees which miraculously appeared from the carcass of a bullock[316].

Now, since Schliemann and Evans[317], the butterfly, which is shown on grave adornments described above, has frequently been identified with the soul of the dead on analogy with modern Cretan folklore. Moreover some gold models of balances with a butterfly engraved on each scale, which were recovered from the Third Shaft Grave at Mycenae, have been cited as examples of Minoan and Mycenaean belief in a *psychostasia*[318]. Butterflies frequently occur in Cretan art[319], but they do not, as Nilsson points out[320], obviously refer to a cult of the dead. The single exception so far seems to be the ring of Nestor[321] which, however, may be a forgery. Again we hesitate to accept that the Minoan or Mycenaean believed in the existence of the

[314] *Rel. Preh.* 214.
[315] A good example of this difficulty occurs on the Ring of Nestor (Evans, *J. H. S.* 45 [1925] 55, fig. 47; *P. of Min.* II, 482 f. and fig. 289; III, 145 ff., figs. 95 ff.; *Earlier Rel. of Greece* 26 ff. and figs. 8–11. The upper left span of the ring shows two female figures in conversation, above whom float chrysalises and insects identified for Evans by an entomologist as butterflies, and for Nilsson *(M. M. R.* 45 f.) as hymenopters by another entomologist. The creatures are larger than life, and the untrained observer could easily describe them as bees. This ring is called a forgery by H. Biesantz, *Kretisch-Mykenische Siegelbilder*, 112 ff., Pl. 9, 55 a, b.
[316] Virg., *Georg.* IV, 281 ff. Zafiropulo, *op. cit.* 40, believes that bees and bulls were associated at least as early as the Middle Bronze Age.
[317] H. Schliemann, *Mykenae*, 193; 229; Evans, *P. M.* III, 151 f.; cf. *Earlier Rel. of Greece* 28.
[318] These were discussed, with references in Dietrich, "The Judgment of Zeus", *R. M.* 107 (1964) 121 f.
[319] The best examples are collected by Evans, *ibid.*
[320] *Gesch.* I, 198; cf. *Opuscula Selecta*, Lund 1951, I, 451.
[321] See n. 315, and cf. Nilsson, *M. M. R.* 43 ff.; *Gesch.* I, 198.

soul, a concept which developed relatively late in Greek thought. And it must be remembered that Aristotle was the first authority to use the word *psyche* in the sense of butterfly or moth[322].

There is not much weight, then, in an identification of soul with butterfly in Bronze Age Crete. Nilsson suggests[323] that the association of butterfly and soul, or spirit of the dead, arose not before the sixth century B.C., and then from the prevalent idea that the *eidolon* perhaps of the dead was represented as any winged creature. We may suppose, however, that, prior to this time, the bee and butterfly stood in some relationship to the dead in a belief which traced back for many generations. Such insects, as well as chrysalises and honeycomb, among burial gifts cannot always be accounted for as articles of use[324]. Occasionally their religious import is apparent. The key to their probable meaning, and this was already noticed by Evans[325], lies in the presence of the *pupae* from which the insects were destined to be born[326].

These *pupae* or chrysalises, as we remarked above, were symbolic of the continuous reappearance of life from death. They played no part in any philosophical concept concerned with afterlife, nor did they, in the manner of the Greek Mysteries, express the promise of life after death. The chrysalis and honeycomb presumably rather figured in the type of cult observed in the Anatolian shrines and in the Cretan caves and perhaps in some domestic sanctuaries dealing with the eternal cycle of nature. There is no doubt about the significance of the honeycomb pattern, butterflies, chrysalises, etc. in the Anatolian shrine. Their help in interpreting the equivalent symbols in Crete and Mycenae is invaluable: surely the chrysalis or honeycomb in the grave essentially conveyed the same message as the wall painting in the shrine at Çatal Hüyük, or the "flower-like" emblem from the same pattern shown affixed to the "charnel houses" at the Anatolian city[327]. Such evidence is proof of the enormous age, well antedating Minoan culture, of the symbolic representation of the birth of life from death[328].

---

[322] *Hist. Anim.* 551ª 14.

[323] *M. M. R.* 47 and n. 44.

[324] See the discussion in the article cited above n. 318.

[325] See above n. 317.

[326] See e.g. fig. 101 in Evans, *P. M.* III, 150.

[327] See the wall painting in House EVI, 1, *A. S.* 12 (1962), Pl. X, a; 13, Pl. XXVI a, p. 98.

[328] Nilsson, *M. M. R.* 47, says, "I am bound to confess that it would be most astonishing to find this symbolism (the resurgence of life) as early as the Minoan age."

The field of Cretan archaeology and religion has proved fertile, but it has also been well ploughed. The mass of evidence that has come to light has been examined with great care, and from it numerous conclusions could be drawn regarding the historical setting of Minoan civilization as well as its interaction with Mycenaean culture on the mainland. The remarkable similarity of L.M. Minoan and Mycenaean artifacts bears eloquent witness to the latter's debt to an older and superior culture which lent much of its colour to mainland thought. Hitherto, therefore, the researcher has looked in one direction. Modern work, in the main, has been concerned with increasing our knowledge of the Mycenaean world with the help of Cretan practice. The wonderful achievement of the Bronze Age Cretan was recognized and appreciated. It inspired admiration in the minds of archaeologists who were content, however, to acknowledge this phenomenon and explore its impact on the Indo-European northerner without enquiring too far into the factors which themselves contributed to Cretan development. There are distinguished exceptions, of course, and reference was made from time to time to parallel cultural or religious features in e.g. Egyptian custom. The difficulty remained that, until very recently, hardly anything was known of the Aegean Neolithic, so that the gates to an understanding of the wealth of Eastern tradition were firmly closed.

Scholars like Schachermeyr and John Evans are now rapidly widening our horizons of this field. Archaeological study is beginning to throw into clearer focus the links that tied the West to the East by means of migratory movements and cultic imports. Again the task of the religious historian is lightened by the discovery in the East of remarkably well preserved shrines and ritual objects which, if used with caution, can and do offer much help in the evaluation of certain aspects of the Cretan scene. One lesson which must be taken to heart in this connection is the astonishing religious conservatism governing Late Stone and Bronze Age thought. It seems that certain religious features continued to exert great power over men's minds and in this way bridged the vast chronological gap that separated Bronze Age Crete from e.g. south-west Anatolia. Mellaart's excavations, therefore, at sites like Haçilar and Çatal Hüyük are of signal importance to Cretan studies.

The work there is still very much in progress and many parts of the ritual and myth revealed by the domestic shrines are strange, nor did they find a home in the island of Crete. But there remains a nucleus of cult, often vividly portrayed by the decoration and appurtenances of a shrine, which strikes a familiar chord with anyone acquainted with Minoan ritual. The

Anatolian cult had at one time been transferred from a cave to the domestic shrine within the city. No doubt this move in some ways affected, or refined, the cult whose basic significance remained the same, however, because central features of cave cult, like the stalagmite, continued to figure prominently in the new surroundings.

Cave cult played a large part in Cretan religious life from Neolithic times. Here, too, one suspects, the essential features came in time to be transferred to other localities like domestic shrines, although throughout the history of the island the cult also endured in its original home. We examined the more important of these caves in detail together with the numerous finds which in their variety encompassed a large sphere of human activity indeed. From such evidence, and from the traditional legendary material, which survived in historical Greek times, one may conclude that cave cult was concerned with a kind of nature religion dealing not only with birth, growth, and general fertility, but also with death. Burial of the dead, accordingly, fitted in with this type of cult equally well as the celebration of the birth and nurture of the divine male child.

This child, it seems, was the son and companion of a goddess of nature who herself stood in some relationship to particular animals like the bull and the goat. Her concern with birth, human and in all likelihood animal, is evident in the figure of Eileithyia at Amnisos. Furthermore, she was perhaps symbolised, or rather represented, by lime-stone concretions, or stalagmites, which at times served an important, or even central, function that was retained apparently in shrines such as that in the Little Palace.

To this broad and fairly intelligible picture one could add further details by means of speculation. Conjectures along these lines either fall within the limits of the available internal and contemporary evidence, or they are determined by attempts to trace backward Mycenaean and later Greek traditional material. In the last five or seven years, however, the Anatolian discoveries, as well as a somewhat better understanding of the Neolithic Aegean area, have come to hand as a new and welcome source of information. To begin with, Schachermeyr's map of Bronze Age and earlier migration across the Aegean indicates in broad outline that a deeper relationship than that motivated by trade bound the Cretans to the Near East. This point leads to the expectation that archaeological finds in areas like Syria and Anatolia might have some bearing on certain aspects of Minoan culture.

In religion cult affinity is most likely in the old traditional parts which contained the basic features of a common Aegean nature belief. For this reason the discovery of a number of relatively well preserved shrines at

Çatal Hüyük is of great value to our Cretan religious map, because the cult practised in these shrines was a nature cult which had its original home in caves. The correspondence, therefore, which was revealed between East and West may not come as a great surprise, but it does serve to explain some of the Cretan religious material not only connected with cave cult but also with other features of Cretan religion, notably the figure of the bull and the so-called Mistress of Animals. Both of these figures may have emanated from such cult, but in spirit they certainly belonged to it. In other words, the Anatolian finds allowed us to reopen the discussion of a subject which had become exhausted when seemingly all possible permutations of the available evidence had been examined.

The Anatolian material centred on a goddess as the dominant figure in the Çatal Hüyük shrines. She appeared moulded in plaster against the wall, or she was represented by lime-stone concretions, the descendants of the original stalagmites and stalactites, from which evolved a fully anthropomorphic statuette in such a way that both primitive and developed representations existed side by side, thereby explaining the significance of the similar concretions in Cretan caves. This goddess, too, was allied to certain animals, like the bull, in a relationship which suggests either the identity of the two figures, or perhaps their interchangeability in cult. The goddess is pictured at times as giving birth to her animal, the bull for example. Is this offspring her youthful male companion? And do we find a memory of such a belief concealed in the myth of Zeus' birth, or in that of the young tauromorphic Dionysus? Perhaps it would be premature to give affirmative answers to these questions. One definite factor to emerge from this material, however, concerns the figure of the Mistress of Animals who played no minor role in Cretan and historic Greek thought, as witness her appearance on Minoan gems and in the sphere of Artemis. It now seems necessary to revise the present image of the Mistress who not only appears to have developed from the deity worshipped in caves and localities to which her cult had been transferred but also enjoyed a closer kinship with her animals than that of a goddess of wild life, the kind protectress of all creatures.

Again, our increased knowledge of the subject has made it possible to describe within narrower limits the type of cult observed in these caves and shrines. Essentially, of course, it revolved about the hope for nature's continuing bounty. But prayer was particularly directed to a goddess in whose possession lay the produce which her power had allowed to grow, and to whom perhaps were entrusted the dead, for in some way she ensured their rebirth in an unending cycle. The representation of death and birth in Çatal

Hüyük is clear, and for either event, it appears, a special area or portion of the shrine was set aside. Also clear seems the symbolism, shown especially in wall painting, of bee, chrysalis etc., illustrating the idea of birth from death. This evidence is greatly relevant to an understanding of similar finds in Crete, and to the nature of the cult there.

The meaning of the butterfly and bee in Minoan and Mycenaean art and as funeral adornment, or engraved on golden scales which were placed in graves, has for a long time been the subject of argument. Opinions have ranged from describing these insects as decorative motifs to discovering in them symbols of the human soul which somehow was felt to survive after death. Neither extreme is in fact verified by the Anatolian evidence. The long and laborious path to the Greek concept of the immortal soul had scarcely yet been thought of in the western Aegean of the Bronze Age. Nature's proof that all life continued in an eternal cycle was discovered at a perhaps more primitive, but nonetheless imaginative, level of thought. Men of that age saw immortality in other more obvious natural manifestations such as the constantly changing constantly recurring stages of life of the butterfly and bee.

Minoan cult, like that of earlier cultures which had travelled westward, began in the cave where men voiced their hopes and fears regarding their basic beliefs of existence. In the cave it continued for generations, well into historic times. But certain aspects came to move from there to other more sophisticated localities, and coloured a number of Cretan as well as later Mycenaean and Greek religious concepts. How it developed we see from the domestic and palace sanctuaries of the Middle and Late Minoan periods, and from the elaborate figure of the goddess revered there who was destined to leave her mark on the developing Greek religion. Such sanctuaries, together with the cult paraphernalia in them, have been exhaustively explored, discussed and interpreted. So far the fresh Eastern evidence can add only a little to the present state of the question.

Whether the splendid palace goddess did, as one might suppose, arise from the nature deity we are familiar with and whether, therefore, she was identical with the so-called Mistress of Animals, are questions which it may be prudent to leave open for the moment. Nor would we, at this time, be justified in seeking this Mistress in the so-called peak sanctuaries, despite some finds from these sites which have been interpreted as belonging to her cult. No doubt peak sanctuaries incorporated ritual features from cave cult, but this does not necessarily lead to the conclusion that they were continuations of the latter, for parts of our available evidence appear to contradict such a belief. Cult on mountain tops in Crete came into being relatively late and endured for only a short period. The extent of its possible dependence on Eastern tradition is still far from clear, so is its nature and content or influence on subsequent cult forms. Our new knowledge of Aegean religious ideas of this time has yet no more than a limited application to peak sanctuaries. Therefore the discussion of this subject properly belongs to the end in an appendix.

It is with fervent hope that the religious historian looks to the growing interest in linguistic and archaeological studies of Bronze Age and earlier Eastern cultures to enable and stimulate him to reappraise the Minoan religious scene which is of such vital concern not only in its own Aegean context but above all to the developing Greek thought.

III. A MYCENAEAN GODDESS OF NATURE

In the history of the culture and religion of any people there is no such thing as a direct development from primitive beginnings to sophisticated complex ideas. The gods to whom the classical Greek paid homage were not merely civilized versions of beings that had grown along a straight predictable line from vaguely defined nature powers. Nor did they have the same background which might have shaped them into a harmonious whole: the Olympians were quite conscious of their differences, for in Homer they were only too prone to quarrel amongst themselves. Any attempt, therefore, to construct a logical system to explain Greek religious thought is doomed to failure. Sacred beliefs which moved the Greek to worship were not always open to logic but could at times appear contradictory, especially to us who are so far removed from their society. Greek religion, further, as we have already seen, was subject to a variety of influences which easily transcended geographical barriers and crossed lines of race. Classical Greek religion inherited prehistoric Mediterranean culture, it accommodated ideas from the Near East, and well remembered some basic Minoan religious custom.

Such traditional material flowed to the mainland by diverse routes which were traced across the Aegean and the adjoining lands – both to south and north – by migratory movements during, and at the end of, the Early Bronze Age. Crete, too, may have seen the arrival of new people during the Middle Bronze Age[1]. Towards the end of the Bronze Age unrest, upheaval, and invasion, disturbed almost the entire Mediterranean basin and, in Greece at least, seemed to arrest a flourishing culture, so that that part of the world entered a Dark Age, the beginning of the Iron Age. The catastrophic events at the end of the Bronze Age – late in the second millennium B.C. – affected all parts of Greece where the Mycenaeans held sway, whether they experienced violence and destruction, as in the Argolid and generally in the Peloponnese, or not, as for example at Athens.

---

[1] But see now the summary of Dr. P. Warren's paper "The Origins of the Minoans" *BICS* 16 (1969) 156.

Some areas, such as particularly the western portions of the Peloponnese, from flourishing centres became partly or wholly deserted: palaces, like those at Mycenae and Pylos, lay in ruins, while the surrounding settlements seemed no longer to support life. There is, then, some sort of break in the archaeological picture of mainland culture at the turn of the millennium, and it can be, and has been, argued[2], with varying degrees of firmness, that historic Greek society of the sixth and fifth centuries B.C. only indirectly drew from their Mycenaean forebears.

When we deal with religious values, however, with sacred ritual and ceremonial and with divine worship, then we are moving on less changeable ground, for in religious belief there are two aspects apt to endure throughout many generations. One of these consists in the continued sanctity of a consecrated locality, and the other in the conservative persistence of a cult and its divinity in such a locality. It was a rule that invaders did not destroy the gods they found revered among the conquered peoples but admitted them to their own worship. Divine names might change, but the gods' functions often remained remarkably similar. This is not to say, of course, that a particular cult endured in its original form throughout the ages in one and the same locality. Cultic figures in time expanded their spheres of influence, or they became fixed in one of their original aspects: they might receive worship at sites other than their original home. But for all that, their beginnings and their early natures are still transparent to the investigator.

Remember, too, that at the end of the Bronze Age many Mycenaeans were uprooted from their homes: they wandered south to Crete where the change from Bronze to Iron had been more peaceful, and to the East across the Aegean to places like Ionia. To these new settlements they took with them the knowledge of their society at a time when in the homeland "the fires in the hearths of Mycenaean civilization went out one by one"[3]. The record and memory of this society was destined to return to Greece at the beginning of the classical age. Religious conservatism in the Mediterranean area from the Bronze Age, and even earlier, to the historic period was a real factor which must be emphasized even at times in the face of gaps in the archaeological material, especially at the end of the Bronze Age in Greece.

The absence of cult paraphernalia, votive offerings etc., during a par-

---

[2] E.g. C. G. Starr, *The Origins of Greek Civilization*, 56, "Mycenaean civilization is not a system from which historic Greek culture emerged on a straight line."

[3] R. Pettazzoni, *La Religione nella Grecia*, 40.

ticular period, such as the beginning Iron Age, may not in every case signify that one special form of cult had come to an end. There are exceptions, of course, where archaeologists can show that a site was abandoned at a given time, or cult there was interrupted over considerable periods. The Cave of Pan, near Marathon in Attica, is a case in point, for cult in that place began in the Neolithic period and appears to have ceased at the end of the Mycenaean Age only to be reinstituted some six centuries later[4]. We can only guess at the reason for such breaks or the extent of possible change in the cult content over the years. It is no more than reasonable, however, to suppose that memory of the locality's sacred nature brought about a reintroduction of cult which, therefore, most likely was influenced by the original beliefs, even though these might have been misunderstood or reinterpreted. But there is as yet little certainty in these arguments: Mycenaean culture, Mycenaean archaeology, are relatively new subjects, and a number of present conclusions will be subject to correction.

The site of Mycenae was discovered, and excavation begun there, before Sir Arthur Evans' work at Knossos. The history of discovery and work at Mycenae, beginning with Schliemann, and at other Mycenaean cities in the Argolid or in Greece, generally has been well told before by scholars like Mylonas and Wace[5]: It goes back to the middle of the nineteenth century. In spite of such early beginnings, however, our knowledge of Mycenaean society has never been full, but, in some respects, even more fragmentary than that of Minoan Crete. Perhaps the often glittering remains of Bronze Age Crete had seduced many scholars away from the apparently less spectacular Mycenaean settlements. But a more likely explanation lies in the relative scarcity of material remains, in the ignorance, until recently, of the extent of the Mycenaean world, and, again, in the difficulty of dating and classifying the contemporary artefacts.

The Mycenaeans were an Indo-European people, this much was known. They spoke an Indo-European language which was linked with Arcadian and with the Ionian and Aeolic dialects. It is still uncertain when and whence they came to the mainland of Greece. Their earlier home might have been in the north of Europe or ultimately in Asia Minor. They found,

---

[4] P. Alin, *Das Ende der Myken. Fundstätten*, 111; V. R. d'A. Desborough, *L. M.* 43.

[5] G. E. Mylonas, *Ancient Mycenae: Mycenae and the Mycenaean Age*, A. J. W. Wace, *Mycenae: An Archaeological History and Guide*. See also the various reports cited in Starr, *op. cit.* 13 n. 3; 21 n. 2. Alin, *op. cit.*, gives a succinct history of excavations, together with modern bibliographies, as in introduction to the discussions of the various sites throughout Mycenaean Greece.

as has been told before, a developed Bronze Age Mediterranean culture which they assimilated. Their own, which they brought with them, remains mysterious. Unfounded, too, are all claims that the Indo-Europeans imposed a new patriarchal order on the existing matriarchy they found there, for the latter has not yet been established beyond doubt for the earlier ages.

Although the Mycenaeans were thought to be the forerunners of the Greeks, they were credited with little refinement. The image commonly suggested is one of illiterate, barbarian, war-lords who brought with them little more than the new war chariot[6]. Essentially a nomadic race, the Mycenaeans in the south came into contact with settled, agricultural, societies which culturally had developed to a high degree. In their new abode, it was thought, these migrants easily fell subject to the brilliant Minoan culture which totally dominated their society and, of course, their religious beliefs. Until very recently, therefore, Cretan religion and ritual practices were normally imagined to include mainland Mycenaean customs.

Much of this is obviously true, for the superior Minoan world could not fail to impress itself deeply on the tough spirit of the newcomers. But it is unreasonable to deny that the latter did in some way contribute their own share to this world. In fact, much of the historian's mistaken view was due to his lack of material describing the events on the mainland and the activities of the inhabitants there during this period. Such gaps in our knowledge are continually being filled: while yet comparatively little is known of the earliest periods of Mycenaean occupation, the picture of the end of the Helladic Bronze Age is becoming more complete as a result of detailed studies by scholars like Furumark, Desborough, and Alin, to name a few.

Thus, it has been discovered that during the latter half of the second millennium the political power of the Mycenaean realm became enormous, stretching from its centre in the Argolid in all four directions: from Crete to at least Thessaly in the north, and from the western limits of the Peloponnese, across the peninsula, as far as the Aegean islands to Rhodes and Cyprus, and, in all likelihood, on to the coast-line of the Near East. Relative dating of Mycenaean pottery has made possible the construction of a fairly accurate chronological table dividing Late Helladic into roughly five separate Mycenaean phases[7]:

---

[6] See e.g. F. Schachermeyr, *Poseidon*, 54; 148.
[7] E.g. A. Furumark, *The Chronology of Mycenaean Pottery*, 110–115; L. W. Taylour, *The Mycenaeans*, 58; Starr, *op. cit.* 53.

Mycenaean	I	= L.H. I	c. 1550 B.C.
	II	=	c. 1500 B.C.
	III A	=	c. 1425 B.C.
	III B	=	c. 1300 B.C.
III C & Submycenaean		=	c. 1230–1100 or 1050 B.C.

(between Mycenaean & Protogeometric)

The dates above L.H. I are uncertain, and even the subsequent periods, especially the end of the Mycenaean Age, are somewhat arbitrarily divided, as witness e.g. the lively debates concerning the boundaries of III B & C[8].

With the growth of archaeological knowledge at least the height of Mycenaean power and its "Ausklang" began to move into clearer perspective. The revolutionary decipherment of Linear B collapsed the old libel of illiteracy which had become attached to the Mycenaeans. It may well be true that the ability to write belonged to the ruling class alone[9], other communities also reserved such skills for a privileged few, nonetheless the knowledge of letters reflects on the standing and organization of a society. Still more illuminating is the fact that the Mycenaeans used an early form of Greek, and that the tablets mainly consisted of lists and inventories. The latter point has an obvious bearing on the economic structure of a Mycenaean city and its administration. To the religious historian the significance of these tablets, normally stored within, or nearby, the palace, not only lies in the divine names mentioned thereon, and in the religious custom they describe, but also in the relationship which the lists reveal with Near Eastern, and perhaps even Minoan, practice, whatever the date of the Knossian tablets.

The tablets from both Pylos and Mycenae and from Knossos, admittedly under mainland influence, in their descriptions of a hierarchically oriented society show a striking similarity to Eastern custom[10]. In both worlds certain classes of subjects were assigned certain types of labour or worked certain areas of land. The tablets further show quite plainly that the Mycenaean palace was the administrative centre of the city and the home not only of the mortal king but also of the divinity watching over the settlement. Another feature shared by East and West alike is the fact that the palace, like the surrounding possessions whose produce was stored within the walls, was the property of the divinity. These are obvious points which spring to

---

[8] For some references to such discussions see Starr, *op. cit.* 54 n. 5; 6.
[9] Desborough, *L. M.* 242.
[10] Cf. above p. 36.

mind on studying the contents of the tablets, and they will have to be verified, or in part discarded, by detailed analysis and comparison.

The result of this consistently increasing information about the Mycenaean world has been to lend it an individual character beside that of the Minoan Cretans. There can be no question of isolation of one culture from the other. Extremists, who hoped to vindicate their view that the Mycenaeans cut adrift from the world of the Minoans, must be disappointed by the growing weight of archaeological evidence which points to a basic similarity in the religious beliefs of the two. To deny that Mycenaean religious thought carried the deep imprint of Minoan belief and, in part, handed it on to the classical Greeks, would be to argue in the face of evidence and good reason. But we may occasionally be in the position to identify what is typically Mycenaean or Minoan, so that it becomes a feasible task to isolate some distinctive features of mainland religious architecture, votive offerings and cultic paraphernalia. There are two results which emerge from an examination of the evidence. Firstly, it is a fact that influence in matters of religious practice had become a two-sided affair towards the end of the Bronze Age. That is, Mycenaean ideas were liable to make themselves at home in the Minoan world no less than receive their stimulus from the latter. This exchange is quite obvious from the remains, even if the exact strength of the physical Mycenaean presence on the island at the time is still a matter for debate. Secondly, even towards the end of the Bronze Age the Minoans and Mycenaeans were not averse to mixing together their particular traditional forms of religious symbolism, as in the ritual scenes painted on the Hagia Triada sarcophagus, or combining their architectural styles, as in the case e.g. of the mainland Asine shrine. Therefore, the relationship in religious matters between Cretans and Mycenaeans remained so palpably close that it may, in fact, be quite wrong artificially to separate the two peoples on the basis of their worship.

Yet their attitude to life, their very temperaments must have differed, if we judge from the individual art styles of the Minoans and Mycenaeans. The Cretans were free from the heavy martial spirit so evident from the Mycenaean remains. There were no forbidding and bleak fortifications to enclose the Minoan palaces. Their pottery was decorated with motifs which differed from those popular on the mainland[11]. The Cretan perhaps had a closer affinity with nature: he was excitable and given to ecstatic and

---

[11] On these basic differences in art and architecture see also A. Furumark, "Gods of Ancient Crete", *Op. Ath.* 4, X (Lund) 1965, 89 f.

mystic forms of celebration, to judge from many of the scenes on his seals. His art lacked "the innate love of balanced order, the feeling of structural symmetry which are the most essential qualities of Greek art"[12].

On the other hand, the Mycenaean Greek in his new surroundings could hardly have escaped the impact of Cretan and, indeed, Aegean culture. It should not, therefore, occasion surprise to find among the Mycenaean remains a good deal of evidence which points to a largely shared Minoan and Mycenaean belief in basic matters of cult, ritual procedure, and, more important still, in the nature of divinity revered. So similar do some of these religious customs – dealing in particular with aspects of nature and vegetation cult – appear to us, that they are at times as difficult to tell apart as Pythagorean from Orphic belief.

The essence of basic religious ideas, like the figure of the youthful Zeus, was transmitted to later, Greek, times. Zeus' name occurs on the Linear B tablets, and this may mean that the Mycenaean Age, in the latter half of the second millennium, was responsible for the fusion of Indo-European names and religious custom with Minoan belief. A better understanding of such religious and historical developments presupposes the detailed appreciation not only of the affinities of Mycenaean and Cretan belief but especially of their differences which alone can set apart the Mycenaean society and its particular contribution to subsequent Greek thought. Therefore it is a tremendous step forward to be able to single out, with the archaeologist, some features which were peculiar to the Mycenaean world.

Such "material aspects" of this civilization are summarized by Desborough, who says[13] that "prominent in the Mycenaean world ... were the megaron plan of many of the houses, the massive and sophisticated architecture in stone, as found particularly in the palaces, the fortifications and the tholos tombs, the great delicacy and skill of the metalworker in gold as well as in bronze, and the similar ability of his companion worker in ivory, the remarkably high standard reached by the potter, and the very individual style he produced, the language as set down on the tablets, the very distinctive terracotta human and animal figurines used as votive offerings, and the custom of multiple burial." Beyond these points, peculiar to Mycenaean civilization, there is the fact of the remarkable unity, or perhaps rather uniformity, which pervaded the Mycenaean world throughout all of its periods in art, inclusive of pottery, in architecture and even in language.

[12] G. Karo, *Greek Personality in Archaic Sculpture*, Oberlin 1948, 5, cited by Starr, Origins 38.
[13] *L. M.* 241 f.

Unity of this kind may have been due to a central administration, which was made possible by outstandingly good means of communication over a large area by ancient standards. Accordingly, some scholars have come to the conclusion that the empire was governed by one supreme king at Mycenae[14]. This idea of central government may well agree with Agamemnon's position in Homer in relation to other kings, a position which seems similar to that of Zeus in relation to the other Olympians[15]. Greek legend, too, like the story of Eurystheus in the Heracles myth, tends to support a belief in a strong central Mycenaean administration under one royal overlord. If true this arrangement would be of signal importance to the consideration of political and economic aspects of the contemporary civilization. But, true or not, the cultural unity of the Mycenaean empire at that time does clearly imply an equal measure of conformity in matters of religion and ritual.

This is valuable knowledge. Therefore, when we discover certain forms of worship being observed at one centre it seems probable that the same worship, and the underlying beliefs, also obtained at other similar sanctuaries. Imported ritual again, such as for example the Cretan type of cult practised at Asine, would not be unique to this one site (or possibly to the Cretan sanctuaries of Karphi and Knossos) but would, in all likelihood, be diffused through the land. Nor would, conversely, the divinities, appearing on the Pylos tablets, receive their dues there alone, but they would equally expect to enjoy cult from the Mycenaean settlers in Crete[16]. The locality and nature of sanctuaries, too, would obey the same laws whether these were attached to the palace, whether celebrated in a cave, or in shrines built in the open country. On this premise we may often generalize and apply information gleaned from one site to others. We may be able to say not so much what was purely Mycenaean but what was current Mycenaean practice. At the same time we should try to isolate Minoan and perhaps Eastern and Aegean material as well as deduce from such information what type of cult survived into Greek from Mycenaean times.

Cave cult on the mainland of Greece was discussed in the previous chapter. The worship occurring on these sites, such as Parnes[17] for example,

[14] Desborough, *L. M.* 242.
[15] Cf. B. C. Dietrich, *Death, Fate and the Gods*, 210 f.
[16] This point is of obvious importance when trying to separate the deities and ritual on the Pylos Linear tablets from those found on the Knossos tablets, see A. Heubeck, *Aus der Welt der Frühgriech. Lineartafeln*, 99. Such differentiation will remain of doubtful value until it is possible categorically to state that such and such a god never occurred on any Cretan or mainland tablet.
[17] See above p. 93.

in its basic purpose probably agreed with that of Crete and other Aegean areas. The Mycenaean, like the Cretan, most certainly set aside part of his palace for religious ceremonial. Such practice was obviously in harmony with the divine nature inherent in the royal buildings. Nonetheless, there were some differences which separated the structure of palace chapels on the mainland from those in Crete. Differences of this kind were superficial and due, one feels, to individual architectural styles rather than to fundamental disagreement in religious matters.

In the Mycenaean palace a part of the megaron and not, as in Crete, an entire chapel normally served for the performance of cult. Sometimes other areas in the megaron were also involved in the ceremony, and this apparently was the case in Pylos where a libation channel ran from somewhere near the throne[18]. Perhaps even other parts of the Mycenaean palace were devoted to cult: there might have been an altar in the courtyard of Tiryns, or a shrine in the palace at Mycenae[19].

So far the evidence does not suggest, by virtue of basic architectural divergencies, or through the introduction of novel types of sanctuary, that the religion of the Mycenaeans must have signally differed from Cretan practice. Quite to the contrary, there is absolutely nothing to contradict the view that in matters of religious belief the Minoans and Mycenaeans in essence continued a partnership which had been begun during Middle Helladic. The dominant member of this association at first had been the Cretan. Minoan artefacts, particularly those of sacred value, found their way to Mycenaean tombs and places of worship. The famous tripartite palace shrine, crowned with the horns of consecration, and painted in Minoan frescoes, like the one, for example, which faced the west-side of the central court of the Knossos palace, lent its form to Mycenaean cult of the time, as witness the so-called Dove Shrines found in the shaft graves in Grave Circle A at Mycenae[20]. Towards the end of the Bronze Age the Mycenaeans apparently became a more actively contributing member of this partnership, proof of which may be found in the new style places of worship. There are other features which seemingly separated Minoan from Mycenaean ritual. These we shall briefly consider in a moment, but we may anticipate the result of this examination with a general statement that the

---

[18] *A. J. A.* 65 (1961), Pl. 53, Fig. 1.

[19] For the views of Müller and Wace on these points see Desborough, *L. M.* 41 and n. 7; 8.

[20] See e.g. G. Karo, *Die Schachtgräber von Mykenai*, 1930–33, Pl. XVIII, 242–44; XXVII, 26; *J. H. S.* 21 (1901) 191, fig. 65; Jahrb. 30 (1915) 302 ff.

modern habit of strictly dividing Cretan from Mycenaean religion has gone too far. The pendulum began to swing outward as our understanding of Mycenaean civilization grew: all aspects of Mycenaean culture, including religious thought, were separated from that of the Minoans. The tendency has been to deny any real kind of bond between the two cultures, to exaggerate those features of Mycenaean art and custom which appear alien to the Minoan scene. This was a natural reaction to earlier dogma in this century, but it should not be allowed to blind the historian to the common religious heritage both lands enjoyed as members of a wider Aegean family, a heritage which was destined to leave ist mark on classical Greek thought. This does not, of course, imply that we should treat Minoan and Mycenaean practices as identical. The right path must lie somewhere in between.

Political circumstances obviously differed on the mainland: disturbances during Middle and Late Helladic both introduced new ideas and were active in shaping religious concepts, some of which became current in historical times. In Crete the scene was quieter. There appears to have been slight political turbulence during the Bronze Age, and little, if any, evidence is extant which could be interpreted as referring to an invasion from outside at the end of the age[21]. The island cults, therefore, did not at any time suffer a dramatic interruption owing to the arrival of large numbers of new settlers[22]. That is to say, the Mycenaean intrusive elements in some of the Late Minoan shrines, in the form of architectural changes, and the introduction of Mycenaean type ceramics, appear to have become absorbed in the continuing Minoan form of ritual, as, for example, in the so-called Spring Chamber sanctuary at Knossos, at Karphi and at Prinias. This point, conversely, serves as a valuable hint, when compared with the Minoan-Mycenaean mixture of cultic figures and impedimenta at Asine in the Argolid, not of Mycenae's mute acceptance of Minoan practice, but of the interdependence of the two cultures, and of their probable acceptance of an essentially common set of religious ideas.

The features which one might list as possibly testifying to a separation of Mycenaean from Minoan religion at the end of Helladic consist in the institution of Mycenaean sanctuaries isolated from other buildings, the use of different votives and cultic vessels, and the seemingly growing emphasis on the male element in Mycenaean belief. There is evidence to support all

---

[21] Cf. Desborough, *L. M.* 193.
[22] Desborough, *L. M.* 189.

three points. But all of it is very difficult to interpret firstly because it is impossible to establish to what extent each feature was unique only to one group, and secondly for the simple reason that by the end of the Bronze Age what occurred in Crete in connection with cultic ritual may not always have been Minoan.

The Mycenaean, aside from palace and domestic sanctuaries, constructed separate buildings for worship, or temples, in the common form of the megaron. Perhaps we should find one example at Delphi where some votive offerings, belonging to L.H. III B, were discovered beneath Apollo's temple, and a hoard of some one-hundred and seventy-five goddess figurines in the neighbouring Marmaria under the temple of Athena Pronaia[23]. The second discovery may not mark the original site of a Late Helladic shrine but could merely constitute a collection of votive offerings moved there to consecrate the spot where Athena's temple was to be built[24]. The Delphi finds, however, were not associated with other buildings, so that they might well have belonged to separate shrines. Amyclae, outside Sparta, also possessed a L.H. III C shrine which, in all likelihood, stood alone but formed the location of the later temple of Apollo[25].

Additional to the archaeological evidence for the existence of separate Mycenaean shrines, the Linear B tablets may also record an example of such a shrine at Pylos. If Palmer's reading is right[26], the Pylos tablets describe a Posidaion, a sanctuary situated in the city (*wastu*) and separate from the Pakijanes which should most reasonably be looked for within the palace. Some gems of Minoan workmanship, but found at Mycenae and other mainland sites, depict scenes of worship close to what could only have been rural shrines. It has, therefore, occasionally been supposed that the Mycenaeans borrowed this type of rural sanctuary, and presumably the cult that went with it, from Crete[27]. Quite probably there is a good measure of truth in this theory, but nothing of such sanctuaries remains, nor can we tell in what relationship they might have stood to the places of worship outside the palace, if, indeed, they were not identical with the latter.

[23] P. Perdrizet, *Fouilles de Delphes* V, Paris 1908, ii ff.; R. Demangel, *Fouilles de Delphes* II, 5, Paris 1926, 5; 6 ff.; Nilsson, *M. M. R.* 466 ff.; Desborough, *L. M.* 43 f.; 123 f.

[24] L. Lerat, *B. C. H.* 81 (1957) 708 ff.

[25] See Nilsson, *op. cit.* 470 f. for the history of excavation at this site. Cf. Desborough, *L. M.* 42.

[26] L. R. Palmer, *The Interpretation of Mycenaean Greek Texts*, 267 f.

[27] E.g. Taylour, *Mycenaeans* 71.

But there is other evidence for the existence in Late Helladic of temples in Messenia, Attica, and on the islands of Delos and Keos. The most uncertain of these examples is a megaron discovered in 1960 by Marinatos in the small settlement of Mouriatadha, close to Kyparissia[28]. Its date probably is L.H. III B[29], but too little remains to be sure of Marinatos' identification with a temple[30].

A stronger case has been made out by Gallet de Santerre for three separate sanctuaries, or temples, on Delos[31]: the so-called pre-Artemision Ac, the site of the later archaic temple of Artemis, a Temple Γ, which, like the Mycenaean Megaron B at Eleusis, was surrounded by a peribolos, and a building H[32]. The pottery associated with all three of these buildings was exclusively Mycenaean, proving, according to the excavator, that they were constructed in Mycenaean times. Some arguments to the contrary notwithstanding[33], these structures show the existence of an early form of temple on Delos during Mycenaean times. We cannot be certain of the type of cult practised there[34], but we may reasonably suppose that Delos, an otherwise inhospitable island, was a cult centre in Mycenaean times already. This would explain the presence of three separate temples. The site further provides a good example of cult continuity from Mycenaean to Protogeometric and probably classical times[35]. We can say nothing certain, however, about the persistence of the original Mycenaean cult form into historical times. Some changes no doubt occurred in the passage of time, but on the other hand a part of the Mycenaean material must have survived, for Delos, in the classical period, specially belonged to the worship of Apollo and Artemis and their mother Leto, of whom the first two most probably played a part in Mycenaean religion[36].

[28] *Ergon* (1960) 149 ff.; *Arch. Rep.* in *J. H. S.* 81 (1960/1) 12 f.; *A. J. A.* 65 (1961) 232.
[29] *J. H. S., ibid.;* Alin, *Fundst.* 80.
[30] Cf. Desborough, *L. M.* 42.
[31] *Délos primitive.*
[32] *Ibid.* 109; 216. Building H was close to the later Greek Temple G, *ibid.* 93.
[33] See e.g. Desborough, *L. M.* 45 f.
[34] Nilsson, *M. M. R.*, citing the Delian tombs of the Hyperborean Maidens, believes that the cult there was in honour of dead heroes.
[35] *Délos primitive* 213 n. 3; cf. Nilsson, *M. M. R.* 611; Desborough, *L. M.* 244. On p. 46 Desborough is more sceptical. He points out there that the pottery remains from L. H. III C to Protogeometric are not enough "for continuity to be taken as assured."
[36] It may be best, however, not to pursue this point too far, in view of the controversy regarding the time of arrival of Leto's cult in Delos. For arguments for and against Leto's early cult on the island see e.g. E. Bethe, "Leto auf Delos", *He.* 71 (1936) 351 ff.;

The discoveries made by the American excavators at Hagia Eirene on the island of Keos are exciting, because this site, like Delos, provided evidence not only of a Bronze Age temple but also of cult continuity into classical times, as well as of the existence of monumental terracotta statues[37] which Mrs. Vermeule dates "to the period of Kean prosperity in the fifteenth century, when the formal aspects of the temple were laid out"[38]. However, the earliest construction of this temple dates from M.H., although little is left of the contemporary settlement[39]. Associated with the building were some Middle Helladic sherds and some L.M. I pottery. The temple was rebuilt in Mycenaean times (L.H. III). It was rectangular in shape, narrow, and had two rooms one of which was equipped with the familiar benches along one of the side walls. Cult continuity on this site is as certain as for Delos and is graphically accentuated by the later construction of a small shrine within the ruins of the collapsed original temple[40].

Our last example comes from the mainland: from Eleusis in Attica. The earliest settlement there can be assigned to Middle Helladic[41]. Of greater interest to us are the building activities beneath the sixth century Peisistratean Telesterion. These date from L.H. III and carry the clear implication that this area, which in classical times remained a centre of religious cult, was hallowed ground to the Mycenaean settlers. The profusion of ruins from the various periods, superimposed upon one another, make this spot difficult to disentangle, and the honour of having done so clearly and systematically falls to the Greek Archaeological Society of Athens. The work of the Greek scholars allows us to assume that this part was an area devoted to cult, which was probably celebrated first in an early apsidal M.H. building and continued beyond the Peisistratean Telesterion.

During L.H. III[42] two structures were erected here, one of which, the so-called Megaron B, we may with Mylonas identify with a Mycenaean

---

"Das archaische Delos und sein Letoon", *He.* 72 (1937) 190 ff.; Nilsson, *Gesch.* I, 500 n. 3; cf. *M. M. R.* 516 and n. 29.

[37] Representing the goddess, or several of her aspects, or, less likely, the goddess and her female attendants.

[38] E. Vermeule, *Greece in the Bronze Age*, 285. For the "fifteen female figures" (now grown to nineteen, see next note) see p. 217 and Pl. XL A–B.

[39] J. L. Caskey, *A. J. A.* 66 (1962) 195; *Hesp.* 31 (1962) 278 ff.; cf. *I. L. N.* 19 May 1962, 801 ff.; *Hesp.* 33 (1964) 326 ff.; 35 (1966) 367–9 (temple); 369 ff.; Pl. 87–9 (statues).

[40] Cf. Desborough, *L. M.* 44; 244.

[41] Mylonas, *Eleusis*, 29 ff.

[42] Perhaps III C, although this is not certain, see Desborough, *L. M.* 43.

temple[43]. Both were clearly set apart from all other buildings, and Megaron B "stood in a court surrounded by a thick peribolos wall"[44]. Finds associated with this area consisted of L.H. III sherds and four terracotta goddesses two of which in the usual "Psi" form[45]. The cult practised there from the Mycenaean era was apparently concerned with our goddess of nature, and we may suppose that in this original form it continued at the same locality and developed into the famous Mysteries of historical times[46]. There is, in fact, a school of thought which traces the beginning of Demeter's Mysteries back to Mycenaean and contemporary Minoan cult[47]. In support of this argument is the name Eleusis itself which was a pre-Hellenic word, perhaps connected with Eileithyia[48], and the fact that the Minoan kernos occupied a central position in the Mysteries[49].

This theory is exciting and attractive, reflecting as it does, the possibility that already during the Bronze Age the worshipper at Eleusis employed, or was familiar with, symbolism in the celebration of the annual cycle of nature. But, quite frankly, the present state of our evidence does not allow us to draw any such definite conclusions. Mylonas, again[50], identifies Megaron B with Demeter's temple of the Homeric Hymn to the goddess. If we describe the L.H. III Megaron B as a temple, and there is little to be said against this, then certainly it was the abode of the nature goddess. It is another matter, however, whether at that time she really was Demeter,

---

[43] See Mylonas, *op. cit.* 33 ff., for a detailed description of this building. Desborough, *L. M.* 44, is doubtful whether Megaron B was used as a temple.

[44] Mylonas, *op. cit.* 36.

[45] Mylonas, *A. J. A.* 40 (1936) 423, fig. 10.

[46] Desborough, *L. M.* 43, denies continuity for this particular spot from Mycenaean into classical times, "no evidence came to light to show that this spot was used for any purpose at any time between L.H. III and the sixth century". This may be a reasonable conclusion to draw from the absence of good pottery remains for the intervening period, but it is difficult to maintain in view of the continued building activity in that exact area in Geometric and Archaic times. The intricate design of structures of all these periods, from Mycenaean until the Peisistratean structures, is brilliantly shown on Dr. Travlos' plan in Mylonas, *Eleusis* fig. 20.

[47] For a discussion of this point with modern references see Nilsson, *M. M. R.* 468 f.

[48] See Nilsson, *M. M. R.* 519 ff.

[49] Cf. Mylonas, *Eleusis* e.g. 17. Mylonas does not believe in Minoan religious influence at Eleusis. He remarks that no "specimens" of this vessel have yet been found in the prehistoric strata of this area. His own, rather unconvincing, thesis is, *ibid.*, that "this peculiar vessel was developed at Eleusis independently."

[50] *Op. cit.* 38 ff.

especially since that name does not appear on any of the Linear B texts[51]. Until then any close identification with Demeter is hazardous, and the Homeric Hymn is not really positive evidence in this regard, for, although the poem unquestionably contains much old and traditional material, it cannot prove the presence of Demeter's name in the prehistoric temple. More likely is the belief, to which we shall return below, that the goddess at that time was still known as the Mistress, Potnia[52].

The case, then, for isolated temples, particularly on Delos, Keos, and at Eleusis, is strong[53]. These examples, and especially the temple on Keos whose first structure dates from M.H.[54], may well cause a revision of the commonly held notion that such sacred buildings did not belong in the Bronze Age. It is quite another question, however, whether this feature constituted a purely Mycenaean development, and whether the cult celebrated within these temples was altogether un-Minoan in character. The strongest argument against such a conclusion once more consists in the finds at the sacred site at Hagia Eirene on Keos. On chronological and architectural grounds alone one must assume that the cult there was a model of the harmonious coexistence of Minoan and Mycenaean religion.

Purely Minoan isolated cult buildings in the Late Bronze Age are thinly documented. A few 12th/11th century round clay models were found on the island some of which contained a figure of the goddess with raised arms[55]. The sacred nature of the buildings thus represented becomes evident from similar round and rectangular examples dedicated in Protogeometric tombs during the ninth century at e.g. Arkhanes and Khaniale Tekke near Knossos[56]. But similar models of terracotta houses or temples were dedicated in

---

[51] See n. 218.

[52] Mylonas, who feels convinced that Demeter was the first goddess to be revered at Eleusis, finds the origin of the local cult in Thessaly and Thrace, op. cit. 19.

[53] Delos, Eleusis, and Keos are now generally conceded as the only examples of early separate temples. Cf. *Délos primitive* 96 ff.; Desborough, *L. M.* 45 "... in the whole of the rest (apart from Delos) of the Mycenaean and Minoan world there is only one sanctuary, that at Eleusis, which is in no way an appendage of a palace or house, but stands as a shrine in its own right." On p. 43 Desborough casts doubt even on the isolation of the Eleusis temple. Cf. Taylour, *Mycenaeans*, 65: "gods were not venerated in great temples during the Mycenaean period." See also below p. 225.

[54] Above n. 39.

[55] These are discussed by R. Nicholls, *Auck. Cl. Ess.* 16 f.

[56] *B. S. A.* 62 (1967) 64 ff., Fig. 2; 3. Interesting in this connection is an isolated megaron type building beside an open air sanctuary (12th cent.) at Hagia Triada, L. Banti, *A. S. I.* 19/21 (1941/3) 68.

Greece towards the end of the Dark Age[57]. It seems, therefore, that we will not find anything here to divorce Mycenaean from Minoan cultic practice. The isolation of the deity in her own temple was a general feature of the end of the Bronze Age. It may indicate a new religious development away from the purely domestic kind of worship. Did this process suggest a more democratic kind of religious practice? Or did the palace goddess begin to lose her hold over one particular, presumably the royal, family and extend her sphere to cover an entire community? These and related questions are unanswerable, of course, but, whatever precise effect this new feature had on the form of contemporary cult, the appearance of separate sanctuaries roughly seems to coincide with the period when the various aspects of the nature goddess crystallized into the individual functions we meet with in archaic and classical Greece. To this point we shall return below.

The famous Shrine of the Double Axes in Knossos, used during the reoccupation of the palace in L.M. III B[58] but probably continuing Middle Minoan religious practice[59], contained horns of consecration, double axes, and the usual bell-shaped idols of the goddess who was the central figure of cult[60]. The Gournia shrine probably belongs to L.M. III B[61]: it was some way from the palace, and, through having developed from a domestic shrine, may have become a public sanctuary[62] by L.M. III B. The shrine contained snake tubes, horns of consecration, and bell idols of the goddess[63]. One of the most interesting finds associated with this shrine is a vessel on to which was moulded in relief the figure of a child-bearing woman[64]. A similar vase was discovered in the contemporary Kefala shrine[65]. The group depicted most likely refers to our goddess of nature, connected with birth and death, and to her youthful male companion.

[57] See Nicholls, *Auck. Cl. Ess.* 16.
[58] For recent discussions of the destruction dates of the Last Palace at Knossos and the subsequent Reoccupation see M. S. F. Hood, *K.* 4 (1965) 16–44; 5 (1966) 121–41; M. Popham, *The Last Days of the Palace at Knossos* (Stud. in Mediterr. Archaeol. V) 1964; *K.* 5 (1966), 17–24.
[59] See Evans, *P. M.* II, 335 ff.; 332; I, 576. Nilsson, *M. M. R.* 78 n. 2, feels that the evidence regarding cult continuity in this shrine is too thin.
[60] Cf. Desborough, *L. M.* 169; 189.
[61] Desborough, *L. M.* 189; R. W. Hutchinson, *Prehistoric Crete*, 217, places it in L.M. I; cf. Nilsson, *M. M. R.* 82.
[62] Nilsson, *M. M. R.* 80
[63] Harriet Boyd-Hawes, *Gournia, Vasiliki and Other Prehistoric Sites on the Isthmus of Hierapetra, Crete*, Philadelphia 1908, 47 f. Pl. 11.
[64] Desborough, *L. M.* 189.
[65] *Ergon* (1957) 88 ff.; figs. 86; 88.

West of Heraklion, between Candia and Tylissos, lay the Gazi shrine (about L.M. III B or C[66]) which concealed, apart from a snake tube vessel, five interesting bell-shaped idols with their arms raised in the "Segensgestus". Four of these (the head of the fifth is lost) carry ornaments on their heads, consisting e.g. of what are probably poppies, on the largest figure which "looks astonishingly Greek"[67], or two birds flanking a pair of horns of consecration[68]. Other shrines of this period, such as those at Mitropolis (L.M. III B[69]) at Katsamba (L.M. III C[70]), contained the same type of goddess figurines and cult implements.

The form taken by this well-known type of Cretan domestic shrine, some time before the end of the fifteenth century, consisted of an "oblong room entered through a small porch from one of the narrower ends and with a ledge for the images and cult objects at the innermost end of the long room." In other words, we are dealing with an architectural style which was markedly similar to that found in contemporary Mycenaean cult buildings and may indeed have been mainland inspired[71]. In any case, this form of sanctuary survived, or perhaps reappeared, in parts of the Greek world, like Delos and Rhodes, in archaic times[72]. To complete the picture of Minoan and Mycenaean religious interdependence at the end of the Bronze Age we should look at two sets of three domestic shrines, one set in Crete and the other on the mainland, which admirably illustrate this close connection.

[66] Desborough, *L. M.* 189; S. Marinatos, *Eph. Arch.* (1937) 278 ff. – L.M. III C – cf. Alexiou, *K. Ch.* 12 (1958) 191 f. Nilsson, *M M. R.* 101, calls the shrine Subminoan.
[67] Nilsson, *M. M. R.* 100, figs. 24; 25.
[68] *Ibid.* fig. 24. Cf. the similar statuette, crowned with a number of birds, from Karphi, *ibid.* fig. 26.
[69] Alexiou, cited by Desborough, *L. M.* 189. But see Doro Levi, *A. S. I.* 19/20 (1957/8) 392 f.
[70] *B. C. H.* 80 (1957) 351; Desborough, *L. M.* 189. It is uncertain whether the isolated find of a similar idol at Pankalokhori points to the presence there of a shrine, *Anz.* (1933) 297, figs. 6–8; *Deltion* 15 (1933–5) App. 55, fig. 12.
[71] Hutchinson, *Preh. Crete,* 217, who also points out that "there seems to be no obvious Minoan prototype for this kind of shrine." Cf. already Persson's suggestion that the mainland shrine at this time "may be considered as a transitional stage between the small house sanctuaries of the Minoan age and the temples of the Greek age." Cited by Nilsson, *M. M. R.* 114.
[72] The Mycenaeans built this kind of rectangular sanctuary, complete with bench, on Delos, for example, *Delos primitive* passim; Desborough, *L. M.* 44 ff.; Nicholls, *Auck. Cl. Ess.* 6. And there, as well as on Rhodes, it still flourished in archaic times, K. F. Kinch, *Vroulia,* Berlin 1914, 11, Pl. I; A. Plassart, *Ex. arch. D.* 1928, I, 145 ff.; Nicholls, *ibid.;* Nilsson, *M. M. R.* 453 f.

The first of these, discovered by Pendlebury[73], was at Karphi. It probably belonged to L.M. III B[74] but continued in use at least into Protogeometric[75]. A remarkable feature of this site, aside from the evidence of cult continuity, are the distinctive traces of Mycenaean architecture in the city buildings of Karphi, and it has been supposed that some Mycenaean nobles settled there[76]. The sacred accoutrements of the Karphi shrine are Minoan in character, although we note the intrusion of elements which may have been due to Mycenaean or Protogeometric influence, namely the increase in size of the statuettes[77], and the appearance of what may have been a male head, perhaps serving as the top of a vase[78]. At Knossos the shrine of the underground Spring Chamber, in use during III C, was obviously devoted to Minoan type cult of the goddess, to judge e.g. from the hut urn which was found there with the goddess inside. However, in addition to their own cultic implements, the Minoan worshippers also used pots of Mycenaean shape and character[79].

The third site in this context is the Minoan settlement at Prinias, along the way from the north to the southern Mesara. No remains of an actual shrine are extant but the usual snake tubes and fragments of L.M. III C bell idols, which were discovered on the acropolis of Prinias and very much resemble those of Karphi and Gournia, make the presence of a sanctuary there a reasonable supposition[80]. Again, no Mycenaean objects are associated with the probable site of the Minoan shrine, but there are other factors which lend special interest to this place. Prinias, like Dreros not far from the Gulf of Mirabello[81], is of considerable importance to the religious historian, firstly because cult continued to be practised at the site from at least Late Minoan until Geometric times, and secondly because the particular type of cult that endured there was concerned with our goddess of nature and her animals.

No actual Mycenaean presence can yet be shown for Prinias, but this becomes inevitable in view of the fact that on the same site were found the

[73] E.g. *B. S. A.* 38 (1932) 57 ff.; *J. H. S.* 57 (1937) 141 ff.; 58 (1938) 236; *A. J. A.* 41 (1937) 628.
[74] Desborough, *L. M.* 172. But see Nilsson, *M. M. R.* 101.
[75] Desborough, *L. M.* 189.
[76] See Desborough, *L. M.* 172 f.
[77] One of the bell-shaped idols was about a metre high, Nilsson, *M. M. R.* 101.
[78] Cf. Nilsson, *ibid.*
[79] Evans, *P. M.* II, 128 ff.; Desborough, *Protogeometric Pottery*, 236 f.; *L. M.* 180.
[80] Desborough, *L. M.* 182; 190.
[81] Nilsson, *M. M. R.* 455 ff.

remains of two archaic Greek temples which illustrate the persistence of Minoan cult across the Mycenaean Age into Greek times. One of these temples (Temple B) the excavators found to have been constructed in such a way that the interior cultic arrangements distinctly recall those of the Minoan domestic shrine, including, of course, that of Asine on the mainland. That is, along one of the rectangular walls (on the south wall of Temple B) there was a bench, or ledge, designed to hold the votive offerings[82]. The sculptures in the temple portray the goddess and her animals: "they consist of a statue of a goddess seated on a throne and wearing a polos and a stiff garment decorated with animals, a horse, a lion, and a sphinx"[83].

The goddess has been variously interpreted as Rhea or "Artemis, the Mistress of Animals"[84]. However, to assign her a name from the Greek divine vocabulary is a virtually impossible exercise, for she was older than her historic titles: she was, in fact, the same figure as our goddess of nature who dominated the Minoan and Mycenaean religious scene during the Bronze Age. She survived into classical times but in more than one form, when she appeared under the name of Artemis, Athena, perhaps even Demeter and Hera, as we shall see in connection with the Linear B texts. Unanswerable at present, if we may anticipate this much, are the questions as to whether the goddess' multiple forms were thought to represent different aspects of the same figure: this thesis is a likely one, and it would explain the different attributes, like birds, plants etc., which were placed on the heads of many L.M. statuettes (e.g. at Gazi and Karphi) and perhaps referred to particular functions. Nor can one yet tell with precision when such a division of functions occurred in the religion of the western Aegean, although a *terminus ante quem* seems to be the Geometric period. Perhaps such ideas were imported from the East[85].

The Prinias sculptures in essence, therefore, represented the same figure as the goddess of Gortyn who, one supposes, experienced a similar develop-

---

[82] *Boll. d'Arte* 1 (1907) fasc. 8, 28 ff.; *A. S. I.* I (1914) 19 ff.; S. Marinatos, "Le Temple géométrique de Dréros", *B. C. H.* 60 (1936) 214 ff.; Pl. XXVI–XXXI; LXIII; Nilsson, *M. M. R.* 454, who cites – n. 25 – Evans, *J. H. S.* 32 (1912) 284, "A remarkable example of the continuity of the cult forms has been brought to light by the Italian excavation of a seventh century temple at Prinia, containing clay images of the Goddess with snakes coiled round her arms, showing a direct derivation from similar images in the Late Minoan shrine of Gournia."

[83] Nilsson, *M. M. R.* 455.

[84] Nilsson, *ibid.*, who cites the Italian view – n. 28 – that the goddess is Rhea.

[85] Cf. G. E. Mylonas, "Seated and Multiple Mycenaean Figurines, in Aegean and Near East", *Studs. Gold.*

ment. The latter was revered on the Cretan site of Gortyn, perhaps from Neolithic times, but certainly during the Mycenaean and Submycenaean periods and later. She, too, became a "Mistress of Animals". In art she was also associated with lions, griffins, etc., and developed from the Minoan model. Again, if we judge from some of her archaic representations, the Gortyn goddess suffered a similar division into different forms, perhaps a trinity, so that the names of Artemis and Athena came to fit her and her aspects equally well[86].

Until comparatively recently no domestic sanctuary of the Cretan type was known on the mainland, although in the light of the factors of religious correspondence between the two lands one expected them to have existed[87]. Now, in fact, two or three examples of these L.H. III B/C domestic shrines have turned up: one probably at Malthi in Messenia, the so-called Sanctuary of the Double Axes, dated by the find of associated III B/C ware[88], and another at Berbati, in the Argolid[89], belonging to the same period[90]. By far the most important and best-preserved domestic shrine (L.H. III C) was unearthed at Asine on the gulf of Argos[91]. The shrine was attached to a private house (House G)[92] and strongly recalls the Late Minoan domestic shrines, consisting of a rectangular room with a shelf in one corner for holding the votive offerrings. These, in the case of Asine, had fallen below the shelf when discovered. They included, amongst others, Mycenaean type painted idols (five), a kernos type composite vessel, like the many Minoan examples, a stone axe, and the large head of a deity[93].

Architecturally, and by virtue of the offerings found there, the Asine shrine is a striking example of Minoan-Mycenaean cultic interdependence at the end of the Bronze Age[94]. The contents of the shrine recall those of the

---

[86] On the Gortyn goddess see especially Doro Levi, *P. d. P.* 11 (1956) 285–315; Cf. *A. S. I.* (1957).
[87] Cf. Nilsson, *M. M. R.* 114.
[88] N. Valmin, *The Swedish Messenia Expedition*, Lund 1938, e.g. 325 f.; fig. 69, Pl. 24; E 4. Alin, *Fundst.* 76 f.
[89] A. W. Persson / A. Akerström, "Zwei mykenische Hausaltäre in Berbati", *B. soc. L.* 3 (1937/8); Alin, *Fundst.* 38; 40.
[90] The Swedish excavators discovered "zwei Räume mit Anlagen,..., die nur als Hausaltäre verstanden werden können", Nilsson, *Gesch.* I, 344 n. 1, and see fig. 6.
[91] O. Frödin / A. W. Persson, *Asine*, 74 ff.; 298 ff.; 308 ff.; Alin, *Fundst.* 47 ff.
[92] Desborough, *L .M.* 83, supposes that this might have been the residence of the "ruler of Asine".
[93] According to Nilsson, the pointed chin of the head was meant as a beard, *M. M. R.* 114.
[94] This shrine may only have been in use during L.H. III C, Desborough, *L. M.* 42.

Knossian Shrine of the Double Axes, although the goddess was represented by the five Mycenaean figurines. The Asine shrine was in use for only a short period of time[95], and there can be no question of cult continuity into Protogeometric and later at that particular site. However, in conjunction with the admittedly rather thin evidence from Malthi and Berbati, the Asine house bears witness to the mainland practice of Mycenaean cult in Minoan dress. Therefore at the time of writing we can agree with archaeologists who call the household shrine at Asine "perhaps unique in the Mycenaean...world"[96], although future discoveries may add further examples to those known at present. With all its obvious Minoan connections the Asine shrine could not be called a slavish imitation of Minoan practice: it was not the usual small chapel, entirely devoted to cult, but a larger room used, one supposes, for other purposes as well, so that the shelf of offerings came to be crowded into one corner[97]. The cult, therefore, which was celebrated within the shrine had its individual features, but in its essentials it was at home in both Mycenae and Crete.

There are other individual features which one can archaeologically show to have existed in the Cretan, as opposed to mainland, shrines. Such differences were superficial, however, in the wider context of the actual cult and should not be overestimated. The Cretan domestic shrines, for example, housed some articles which seem distinctly Minoan in character. These in the main consisted of double axes, horns of consecration, and the well-known tube-shaped vessels with snakes as handles, used perhaps for pouring subterranean libations. The goddess was most frequently shown in the form of the so-called bell-shaped idols. These remains, particularly the tube vessels and the female idols, recur almost monotonously in all notable shrines on the island at that time. The L.M. III B/C shrine at Hagia Triada, within the palace[98], contained three snake tube vessels, but no statuettes. Nearby, however, south to the east-wing of the palace, in a place called *piazzale dei saccelli* by the excavators, a wealth of sacred relics was found consisting of terracotta bulls, cows, axes, male and female figurines etc.[99].

---

[95] See the previous note.
[96] Desborough, *L. M.* 42.
[97] Cf. Nilsson, *M. M. R.* 114.
[98] L. Banti, *A. S. I.* 3/4 (1941/2) 10–74; L. Pernier and L. Banti, *Guida degli scavi italiani in Creta*, Rome 1947, 7. Hutchinson, *Preh. Crete*, 290, assigns the shrine to L.M. I.
[99] See Banti, *A. S. I.* (1941/2) 28 ff.; fig. 14–25; 52 ff.; figs. 31–68; 40 ff. no. 2. We merely note here, without discussion, Banti's theory regarding the gradual separation

Again, a few cult objects and vessels appear to have been peculiar to Mycenaean ritual. These included the kalathos, with or without figures on the rim[100], and a jug with a special kind of "strainer spout or excrescent cup", and occasionally with snakes moulded or painted on to it[101]. The rhyton, a libation vase, was, of course, also used in Minoan cult. Another kind of vessel in common use on the mainland was the kernos which, however, had an unimpeachable Minoan ancestry. The kernos was a composite vase with "smaller vessels fixed upon a (common) base"[102]. It was a typical part of Minoan cult paraphernalia, perhaps in its earliest form going back to E.M. II[103]. Thus its employment in Mycenaean ritual, as e.g. at Eleusis[104], argues for an acquaintance with Minoan ways.

There was very little in the Minoan religious repertoire which would have struck a Mycenaean as totally alien to his belief, so that he was not above following the Cretan artist's model when depicting scenes of cult or divinities[105]. We do not wish to suggest that there was absolute identity of Minoan and Mycenaean cult, but, as has been said earlier on, a kind of partnership which in a number of respects endured after the end of the Bronze Age. And this point will be raised again in the next chapter. At the moment it is important to stress one conclusion, namely that archaeological evidence for the last years of the Helladic period does not establish any basic difference between mainland and Cretan religious beliefs, despite the presence of some dissimilar features in both centres. For example, the shape and appearance of Minoan and Mycenaean female idols differed from one another. But should we not read these as different forms, or representations, of the same goddess in essence, particularly in view of the peaceful coexistence of Cretan and mainland cult in shrines like that of Asine[106]?

·From L.H. III A very many stereotyped terracotta statuettes were produced on the mainland. These were types of handmade, probably goddess, figurines which in their crudely stylized forms somewhat resembled the

of the Minoan shrine from the palace. According to her, the Minoan shrine became an independent place of worship after M.M. III (*op. cit.* 40 ff.). On this point see Nilsson, *M.M.R.* 77 n. 1.

[100] Desborough, *L. M.* Pl. 7 a; b.
[101] *Ibid.* 40; Pl. 7 c; d.
[102] Nilsson, *M. M. R.* 135; figs. 44 ff.; cf. A. Furumark, *The Mycenaean Pottery* 69.
[103] Evans, *P. M.* I, 76; fig 43 a; b.
[104] Nilsson, *M. M. R.* 450.
[105] F. Matz, *Kreta, Mykene, Troja*, 140: "Die Typik (of representing cult scenes and deities) bleibt aber die kretische."
[106] Nilsson, *M. M. R.* 110 ff. and fig. 32; Desborough, *L. Myc.* 42.

Greek letters "Phi", "Tau" and later on "Psi"[107]. They have been found in tombs, houses, and sanctuaries, and their significance has been much debated[108]. Now, their style seems to have been a mainland contribution, but the distinctive gesture of their upraised arms, particularly in the case of the "Tau" and "Psi" figures, was inspired by representations of the Minoan goddess[109]. Besides these schematized figures, contemporary wheelmade terracottas have also come to light in Mycenae and Pylos. These are in the form of cylindrical idols. Their connection, therefore, with Cretan goddess figures, like the famous "Poppy Goddess" at Gazi, is obvious, although their artistic style is purely Mycenaean[110]. Both types of figures were often associated with statuettes of animals, notably the bull, and this is a point of considerable interest in view of what was said in the last chapter about the nature of the goddess who is represented by these figurines[111]. Incidentally, the animal figures remained important to cult throughout the Dark Age in Crete and Greece[112]. Neither were the crude Late Mycenaean goddess figurines forgotten on the mainland, but we find their descendants in archaic Greece, especially in Boeotia and Corinth[113].

Finally, votive offerings, or divine representations, of male figures were rare in Minoan cult at all periods, whereas in Mycenaean religion on the mainland, or in Crete under Mycenaean management, a male figure may have played a more than peripheral part in religious ceremonial. At any rate some evidence has been produced, according to which male figures were dedicated in Mycenaean shrines. This change of emphasis from a female oriented religion would agree well with later Greek thought, and with the mention of a number of gods, familiar to classical Greece, on the Linear B tablets. But once more archaeology serves us poorly in this respect. Exam-

---

[107] Furumark, *Chronology* 87 ff.; E. French, "The Development of Mycenaean Terracotta Figurines", *B. S. A.* 66 (1971) especially pp. 108–150. See also R. A. Higgins, *Greek Terracottas*, 14.

[108] Sometimes they are denied divine status and are described as nurses placed within the tomb beside the body of a child, cf. Mylonas, *Eleusis* 51 f., who even believes the female figures on the famous ivory group from Mycenae to be nurses. He is altogether opposed to finding Minoan influence in Helladic Greece, with special reference to Eleusis, e.g. *op. cit.* 19.

[109] See Nicholls, *Auck. Cl. Ess.* 3; 4.

[110] Higgins, *Terracottas* 15 f.; Fig. 9, Pl. 5 d.

[111] Above p. 111; 114 ff.

[112] Nicholls, *op. cit.* 13, who contradicts Higgins, *op. cit.* 17; 18; 20 f.

[113] S. Mollard-Besques, *Les Terres Cuites Grecques*, Paris 1963, 44 f. and Pl. VI, 1, 2, 4.

ples of 13th/12th century idols of gods in Crete and on the mainland are difficult to identify from the extant material.

Curiously enough the strongest example cited in this connection is at Asine, in the 12th century domestic type shrine of obvious Minoan ancestry. It consists of a comparatively large wheelmade head, surrounded by the usual Mycenaean "Psi" figures, as well as by figures of the Minoan goddess with raised arms[114]. The evidence is inconclusive, however, because there can be no certainty about the sex of the divine figure of which only the head survived. Nilsson is convinced that in this case we are dealing with a god, namely the "Lord of Asine" or Zeus with his thunderbolt[115]. To Evans, Persson, and more recently to Nicholls, the head was part of a goddess[116]. The impasse is unlikely to be resolved. The Asine head has stylistically been compared with the 10th/9th century head from Kalokhorio, Crete, in the Pediadha Plain[117], with the famous 13th century stucco head (female) from Mycenae, and a slightly smaller, but more or less contemporary, head from Tiryns[118].

The background to cult and divine worship was probably the same in both Crete and on the mainland, although at present it is impossible to establish accurately how far different aspects of the chief goddess had been isolated by the Mycenaeans, or what distinctive flavour the latter might already have imparted to individual aspects, such as the later so prominent warlike Athena. One should also remember that at this moment no decisive evidence exists from any source regarding the whole range of mainland and Cretan Bronze Age cult, the number of divinities worshipped, or the exact procedure of ritual.

If our previous examination of Cretan cults, and if what has been said about Mycenaean religion thus far, brought to the foreground the central figure of a goddess of nature, particularly concerned with life and death, who was associated with a number of animals and with a closely allied youthful male god, we would still be wrong to infer that these two deities

[114] *Asine*, 308; fig. 211. For another Minoan male figurine (M.M.) from Hagios Stephanos see E. French, *B. S. A.* 66 (1971) 148.

[115] The pointed chin of the head is explained as a beard by Nilsson. The thunderbolt is supposed to be represented by the axe which was also discovered among the votive offerings, *M. M. R.* 114; cf. Taylour, *Mycenaeans* 67. Cf. n. 93.

[116] Evans, *P. M.* IV, 756; A. W. Persson, *Preh. Rel.* 100 n. 1; Nicholls, *Auck. Cl. Ess.*

[117] S. Alexiou, *K. Ch.* 12 (1958) 216 n. 127; Pl. 10, fig. 3; cf. Desborough, *L. M.* 190. Nicholls, *Auck. Cl. Ess.* 6 is unconvinced by this comparison.

[118] Nicholls, *Auck. Cl. Ess.* n. 51; 52. One certain and one possible male figurine have also been identified in Athens and at H. Triada respectively, *B. S. A.* 66 (1971) 148.

and their attendant animals were the only objects of cult. Such ideas would fly in the face of the written evidence of the Linear B texts, as well as contradict our knowledge of the multiple figure at e.g. Gortyn in Crete and Hagia Eirene on the island of Keos, not to mention those cult localities which, like the Minoan peak sanctuaries, point to separate and individual forms of cult. Professor Furumark correctly remarked that to speak only of one goddess and her spouse in Minoan religion was equally misleading as to discover a great number of gods[119]. The same, we may add, obviously applies to Mycenaean belief. More in accordance with the evidence is another conclusion which in some manner associates the other divine figures with a central goddess of nature who could, we recall, appear to her worshippers in a number of forms, both human and animal[120]. It seems that such figures must be taken to represent different aspects, perhaps epiphanies – in Furumark's words – of one main divinity. They represented, one might say, different departments of a wide range of religious belief which covered the most important spheres of contemporary society. If we are right, even in general outline, and no one can yet venture beyond a general picture, then we need not be surprised at the strong position in Late Bronze Age cult of the chief goddess, beside whom indeed there appear the names of other figures on the tablets who had a common bond with her.

There are numerous remains of sanctuaries and cult sites throughout the Mycenaean world. The evidence for these has been collected and published in the relevant archaeological reports which it is unnecessary to repeat in detail[121]. However, in practically every instance a good deal of uncertainty attaches to the question of how far Mycenaean cult, or portions thereof, continued at these sites into historic times. Viewed from the archaeologists' camp, there seemed to be a definite break at the end of the Bronze Age. The ceramic scene suggests the arrival of new population elements at that time, who put an end to religious and social customs, who conquered or destroyed Mycenaean settlements, but who, especially in the Peloponnese, did not always deign to inhabit their newly won territory. This picture, for example, presents itself at many of the Late Mycenaean sites examined by

---

[119] Furumark, *Op. Ath.* (1965) 96.
[120] Cf. Furumark, *ibid.*
[121] For a brief survey of some of the important Mycenaean sanctuaries see Nilsson, *Gesch.* I, 338 ff. For discussions of the evidence and references to Mycenaean archaeological work see e.g. F. H. Stubbings' three chapters in the *C. A. H.*² vol. II, chapters 14, 22 (a), 27, together with the relevant bibliographies. See also Alin, *Fundst.*; Desborough, *L. M.* with bibliographies.

Desborough. If one rigorously argues this case, and believes in addition that those sanctuaries, or sanctuary sites, which the later Greek also thought sacred, survived the Dark Age as dim memories, or perhaps because of the influence of Homeric epic, then, surely, "there is no longer any need to suppose that there was continuous worship at any of the... places which were holy to the Mycenaeans"[122]. The religious historian is not so easily persuaded that there was a dramatic break in mainland culture at the end of the second millennium. Nilsson some years ago correctly stated that in general continuity of site implied continuity of worship. The divinities mentioned in the Mycenaean texts, the survival into Greek legend of Mycenaean as well as Minoan belief, are further eloquent witnesses that some important portions of religious practice lived through the Dark Age. This question of continuity will be fully discussed in the next chapter, together with a survey of the sites where cult most likely survived the end of the Bronze Age. At present we should, however, admit that a detailed definition of what was new or old in classical religion, in other words, what had endured in belief from the Mycenaean period, is still beyond our reach. These, in fact, are areas "of which", as Desborough readily concedes[123], "archaeology can tell us nothing."

To a certain extent, therefore, we are bound to move in the dark regarding religious development during and after the Mycenaean Age. But there are places where cult persisted in association with certain deities who came to hold an important place in classical Greek religion. Continuity at such sites seems certain, although archaeological evidence in some instances suggests that occupation ceased, and consequently religious worship was abandoned occasionally for considerable periods of time. In these cases it was not a true cessation of cult apparently, but an interruption after which for some reason or other cult was resumed at the identical site. With this picture, unlikely as it may seem, we cannot argue for lack of evidence to the contrary. We may claim, however, that, possible interruptions of cult notwithstanding, the type of deity revered in a particular locality, and the nature of his cult there, in essence remained the same. That is not to say, of course, that god and cult in one place survived the passage of centuries unaltered and intact; but the form of worship and ritual in later ages should still reveal some aspects of the deity's early nature and function at such an ancient site.

[122] Desborough, *L. M.* 46.
[123] *Ibid.* 244.

It is no coincidence, then, that those Mycenaean cult localities whose sacredness endured in classical Greek times came to be devoted in the main to the worship of Athena, Artemis, and her brother Apollo[124]. Apollo has not yet been clearly identified on the tablets[125], but Athena and Artemis were familiar names to the Mycenaeans. The functions which these deities exercised were concerned with nature and the government of the city. In Mycenaean times these functions were certainly compatible, because they were gathered in the one sphere of the Potnia. Traces of this tradition persisted, for example, in the classical cult – on Mycenaean sites – of Artemis Aphaea in Aegina, and that of Alea Athena in Tegea[126]. The votive offerings found on the sites of Late Mycenaean cult, usually consisted of the stylized figures of the goddess and figurines of her animals, like the bull and horse.

South of Sparta, at the site of the modern Hagia Kyriaki, was the sanctuary of Amyclae[127]. No buildings remain on the sacred hill where later Apollo's throne was set up concealing within its base the tomb of Hyacinthus. The area was inhabited from Early Helladic, but the votive remains discovered there must have come from a sanctuary of L.H. III B/C[128]. These were composed of seventy-five goddess figurines and a number of statuettes of bulls and horses. Unbroken continuity of cult at this spot, after the Mycenaean era, cannot be proved an archaeological grounds. Protogeometric sherds have been found at the site, but no examples of connecting Submycenaean ware[129]. But continuity may be assumed from the survival there into historic times of the cult of the pre-Greek Hyacinthus[130]. At Epidaurus

---

[124] The odd man out, as it were, may be Aphrodite and her temple over a possible L.H. III B site at Kolonna in Aegina. But it seems uncertain that this site was the locality of a Mycenaean sanctuary, see Desborough, *L. M.* 119, with modern references.

[125] See below n. 245. Cf. Heubeck, *Frühgr. Lineartafeln* 99. This does not mean that we should follow Heubeck and Nilsson, cited here, in describing Apollo as "einen relativ späten, nachmykenischen Zuwanderer aus dem Osten."

[126] Add to these examples the archaic Greek temples at the site of the L.M. III C shrine at Prinias, associated by Nilsson with Artemis, see above p. 145.

[127] Alin, *Fundst.* 92 f.

[128] See E. Buschor, "Vom Amyklaion", *A. M.* 72 (1927) 1 ff.; *Gn.* 2 (1926) 120 (preliminary report). On the figures see Tod-Wace, *A Catalogue of the Sparta Museum* 221 f.; 236; 244 ff.

[129] Alin, *ibid.*

[130] Cf. Nilsson, *M. M. R.* 471; Desborough, *L. M.* 42, points to the absence of ceramic links at Amyclae, but concedes that "the memory at least of the spot's being sacred survived."

we meet a similar picture of probable cult continuity into historic from Mycenaean times, although there are some gaps in the archaeological evidence[131]. Here an archaic sanctuary was built for Apollo Maleatas on the site of a Mycenaean shrine from which some goddess and animal figures have been recovered. Pottery remains point to a settlement at this spot as early as Early Helladic, while the votive offerings chiefly belong to L.H. III[132].

More rewarding, for the wealth of Mycenaean remains, is the site of Delphi. Beneath Apollo's temple and the Great Altar, to the east of it, lay objects, such as a lime-stone rhyton in the shape of a lioness' head and resembling a libation vessel from the Treasure Chamber of the Knossos palace[133], and some "Phi" shape goddess statuettes, as well as some figurines of bulls[134]. Other Mycenaean objects, mainly of L.H III B, came to light in the near vicinity, including the remarkable figurine of a nude woman sitting on a three-legged chair[135] which Poulsen identifies as the image of a goddess[136]. There is good evidence at Delphi of cult continuity[137], but the remains nearby, or beneath, Apollo's temple are not associated with any contemporary buildings[138]. They are scattered, in fact, in such a way as to make it impossible to pinpoint the exact location of Mycenaean cult, which, how-

---

[131] I. Papadimitriou, *Praktika* (1948) 101; (1949) 94 ff.; (1950) 194 ff.

[132] Cf. Nilsson, *Gesch.* I, 342; Desborough, *L. M.* 42 f.; 78. Desborough also concedes, p. 43, that at least the memory of cult survived in this area.

[133] P. Perdrizet, *Fouilles de Delphes* V, Paris 1908, 3, fig. 13 b; Evans, *P. M.* II, 832 f., figs. 544; 545; 549. Cf. *B. C. H.* 64/5 (1940/1) 270, fig. 33. Nicholls, *Auck. Cl. Ess.* 8 ff. discusses the development of these rhyta in the shape of animals and comes to the conclusion that they were copies of Cretan models but ultimately went back to a general Aegean type of ritual vessel which was introduced into this area at the beginning of the second millennium

[134] Perdrizet, *op. cit.* 14 f.; L. Lerat, *B. C. H.* 59 (1935) 275 ff.; 329 ff.; 74 (1950) 323; 85 (1961) 357 ff.

[135] Nilsson, *M. M. R.* 305, fig. 149. Another similar example was found under Athena's temple in Marmaria, p. 467. For the type of naked or dressed goddess on a throne on the mainland and on the islands in Mycen. times see Higgins, *Terracottas* 14, Pl. 4 A, C (throne). This type "reappears" in Attica during the Dark Age (1100–700 B.C.), *op. cit.* 22, Pl. 7 A, F, G.

[136] F. Poulsen, *Delphi* (transl. from the Danish, 1924) ch. II. But see Nilsson, *M. M. R.* 467.

[137] Nilsson, *ibid.*; Alin, *Fundst.* 130, shows that, in spite of extensive destruction through fire at the end of L.H. III B, there is clear evidence of continuity of settlement across Protogeometric into Geometric times. Cf. Desborough, *L. M.* 44, with the usual reservations.

[138] See references in n. 134 above.

ever, one would be inclined to seek in the same area where the later temple was built.

Less than a mile down the modern road from Delphi lies Marmaria, another site which concealed a great deal of Mycenaean religious material below the temple of Athena Pronaia[139]. The finds included some one-hundred and seventy-five goddess figurines which had been transferred from near by and heaped together there to mark the sacredness of the place where Athena's archaic temple was erected[140]. Whatever the precise position of the original Mycenaean sanctuary in Delphi (perhaps under Apollo's altar)[141], it is possible that Marmaria's history did not go back to the Bronze Age[142]. What is of enormous interest to the religious historian, however, is the association in the Greek mind of the well known Mycenaean statuettes of the goddess and her animals with the person of Athena. The bond between them is obvious, exactly as in the case of the Cretan Prinias[143], and is emphasized in this instance by the thought, which motivated the builders of Athena's temple, to consecrate the new site by burying within the earth the relics of her earlier cult at Delphi. The Greek Athena, in fact, embodied and continued the Mycenaean nature goddess, or one of her particular aspects, with whom we are familiar from the many Late Minoan and Helladic sanctuaries in Crete and Greece. The Bronze Age goddess had certain affinities, we already noticed, with animals and a male companion, and we may expect her to have possessed the same features in Delphi[144], judging by the presence of the usual figures of the goddess and her animals[145].

We note two other Greek sites where Mycenaean cult in historical times passed into the hands of Athena or Artemis[146]. The first of these is at Tegea in Arcadia, where, from below Athena's temple, some Mycenaean sherds have come to light (probably L.H. III C)[147] which indicate that this area was used as a Mycenaean sanctuary. The Bronze Age remains from there are

---

[139] R. Demangel, *Fouilles de Delphes* II, 5, Paris 1926, 13 ff.; 15 n. 2.
[140] L. Lerat, *B.C.H.* 81 (1957) 708 ff.
[141] Cf. Desborough, *L.M.* 124.
[142] See Lerat, *ibid.*
[143] See above pp. 145 f.
[144] Cf. above e.g. 117.
[145] On the problems surrounding the age and history of Apollo's cult at Delphi see Appendix II.
[146] For other examples cf. Nilsson, *Gesch.* I, 340 ff.
[147] Alin, *Fundst.* 74; Desborough, *L.M.* 87.

scanty in number, but they do prove Mycenaean occupation, and they are important to us in that we are given another example of the succession of Mycenaean cult into the domain of the goddess Athena. The goddess was revered in this temple under the title of Alea Athena, that is, she was, like Athena Itonia – presumably with reference to a Thessalian town Itonos –, a localized city goddess or protectress of the city[148]. She therefore in this place exercised functions which were compatible with those of the Cretan and Mycenaean goddess who was attached to, and protected, the palace as well as its occupants.

The other site is on the island of Aegina where the precincts of the splendid temple of Artemis Aphaea have yielded remains of Mycenaean cult from L.H. III B[149], including terracotta figurines of the goddess and her animals[150]. Aphaea was a goddess of Cretan religion, but both her close relationship with other Minoan figures, like Diktynna and Britomartis, and her invocatory name, suggest that she was no more or less than a particular aspect of the chief goddess revered in Bronze Age Crete and Mycenae[151]. All the aspects relating to cults of nature and the wilds in historical times fell within the ambience of Artemis who gathered such titles into her own sphere of cults[152].

No unified picture of Mycenaean religion can yet emerge from our survey: obviously our knowledge is still too fragmentary at present for many definite conclusions to be drawn. Nonetheless, the evidence already available should put the historian on his guard against underestimating on one hand the religious connections between, and interdependence of, Late Bronze Age Minoan and Mycenaean cult, and on the other against lightly assuming that a total break separated the Bronze Age from the classical Greek world. Not only faint memories of religious practice survived the Dark Age into classical legend but actual sites of Mycenaean worship continued to be used, in some cases, one suspects, without any greatly significant temporal interruptions or fundamental changes to the nature of the cult.

---

[148] Herodotus I, 67; Strabo VIII, 388; cf. *B. C. H.* 25 (1901) 256; 45 (1921) 403; Nilsson, *Gesch.* I, 388; 434 (Alea). Dittenberger, *SIG²*, 642 A. 2; cf. Nilsson, *Griechische Feste* 89 (Itonia).
[149] A. Furtwängler, *Aigina, das Heiligtum der Aphaia*, Munich 1906, 370 ff.; 432; 434 f.; Pl. 122, 7 and 11; Pl. 127, 2 and 3.
[150] *Ibid.* Pl. 109.
[151] Cf. Persson, *Preh. Rel.* 129 f.; Nilsson, *Gesch.* I, 312.
[152] On the probable Mycenaean site of Kolonna see n. 124 above.

Local differences apart, and these include the specifically Mycenaean developments outlined above, both Late Minoan and Late Helladic cult centred about the figure of a goddess, her animals, and an associated male deity. The goddess, or certain of her aspects, we noticed, endured into historical times mainly within the ambience of the goddesses Artemis and Athena. This goddess pervaded all parts of Bronze Age society about the royal palace. In particular she was concerned with nature cult, an important feature of which was the cycle of birth and death. We should expect, therefore, that whatever evidence exists of a so-called cult of the dead in Crete and Mycenae will in the main agree with our account. In other words, any cult concerned with the dead should form an integral part of nature cult, in such a way that the ritual for the dead was intimately connected with the celebration of birth and growth in nature. What evidence is there in Crete and Mycenae of a cult of the dead and what was its nature[153]?

In Crete it is possible to trace some concern with the dead, expressed by gifts and votive offerings accompanying the dead. A similar interest in the dead is evident from the performance of burnt sacrifice or other ceremonial associated with burial, throughout the Bronze Age, from the Cretan type tholos to the painted larnakes, or coffins, in L.M., such as the famous sarcophagus of Hagia Triada[154]. It is wrong, therefore, to doubt the existence of such a cult on the grounds of the relative scarcity of finds in Crete[155] compared with the lavish gifts found in, for example, the shaft graves at Mycenae. The practice of inhumation, almost universal in Crete and on the mainland[156] until the end of the Bronze Age, was, it seems, a necessary condition of a cult associated in some way with the dead. Again, in Crete the mode of burial in the Minoan circular tombs, in larnakes, or even in separate buildings, like the famous L.M. Temple Tomb at Knossos, suggests that some importance remained with, or perhaps a future existence awaited, the deceased. The same can be said of the persons buried in the Mycenaean shaft

---

[153] For a brief survey of Cretan burial customs see J. D. S. Pendlebury, *The Archaeology of Crete*, 279; 281; 287; Hutchinson, *Preh. Crete* 228–31; I. Pini, *Beiträge zur Minoischen Gräberkunde*, Wiesbaden 1968. A short and good description of Mycenaean customs can be found in Taylour, *Mycenaeans* 74–88.

[154] Cf. Hutchinson, *op. cit.* 228 ff. but see n. 157.

[155] E.g. Nilsson, *M.M.R.* 440 f.

[156] With a few exceptions to prove the rule. Van Effenterre, *Et. C.* 1948, ch. 2, for example, finds some instances of cremation in the cemetery of Olous. Sinclair Hood also discovered at Knossos an instance of cremation in a pithos, cited by Hutchinson, *op. cit.* 230. In the Mycenaean world there are examples of cremation in e.g. Perati, Kos and Rhodes, Desborough, *L. M.* 71.

graves of Middle Helladic, and the splendid tholos tombs which continued into Late Helladic. Also the gifts found there, ranging from articles of use to votive figurines, point to a cult, and so do the many marks left by ritual ceremonies and fires at least on the mainland.

These are well known facts, of course, and there are a good many discussions of the evidence concerning some sort of cult of the dead[157]. The weight of this evidence speaks for the existence of such a cult in the Mycenaean world, whatever form it took. It is, therefore, worth remembering in this connection that, especially during the Late Bronze Age, any Mycenaean type of worship most probably resembled Cretan practice, particularly in view of the probable influence exerted by the former on the burial customs of the latter, and because of the mixture of other religious customs apparent from the remains of contemporary sanctuaries both in Greece and in Crete. In fact, it has been supposed that the scenes of cult painted on the Hagia Triada larnax provide an instance of such a syncretism of Mycenaean practice and Minoan belief[158].

This last point aside, however, while there is general agreement concerning the observance of such a cult, scholars widely differ with regard to the nature, significance, and procedure, of this cult. Divergence of this kind is entirely natural, not only because of the poor and fragmentary state of our evidence, but particularly for the reason that the historian is compelled to deal with separate forces of influence which worked on Late Mycenaean and Minoan ritual from the Near East and from Egypt. Another point easily lost sight of over the many centuries since this worship was instituted is that a cult concerned with the dead most probably passed through various stages which may not have drastically differed in some basic concepts of religion, but which, if considered as a whole, are bound to confuse. A development of cult may already have occurred, for example, between the time when the shaft graves at Mycenae were dug to receive the first dead in the sixteenth century, and the moment in the thirteenth when Grave Circle A was specially included in the last fortifications of the citadel.

[157] See e.g. Karo. *Schachtgräber*; C. W. Blegen / A. J. B. Wace, "Middle Helladic Tombs", *Symb. Osl.* 9 (1930) 28 ff.; Mylonas, *Anc. Mycenae*, on Grave Circle B; Nilsson, *M. M. R.* ch. 17; Mylonas, "The Cult of the Dead", *Studs. Rob.* I, 64–105; *Mycenae and the Mycenaeans*; Ch. Starr, *Origins* 175. Most recently Pini (*op. cit.* 31 f.) connects the cult of the dead with divine cult in Crete from Neolithic until M.M. III. According to him the only evidence of a cult of the dead in L.M. comes from the Temple Tomb (p. 71).

[158] On this point and on the subject of Mycenaean influence on the island's burial customs during L.M. see Nilsson, *M. M. R.* 440 f.; 442.

It is just possible that by then the distinguished, perhaps royal, figures buried there had, in the minds of their descendants, achieved an eminent status which could have been that of hero. This is certainly true of Mycenaean graves which, together with their cult, survived the catastrophe at the end of the Bronze Age and continued into the Geometric period[159], or which, after a long temporal gap, were rediscovered sometimes as late as the classical age. The latter instance is illustrated by the case of the tomb of the so-called Hyperborean Maidens, on Delos, which the Athenians opened during the purification of the island in the fifth century. This originally Mycenaean tomb then became the locality of a hero cult[160]. At the moment we are not so much concerned with the developments or changes which a cult about the grave of the dead experienced until historic times, often under the influence of the poets and of Homer in particular. It would be more interesting to know the original motives surrounding such a cult which might have been observed in honour of all members of a Bronze Age society or perhaps merely for a privileged few. An understanding of the reasons for instituting a cult of the dead would reveal something of the beliefs regarding life after death.

To begin with, Mycenaean, and indeed Cretan, custom concerning the treatment of the dead should fit into the contemporary Aegean religious context. It is extremely unlikely that either civilization was altogether immune from outside stimuli in the cult they offered to the dead. Therefore, to view such a particular form of cult in isolation is just as mistaken as the attempt to describe the whole religious life of these peoples without reference to outside influences which, when they were imported into their lands, at least helped to shape some basic sacred concepts. Fortunately this last point is not always forgotten. Many scholars who discover a cult of the dead in Crete and especially in the Mycenaean world find evidence of extraneous influence. But should we only, or even predominantly, look to Egypt in this connection? Schliemann and others, like Marinatos, Karo, Persson, Picard[161], Mylonas[162], and Nilsson[163], find, especially at Mycenae, the mark of Egyptian custom.

---

[159] See Mylonas, *Studs. Rob.* 105.
[160] Cf. Nilsson, *M. M. R.* 612.
[161] See Picard, *Religions Préh.* 288 f., where further references are given.
[162] *Studs. Rob.* 105.
[163] *M. M. R.* 438 f. On Nilsson's derivation of the concept of Elysium – the Isles of the Blest – from Egypt see *op. cit.* 625.

Certain features of the finds from the Mycenaean shaft graves, such as the gold masks[164], and the mummified body in the First Shaft Grave[165], do suggest a knowledge of Egyptian ways. But most certainly in Mycenae and in Crete other forces were at work in determining the nature of funerary cult. We must stress, then, that a broader perspective of Mediterranean beliefs is necessary, in order to form some kind of impression about the nature of this cult in Crete and on the mainland during the Late Bronze Age. In his chapter on "Jenseitsvorstellungen"[166] Joseph Wiesner ventures to add a wider view of common Mediterranean beliefs to his discussion of the scenes on the Hagia Triada sarcophagus. Some of his ideas may no longer be defensible in the light of recent discoveries, but this method is valuable in that it resists narrow interpretations which are motivated only by internal evidence from Cretan and Mycenaean sites. In this way we obviate the error of explaining the origin of the Bronze Age cult of the dead by specialized aspects it came to assume during subsequent periods.

It is doubtful, for example, that, wherever funerary cult can be shown to have obtained in Crete and Mycenae, we should think of it as a cult of a deified king patterned on the Egyptian model[167]. Nor can we assume at present that the cult about the Mycenaean shaft graves in the sixteenth century already was a cult of heroes[168], whether this arose from a cult of ancestors[169], or from a belief in the superhuman powers of the king which were felt to continue after his death[170]. Hero cult undoubtedly existed in Greek, and most likely in pre-Greek, times: traces of it do appear in Homeric epic. Cult of this kind, in all probability, was a Greek development, begun perhaps as early as the concluding years of Mycenaean influence, and deriving from a more universally spread type of worship in the Bronze Age. That is to say, our understanding of the growth of hero worship out of a more general cult of the dead will contribute little to an appreciation of the beginning and early significance of the latter.

[164] Cf. Karo, op. cit. 180.
[165] H. Schliemann, Mykenai, 340 f. and fig. 454.
[166] J. Wiesner, Grab und Jenseits (RGVV XXVI), Berlin 1938, 199 ff.
[167] Nilsson, M. M. R. 438; cf. Mylonas, Studs. Rob. 105.
[168] Picard, Rel. Préh. 291.
[169] This belief, which enjoys a great following, goes back to F. de Coulanges, La Cité Antique[19], Paris 1905, e.g. 15–20; 30; 31–38.
[170] Mylonas, Studs. Rob. 105. Mylonas does not believe a general cult of the dead existed in Helladic times. This type of cult, he says, became popular in post-Mycenaean and Geometric times, when it was associated with ancient graves and relics and served the purpose of immortalizing a leader.

In some respects Minoan burial custom differed from that current on the mainland[171]; but both societies shared two features in their funeral rites which will accord with what we might consider to be necessary conditions for funeral cult. The first consists in the curious fact that the paraphernalia and votive objects, employed in the cult of the dead, did not signally differ from those in common use on other religious occasions. The second feature, yet more puzzling than the first, concerns the light hearted manner, not to say contempt, with which the remains of the dead were treated. Xanthoudides, for example, has cited instances of fires lit for sacrificial purposes, that is after the actual burial, in the E.M. circular tombs in the Mesara of southern Crete, which caused the bones to turn black "from exposure to the heat and smoke at close quarters"[172]. These two points are obviously of great importance. We must briefly consider them and draw from them our conclusions about the probable nature of the forms of a cult of the dead.

Apart from the usual adornments and normal implements of daily use, the specialized paraphernalia of cult most commonly discovered with Minoan burials were the curious tube-shaped vessels with snakes as handles[173], and the goddess idols, whatever their precise significance[174]. The identical cult vessels and idols, which Nilsson believes to belong to house cult[175], formed essential parts of a cult of the dead and of domestic cult.

---

[171] On the peculiarly Minoan pithos and larnax burials see Hutchinson, *Preh. Crete* 230; Cf. Desborough, *L. M.* 187. Cf. K. Branigan, *The Foundations of Palatial Crete*, ch. 8.

[172] S. Xanthoudides, *The Vaulted Tombs of the Mesara*, 1924, 134. For a slightly different view see Branigan, *op. cit.* 171.

[173] See Nilsson, *M. M. R.* 317 ff.; Gesch. I, Pl. I; II; Picard, *Rel. Préh.* 205 f.: "ils viennent en général de nécropoles."

[174] Idols were placed in Cretan tombs from E.M. They became much rarer as funeral offerings in subsequent periods, but do occur, especially during L. M. Nilsson, *Gesch.* I, 286, believes that the majority of such idols originally belonged to house cult, and that funeral idols of E.M. were placed with the dead in imitation of Egyptian practice (perhaps as the equivalent of *oushebti*, Picard, *Rel. Préh.* 49), while the numerous L.M. grave idols found their way into tombs under Mycenaean influence. This view has, I think, been successfully contested by Picard, *op. cit* 204 f., who cites, with references, a number of examples of Cretan goddess idols in tombs. Of course, the significance of these idols, even their divine nature, is debatable, and we will note at this point the important find in the Mavro Spelio Cemetery, Knossos, of an L.M. III idol of a goddess holding up in her arms the figure of an infant (Evans, *P. M.* II, 2, 556 f.; Suppl. Pl. XXI B).

[175] See the previous note. Cf. Branigan, *op. cit.* 171.

This relationship between the implements of funeral cult and those found in sanctuaries was the same in the Mycenaean sphere. Desborough remarks[176] that "cemeteries produce the material for the cult of the dead", and he goes on to enumerate such material, including the "kalathos with figurines on the rim" (Pl. 7 a, b), a jug with a special "strainer spout or excrescent cup", often decorated with snakes, like the Cretan tubes (Pl. 7 c, d), libation rhyta, and the composite vessel mentioned above. Together with these implements the Mycenaean graves also contained massive numbers of the well known types of terracotta figurines of a goddess and her animals, notably, again, the bull. Yet Desborough's close division between the utensils for the cult of the dead and for sanctuary worship breaks down, as he himself admits[177], because no such division existed in the minds of the Mycenaeans. These points must invite the conclusion for Crete, and in particular for Mycenaean religion, that either a cult of the dead did not exist – the dead person perhaps being imagined to continue his daily habits quite meaninglessly after his burial –, or that such a cult belonged to, and was part of, the form of worship observed in the sanctuaries[177a].

The second striking feature of burial custom in Crete and on the mainland is the surprisingly slight regard paid to the remains of the deceased. Not only, as we saw, were fires, obviously lit for religious purposes, allowed to scorch the bones of the dead, but, during E.M. and probably later, one burial site served for many: "some of them contained the bones of many hundreds or even thousands of bodies"[178]. It is true that during L.M. the Minoan habit of placing the dead in pithoi and larnakes did not lend itself to what might be called multiple burial, and in that they differed from Mycenaean custom[179]. But the difference, one suspects, lay in the form of, rather than in the spirit behind, the burial, for we noticed that even in L.M. many such sarcophagi could be placed in the same cave or rock shelter as at Pyrgos, not far from Knossos[180]. Also, the similarity of Minoan and Mycenaean attitudes in this respect is revealed by the famous scene of

---

[176] *L. Myc.* 40.

[177] *Ibid.*

[177a] Cf. Pini, *op. cit.* 29 ff., who points to the connection in Crete between tomb and cult building from E.M. He also maintains that the architecture of the Temple Tomb at Knossos was based on that of the palace.

[178] Xanthoudides, *Tombs of Mesara* 134.

[179] See Desborough, *L. M.* 187.

[180] Nilsson, *M. M. R.* 55 f.; cf. above pp. 79 ff.

funeral cult which, though painted on the Hagia Triada larnax, betrays Mycenaean influence[181].

On the mainland, *mutatis mutandis*, the picture is virtually the same from the period of the Mycenaean shaft graves, that is about the sixteenth century. With a few exceptions the graves of the two Circles at Mycenae were used for more than one burial. Of the six graves in Circle A only one, Grave II, had a single burial[182]. The tholoi, again, tell a similar story. Only a very few of these tombs escaped the attention of robbers. The best preserved is at Pylos, and from its remains it is possible to see not only an admixture of Cretan practice, e.g. pithos burial, but also that multiple burial obtained there. As one burial followed another the earlier remains were usually unceremoniously crammed into pits, or trenches, dug for the purpose, or even simply pushed aside to make room for the new arrival. There did, however, seem to be an apparent distinction in practice between the western and eastern Peloponnese, for undoubtedly the princely tombs of Mycenae, as far as one can gather from the extant shell, might have been reserved for one, or only a few, burials. Yet even in the east there are examples of tholoi as multiple burial grounds if the "semi-circular pit along the wall" of the Lion Tomb at Mycenae was dug to receive the discarded bones from earlier burials[183]. The chamber tombs of Late Helladic are well known, of course, as multiple burial grounds[184].

These, then, were distinctive features of both Minoan and Mycenaean funeral practice: the apparent absence of any really clear division between funeral and other cult, and the habit of communal burial with its implied disregard of any idea of sanctity that might have been attached to the mortal remains[185]. These two aspects are bound to lie at the root of what cult there was concerning the dead. It seems unwarrantable to argue that a ceremonial was not observed during or after burial, and to doubt that some kind of religious belief was involved in such ceremonial, in the face of the circum-

---

[181] See above p. 159.

[182] See e.g. Taylour, *Mycenaeans* 74 f.

[183] See Taylour, *op. cit.* 80 ff.; cf. M. S. F. Hood in his review of Vermeule's book, *Greece in the Bronze Age*, in *J. H. S.* 86 (1966) 266.

[184] Desborough, *L. M.* 242.

[185] Cf. Vermeule, *Greece in the Br. Age* 299. Mrs. Vermeule also compares the similar practice of using shaft grave, tholos, and chamber tomb as "family receptacles", *op. cit.* 297 ff. On p. 299 she makes the important point that, since "these tholos customs (of burial) were shared by families using chamber tombs, ... there was no social distinction in the ceremonies."

stances surrounding the burial. Other indications of cult include the gifts, together with symbolic representations of the goddess[186], as well as clear indications, mentioned above, that sacrifice and sacrificial fires belonged to the occasion.

Some are ready to deny that the Mycenaean Greek practised any form of a cult of the dead[187]. What should be questioned, however, is not the existence of a cult, but its nature and the ideas concealed behind it. For an appreciation and understanding of this we are bound to recall the cults discussed in the previous chapter, in particular the type of worship which originally obtained in Cretan caves whence it was transferred to other religious sites. Cretan cave cult had much in common with Neolithic Anatolian practice, as at Çatal Hüyük, a source from which no doubt it derived some of its own ideas that were handed on to, or perhaps shared with, the peoples on the mainland. In connection with this cult it was noticed that there did not appear to exist a clear distinction between the worship the living offered to their divinity and that connected with the dead.

In Crete the dead at times shared their cave with the worshippers of nature cult[188]. In Çatal Hüyük, again, the dead were buried, in a secondary burial, in the same sanctuary where the goddess had her home, the only division being that the eastern portion of the sanctuary, more often than not, belonged to the dead[189]. Their bones received the same slight regard as we observed in Minoan and Mycenaean burials. Associated with the dead and with the goddess in these shrines, both in Anatolia and in Crete, we found a number of animals, notably the bull, the same creature, in fact, which, as a terracotta model, so often found its way into Mycenaean graves beside the female figurines. In none of these cases is there a noticeable distinction between the dead and the worship of the goddess concerned with nature cult, and with birth in particular. This juxtaposition of the living and the dead, taken together with the apparent "callous disrespect" shown

---

[186] Not to mention the famous golden balances with butterflies engraved on each scale from the Shaft Graves, e.g. Vermeule, *op. cit.* 298; Pl. XLVIII A, cf. below.
[187] Mylonas, somewhat cautiously, *op. cit.* 105. But Mrs. Vermeule is quite firm in her judgment that (*op. cit.* 305) "no cult of the dead was ever practised in any Mycenaean tomb during the Bronze Age." Cf. Pini (*op. cit.* 72): no cult of the dead on the mainland before Protogeometric. Pini (pp. 71 ff.) also discusses other modern views for and against such a cult in the Bronze Age.
[188] This is denied by Faure, see above pp. 89 f.
[189] Above p. 104.

for the remains of the dead, provide a vital indication of the nature of a cult of the dead which persisted through the Bronze Age.

To believe, therefore, with Mylonas[190] that the Mycenaean imagined the soul of a person to remain with his body only until the flesh had decayed from his bones would involve the presence and knowledge of more sophisticated philosophical concepts than we are entitled to expect in Greece during the second millennium. Ideas of after-life, and particularly of the existence of the human soul, more properly belong to the sixth century[191]. During the Bronze Age interment in a shrine or consecrated area more likely gave the worshipper the promise of new life. His burial and, as it were, temporary disappearance from the company of the living, were merely a part of a constantly recurring natural cycle whose continuance was ensured by the goddess of nature and birth[192]. We saw that symbols of this cycle[193] were the butterfly and chrysalis which constituted some of the central motifs in Çatal Hüyük shrines on the east wall of death. Similar signs were also at home in Cretan tombs, and they belonged e.g. to the Mycenaean shaft graves, engraved, for example, on the famous golden scales[194].

The figure of the goddess of nature, of birth and death, dominated the religious scene still in the Late Bronze Age. This is the impression which is most consistently left in the mind of the historian, in spite of the often fragmentary information at his disposal. Further evidence that will come to light in the course of time no doubt will help to diversify our appreciation of Mycenaean religion, but it is unlikely to displace our goddess from her position of prominence. It is unfortunate that for the understanding of Mycenaean society Homeric epic is a rather inadequate source[195]; nor is it possible to extract much accurate information about prehistoric times from the bulk of Greek mythology. Nilsson's thesis, proposed in the Sather Classical Lectures of 1932[196], that the most important Greek legends were formulated in Mycenaean times, has recently been attacked but without any real success[197].

---

[190] Cited by Taylour, *Mycen.* 88. This is also suggested by Branigan, *op. cit.* 176. For similar ideas see also Pini, *Min. Gräberk.* 73 f.
[191] Cf. above p. 126.
[192] Cf. above p. 105.
[193] E.g. above pp. 119 ff.
[194] See above p. 120.
[195] See e.g. Vermeule, *op. cit.* X; 306 ff.; Heubeck, *Frühgr. Lineartaf.* 72 f.
[196] M. P. Nilsson, *The Mycenaean Origin of Greek Mythology.*
[197] See Appendix III.

Even without such aids, although no full history of Mycenaean society can yet be written, the picture of Mycenaean nature cult with its central goddess remains sufficiently clear. The goddess eventually was the same as the figure of cave cult and of Minoan and Mycenaean domestic cult. What we cannot estimate at present is the degree to which by the end of the Bronze Age this goddess had already become diversified in her functions, representing differing aspects of cult, such as birth, nature and the wilds, the palace and so on. Nor is it possible to understand the contemporary development of the male figure associated with the goddess, or, of course, the intrusion into this religious complex of other gods. The goddess, most likely, was known under the invocatory title of Potnia, Lady or Mistress, a name which, in the context of the goddess of nature and her paredros, apparently survived in Eleusinian cult. Centuries later the hierophant, during the celebration of the Eleusinian Mysteries, still called out that "the mighty Potnia had born a strong son": ἱερὸν ἔτεκε πότνια κοῦρον, βριμὼ βριμόν[198]. Potnia, in the position of a central goddess, occurs on the Linear B tablets. The Mycenaean scribes, it seems, used this title to describe the goddess who governed the vital parts of contemporary society from her palace. This, of course, has yet to be established. Nevertheless, despite their present limitations, these texts offer some sort of control of the Mycenaean cultic scene which we have outlined with the help of other sources. This much, however, we may anticipate without undue prejudice: it would be strange if the Eleusinian Lady had no ties with, or memories of, the Bronze Age Potnia.

John Chadwick in a recent review[199] suggests that "The study of the (Linear B) texts has reached a stage at which cautious conclusions can be reached." Such conclusions mainly concern "some facts about the economic situation" of the Mycenaean world. Perhaps such optimism is less justified

---

[198] Hippolytus, *refut. haeres.* V, 8, p. 164. A Christian author whose information is not entirely reliable on this point. The tradition recorded in these words is ancient, however, in the light of other and older witnesses, cf. A. Körte, *ARW* 18 (1915) 124; Nilsson, "Die Eleusinischen Gottheiten", *ARW* 32 (1935) 126 = *Opuscula Selecta* II, Lund 1952, 605; *M. M. R.* 559; *Gesch.* I, 662. A strong memory of the "Divine Child" Pluto – cf. above pp. 14 ff. –, and of cave cult, may have survived in Eleusis in the Ploutonion. The evidence is late and somewhat confused, because in historic times traditional pre-Greek elements had become contaminated with the Eleusinian rites – cf. Nilsson, *Opusc. Sel.* 581 ff. –, but enough is extant to show that the famous cave, thought of as an entrance to Hades, was sacred to Pluto in the sixth century and earlier, cf. Mylonas, *Eleusis* 99 f.; 139; 148.

[199] *J. H. S.* 86 (1966) 215.

in relation to Mycenaean religious belief. One surprise that awaits the reader of the texts concerns the familiarity of the Mycenaean, as early as the thirteenth century B.C., and perhaps earlier, with a number of the important figures of the Olympian family, beside whom there exist the titles, like wanax, potnia, erinys and hero, which speak of age old beliefs. Of course, very many grave difficulties still attach to the transliteration and interpretation of individual words: often too little is known about the context of a particular religious name or title. Other words can be interpreted in a variety of meanings. Examples are too well known to cite in detail. A great part of this difficulty arises out of the system of writing. Some textual discussions are liable even to leave the non-philologist with his head spinning in confusion; confusion, however, mainly on points of detail.

But it may still be too early to integrate the information derived from the tablets with archaeological data and cultic ritual sufficiently for a unified picture to emerge. Especially hazardous in the present state of our knowledge seems to be the practice of closely comparing Near Eastern with Mycenaean ritual features, as they apparently are described in the Linear B texts[200]. Equally contentious are constructions of elaborate festal calendars on the strength of relatively sparse words whose interpretation must still be open to doubt[201]. There is much that is persuasive in these arguments, but we

---

[200] G. Pugliese Carratelli, "Aspetti e Problemi della Monarchi Micenea", *P. d. P.* 15 (1959) 405.

[201] This, for example, has been done from the Pylos Fr Series (1955), the Oil Tablets, where in occasionally uncertain contexts a few words [e.g. reke(e)toroterijo (Fr 343 + 1213; Fr 1217) – etymologically interpreted as λεχεστρωτήριον (E. L. Bennett, cited by Palmer, *Interpretation* 251; cf. the debate concerning the seemingly related tonoeketerijo [Fr 1222], Palmer, *op. cit.* 252), porowito ("neutral nominative" πλωϝιστός Fr 1218; 1221; 1232), dipisijo(i) (Dat. δίψιοι Fr 1220; 1231; 1232; 1240; cf. W. K. C. Guthrie, "Early Greek Religion in the Light of the Decipherment of Linear B", *BICS* 6 [1959] 45), and keseniwijo (Gen. Plur. of ξένϝια Fr 1231)] have been taken as a reference to the Greek Anthesteria (Palmer, *op. cit.* 253 ff.; *Mycenaeans and Minoans*², 137 f.). A part of the argument certainly is attractive, but, the uncertainties of context and interpretation of individual words apart, too many problems make a close comparison with the Anthesteria unconvincing. These were a compound of festivals of which the last day – the "Seelenfest" in question – did not belong to Dionysus (for sources and discussion see my paper "A Rite of Swinging during the Anthesteria", *He.* 89 [1961] especially 42 ff.), nor is there any evidence that *lectisternia* were celebrated in the course of the three day festival, or indeed *xenia* or *theoxenia* which, in reasonably close proximity to wanaktes (?) (wanakate, e.g. Fr 1220; 1227; 1235), would point to a house or domestic cult connected with the Dioscuroi (for this see below pp. 186 ff. and cf. Carratelli, *op. cit.* 410; J. Puhvel, "Helladic Kingship and the Gods", *Minoica*, 332).

are clearly not so far that we can safely establish from any of the available sources, be they archaeological, linguistic, or literary, a concise plan of many religious festivals, ritual events, or even, in every case, the exact divinities involved on such occasions[202].

This is particularly true of Minoan and Mycenaean cults which, though often related, are extremely difficult to define accurately beyond certain general traits dealing with important aspects of nature religion. Mycenaean religious thought, particularly in the case of cave and domestic cults, owed a great deal to outside, including Minoan, sources. This point should be well remembered when examining Linear B titles like Wanax and Potnia. On the other hand, the tablets, when the interpretation is certain, offer considerable assistance to the student of Greek religion, provided the names and cultic epithets are read at their face value.

One of the first notable points to emerge from the study of Mycenaean Greek is the uniformity of language throughout the Mycenaean world[203], certainly in the thirteenth century, that is at the end of the Bronze Age[204]. Such evidence of a widely shared language does tend to bear out the theory of a general acceptance of some basic cult features which obtained throughout much of the Aegean world from the Early Bronze Age[205]. To this knowledge we may add the fact that a tenacious conservatism pervaded the religious beliefs of most cultures of the Aegean, including, of course, the Minoans and Mycenaeans.

We are specifically concerned with a vegetation cult at whose centre there was a goddess, related to, or perhaps identical with, the famous deity

---

[202] Palmer's equation of metuwo newo (Gen. of date, Fr 1202) with the Pithoigia (first day of the Anthesteria), *Interpret.* 253; *Myc. and Min.* 137, surely is beset by grave doubts when set beside the datives matere teija (Ματρεὶ Θείᾳ) on the same tablet, whoever this Divine Mother was meant to be.

[203] Cf. e.g. Puhvel, *Minoica* 327, who uses the happy expression of a Helladic *koine* in the Mycenaean world.

[204] C. W. Blegen, "A Chronological Problem", *Minoica* 61–66, makes the very plausible suggestion that the Knossos tablets may belong to the debris from the destruction – end of L.H. – of a Mycenaean palace at Knossos, so that their date, like that of the tablets from Pylos and Mycenae, would be the end of the thirteenth century B.C. We cannot now take issue with the extensive modern literature concerning the chronological problem, but merely wish to cite Blegen's interesting opinion. In this context a noteworthy comment comes from Prof. E. Grumach who says, "Epigraphische Mitteilungen", *K.* 5 (1966) 171, "Tatsächlich ist nicht einzusehen, warum Linear B nicht auch nach der Zerstörung von Knossos in Kreta geschrieben sein und sich ähnlich wie auf dem Festland bis ans Ende der Bronzezeit erhalten haben soll."

[205] See e.g. my "Some Eastern Traditions in Greek Thought", *A. C.* 8 (1965) 13; 15.

whom Studniczka some seventy years ago gave the Homeric name of *Potnia Theron*[206]. The relationship in cult between the Potnia and her male companion is difficult to define from archaeological remains. Therefore it is exciting to notice that the same curious ambivalence between divine and human nature – in the figure of the king[207] – may well be reflected in the position of the w̄anax on the tablets. These are yet vague data, mainly owing to the uncertain context in which wanax, for example, and potnia appear on the tablets, but it is useful to know what evidence we may expect from the written sources in the light of archaeological discoveries.

In this chapter we cannot pursue the growth of this goddess, or one of her aspects, into the figure of the palace goddess. But this part of her history is plain from the extant evidence. Equally certain is the archaeological evidence which, in all likelihood, shows her cult to have been observed in shrines such as the underground Spring Chamber at Knossos in L.M. III C (c. 12th cent.)[208], and the sanctuary at Karphi from at least as early as L.M. III B (c. 13th cent.)[209]. At these sites there continued a cult which may have been predominantly Minoan, but which could not materially have differed from that observed on the mainland in sanctuaries like the house sanctuary at Asine in the Argolid[210]. In this last shrine a mixture of Mycenaean type religious architecture with Cretan cultic paraphernalia bears lively witness to the persistence of largely shared Minoan Mycenaean practice[211] until the end of the Bronze Age. The type of domestic cult practised at these and, no doubt, other sites one would expect to find reflected in the written records. From other sources it appears that at the centre of the cult was a goddess, or perhaps, at a later period, several aspects of the same goddess, as is well illustrated by the idols from e.g. the Submycenaean sanctuary at Gazi[212]. Her history is old, probably going back to the Neolithic period[213], and her original cult locality may well have been

---

[206] F. Studniczka, *Kyrene* (1890) 153 ff.; cf. Homer, *Il.* 21, 470.

[207] Cf. *A. C.* 8 (1965) 19 ff.

[208] Evans, *P. M.* II, 128 ff.; Desborough, *Protog. Pott.* 236 f.; *L. M.* 180.

[209] Desborough, *L. M.* 172.

[210] *Asine* 298 ff.; Desborough, *L. M.* 83; 190.

[211] Cf. Nilsson, *Gesch.* I, 344. The same probably applied to the Minoan type house chapels at Berbati near Mycenae, Persson-Akerström, *B. soc. L.* 1937/8, III. See above p. 147.

[212] Nilsson, *Gesch.* I, 267; *M. M. R.* 100, figs. 24; 25. See above p. 144.

[213] See above pp. 8 ff.; 110; 125.

the cave[214]. In her domestic shrine the goddess had become a protecting deity, hence her attribute of the snake[215]. This point is of considerable significance not only to an understanding of the developing Greek religion, where the protecting deity *par excellence* was to be Athena, but also to a possible identification of this figure with a particular divine name on the tablets.

The goddess, or perhaps more accurately certain of her aspects, made her mark on Mycenaean and Greek religion, and, apart from the snake, she retained from her past history as goddess of nature, birth and death, some attributes even in her domestic cult to the end of the Bronze Age. Such attributes included her association with the tree[216] and some animals, not all of whom, however, obviously survived into classical times connected with the protecting deity. These, we noticed, were chiefly the bird, bull, ram or goat. To these creatures the goddess stood in a relationship which was more intimate than that suggested by an attribute, symbol, or companion, to deity, for one suspects that the goddess could appear as, or be represented by, any one of these animals on its own in what, for lack of a better term, one might describe as an epiphany[217].

In classical Greece this pronounced relationship of what originally was a nature goddess with her animals survived in popular belief and in myth. The protecting deity, like Athena, did indeed retain a memory of her relation-

---

[214] For the probable transference of cave cult to palace and house sanctuaries see above p. 110; 92.

[215] The snake, though a chthonic creature, was a protector of the house and eventually city, and in historial Greek belief came to be associated with Athena, Zeus Ktesios, and the Dioscuroi. Cf. Herodotus' story in VIII, 41. See also Nilsson, *M. M. R.* 498; *Gesch.* I, 289 f.

[216] Cf. e.g. the bronze tablet from the Psychro cave (prob. L.M. I), Evans, *P. M.* I, 632, fig. 470; cf. Nilsson, *Gesch.* I, Pl. 7, 3; Willetts, *Cretan Cults* 145 f.

[217] Cf. above p. 110 and notes; 125. For the well known function of the bird in this connection see also e.g. Nilsson, *M. M. R.* 330 ff.; *Gesch.* I, 290 ff.; F. Matz, *Göttererscheinung, passim.* For the snake see Nilsson, *M. M. R.* e.g. 332; 340. The association of goddess, bull, and goat, appears predominantly from cave cult where the many finds of bucrania and horns represented the whole animal (cf. Schachermeyr, *D. min. Kultur,* 157): e.g. at Patso, Nilsson, *M. M. R.* 67 (cf. the bucrania and oxe-shaped rhyta discovered in the Psychro cave, *op. cit.* 63, as well as the bronze plaque cited in the previous note), on a cave scene from a sealing from Knossos, Schachermeyr, *op. cit.* fig. 72 d. The bull played a similar role in probably basically related cults such as at Çatal Hüyük, J. Mellaart, *A. S.* e.g. 13 (1963) 52 ff. For the goat see some Knossian sealings reproduced in Matz, *Kreta, Myk., Troja* Pl. 54. By far the best evidence for the part played by the bull and goat in this connection, and the strong hold this kind

ship with the bird and the snake; but at a time of more specially defined functions other great divinities, connected with nature and wild life, had also become involved with zoomorphic cult figures. Of these we are familiar with Artemis and Demeter in particular[218]. Such cult figures became minor and half-forgotten traits in the diversified functions of these great goddesses. In the Bronze Age, however, this association of nature goddess and animals, one suspects, was yet strongly felt in Minoan worship even in the confines of the palace sanctuary. Then, too, we saw, the goddess may have had different names to describe her separate aspects before she found her place in Mycenaean worship. Beside her there was a male companion, or paredros, at once her child and her husband, who was symbolic of the growth and decay of vegetation.

The subject of the so-called "Divine Child" need not again detain us[219], but it conceals two points of vital concern to an understanding of Mycenaean religion. The male child, though he died and was reborn at periodic intervals, obviously was divine: yet there is some body of evidence which brings him close to the figure of the Minoan, and presumably Mycenaean, king, or priest-king, in a tradition that, in all likelihood, travelled West from the Near East in the course of the Bronze Age[220]. If this relationship was a fact, and there is little reason to suppose that it was not, we have another good instance of hazily defined limits in religious thought: where did the borderline lie between divine and mortal? Was the separation as indistinct as we saw in the case of the goddess and her animal? With the exception of Egyptian practice, there is no convincing evidence to prove

of concept had over popular imagination, comes from the memory of Greek myth, where both animals, associated with the "Divine Child", like Zeus and Dionysus, occurred as children both of the goddess and, in the case of e.g. Amaltheia, of the nature goddess herself. Cf. the sealing from Knossos showing the goat as foster mother suckling the babe, Evans, *P. M.* III, fig. 326; cf. Nilsson, *Gesch.* I, 321.

[218] This association is not yet apparent from the Linear B tablets in the case of Demeter and Artemis. While the name of Demeter has not been established on the tablets beyond all reasonably doubt (damate on PY En 609 is still under dispute, M. Ventris / J. Chadwick, *Documents in Mycenaean Greek*, 242; J. Chadwick / L. Baumbach, "The Mycenaean Greek Vocabulary", G. 41 (1963) 184, with further refs.), Artemis (atimite [Dat.], atemito [Gen.]) was not obviously associated with animals (PY Es 650; Un 219. The word aikiwaro, on the first tablet – Ventris / Chadwick, *op. cit.* 127 – probably has nothing to do with the goat). This is a point worth remembering when discussing the early history of the so-called Mistress of Animals.

[219] See above pp. 14 ff.; 88 ff., with the relevant references to modern discussions of the topic.

[220] See above pp. 37 f.

the divinity of the king, or priest-king, in either East or West[221]. Perhaps, then, we should not be too dogmatic in looking for the precise nature of the wanax beside the figure of potnia. The second point consists in the fact that the "Divine Child", like his mother, was equally closely allied to certain animals, and the bull in particular. The best known figures to survive into classical times were the youthful Zeus, shown e.g. as Velchanos in human and bull shape (also associated with the cock) on classical coins from Phaistos and Gortyn[222], and, of course, Dionysus, often tauromorphic in historical times[223], who is a good example of the male child and the companion of a great goddess of nature[224].

Both figures, and their animals, were a primary force in Aegean religious thought of the Bronze Age. Their cult had at one time been observed in cave shrines where it enjoyed a long history, which in the case of the Near Eastern sites, like Çatal Hüyük, probably went back to the Stone Age[225]. They were admitted to domestic cult from as early as M.M.[226], although this did not mean that their worship in caves came to an end at the same time. A more likely explanation is that the domestic form of worship suffered some change, or experienced a special bias, towards the goddess' function as a protectress of the particular abode where she was honoured, and that her relationship with the male figure now had a special significance with respect to the king of the palace that housed the shrine. This remains conjectural at present, but clear is the prominent position in cult the nature goddess enjoyed at the time together with her male companion. This kind of belief should appear in both the monumental and written evidence of the late Minoan and Mycenaean periods, especially when memories survived

---

[221] Cf. above p. 33 n. 155. See also L. A. Stella, *La Civiltà Micenea*, 52, who collects all the references to modern discussions of the subject, *op. cit.* n. 15. Stella, *ibid.*, cites the figure of the Sumerian *lugal* as an interesting example of the mixture of divine and human qualities.

[222] Notice that this temple was built on the ruins of the Hagia Triada palace, Nilsson, *M. M. R.* 464; *Gesch.* I, 323. The coins are reproduced in A. B. Cook, *Zeus*, Cambridge 1914–40, I, 527 ff., figs. 391–400; II, 946, figs. 838–41. Cf. above p. 116 n. 282.

[223] In Thespiae, Elis, etc. see p. 117 n. 284. For the mother and child in human form in cave cult see the L.M. III statuette of a woman and child found in a tomb at Mavro Spelio, E. J. Forsdyke, *B. S. A.* 28 (1926/7) 243; Evans, *P. M.* II, 556 f., fig. 327; cf. above n. 174. Nilsson sees Mycenaean influence here, *M. M. R.* 300; 304 f. Cf. Picard, *Rel. Préh.* 205. See also the L.M. III B vase with a child-bearing woman from Gournia, Desborough, *L. M.* 189.

[224] See above p. 116; 117 n. 285.

[225] See above pp. 94 ff.

[226] See above n. 214.

into Classical and Hellenistic times regarding figures like the Zeus Kretagenes, Dionysus, and others, such as Hyacinthus[227]. Erechtheus, in particular, is a good example of the connection of the male paredros with the Mycenaean king. Erechtheus is a "Nebenform" of Erichthonius whose name and myth class him among the "Divine Children"[228].

The archaeological picture for these figures is there, but, viewed by itself, may not always convince, because some artefacts are open to misinterpretation while others add problems of their own. Female and animal statuettes were ubiquitous votive offerings at Late Bronze Age Cretan and mainland cult sites. But male images were rare[229]. Perhaps, apart from the seals mentioned above[230], we should discover examples of the paredros type on gems, plaques, etc. where an often youthful male figure has been identified with a *Potnios Theron*[231]. Again, archaeology so far remains silent about the fortunes of religious cult after the end of the Mycenaean era. We noticed that, with few exceptions, there is no proof of cult sites, let alone the nature of the cult, enduring beyond this time[232]. Yet, without entering the discussions about the migratory movements in Greece at the end of the Bronze Age, subsequent Greek beliefs and traditions testify to the existence of such a religious continuity, perhaps in modified form in view of Mycenaean architectural developments[233].

Most interesting in connection with what was said above concerning different aspects of the nature goddess and with some later Greek religious traditions are the archaeological finds which point to more than one goddess, or two aspects of the same goddess, associated with the youthful male figure. The best example is the famous Mycenaean ivory group of two women and a boy found in 1939 on the acropolis of Athens, at the site of the Mycenaean palace[234], looking forward perhaps, as Picard supposes, to

---

[227] Cf. his Mycenaean cult at Amyclae, above p. 154; cf. Nilsson, *Gesch.* I, 340, and the festival of Artemis Hyakinthotrophos in Cnidos *SGDI* 3502; 3501; 3512, an epithet which shows Artemis' connection with this type of nature goddes, cf. Nilsson, *Gesch.* I, 317.

[228] See Nilsson, *ibid.* with references. T. B. L. Webster, *From Mycenae to Homer*, 107.

[229] See above p. 150.

[230] See n. 217 above.

[231] Collected by J. Charbonneaux, "Deux grandes fibules géométrique du musée du Louvre", *Préh.* 1 (1932) 226 f. See also the instances cited by Picard, *Rel. Préh.* 80 f.

[232] For Desborough's views see above p. 153.

[233] See above pp. 152 f.; cf. Desborough, *L. M.* 244.

[234] A. Wace, *J. H. S.* 59 (1939) 210, Pl. XIV b, c. The triad is of Minoan workmanship, see e.g. Picard, *Rel. Préh.* 104, but for our purposes it is of little importance whether

the two Eleusinian deities and the young Dionysus *parapaizon*[235]. The problems attaching to the divine plurality, and particularly trinity, will be mentioned again below. At the moment we should merely note that this plurality was a feature of Minoan and Mycenaean cult[236], and that the two goddesses with the young male probably were aspects of the same nature goddess[237] and her paredros[238]. Furthermore, such a concept of divine plurality, or trinity, survived into Greek times[239] where it always fell within the domain of chthonic cult[240], and that type of cult in particular which was associated with deities protecting the house (also chthonic)[241].

To what extent can the written evidence of the Linear B tablets resolve the problems surrounding this all-important cult, or give proof of continuity by linking Mycenaean and Minoan religion with what is known of Greek practices? Regarding the plurality, or trinity, of divine figures the texts are disappointing[242], with the possible exception of the Pylian wana(o)

it belonged to Minoan or Mycenaean cult, see also Vermeule, *Greece in the Br. Age*, 220.

[235] *Rel. Préh.* 104. This interpretation is contested by Nilsson, *M. M. R.* 313 n. 20; XXIV, on rather uncertain grounds.

[236] Cf. e.g. the typical Minoan tripartite shrines, paralleled on the mainland by the similar gold models from Mycenae – *Jahrb.* 30 (1915) 302 ff. (cf. above p. 136), and see the M.M. III – L.M. I chapel at Hagia Triada with separate bases for three idols, Picard, *Rel. Préh.* 109.

[237] Picard, *op. cit.* 183, believes that this triad form developed under the influence of the East.

[238] Fine examples of the part played by the bull in this cult come from Knossos and Tylissos where similar groups of two goddesses, flanking the forepart of a bull, were found. Refs. in Picard, *op. cit.* 104.

[239] It still is somewhat uncertain, however, to what extent we can connect this type of trinity with the well known ones, from archaic times, of Zeus, Hera, Dionysus in Sparta – Orthia's sanctuary –, Delos, Lesbos, Samos, etc., Picard, *Rel. Préh.* 120; 159; 243. Cf. Doro Levi, *P. d. P.* 11 (1956) 294.

[240] Dietrich, *Death, Fate and the Gods* 101 f.; 171.

[241] See the Dioscuroi who formed an ancient trinity with the Minoan figure of Helen in Laconia and Asia, Picard, *op. cit.* 109. Most interesting in this connection are the three goddesses, or three aspects of the same goddess, at Gortyn where the cult paraphernalia – e.g. the kernoi – and monumental remains give evidence of a cult continuing from Minoan to Roman times. The goddess, or trinity, with snake etc. eventually became Athena the Protectress, see Doro Levi, *P. d. P.* 11 (1956) 285–315.

[242] Occasionally different divinities are mentioned together as the recipients of offerings, but there is no evidence of any close cult association between them. Perhaps the word tiriseroe (*triseros*) is relevant here (PY Fr 1204; Tn 316). It is usually identified with Tritopator, B. Hemberg, *Er.* 52 (1954) 172–90; Ventris / Chadwick, *Docs.* 289; Palmer, *Interpretation* 241; 263 ("Clan Ancestor" [?]); cf. Chadwick / Baumbach, *G.* 41 (1963)

soi (e.g. PY Fr 1222; 1219) which could be a dual form of a goddess *anassa*[243]. Such possible identifications apart, the tablets show knowledge of a pantheon which included the general terms *theos, theoi*[244], as well as a number of divine names known from classical Greek religion, although not all of them were destined to be readily admitted to the Olympian family. These names are Poseidon, Zeus, Dionysus, Hermes, Athena, Hera, Artemis[245]. Other divine names, which came to be absorbed by other deities, or which disappeared into popular cult, include Eileithyia (KN Gg 705) at Knossos, Erinys (erinu Kn Fp 1, Fs 390), a Dove Goddess(?) (pere- PY Tn 316), and deities or daemons of the Winds[246].

201; 250, but some doubt still attaches to the exact significance of the word, see e.g. A. Sacconi, *P. d. P.* 16 (1960) 171; Stella, *Civiltà* 248.

[243] Ventr. / Chadw., *Docs.* 411; Chadw. / Baumb., *G.* 41, 172; Palmer, *Minos* 5 (1957) 91; T. *Phil. Soc.* 6 (1958) 20; *Interp.* 249 ff.; Puhvel, *Minoica* 332 f. (also *anasso* = female paredroi of Poseidon at Pylos, Guthrie, *B. I. C.* 6 [1959]). M. Lejeune, *R. Et. A.* 64 (1962) 15, shows, however, that wanasoi could be the loc. dat. plur. of a masc. or neut. derivative of wanax, as well as the dat. dual of wanassa (presupposing an asyndeton on the tablets). Pugliese, again, *P. d. P.* 15 (1959) 410, believes that wanasoi is the name of a festival. We are, alas, some way still from identifying wanasoi with "Demetra, Madre divina e la sua Figlia fanciulla", Stella, *Civiltà* 234.

[244] E.g. PY Eb 297; 704 (teo – acc., dat.), Eb 416, En 609 (gen.), Fr 1226; Fr 1355 (dat. plur. or poss. dual) etc. In Knossos dedications to "all the gods" (pansi theoi'i) are frequent, Ventr. / Chadw., *Docs.* 127; Chadw. / Baumb., *G.* 41, 202 with modern refs. Uncertain is Stella's conjecture, *N.* 5 (1958) 21, that the *theoi* refer only to minor gods on analogy with Babylonian, Hittite, and similar Near Eastern practice. Nor does their presence on the tablets prove or disprove that Mycenaean religion was either matriarchal or not, *P. d. P.* 15 (1959) 259. The Knossos and Pylos tablets are taken together in this survey. There are some local differences between Crete and the mainland (cf. Heubeck, *Frühgr. Lineart.* 99), but we have no means yet of telling to what extent these are due to chance.

[245] Ventr. / Chadw., *Docs.* 125 ff. Ares is never clearly named, although he may be referred to by the name enuwarijo *(Enyalios)* KN V 52, Ventr. / Chadw., *Docs.* 126; Chadw. / Baumb., *G.* 41, 192. The same probably applies to Hephaestus: apaitijo (KN L 588) may refer to a sanctuary or festival, Ventr. / Chadw., *Docs.* 127, Stella, *Civiltà* 246 n. 69. Nor can one yet confidently assert that pajawo- (KN V 52 *Paieon [Paian]* cf. KN Fp. 354) refers to Apollo. Paean as "Götterarzt(?)" originally was an independent figure who perhaps even in Homer was not always fully identified with Apollo, see Nilsson, *Gesch.* I, 543. It is equally interesting to note that Paean was an epithet, or title, of other deities, too. Thus, for example, it appears from the song of Philodamus of Skarpheia *(B. C. H.* 19 (1895) 393 ff.) that Dionysus carried this title when he received sacrifice during the Pythian Games. Cf. Nilsson, *Gr. Feste* 161. Demeter's presence on the tablets is also uncertain, see above n. 218.

[246] Offerings of oil to the priestess of the Winds, anemo ijereja, KN Fpl.; Fpl. 3. If Palmer, *Interpret.* 220, is right, iqojo, on PY Eq. 59, may refer to a god Hippos. On

To return to the positively identified names belonging to the Greek pantheon, we notice that the gods, including Zeus and Hermes, generally share a common trait, that is their connection with chthonic cult. From what has been said above, it is possible to be yet more precise and compare all these gods with the male figure associated with the nature goddess. This is obvious in the case of Dionysus and Zeus. Once Zeus is called Dictaeus on a Knossian tablet[247], a title which, referring to the Dictaean cave and birth place, quite closely defines his function as male paredros. Again, Poseidon, the chief god of Pylos on the tablets, falls into the same group mainly by virtue of his name as husband of Earth[248], by his close association with Potnia and Pylos, and by his identification with the figure, or title, of wanax which extends through Homer to classical Greek cult[249]. These points ally Poseidon with the so-called "Divine Child", and we find further valuable evidence of this alliance on one Knossos tablet (Ma 719) where Poseidon (his epithet Enesidaon) is the recipient of offerings in Eileithyia's cave at Amnisos[250].

Hermes' case is not quite so readily pleaded, partly because of his clearly defined and inferior status in Greek religion. Herodotus called him an ancient "Pelasgian" god[251]. He was a chthonic figure whose cult home was Arcadia where many ancient religious practices survived into historic times[252]. In Mycenaean Greek his name was written *emaa*, without the

---

Iphimedeia (KN 02) see Ventr. / Chadw., *Docs.* 288; on Diwia (diuja: PY An. 607; Cn. 1287; Tn. 316) see *op. cit.* 288; Stella, *Civiltà* 235 f. and 236 n. 33 for further references.

[247] dikatajo diwe receiving oil (KN Fpl.). For modern discussions of this reading see Stella, *op. cit.* 241 n. 55.

[248] *Posis Das*, Kretschmer, G. I (1909) 27 ff.; 14 (1926) 201; 15 (1927) 187; see also Schachermeyr, *Poseidon* 13 f.

[249] Where, together with Zeus, he is the most frequent carrier of the title, see B. Hemberg, *Anax, Anassa und Anakes*, 8; cf. Nilsson, *Gesch.* I, 407. There was a cult of Poseidon Wanax near the Acrocorinth where many clay tablets with this title were found in 1879, see O. H. N. Fowler, "Corinth and Corinthia", *Corinth* 1 (1932) 9; cf. the *anax heros* in Attica at Laciadae, whose name Phytalos connects him with Poseidon, Schachermeyr, *Poseidon* 36; Hemberg, *Anax* 17.

[250] See note 305 below. The evidence does not, however, justify any close analogies between Poseidon's cult and Eastern practice, see especially Palmer, *T. Ph. Soc.* (1958) 7-9; *Interpret.* 258, who makes a comparison between the Greek god and the Sumerian Enki. On this point see also Pugliese, *P. d. P.* 15 (1959) 405.

[251] II, 51.

[252] See Nilsson, *Gesch.* I, 503.

digamma, a point which upset a number of traditional etymologies[253]. Of more immediate interest to us, apart from his ancient cult and chthonic nature, is his probable connection with cave cult. This, quite frankly, it is now impossible to prove, but a hint of his old nature may be concealed in tradition (*Hom. Hymn. to Hermes*), for, like Zeus, he was born in a cave. Hermes' cave was on Mt. Cyllene, Arcadia[254]. We also note here that the youthful Hermes carried the title of anax in Imbros and Ephesus[255].

If all the gods appearing on the tablets can be shown to have been connected with the figure of the male companion of the nature deity, it remains to be seen to what extent the goddesses mentioned fit the picture of such a cult which was transferred from cave shrines to domestic and palace sanctuaries. The names certainly established are Athena, Hera, Artemis and Eileithyia. Now the Greek Athena and, in all likelihood, Hera arose from the figure of the Minoan and Mycenaean "Palastgöttin"[256]. Their attachment to certain animals (snake, bird, and cow[257]) found in the type of cult under discussion in some form survived into historical times. Artemis was no goddess of the palace but the Greek goddess of the wilds, yet she belonged to the same stratum of worship from which, at least in part, the domestic cult of Athena derived. She was a goddess of fertility and vegetation, and as such associated with tree cult[258] as well as closely allied, of course, with the animal world[259]. Also Eileithyia came to be identified with her. Eileithyia was a Minoan figure who received worship in her cave at Amnisos as a goddess of birth, that is exercising one functions within a larger complex of cults

[253] But probably not that of Nilsson, *ibid.*, who derived the name from "cairn" (*erma*), see Chantraine, *R. Phil.* 31 (1958), 244.
[254] The chthonic Hermes Cyllenius occurs once in Homer as Psychopompus, *Od.* 24, 1 ff. Interesting in this connection is Hermes' juxtaposition with the chthonic Moirae in cult, as at Kos – inscr. in A. Maiuri, *Nuova Silloge Epigraphica di Rodi e Cos*, Florence 1925, 452, and in Orphic belief, Dietrich, *Death, Fate* 69.
[255] For references see Hemberg, *Anax* 45 f.
[256] The best discussion of the evidence in Nilsson, *Gesch.* I, 345 ff. Cf. the close association of Athena and Artemis with Mycenaean cult localities and sanctuaries, above p. 154.
[257] Although the significance of Hera's common epithet *boopis* cannot be explained satisfactorily. If W. Pestalozza is right, the title connects her with Oriental types of cow-goddesses and bull-gods, all of whom, according to him, were identifiable with the Mediterranean type of nature goddess, *Ath.* 12 (1939) 105 ff. = *Religione Mediterranea*, 1951, 151 ff. For modern discussions of the etymology of Hera see Dietrich, *Death, Fate* 25 n. 3.
[258] Nilsson, *Gesch.* I, 161; 486 ff.
[259] The *Potnia Theron*, cf. Nilsson, *Gesch.* I, 227.

concerned with the celebration of the annually recurring vegetation cycle[260]. Eileithyia, again, was part of an entire group of similar Minoan goddesses such as Britomartis, Diktynna, Ariadne, and Aphaea, all of whom were absorbed by the Greek nature goddess Artemis.

The functions of all these goddesses, therefore, one must suppose to have been compatible: the spheres of the palace goddess and the chthonic goddess of fertility and birth originally were related. Indeed, Hera's epithet of Eileithyia in Argive cult is a sign of this fact[261]. What we cannot tell from the written evidence is the extent to which all these goddesses had already become departmentalized in the Mycenaean Age along the lines suggested, for example, by Guthrie[262], who proposes that at that time there were three distinct types of goddess 1) an Earth Mother, 2) a Mountain Mother, 3) a Snake and House Goddess. Archaeological remains do not especially support this thesis[263].

More immediate perhaps is the difficulty occasioned by the juxta-position on the tablets of pre-Greek, probably Minoan, and Greek divine names. By the time these were recorded, Cretan deities, who belonged to the type of cult under discussion, evidently had come to meet with, and be absorbed by, similar or, in fact, equivalent Greek figures brought south with them by the Mycenaeans. In the case of the male gods this could apply to all the names[264], while Minoan, or at least Aegean, goddesses seemed to enjoy equal prominence beside Olympian figures. Thus Athena[265], and Eileithyia[266] stand beside Hera[267] and Artemis, whose etymological meaning is still problematical[268], whose nature, however, was Mycenaean Greek[269].

---

[260] See above pp. 87 f.

[261] Hesych, s. v. Εἰληθυίας. The age of this cult is obscure, cf. Nilsson, *Gesch.* I, 432. Cf. Pausanias, V, 3, 2, who tells of a cult of "Mother" Meter Athene at Elis. According to Nilsson, *Gesch.* I, 442 ff., this is a later trait of Athena's nature; but see Schachermeyr, *Poseidon* 19.

[262] *BICS* 6 (1959) 35–46.

[263] The case is particularly hard to prove for an Artemis type Mountain Mother, see Appendix I.

[264] Although "Da" in Poseidon may be Aegean, Schachermeyr, *Poseidon* 123.

[265] For Athena see Kretschmer, G. 11 (1921) 277; Nilsson, *M. M. R.* 419 ff.; *Gesch.* I, 349; Schachermeyr, *op. cit.* 123.

[266] See Persson, *Preh. Relig.* 130; Nilsson, *Gesch.* I, 313.

[267] Probably a Mycenaean goddess, perhaps derived from *heros*, Nilsson, *Gesch.* I, 350; *M. M. R.* 501. With the appearance of *era* on the tablets all etymologies from Ἥρϝα

As a member of the Greek Olympian family Artemis had, like a number of her peers, arrogated a variety of other cults. From the Minoan sphere she assimilated the functions of our nature goddess, or perhaps more probably, her various aspects. This is reflected in Artemis' identification with the now shadowy Minoan figures mentioned above. All these latter figures, and one might well discover that Athena belonged here too, appear to have been invocatory names[270] which presumably described the salient facets of the nature goddess. The Cretan tendency, which incidentally was handed down to the Mycenaean Greeks, to call to their goddess to appear to them (perhaps together with her male companion) may be gathered from the prominent position in the texts of other invocatory names, such as Wanax, Wanassa and Potnia, whose sacred nature is certain from the context[271]. Any discussion of these last three figures, and there has been a great deal, is bound to take into account not only their probable relationship with the other deities mentioned[272] but also their position regarding the type of cult under discussion.

We know from later usage that all three were invocatory names[273]: Wanax and Wanassa signified the King or Lord, and the Queen or Lady. Potnia, too, meant the Lady or Mistress, although the true etymology of the first two is shrouded in mystery equal to that surrounding Athena[274]. The fact that these figures, like Potnia, with obvious appellative names fit the picture of actual deities of cult concerned with vegetation, rebirth etc., is of great significance to their interpretation, and it is one that has to be answered by the modern school of thought which – arguing from the

---

come to an end, see H. Frisk, *Griech. Etymologisches Wörterbuch*, Heidelberg 1960, 642. F. R. Schröder's idea, "Hera", *Gym.* 63 (1956) 57–78, to equate Mycen. *era* with Germ. "Jahr" and call Hera a "Jahresgöttin" is a little adventurous, cf. above n. 257.

[268] Nilsson, *Gesch.* I, 309; cf. Schachermeyr, *Poseidon* 123, who leaves open the question whether Artemis is a Greek or pre-Greek word.

[269] Cf. Nilsson, *Gesch.* I, 307 f.

[270] See Persson, *Preh. Relig.* 127 ff.

[271] Perhaps this custom, mentioned here, explains the usage on the tablets of the general god or gods, see n. 244 above; cf. the Eleusinian *Theos* and *Thea*, Persson, *op. cit.* 150. If true, this need not necessarily conflict with the Homeric concepts and usage of such terms.

[272] For up-to-date bibliographies on Potnia see e.g. Chadw./Baumb., *G.* 41 (1963) 238 f.; Stella, *Civiltà* 228–34, with the relevant notes.

[273] Cf. Stella, "Le Iscrizioni Pilie 1955 nel Quadro della Civiltà Micenea", *P.d.P.* 15 (1959) 258.

[274] See Lejeune, *R. Et. A.* 64 (1962) 11 ff. For a probable etymology of Potnia see Chadwick, *M.* 5 (1957) 123.

tablets alone – believes in e.g. Potnia as a general title applicable to most great goddesses[275]. If this were true, how could we account for the custom which allows the name Potnia to stand more readily with figures like Artemis, Athena, and Demeter, than Themis, for example, or Nemesis, or Hekate?

Discussions of Potnia and of Wanax have enormously multiplied over the last ten years. It would take too long to evaluate the various results arising from them. The searching and detailed studies, however, by scholars like Chadwick, Guthrie, Palmer, Pugliese Carratelli and Lejeune have largely helped to crystallize the religious concepts of which Potnia was part, namely the sphere of our now familiar nature goddess who was concerned with birth and vegetation[276]. Beside her we may now place the related goddess of the palace, so that we can be more precise than e.g. Chadwick who calls Potnia a pre-Greek mother-goddess[277], or Guthrie who describes her as a "universal Mother Goddess"[278]. Most generally the Potnia of the tablets has been identified with Artemis (or Demeter)[279], or with Athena[280], on grounds which do not always appear mutually exclusive. In the light of Bronze Age cult it seems rather more probable that Potnia will fit both Athena and Artemis, and certainly Demeter, should the last name also clearly be found on the tablets. Furthermore, provided we are on the right path in our estimation of contemporary cult practice, the tablets, reflecting Mycenaean thought and custom, well illustrate a point of religious development where our goddess, and presumably her separate aspects, were in the stage of becoming integrated with the figures of particular deities whose names in the course of time were elevated to prominence and entirely independent worship. In other words, the Greek Artemis, for instance, carries with her to her personal functions and cult these traits of a Minoan figure whose

---

[275] Partly from the later usage of Potnia in literature, and partly from the fact that Potnia on the tablets usually is found together with a genitive, adjective, etc. For some of the refs. see Dietrich, *Death, Fate* 102 n. 3.

[276] For bibliographies see e.g. Stella, as cited in n. 272 above, and Palmer, *Interpret.* 381–402. Cf. already Picard, *Rel. Préh.* 78. Perhaps, therefore, Potnia can be identified with the Divine Mother (matere teija) from PY Fr. 1202, see E. L. Bennett, *The Olive Oil Tablets of Pylos*, 26 f.; Guthrie, *BICS* 6 (1959) 40.

[277] *M.* 5 (1957) 123.

[278] *Op. cit.* 39.

[279] E.g. Chadwick, *op. cit.* 122 ff.; Stella, *N.* 5 (1958) 31 ff. In *Civiltà* 228, Stella inclines more to an identification with Athena; Palmer, *T. Ph. Soc.* (1958) 9 f.; *Interpretation* 250.

[280] E.g. Pugliese Carratelli, *P. d. P.* 15 (1959) 415.

history came to be lost in myth. On the Mycenaean tablets we find her and Athena side by side, as it were, with the names of Potnia and Wanassa[281], showing thereby quite plainly that the process of integration was already in being in the thirteenth century B.C., although we can only guess at the extent of cultic departmentalization at that time. On the tablets there are still hints of Potnia's nature which echo a) her general association with nature cult, b) her connection with animals like the bull (perhaps even the goat), and c) her functions in house cult.

On PY An 1281 Potnia has the epithet Hippeia (potinija iqeja)[282]. Other evidence from Knossos speaks of animals belonging to Potnia's sanctuary[283]. More exciting is the mention of the goddess, together with bucrania, on decorated jugs described on tablets in the Pylos Ta series[284]. Here Wanassa's association with the bull[285] agrees with the impression we formed of the goddess and her paredros worshipped in caves and eventually in domestic sanctuaries. We also recall the frequent juxtaposition of goddess male companion and bull in plastic art, as for instance in the groups found at Knossos and Tylissos[286]. Potnia's connection with the city, on the other hand, and particularly with the palace within it, also plainly emerges from the texts. In Pylos she was, in Palmer's words, the chief goddess of the city[287]. There

---

[281] Potnia and Wanassa on the tablets most likely describe identical deities, or possibly two aspects of the same deity, rather like the Cretan figures Britomartis and Diktynna – see Persson, *Preh. Rel.* 128; Nilsson, *M. M. R.* 510 f. Like Potnia, Wanassa on the tablets and in Homer exclusively belonged to cult vocabulary – Lejeune, *R. Et. A.* 64 (1962) 15 – but became secularized in subsequent literary usage, although it predominantly remained the title of Athena and Artemis – Hemberg, *Anax* 7–12; Puhvel, *Minoica* 332. Interesting in this connection is a second century B. C. notice from Perge, according to which Artemis was still revered there with the epithet Wanassa, together with her youthful male paredros (Adonis), see Hemberg, *op. cit.* 20. The tablets do not, in fact, offer any clear objections to this interpretation, since the meaning of forms like wanasoi, wanasso is undecided, see above n. 243, and especially Lejeune, *R. Et. A.* (1962) 11–15, and Chadw. / Baumb., G. (1963) 172 for further literature.

[282] Palmer, *Interpret.* 226; *Mycen. and Minoans* 110; 148; Pugliese, *P. d. P.* (1959) 415.

[283] KN G 280 = Ventr. / Chadw., *Docs.* 90; DZ 930; DZ 943 = Ventr. / Chadw., *Docs.* 73; DZ 946; cf. Pugliese, *P. d. P.* (1959) 415.

[284] PY Ta. 711; Ventr. / Chadw., *Docs.* 332 ff.; Palmer, *Interpret.* 340.

[285] For the adjectival form wanasewija see Lejeune, *R. Et. A.* (1962) 16 ff.

[286] See e.g. Picard, *Rel. Préh.* 104; 109; 114; 245. The goat, the other animal which was identified with our goddess, does appear on the tablets but never obviously associated with Potnia or Wanassa. Once perhaps, also in the Ta Series (Ta. 641), we may have a description of tripods decorated with "goat-handles" Or "goat-head" protomes, Palmer, *Interpret.* 343 f.

[287] E.g. *T. Ph. Soc.* (1958) 34.

apparently she had a shrine at Pakijane(s)[288], a religious site or sanctuary most likely attached to the palace[289]. Again, if Palmer's reading of dapuritojo potinija = Λαβυρίνθοιο πότνια on the Knossos tablet Gg 702 is correct[290], then we have written evidence that the palace was Potnia's home in other cities beside Pylos.

In fact, Potnia, and probably Wanassa, in the Mycenaean texts comes closest to the figure which can, from archaeological evidence, be shown to have held a predominant position in Cretan cave cult, and in Cretan as well as in Mycenaean domestic cult. Her image in the texts is perhaps not very sharp but the descriptive genitives and adjectives attached to her name will, when fully interpreted, no doubt explain in greater detail her already diversifying functions which should nevertheless still betray their original ties with earlier cult. Potnia, then, was a goddess in her own right. She was the Lady or Mistress who was, most probably in various forms or aspects, worshipped in Crete as the most important cultic figure from the beginning of the Minoan period. Thence she also found a home in the Mycenaean palace. At this time, we suspect, she yet was intimately bound up with her animals, especially the bull, and with her male companion. The latter has, of course, been recognized by Palmer in the figure of the Wanax, the King, who appears beside the goddess on Pylian tablets[291]. Potnia, however, was not the same as the general Eastern Mother Goddess[292], but more specifically she corresponded to the developed figure in Minoan cult whose functions included the provinces of birth and death, who was associated, or even identified, with her animals[293], who furthermore had her cult in caves whence it was transferred, probably some time during M.M., to domestic or palace sanctuaries[294].

From what is known of Minoan and Mycenaean cult practice the Wanax fits the part of the male companion as well as one can expect from the avail-

---

[288] Palmer, *Interpret.* 83; 192; 231.
[289] *Op. cit.* 267 f.; Pugliese, *P. d. P.* (1959) 416. Apart from Pakijane(s), the Pylos tablets also mention a Posidaion, probably the cult locality in honour of its chief god. It seems, however, that the Posidaion was located in the *wastu*, that is away from the palace, Palmer, *ibid.*
[290] *Op. cit.* 238.
[291] E.g. PY Un. 219 (on this tablet *anakate* is marked as a doubtful reading by Chadw./ Baumb., G. (1963) 172, because of the absence of w-), Palmer, *Interpret.* e.g. 83; 249; 267; *Mycen. Min.* 133 f.
[292] Palmer, *Myc. Min.* 135.
[293] It is quite possible that the bull and male child were thought of as interchangeable.
[294] See above n. 214.

able evidence. Nevertheless not everyone is prepared to accept this interpretation, mainly because of the ambivalence between divine and human nature in the usage of wanax on the Linear B tablets and in literature[295], and because, until now, there has been no satisfactory or convincing explanation of the relationship between the wanax and lawagetas on one hand[296], and that between the wanax and basileus on the other[297]. However, the double standard, so to speak, of wanax on the tablets from our earlier discussion appears to coincide with the ambiguous nature of the male consort in Minoan and, if we are right, in Mycenaean religious thought[298].

In support of the identity of the wanax and the paredros in the goddess' cult we expect to find further corroborating evidence which points e.g. to wanax' chthonic and, if possible, youthful nature, as well as to his close association with domestic and palace cult in such a way that with his goddess he reflects the development of a vegetation cult, primarily concerned with birth and death, to a cult devoted to the protection of the palace where it was housed. Beyond indicating the close connection of Potnia and Wanax

---

[295] See e.g. Hemberg, *Anax* 42; Lejeune, *R. Et. A.* (1962) 14; Guthrie, *B. I. C. S.* (1959) 42.

[296] See e.g. Lejeune, *op. cit.* 18; Pugliese, *P. d. P.* (1959) 420.

[297] On the tablets the lower rank and secular nature of basileus seem clear – e.g. Pugliese, *op. cit.* 429 f. –. Yet in later usage this distinction is occasionally blurred. Puhvel, for example, *Minoica* 329, argues that in Homer basileus and wanax were interchangeable titles. However, according to G. Calhoun, *T. A. P. A.* 66 (1935) 4, the gods in Homer were never addressed as basileis. Thus there seems to be a clear distinction between wanax and basileus on the level of their mortal or immortal nature. But later usage is not entirely unambiguous even in this respect, when we consider the figure of the *archon basileus* in Athens and the part played by his wife, the *basilinna*, in the *Hieros Gamos* during the Choes – L. Deubner, *Attische Feste*, 100. Also contrary to a clear division of the two words is the juxtaposition of basileus and wanax in the dynastic terminology which, according to Aristotle (fr. 526 [Rose]), obtained in fourth century Cyprus, cf. Pugliese, *P. d. P.* (1959) 431. Puhvel, *Minoica* 328 f., speaks of basileus as a local pre-Hellenic ruler who became the vassal of the Helladic wanax. He also sets out a theory, following which Homer knew of two kinds of kingship: 1) a hereditary ruler, like Agamemnon, who was given his kingship by Zeus, and 2) a ruler who stood in a special relationship with the Minoan snake or palace goddess like Odysseus and Athena. The latter kingship is said to have been founded on a purely religious concept of royal power. On the position of the wanax and basileus, and the former's change during the Dark Age to the basileus, see Webster, *Mycen. to Homer* 11; 143.

[298] Palmer, *Interpret.* 267 n. 2, in this connection cites an interesting sentence from Guthrie (F. M. Cornford, *Principium Sapientiae*, Cambridge 1952, 257): "One, at least, if not only, starting point of anthropomorphism is the divine man, the king who also represents the god."

in Pylos[299], and the latter's divine as well as royal nature, the tablets do not really help in this search[300]. For more information we are obliged to go to literary and especially later cult usage.

As often in this respect, Homer is a difficult authority to use. While he has numerous echoes of popular religious belief, it is a complicated process to isolate these without the help of external sources, because often religious thought had been adapted to serve the literary needs of the poem. Thus, as in the case of Potnia, the usage of wanax in the *Iliad* and *Odyssey* becomes more diffuse[301], thereby setting an example to be followed in post-Homeric literature. Yet we notice that, beside Apollo, the divinities in Homer most frequently to carry the title of wanax were Poseidon and Zeus. Of greatest value to us, however, are the Homeric researches which, some thirty and more years ago, discovered that the Homeric wanax "designated a man in his relation to property, treasures, domestic animals etc.", and that the title meant not only King, but specifically "Beschirmer" or "Schützer"[302].

The usage of wanax after Homer has been concisely classified by Lejeune[303] under three headings: wanax appears 1) in epic heritage poetry, 2) in traditional epithets belonging to certain divinities, notably the Dioscuroi and Kabiroi, 3) in Cypriot official titles[304]. Of these three groups the connection of wanax with the Dioscuroi is of the greatest moment with reference, in fact, to all three areas where we hope to gather evidence about wanax' nature. His chthonic associations are vividly portrayed by his close affinity with Poseidon who carried the title as "Herr der Unterwelt"[305].

---

[299] See above n. 291.
[300] For the usage of wanax, and related forms, on the tablets see Ventr./Chadw., *Docs.* 411; Palmer, *Interpret.* 461; Chadw./Baumb., G. (1963) 172.
[301] See Hemberg, *Anax* 7 ff.
[302] See Calhoun, *T. A. P. A.* 66 (1935) 4; C. Angermann, *Zur griech. Etymologie und Wortbildung*, 1870, 120 ff., cited by Hemberg, *Anax* 8 and n. 7.
[303] *R. Et. A.* (1962) 11.
[304] See n. 297 above.
[305] See Schachermeyr, *Poseidon* 31; 36; n. 71, who follows L. Malten, "Das Pferd im Totenglauben", *Jahrb.* 29 (1914) 193, who generally describes wanax as a chthonic title. Cf. U. v. Wilamovitz-Möllendorff, "Über die ionische Wanderung", *Sitzb.* (1906) 66: "Dieser Name (Wanax) bezeichnet immer den Herrn der Unterwelt." Cf. Hemberg, *Anax* 17 f. A further pointer to the chthonic nature of Poseidon Wanax (see n. 249 above) comes from the title *enesidaone* which the god carries on Knossian tablets, e.g. Ma. 719; Gg. 704(?), Ventr./Chadw., *Docs.* 309; Palmer, *Interpret.* 302; Stella, *Civiltà* 237. *Enesidaone* recalls *Ennosidas* (Pindar), *Ennosigaios*, *Enosichthon* (Homer, *Il.* 13, 34; 7, 445), cf. Ventr./Chadw., *Docs.* 309. Ma. 719, where *Enesidaon*'s offerings are given up in the Amnisos cave, connecting him there with Eileithyia's cult – cf. Palmer,

They also appear from later cult practice, as well as from the use of wanax to describe figures like the Dioscuroi[306]. The basic meaning of Protector, inherent in wanax, beside that of Lord and Master, and his connection with domestic and vegetation religion, by virtue of his chthonic nature, probably never died out in the sphere of cult. In the same tradition wanax (and wanassa) in literature remained apt epithets of those deities who, with the possible exception of Apollo, originally were concerned with vegetation and house cult[307].

There is, however, some archaeological and written evidence which knows of occasionally pre-Hellenic cults (mainly in central Greece), at whose centre there were plural figures of anaktes or anakes. Such cults, despite much obvious contamination, constitute useful source material for the interpretation of wanax in Minoan and Mycenaean religion. This evidence has been examined in a detailed study by Hemberg[308] whose results show that in the majority of instances, when identifiable, the carriers of this title were the Dioscuroi or related figures[309]. Plurality in these cases often signified two or three figures[310] with whom a goddess was generally associated[311]. The Dioscuroi, like the similar Kouretes, Korybantes, Kabiroi, and Daktyloi, played an important part in Greek popular religion, and they deserve a separate treatment which we cannot entertain here. What is known of their cult – such figures tended to receive private rather than public worship[312] – both appears to make anakes a suitable title for them and serves to substantiate the picture we have formed of the Mycenaean wanax.

In tradition Helen was the sister of the Dioscuroi. But originally she was a Cretan figure. Therefore, and because all three were connected with tree cult[313], the Dioscuroi, like the Kouretes[314], probably had been part of Minoan

    ibid. –, is, of course, an invaluable indication of this god's association with the goddess of vegetation, birth (and death) in cave cult, cf. the discussion of Poseidon above p. 177.

[306] See e.g. Hom. *Il.* 3, 243 f.; *Od.* 11, 300 f.
[307] Cf. Hemberg, *Anax* 45.
[308] *Op. cit.* 14–44.
[309] *Op. cit.* 47 n. 1. See also Pugliese, *P. d. P.* (1959) 410, and cf. Puhvel, *Minoica* 331 f.
[310] Hemberg, *Anax* 46.
[311] *Ibid.*: "Die Mehrzahl dieser Kulte (with reference to wanax) läßt im Hintergrunde eine Göttin entdecken."
[312] See Nilsson, *Gr. Feste* 419; 422.
[313] Cf. n. 241; see Nilsson, *Gr. Feste* 418; *Gesch.* I, 315.
[314] Their part in the myth of Zeus Kretagenes is well known. Their name is closely bound up with Cretan religion, Nilsson, *M. M. R.* 543 f. In Apollodorus, *Bibl.* 3, 3 ff., they are also made to take a part in Glaucus' resurrection; cf. Picard, *Rel. Préh.* 117.

religion[315]. In Greece, either on their own or when identified with the Anakes[316], the Dioskuroi were thought of as children[317]. They were, in fact, "göttliche Kinder", children-gods, who were named either Anaktes or simply the sons of Zeus, the *Dios kouroi*[318].

These children, or youthful gods[319], were attached to house cult[320]. They had, in fact, clear links with Minoan house cult and the goddesses revered there. As house and chthonic deities their animal was the snake[321], and one of their common symbols consisted of two amphoras surrounded by snakes in such a way that they resembled the famous tube-shaped vessels which belonged to the cult inventory of the Minoan snake and palace goddess[322]. The close association of these child gods with the palace goddess has in some modern discussions earned them the description of the assessors of the Minoan goddess[323]. This association they continued into historic times when they had a cult in Brasiae, for instance, together with Athena[324].

On the mainland their cult seems to have centred in Laconia, and in Sparta in particular[325], where, yet as central figures in house cult, they

---

[315] F. Chapouthier, *Les Dioscures au service d'une déesse*, Paris 1935, denies that the Dioskuroi were originally Minoan figures. This does not, however, apply to the child gods, anakes, concealed behind the name of Dioskuroi.

[316] *anake*, Hemberg, *Anax* 34, in Athens.

[317] In Lerna, Epidaurus, and Argos; cf. the *Anaktes Paides* at Amphissa whom Pausanias, X, 38, 7, equates with the Dioskuroi, the Kuretes or the Kabiroi.

[318] For Nilsson's thesis, regarding their early history and how they came to be identified with Zeus, see *M. M. R.* 542. On the other *kouroi*, the Kuretes, and attendants of Zeus, see *op. cit.* 543 ff.

[319] Cf. their foot-high images in Pephnos, Paus. III, 26, 3, and the three small images of them in Brasiae, Paus. III, 24, 5.

[320] Nilsson, *Gr. Feste* 419.

[321] Their connection with horses, in all likelihood, was a later development, Nilsson, *M. M. R.* 541.

[322] Cf. Nilsson, *ibid.* Picard, *Rel. Préh.* 196; 198, connects the Dioskuroi house gods with the many pillars in the Cretan palaces which seem to have possessed more than a structural significance.

[323] See Picard, *op. cit.* 113; 159.

[324] Pausanias, III, 24, 5, describes three small pictures beside one of Athena. He identifies the children with the Dioskuroi or Kabiroi. Cf. Nilsson, *Gr. Feste* 418 n. 2; "Kabiren waren sie sicherlich nicht." In Tomi the Dioskuroi, as saviours of the city, received, together with the Mother of the Gods, an annual sacrifice, *Öst. M.* 14 (1891) 22 ff., No. 50, 35 ff. Cf. the Mysteries in Samothrace in honour of the related Kuretes or Kabiroi – Strabo, 10, 472 – and the Mother Goddess, see also Nilsson, *Feste* 399 f.

[325] Nilsson, *Gr. Feste* 417.

became the protectors of the Spartan kings[326]. Their other common representation, the *dokana*[327] entwined on either side with snakes, which appears on a number of Spartan monuments and reliefs[328], symbolically expressed the Dioskuroi's spirit as house and protecting deities. And it is remarkable to observe that these figures, whose original sphere of interest was so closely interwoven with that of the palace goddess, did also share with her the same development, for, like Athena, from deities concerned with the safety of one house or palace they saw their functions extended so that they became warrior-gods and protectors of the entire city[329]. Thus the chthonic nature of the Dioskuroi, the fact that they were imagined as children[330], and their affinity with house cult and the house goddess[331], explain their identification with the figure of the wanax, the Lord and Protector, for this is a later step whose date can no longer be determined[332].

It is, of course, not our present concern to attempt to isolate the early history of the Dioskuroi beyond the evidence their cults can furnish towards an understanding of the wanax. We note here, however, that the fate of the Dioskuroi, as the youthful house gods, brought them close to some aspects of Zeus which made him one with the Cretan "Divine Child". The Dioskuroi, the Sons of Zeus, whatever figures of prehistoric cult they represented, were drawn into the realm of the Indo-European Zeus[333] in the same, at present rather mysterious, way as the Kouretes who helped to prevent the discovery of Zeus the infant in his Cretan cave. This is obvious in the field of private house cult where Zeus, with the epithets of Ktesios, Philios, or

[326] Nilsson, *M. M. R.* 541. As house gods the form of worship or sacrifice which would most please the Dioskuroi are *theoxenia*, often celebrated in their honour, Nilsson, *Gr. Feste* 418 f.; and it is interesting that this kind of festival may well be mentioned on the Pylos Oil Tablets together with Potnia: Fr 1231 – potinija dipi [si] joi kenesiwijo. See also above n. 201.

[327] ἔστι δὲ δύο ξύλα παράλληλα δυσὶ πλαγίοις ἐπεζευγμένα, Plutarch, *de frat. am.* 478 A.

[328] Cf. the fifth century relief reproduced in Nilsson, *Gesch.* I, Pl. 29, 4.

[329] Cf. Nilsson, *Gesch.* I, 410.

[330] Sometimes they were shown in swaddling clothes, Nilsson, *M. M. R.* 541.

[331] Dörpfeld, in the course of his excavations at Olympia, brought some evidence to light which also appears to connect child gods (the Kuretes) with cave cult. At the foot of the hill Kronion, in the "Idaean Grotto", there was practised a cult in honour of Sosipolis (child and snake god), the Kuretes and Daktyles. For refs. see Picard, *Rel. Préh.* 208.

[332] Cf. Hemberg, *Anax* 47: "Dass Anakes von Anfang an nur die Dioskuren bezeichnete, ist völlig ausgeschlossen."

[333] For Nilsson's explanation, that the Sons of Zeus represented the many child god cults which Zeus had absorbed in Greece, see *M. M. R.* 542.

Meilichios – in the form of a snake –, performed essentially the same functions as the Sons of Zeus[334]. How it came about that Zeus and his sons were identified with this type of cult we do not know, we may nonetheless assume that their names covered other figures whose worship reached back to Minoan and Mycenaean religion where they had a place in the most important cult of the palace and, perhaps, city: that of the male child beside the goddess of nature and birth in particular.

From all the varied evidence we may safely suppose that these figures answered to the invocatory title of Wanax and Potnia or Wanassa. The Lord and Mistress survived, as we saw, the post-Mycenaean Dark Age, but the same cannot be said of the cult originally associated with them. Their greatest impact always was to be on popular cult, while literature was inclined to ignore their kind of worship; and for this perhaps we must blame the influence of Homer, because no deity was readily admitted to Mt. Olympus and official cult, unless he or she, like Athena, Hera, and Artemis, first cast off her affiliation with chthonic ritual and nature religion. The wanax, the chthonic divine child in Greek religion, went underground, as it were, he belonged to popular worship. The figure of Potnia, on the other hand, suffered considerable change. She became departmentalized and, as chief goddess of the city – also representing or watching over numerous activities ranging from war to the daily work of the society within it –, or as Mistress of Animals, found a place in the foremost ranks of the Olympian family. Such changes notwithstanding, some chthonic aspects Potnia retained, and these, too, were submerged in that sphere of popular cult which normally fell within the province of Demeter.

The picture, then, we have drawn of the goddess and her male companion and of their cult, which began at least in Minoan and Mycenaean times, seems reasonably lucid. Our knowledge, however, of the early Greek period is not so firmly grounded that we can close our account without raising yet larger problems which, on our present evidence, defy solution. The child-gods, who in classical times were identified with the Anaktes, generally occurred as two, three, in number, or sometimes loosely in the plural. This multiplication was not an uncommon feature of popular belief in chthonic beings. Therefore it hardly surprises to discover that the chthonic aspects of Potnia, too, when worshipped in Greek cult, appeared in the

---

[334] See e.g. Nilsson, *Gesch.* I, 403 f.; 414; 416 and n. 1. See also the interesting account in J. Harrison, *Prolegomena* 13–28; 355 f. Picard, *Rel. Préh.* 113, supposes that Zeus Ktesios was the successor of the Kretagenes.

plural number[335]. The Anaktes and Potniae shared this feature with a great many other figures of the same ambience, some of whom had in the course of time declined from important positions in local cult. Many such figures have been classified, not always accurately, under the large headings of daemons and heroes, and they all have in common their ultimate beginning in chthonic cult[336].

The part played by the Potniae in Greek religion has been fully discussed elsewhere[337], and it appeared that they were similar to plural cult figures like the Erinyes, Eumenides, and Semnae[338], and that all of them were closely allied with the Eleusinian Demeter. Chthonic figures in Greek thought – and the Moirae, too, fall under this heading – often received worship as dualities, trinities, or in plural number[339]. One could suppose, therefore, that this multiplication of beings of lesser import in Greek cult constituted a later development, were it not for some Bronze Age archaeological remains depicting several deities side by side[340], as well as for some hints[341] of similar groups of two or three on the Linear B tablets. Such evidence[342] speaks of older traditions than one has suspected.

Perhaps here we are dealing with different aspects of our nature goddess, and this seems most likely. The question must remain open, however, at least until we can satisfactorily explain the collective gods in Mycenaean religion and their relationship with the named gods including the figures of wanax, wanassa, and potnia. To solve this problem would be to illumine one of the deepest shadows which at present obscures the development of early Greek religion.

---

[335] Cf. Chadwick, *M.* 5 (1957) 122 f.

[336] There are at least two interesting notices connecting, in historical times, the Anax or Anaktes with a hero. In Athens, for example, the Dioskuroi had the same priest as the *heros epitegios*, cf. Hemberg, *Anax* 35. In Laciadae (Attica) Pausanias mentions the figure of the *anax heros Phytalos*, cf. above n. 249.

[337] Dietrich, *Death, Fate* 100 ff.

[338] Cf. H. Usener, *Götternamen*, Bonn 1896, 225: "Wir ahnen, dass hinter den beiden eleusinischen gottheiten und den Eumeniden der ungetheilte begriff der Πότνιαι steht, die mit jüngerem namen zu Athen als Σεμναί ... verehrt wurden."

[339] Dietrich, *op. cit.* 89 f. We may add to this group the two Smyrnaean Nemeseis, *op. cit.* 170 f.

[340] Two female figures and one male child, or two male figures, together with a goddess.

[341] See above n. 242; 243.

[342] Some in Picard, *Rel. Préh.* 113; 159; 193 f. Cf. above pp. 174 f. and see n. 229.

IV. THE PROBLEM OF CONTINUITY IN THE DARK AGE

The Greek Dark Age embraces the period from the end of the Mycenaean, about 1100 B.C., until the beginning of the Archaic Age, very roughly about 650 B.C. These four hundred and fifty years mark the period least known and understood by modern historians. Towards the end of the second millennium the brilliant Mycenaean culture decayed and there ensued a prolonged era of poverty and darkness from which eventually emerged a people in the ferment of social and political revolution that gave form to the classical Greek age. What occurred in the interval is as little known as the forces which caused a renewed "Sturm und Drang", a fresh artistic and political drive in the Greek peoples of the mainland. Perhaps the turning point came as early as the eighth century when the forerunners of the monumental temples began to rise throughout the Greek world, when life-size sculptures of the gods and goddesses were fashioned to be set up in the new divine houses.

Perhaps this was the time when the Greeks, awaking from the somnolence of some centuries, became conscious of their heritage, devised myths concerning the Bronze Age heroes, or instituted hero cults about the tomb of some forgotten Mycenaean king or nobleman. "It is time", says Chester Starr, "we gave over interpreting human development as a slow evolution of Darwinian type; great changes often occur in veritable jumps."[1]

Much new development in social institutions, reflecting the changes in artistic forms, undoubtedly took place from the eighth century. But we have no means of telling the weight of inherited tradition which went into such changes. In other words, there is no infallible guide to separate the new from the old Archaic Greek institutions. This particularly applies, as we shall see, to religion where older ideas regarding the dates of temple construction and divine sculpture will have to be revised in the light of new archaeological discovery. One major cause which is sometimes said to

---

[1] C. G. Starr, *The Origins*, XII.

have contributed to the Greek Dark Age is the loss of the skill of writing. Quite probably only a few Mycenaeans knew how to use the linear script, and they might have taken their knowledge with them to the grave at the end of the Mycenaean Age. The fact that there are no extant written records during the intervening period until the adoption of the Phoenician alphabet in the eighth century seems to suggest that the Greek world reverted to illiteracy for some hundreds of years. Whether or not the wilful abandonment of such a basic skill is a reasonable supposition, there is another possible answer to the lack of records. That is that chance, or the workings of time, destroyed writing materials which were not as durable as the baked clay tablets of Pylos or Knossos.

The sealed tablet (*pinax pyktos*) containing Bellerophon's death warrant was not of clay. The famous story was first told, if Webster is right[2], in the fourteenth century. The Mycenaean origin of the myth is further reflected in the relationship between Bellerophon's grandson Glaukos and Diomede who meet before Troy in the *Iliad*. Is it possible though that Proitos' *semata lygra* survived in a strong mythological tradition[3] which was handed down by people who could not write? There are other more obvious difficulties. One will find it hard to believe that the early Greek form of writing survived in Cyprus, for example, in unbroken continuity, or persisted as a script in parts of Eastern Crete, but disappeared on the mainland without a trace[4].

The case regarding the practice of writing during the Dark Age is far from closed. It seems, in fact, that this so-called Dark Age is largely of our own making, that we deny to the Greek world a continued knowledge of the past and a certain kind of natural development because of our ignorance of events immediately after the Bronze Age. We are here concerned primarily with religious beliefs and ritual which owing to their conservative persistence are perhaps easier to trace than political circumstances. These observations are not meant to explain away a number of

---

[2] T. B. L. Webster, *From Mycenae to Homer*[2], 25; 117.

[3] It did not find its final form probably before the eighth century. Cf. J. Wiesner, *Olympos*, 127. T. J. Dunbabin, *Studs. Rob.* II, 1179, believes that Corinth claimed Bellerophon as her own in the eighth century.

[4] On this point see also A. J. B. Wace, *Mycenae*, and A. Severyns, *Grèce et Proche-Orient avant Homère*, 200 f. An opposed view can be found in J. Chadwick, "The Greek Dialect and Grk. Pre-History", *G.R.* 3 (1956) 49 n. 1, now in *Language and Background of Homer*, 117 n. 1. Cf. I. G. Nixon, *The Rise of the Dorians*, London 1968, 5 f.

more or less drastic changes which evidently marked the turn of the millennium. To attempt such would be foolhardy. We should not, however, overlook the possibility that changes may have come about from within, that is, that they represented an organic development rather than revolutionary innovations imposed by outside alien forces. The support for such a supposition obviously must come from an appreciation of historic events at the end of the Bronze Age.

Unfortunately nothing precise emerges from an examination of the often confusing evidence of the period. Certainly there is no compelling reason to assume that the end of the Bronze Age marked a clean break in every department of Greek culture. The main sources of information consist of oral tradition recorded by classical Greek historians, of linguistic evidence, which seems to bear out the results of the former, and of the interpretation of archaeological material. The turning point in the fortunes of the prosperous but possibly over-extended Mycenaean empire historians believe to have been the Trojan War. The prolonged absence of the Mycenaean nobles caused strife and revolt at home[5]. Many heroes returning home found their affairs in disorder[6]. On the mainland military activity, reflected in the Linear B tablets and in added fortifications to cities at the time, describe a period of nervousness which was contemporary with, and in some instances antedated, the traditional date of the Trojan War. New walls were built, old fortifications were strengthened at Mycenae, Tiryns, and Athens. A wall, constructed across the Isthmus of Corinth, makes clear that not only domestic difficulties were anticipated, but invasion from the north had become a real threat[7]. Tradition, in fact, as well as some archaeological remains apparently record the arrival of invaders who broke through to the Peloponnese, put the weakened Mycenaean civilization to the torch and presumably imposed their own more primitive culture on the old. These invaders are usually identified with the Dorians, who were connected with the mythical sons of the Heraclidae. But we shall see below how little such people affected Greek culture.

On the face of it, it would appear that events at the time progressed in an historically orderly manner. The flourishing Bronze Age came to an abrupt halt on the arrival of the newcomers who, together with the palaces, effectively crushed the theocratic administration under the protection of

---

[5] Cf. Desborough, *L.M.* 223.
[6] Cf. F. H. Stubbings, *C.A.H.*², ch. XXVII, II, 16.
[7] Stubbings, *op. cit.* 14.

the city gods. The foreign lords brought their own system of government, their religious festivals[8] and in short, making a clean break with what had gone before, introduced a new era recognizable by changed modes of burial and novel art forms. The simplicity of this arrangement is deceptive and conceals some major flaws of which timing is the most serious. It soon becomes obvious, even after a cursory study of the evidence, that there was no single attack or southward migratory movement which swept all before it in the Peloponnese. The Dorians indeed are an elusive people. Their language was Greek, like that of the Achaeans, with whom their fortunes were intricately interwoven through e.g. the Delphic myth of Deucalion and, of course, through their connection with Heracles' family. Both myths most likely were of Mycenaean origin[9], so that, for example, Heracles' connection with the Dorians was not a wilful fabrication made in Archaic times by Greeks who wanted to integrate Achaeans and Dorians in one common heritage[10]. Troubling, too, are the two Homeric references to a pre-Trojan War Dorian presence in Crete[11] and in Rhodes[12].

The massive evidence from the major Mycenaean sites, so painstakingly gathered by archaeologists, shows quite plainly that the mainland was not subject to one unique invasion at the end of the Bronze Age, but that several stages of attack, from within or without, and destruction were involved covering a considerable period of time over more than a century. In the case of the famous city of Mycenae alone, disaster came in three separate waves which extended from some time in L.H. III B until about the end of L.H. III C[13]. Again some sites, like Pylos in Messene, were deserted after destruction; others, like Tiryns in the Argolid, or Amyclae in Laconia, or further north Iolkos in Thessaly, continued to be settled. Others again, like Athens, were left untouched. The chief moral to be drawn from such information is not that there were no intrusive elements in the Greek world of the Late Bronze Age, but that these infiltrated the scene rather than burst upon it, and that over a longish period they assimilated with the native Achaeans. Such conclusions, of course, are of great

---

[8] A. Andrewes, *The Greeks*, 34.
[9] Cf. e.g. Wiesner, *Olymp.* 104; 138; M. P. Nilsson, *The Mycen. Origin of Greek Mythology*, 187 ff.; Webster, *Mycen.* 104; 125.
[10] This is the usual interpretation of Heracles' Dorian ties, e.g. Desb., *L. M.* 247.
[11] *Od.* 19, 177.
[12] *Il.* 2, 653 ff.
[13] Desb., *L.M.* 73 ff. This is questioned by G. E. Mylonas, *Hesp.* 33 (1964) 376 ff.

moment to a consideration of continued cultural and particularly religious forms.

If we examine the three major sources of information for the disturbances at the end of the Bronze Age – traditional, linguistic and archaeological mentioned above – we do find a history of popular movements and conflict which reflect the upheavals throughout much of the Mediterranean at the time. The beginning of the end in Mycenaean Greece was usually connected with the Trojan War. And the sack of Troy, according to the one traditional date, among many, which does not clash with archaeological data, was about 1250 B.C.[14], a time which also agrees with Hittite written records of Achaean activity in that part of the world[15]. It is highly probable, however, that the war about Troy VII A was not the only occasion of Mycenaean attack, and that the importance of that particular siege was exaggerated by Homeric epic, so that there would be little cause to connect – except by purely chronological coincidence – the disasters on the mainland with it, or even believe that the Mycenaeans in this over ambitious undertaking sapped their strength and opened the way to warlike invaders at home[16].

Whatever the reason, intrusive elements arrived in Greece towards the end of the millennium, and the traditional accounts of new arrivals at that time essentially must rest on fact. Such accounts are highly involved and naturally contain some elements added in the sixth century and even later[17]. Two features distinguish all of them. Firstly the period of invasion, and the consequent migration of the displaced peoples on the mainland within Greece and east across the Aegean, occupies no more than one hun-

---

[14] Herod. II, 145. On these trad. dates see esp. J. Forsdyke, *Greece before Homer*, 62 ff.; C. W. Blegen et al. *Troy III* 18; *Troy IV* 9; 12. But see Mylonas, *Hesp.* (1964) 366 (c. 1200 B.C.).

[15] See e.g. Desborough, *L. M.* 249.

[16] See also S. Dow, "The Greeks in the Bronze Age", *XI ConSchist* 33 n. 65 = *Lang. and Backgr. of Homer* 172 n. 65.

[17] E.g. M. B. Sakellariou, *La Migration Grecque en Ionie*, maintains that the story of the passing through Athens of the Pylian refugees on their way to Ionia is a sixth cent. invention. Excellent treatments of the literary traditions concerning the end of the B.A. and the subsequent migrations can be found in Desborough–N. G. L. Hammond, "The End of Mycenaean Civilization and the Dark Age", *C.A.H.*² II, ch. XXXVI, Cambridge 1962; Webster, *Myc. to Hom.* ch. 5; Desborough, *L.M.* 246 ff., on whose summary my brief account is chiefly based. See also F. H. Stubbings, "The Recession of Mycenaean Civilization", *C.A.H.*² II, ch. XXVII.

dred and fifty years[18]. Secondly all chronological computations were arrived at by a more or less fictitious, but certainly forced, series of generations. This is particularly evident in the case of the Spartan royal family which from historical times is traced back directly across the Dark Age to Heracles. In this way ancient historians managed to connect the Heroic Age with their own and combine transmitted historical fact and mythological material together with later invention into a causally as well as chronologically plausible narrative.

Oral tradition records several incursions into Greece from the north and north-west. The principal group of these were the Dorians who attacked the centre of the Mycenaean realm, fought with and defeated Orestes' and Hermione's son Teisamenos and divided his kingdom threefold. Temenos and his son obtained the Argolid, Cresphontes Messenia, while Laconia went to the sons of Aristodemos[19]. Teisamenos in turn took over Achaea while the displaced Ionians first moved to Athens and thence across the Aegean to Ionia[20]. Apart from the Peloponnese the Dorians, according to tradition, took the Megarid and eventually, too, crossed the Aegean to Melos[21], Thera[22], to Crete, the Dodecanese islands, and to the nearby coast of Asia Minor[23]. In Attica the Dorians met with successful resistance, reflected in the famous episode of Codrus, himself a descendant of the exiled Pylian Neleus[24], so that Athens remained unscathed. With the exception of Arcadia, which also remained untouched, these invasions, moves and counter moves, account for the position in the Peloponnese and in Attica, and they probably also explain the Dorian and Ionian migrations to the south and central portions of Asia Minor and to the adjacent islands.

Comparatively lesser movements, following tradition, involved for example the Aetolians, who, in the wake of the Dorians, seized Elis, and the Thessalians. The latter, also coming from the north[25], settled in central Thessaly evicting the local people, perhaps invaders themselves, who moved into Boeotia. The dispossessed Aeolian people again moved eastward across

---

[18] Thus, according to Thucydides 1, 12, 3, the Dorians came into the Peloponnese and settled there within eighty years of the sack of Troy.
[19] Paus. II, 18, 6 ff.
[20] Herod. I, 145 f.
[21] Thuc. 5, 84, 112.
[22] Herod. IV, 147.
[23] Strabo 653.
[24] Paus. VII, 25, 2, Cf. Sakellariou in n. 17 above.
[25] Herod VII, 176, specifies Thesprotia as their place of origin.

the Aegean and settled in Aeolis[26] and the northern parts of Asia Minor. The Thessalian movements are said[27] to have occurred prior to the Dorian arrival in the Peloponnese, while Strabo (582) speaks of an interval of four generations before the Aeolian migration was complete. This migration therefore, begun before the Ionian eastward move, would have extended at least over the same period of time as the Ionian settlements.

The discussions on points of detail aside, the ancient authorities agree that invasion and migration were complete within a space of rather less than two-hundred years. This would mean that, if we take Herodotus' date of 1250 B.C. for the fall of Troy, the Greek scene was settled once more, and the Asian colonies founded, by about 1100 B.C.[28]. The more obvious weaknesses of the oral tradition apart, it is vital to establish two points from all of these stories immediately, before discussing the linguistic evidence. Firstly the Dorians as a separate racial entity remain curiously elusive, and secondly their connection with the Heracles family seems to go back some four generations before their irruption into the Peloponnese[28a]. Herodotus' account in I, 56 implies that the name of these nomadic people was changeable according to their location at a given time[28b]. Immutable only were the names of the three traditional Doric tribes[28c] which successfully attacked the Peloponnese three generations after Hyllus' death. But the eponyms of these tribes were Heraclids, that is, of course, genuine Achaeans who traced their descent to Perseus, king of Mycenae[28d]. It would be interesting to pursue further the close connection between these "foreign" Dorians and Mycen. Heraclids, their common haunts in s. Epirus, Crete, and Rhodes (through the sons Thessalus and Tlepolemus), but at the moment it must suffice to establish their proximity to the Mycenaean world.

A good deal can be learnt of this period from a study of the dispersion of the Greek dialects in the Aegean. This linguistic control tends to confirm the geographical distribution of the migrating peoples towards the end of the Bronze Age, but it can tell us virtually nothing about the order

---

[26] Thuc. 3, 33; 8, 5, 2.
[27] Thuc. 1, 12. The Boeotians arrived in Boeotia sixty years after the Trojan War, and the Dorians invaded eighty years after the War.
[28] Desb., *L.M.* 248.
[28a] Cf. the story of Aigimius' promise to Heracles, Diod. Sic. 4, 37, 3; 58, 6.
[28b] Cf. Hammond, *op. cit.* 30.
[28c] Hammond, *ibid.*
[28d] Herod. 5, 72, 3.

of events or about the precise length of time during which the various movements were accomplished.

Studies of the Greek dialects have to rely on evidence as late as the seventh century. The results of the most recent work, however, are a fairly reliable guide to the Greek scene in the second millenn. B.C.[29]. The most immediate effect of the fresh treatment of this subject has been a revision of the previously accepted Greek migration doctrine which postulated a threefold invasion of the mainland from the beginning of M.H. These three waves were believed to consist of Ionians, Achaeans, and Dorians. The last remain in their place at the end of the Bronze Age, but the first two groups now disappear for the following reasons. The evidence suggests that the Greek language was divided into two main groups: East Greek and West Greek. The latter was the dialect of the newcomers from the north and n.-w. whose tongue in part replaced and in part, as in Attica, changed the existing East Greek dialect. East Greek was spoken earlier in the Peloponnese, generally in s. Greece and also in parts of the land north of the Isthmus, like Boeotia and Thessaly. All these areas we know to have been Mycenaean, so that we may suppose the people living there to have used a common speech. It follows, too, that classical Greek dialects, like Ionic, Attic, and Aeolic, were the product of a development which occurred after the advent of W. Greek. Therefore, far from reflecting prior invasions into Greece by Ionians and Achaeans[30], such later evolved dialects, when placed beside West Greek, Doric, help to draw a geographical plan of the settlement and migration scene in Greece and the eastern Aegean after the Bronze Age.

The plan, in fact, is largely in agreement with the movements and dispositions of Greek peoples according to the literary tradition. Thus the Aeolic tongue of the inhabitants of Aeolis, for example, and Lesbos in the east can be shown to have evolved from the dialect spoken in Thessaly and Boeotia: it was taken east by the people displaced in the

---

[29] The pioneer work in this field was done by W. Porzig, "Sprachgeographische Untersuch. zu d. altgriech. Dialekten", *Ind. F.* 61 (1954) 147–69; E. Risch, "D. Gliederung d. griech. Dial. in neuer Sicht", *M.H.* 12 (1955) 61–76. Their findings are summarized by Chadwick, *G.R.* 3 (1956) 38–50, see also his "The Preh. of the Greek Language, *C.A.H.*² II, ch. XLIX, and C. D. Buck, *The Greek Dialects,* Chicago 1955. For a somewhat different theory see N. G. L. Hammond, *B.S.A.* 62 (1967) 104 and n. 26.

[30] Achaean was frequently equated with Aetolian. Prof. Burkert kindly pointed out to me that Risch believes Aeolian to be closer to North West Greek than to Mycenaean/Ionian.

second millennium. Ionic again in similar fashion travelled eastward from southern Greece, Attica in particular, and also probably from the Peloponnese, while Doric expanded to areas of southern Asia Minor, like Rhodes, and most likely directly southward to Crete. Before the arrival on the scene of West Greek the Mycenaean world in all likelihood spoke a common dialect. This was certainly true for southern Greece and the Peloponnnese, but one might also include the Mycenaean lands north of the Isthmus. If there were local differences they must have been minimal, but it may be possible to speak of proto-Ionic used mainly in Attica, proto-Arcadian in the Peloponnese, and proto-Aeolic in Thessaly and Boeotia.

The decipherment of Linear B, the Mycenaean script, has helped to clarify this picture[30a]. Despite the relatively scanty evidence from this source – so far only a few sites have yielded examples of the script – Linear B tends to confirm the findings of the study of later dialects. From it, for example, it is evident that the language of the Peloponnese and southern Greece was the ancestor of Arcadian. Linear B further had strong links with what has been called proto-Ionic and proto-Aeolic, showing, of course, the close communal tie between all of these. Of great interest again is the fact that the Mycenaean script possessed some archaic features which are not found in any classical Greek dialect. These the script apparently preserved until about 1200 B.C. when the impact of West Greek set in motion the developments found in the languages of classical times. The coming of the traditional Heraclidae with their new dialect affected, and in some instances broke up, this linguistic community. All accounts agree, however, that mountainous Arcadia was spared, and it is in this area that a dialect form most closely related to ancient Mycenaean survived the troublous events of the ending Bronze Age[31]. The same archaic

---

[30a] For an account of the numerous linguistic difficulties of the Lin. B decipherment see E. Grumach in W. Hausmann (ed.) *Allgemeine Grundlagen der Archäologie*, Munich 1969, 259–67.

[31] An interesting linguistic reflection on historic events is the temporary influence – c. 1000 B.C. – of Doric on Ionic. Attica, according to tradition, also resisted the invaders. But the linguistic facts suggest that in this area, too, the Dorians left their mark. It seems that the features in which Ionic differs from Arcado–Cyprian are those which agree with Doric. The break, however, of Ionic into Attic and Ionic was a later internal development which has nothing to do with Doric dialect, *G.R.* (1956) 44. For the theory that the newcomers to Attica, who infused Doric elements into Ionic, consisted of a mixed population of Mycenaeans from the Argolid and Dorians see C. G. Styrenius, *Sub. St.* 163.

language form, Arcado-Cyprian, had in Late Mycenaean travelled to Cyprus with groups of settlers, presumably refugees, and there went its own highly conservative way even resisting the new alphabet in the eighth century.

A general map of the dispersion of Greek dialects would look as follows:

East Greek

Arcado-Cyprian (Arcadia, Cyprus)   Ionic   Aeolic (Thessaly, Boeotia,
                                   (Attica)   Aeolis, adjacent islands)
Attic   East Ionic (Ionia & adj. islands)   Central Ionic (Cyclades)
                                             West Ionic (Euboea)

West Greek

N.W. Greek (Phocis, Locris, Aetolia, Elis)   Doric (Laconia, Argolid,
                                              Corinthia, Megarid, S. Cycl-
                                              ades, like Thera, Melos.
                                              Crete, Dodecanese, parts of
                                              s. coast of Asia Minor[32].

The knowledge gained from an examination of the geography of dialects does, albeit in very general outline, reinforce the oral tradition regarding the progression of events. The picture that emerges is one of intrusion from the north some time in Late Helladic into Greece followed by an eastward movement, which included some of the intruders themselves, and a series of new settlements along the lines suggested by tradition. However, what linguistic studies tell even less than the traditional stories, is the magnitude of the incursions, the time involved in migration to and from Greece, and especially the cultural impact of the newcomers on established customs and beliefs. The Dorians, if we must give this name to the invaders, we have to remember were "no unintelligible foreigners". "A Dorian would, it seems, have made himself understood in thirteenth century Mycenae more easily than a Spartan in fifth century Athens[33]."

How far does the presently available archaeological evidence point to the same conclusions as the oral accounts and the linguistic studies? There is, in fact, much physical evidence of destruction in large parts of the

---

[32] Aeolic was subject to Ionic influence in Aeolis and also assimilated N.-W. Greek features in Boeotia, in W. Thessaly and, to a lesser extent, in E. Thessaly. To the group of areas where Doric was spoken add Acarnania & Corcyra, but prob. only after Corinth. colonization there in 8th/7th century. Messenian Doric may go back no further than the Spartan conquest of the territory also in 8th/7th century.

[33] Chadwick, G.R. (1956) 48 f.

Mycenaean world: in Thessaly, at Iolkos, at a number of Boeotian sites, like Gla and Eutresis, and particularly in the Argolid. The archaeological dates of such disturbances generally belong to about 1200 B.C., but in some cases, as in Mycenae for instance, extend to the end of L.H. III C. There cannot therefore, as in the case of the Norman invasion of England, have been one wave of foreign intruders which laid low the Mycenaean strongholds and took over the government of the empire.

The archaeological picture can be briefly described in this way[34]. In Thessaly the palace at Iolkos was destroyed early in L.H. III C[35], but there is no real evidence of outside intrusion or foreign occupation[36]. In Phocis the fortress in Krisa succumbed late in L.H. III B[37]. Gla, too, in Boeotia, was destroyed at the same time[38], while Eutresis was abandoned in L.H. III B/C[39]. Other notable sites destroyed about this time, apart from the Argolid, include the Messenian Pylos and Zygouries in Corinthia, as well as the Menelaion in Laconia[40]. To these outright destructions we should perhaps add some fairly extensive areas which were deserted at the end of the Bronze Age. Such were established settlements on the mainland south of Thessaly in the Argolid, in Laconia, Elis, Messenia, and to some extent in West Attica[41]. Many of the people, probably displaced by migratory movements at the time, moved, according to archaeological surveys, e.g. to Achaea at the northern end of the Peloponnesian peninsula, and particularly eastward to Attica and its east coast[42]. Such wide-spread disturbances are difficult to interpret as entirely due to internal strife as Desborough points out[43]. The archaeological destruction dates on the mainland are pretty close to the time traditionally assigned to the fall of Troy, namely 1250 B.C. Nevertheless there appears to be very little

[34] Desborough, *L.M.* 250 ff.
[35] Theocharis, *Ergon* (1956/60/65), *Arch.* 11 (1958) 13 ff.
[36] T. C. Skeat, *The Dorians in Archaeology*, 48, speaks of an incursion into n. Thessaly by a Macedonian group–unknown to tradition, Desb., *L.M.* 250.
[37] *B.C.H.* 61 (1937) 326; Desb., *L.M.* 125.
[38] *B.C.H.* 18 (1894) 284 f.; *Ergon* (1957) 29; Desb., *L.M.* 120.
[39] Desb., *ibid*. Mr. Desb. privately informed me that there may be some as yet unpublished evidence of a late III B destruction at Thebes.
[40] Desb., *L.M.* 221.
[41] Desb., *L.M.* 221 ff.
[42] *Ibid*.
[43] *Op. cit.* 250.

in the archaeological material which could be construed as outright contradiction of the traditional tale concerning the newcomers from the north at the end of the Bronze Age.

Despite such superficial agreements, however, there are some serious objections to be made against any convenient inference that the Dorians, or a similar single group, were responsible for the havoc wrought on so many Mycenaean sites. The most obvious difficulty to arise concerns the painfully wide temporal gap between the times of destruction and desertion – about 1200 B.C. – and the period when renewed settlement can be archaeologically proven for some of the abandoned areas. The time involved extends over something like two-hundred years, certainly for the Argolid and the southern Peloponnese[44]. A perhaps more grievous problem is that some of the centres of destruction continued to be occupied by apparently the same people – the Mycenaeans – even after the disasters. If we take the upheavals in Greece at about 1200 B.C. as due to intrusion from outside, then we are left with the puzzling conclusion that the invaders did not retain and occupy their conquests. Thucydides' express statement that the Dorians on arrival "held the Peloponnese" must be wrong[45], for extensive settlement in the Argolid did not apparently take place before 1075[45a] while the date in southern and south-west Peloponnese may be as late as the turn of the millennium.

The effect of this gap on traditional accounts is to upset the smoothly flowing continuity of e.g. the Spartan royal genealogical line back to Heracles, or the take-over of the Argolid by the Dorian Temenos. Perhaps there is some substance to Rhys Carpenter's theory that climatic conditions temporarily made habitation of these areas difficult[46]. Perhaps again we must suppose later waves of invaders to have been responsible for renewed settlement late in the eleventh century, as was suggested by Desborough[47]. In proportion, however, to the increasing clarity of the archaeological picture, the historian's conviction grows that the Dorians must be discounted as a strong disruptive force in Late Bronze Age Greece. Changing art styles, architecture, and building forms in general, as well as destruction

---

[44] Desb., *L.M.* 252.
[45] 1, 12, 3.
[45a] Mr. Desborough informs me that the Argolid may have been settled (possibly by newcomers) before 1100 B.C.
[46] R. Carpenter, *Discontinuity in Greek Civilization*, Cambridge 1966.
[47] *Op. cit.* 252.

levels, may seduce the unwary, especially in the absence of literary sources, into a belief in absolute breaks at certain clearly marked periods.

Greece had earlier been subject to two such major breaks in its history: one that heralded the Bronze Age at the beginning of Early Helladic, and the other at the time of transition from Early to Middle Helladic. Yet not every major site was archaeologically involved but may to some extent have continued its own culture or successfully fused with new elements without fundamentally disturbing its cultural, and particularly religious, continuity. Eutresis in Boeotia, for example, shows only vague signs of a transition from Neolithic to Early Helladic[48]. Again Berbati, in the Argolid, has no E.H. strata at all, but M.H. directly succeeds Neolithic. "Evidently Berbati, obscure and withdrawn, was not interfered with by the E.H. folk"[49]. At other sites, like Lerna, also in the Argolid, there is no sharp break or destruction before Early and Middle Helladic but a fusion or blending of both periods[50].

We must treat with equal caution the traditional stories of overwhelming onslaughts at the end of Late Helladic of Dorian invaders who carried all before them. In any case physical presence and perhaps even domination need not imply drastic harm to inherited custom, as is evident in Crete. There may have been instrusion in Crete some time in L.H. III C[51]. If there were invaders (Dorians?), their arrival had little impact on cultural continuity: the natives fled to the mountains with their goddess, shrines and all[52]. Resistance to dramatic innovation in Crete then was probably as strong as when the Mycenaeans established themselves there in the fifteenth century or earlier.

What then is one to make of the Greek scene at the end of the Helladic Bronze Age? The wide-spread destructions of L.H. III B/C and the depopulation of certain sites cannot be explained away as simple localized phenomena[52a], because not only Greece but much of the Aegean world was affected by disturbances at the time. For our purposes, however, at least as an equally plausible alternative to predominantly foreign agents as dis-

---

[48] H. Goldman, *Exavations at Eutresis in Boeotia*, Cambridge Mass. 1931, 7; 77–93; S. S. Weinberg, *A.J.A.* (1947) 172 f.

[49] Dow, "The Greeks in the Bronze Age", *Lang. & Backgr. of Homer* 166 f. n. 10.

[50] J. L. Caskey, *Hesp.* (1957) 162; cf. Dow, *ibid.*

[51] Desb., *L.M.* 253. Popham believes that intrusion in Crete occurred early in III C, *B.S.A.* 60 (1965) 316 ff.

[52] E.g. Starr, *Origins* 81.

[52a] Cf. the theory of local social upheavals, M. Andronikos, *Hell.* 13 (1954) 221–240.

turbing factors, it is important to consider the possibility that what occurred in Greece at the time was the result of an organic development set in motion and continued by principally Mycenaean forces. Dorians, or rather north and north-west Greeks, there were, but perhaps they had been there some time before the final catastrophe and had fused with the local people[53] without materially altering their language, art, and existing cultural patterns[54], and to this point we shall briefly return below. One thing, however, is already clear from the present state of our knowledge: not really one single feature in art or custom which could possibly be described as new at the end of Bronze, can effectively be connected with a Dorian arrival[54a]. To appreciate the validity of this claim one need merely look at what is already known of the transitional phase between the end of Mycenaean and the beginning of Protogeometric, that is, the crucial period of about one-hundred years between 1125 and 1035 B.C.

Those relatively few years are vital, because it is during that time that new forms should signal a break between old and new, when intrusive elements established their own customs. The period is named Submycenaean after the style of pottery which was found in contemporary burials. Submycenaean, in fact, describes a style which is distinctly Mycenaean although in debased form. From it arose Geometric design at about the turn of the millennium as a natural, organic, and internal, development of Mycenaean styles. It would seem then that historically Submycenaean, at least as far as the pottery is concerned, is an artificial division, because Mycenaean decorative motifs show a continuation of ideas and designs which "links firmly onto the sub-Mycenaean... and leads directly toward the later Geometric style"[55]. The borderline even between Submycenaean and Protogeometric is vague and occasionally so fuzzy that an experienced archaeologist can find it difficult to tell when he has passed from one period to the

---

[53] Desb., *L.M.* 242; 252; 253; J. Deshayes, *Argos. Les fouilles de la Deiras*, Paris 1966, 251. Nixon, *Dorians* 102, calls the Dorians "fringe" Mycenaeans.

[54] Desb., *L.M.* 252, favours the view that the invaders, after causing their destruction, moved elsewhere or returned without leaving another trace to their place of origin.

[54a] Cf. G. E. Mylonas, *Mycenae and the Mycenaean Age*, 230. But on p. 232 Mylon. agrees with Desb.'s view that the Dorian invaders brought a new culture to Greece in L.H. III C. Cf. Mylonas, *Mycenae's Last Cent. of Greatness*, where the same conclusion is implied on p. 38.

[55] Starr, *Orig.* 89, see also A. D. Lacy, *Grk. Pottery in the B.A.*, London 1967, 286.

other[56]. In great part such difficulties are due, of course, to the as yet inadequate exploration of Submycenaean strata. However, even when this is done it seems doubtful whether the results will warrant the assumption that a new and strange culture found its way onto the Mycenaean scene in the final years of Late Helladic and set aside what had gone before. The appearance of Protogeometric pottery no longer serves as evidence in this respect.

Other kinds of archaeological data may fare no better, for such evidence on its own very rarely leads to convincing conclusions about foreign intervention in the *cultural* scene. There are a few new types of artefact, a few customs which make themselves noticeable particularly at this time, but none of them can be shown to have any connection with a Dorian arrival[57]. These are, exclusive of the Geometric pottery, some types of pin (bronze and iron), fibulae, and the methods of burial in cist tombs generally superseded, in Attica at least, by cremation in Protogeometric. Submycenaean pottery was first isolated to any degree in West Attica, namely in two cemeteries, the Kerameikos in Athens[58], and at Salamis[59]. This discovery, which was made before more was known of the Submycenaean period in other parts of the mainland, suggested that the impetus to Submycenaean came from Attica. The fact, too, that the Submycenaean vases were recovered from cist tombs seemed to be significant[60]. Such tombs contained single burials and therefore contrasted with the common Late Mycenaean mode of multiple burial in chamber tombs. This evidence led Desborough to suppose that western Attica had at that time witnessed the arrival of new peoples whose movements were not mirrored in the traditional accounts[61].

Since Desborough wrote, a number of facts have come to light which further illuminate the scene and also show how little value is to be attached

---

[56] E.g. some seven vases found in a cist tomb at Mycenae. These, according to Megaw, *J.H.S.* Arch. Rep. 1964/5, 10, were "painted in that Submycen. style classified by V. Desborough as Early Protogeometric."
[57] Cf. Dow, *op. cit.* 165 n. 2.
[58] W. Kraiker–K. Kübler, *Kerameikos: Ergebnisse d. Ausgrabungen,* Berl. 1939, vol. I. Later reports in IV (1943); V, 1 (1954); VI, 1 (1959); G. Karo, *An Att. Cemetery,* Philad. 1943. The Kerameikos cemetery is the best example of continuity of pottery style from the end of L.M. to Geom. in Attica, cf. Starr, *Orig.* 84 ff.
[59] Desb., *L.M.* 37; 231.
[60] "Pit graves lined and covered with stone slabs", Desb., *L.M.* 37.
[61] *Op. cit.* 252 f.

to burial customs as evidence concerning Dorian interference. It seems clear now that neither Submycenaean cist burial, nor the practice of single burial in these graves, is reason enough to postulate the arrival of new elements. Cist graves were no new phenomenon to Greece in Submycenaean times, but they were in use throughout Middle Helladic beside the common shaft and pit graves[62]. Examples have been found in many parts of Greece[63] which seem to argue in favour of this mode of burial as an established practice. In fact Styrenius, in his recent study on Submycenaean Greece, believes in a survival of cist graves from Middle Helladic[64]. In Eleusis, for example, so Desborough himself testifies, cist graves were used until L.H. III B/C[65]. No single mainland site so far shows continuity of cist graves from Middle Helladic until Submycenaean[66], so that conceivably the use of cist graves could have been discontinued after M.H. not to be reintroduced until the arrival of new peoples on the scene. It is difficult, however, to subscribe to such a view when current archaeological work continues to uncover new examples of cist tombs in Greece. At least the Attic examples in Salamis and the Kerameikos can no longer argue the presence of foreign elements. Cist graves were not the only form of inhumation in Submycenaean although they were the most common.

Other forms of earth cut graves in use included the shaft and pit grave, which continued until Protogeometric and during Protogeometric outside Attica[67]. Thus, prior to universal adult cremation in Attica, cist tombs by no means displaced all other types of inhumation. What is more important still, and may well explain the feature of single burial in cists as opposed to the more common Mycenaean habit of multiple burial, is that these pits lined with stone slabs occasionally occurred in Mycenaean times in association with both tholos and chamber tombs. That is, a tholos tomb may contain

---

[62] *Symb. Osl.* 9 (1930) 28 ff.
[63] P. Ålin, *D. Ende d. Myken. Fundstätten*, 44; 53 (Argolid incl. III B); 61 (Korakou, Corinthia); 67 (Achaea); 72 (Elis); 75 (Arcadia); 90 (Messenia); 97 (Laconia); 102; 116 (Attica incl. III A & B); 124 (Boeotia); 134 (Phthiotis & Phocis); 147 (Thessaly). A general survey of all Greek examples can be found on p. 148.
[64] Styrenius, "The Vases from the Submyc. Cemetery on Salamis", *Os. Ath.* 4 (1962) 121; *Sub. St.* 161.
[65] "The Greek Mainland, c. 1150–1000", *Proc. PS*, 1965, 221; cf. Mylonas, *Eleusis*, 31; 33.
[66] Desb., *L.M.* 33; 114; cf. the concession made on this point by Styren., *Sub. St.* 162.
[67] Styren., *Sub. St.* 153 f. In Attica during Protogeom. cist tombs were exclusively used for child burials. Outside Attica, however, inhumation continued generally during that period, *ibid.* and n. 3 for examples.

an individual cist-like grave for a single burial in, as it were, a multiple burial ground[68]. The same separation of single cists can be found in chamber tombs[69]. Whether or not this practice lies at the root of the common Submycenaean single burial, or whether this custom bears witness to the general material poverty of the period[70], it is quite plain that the number of single burials in Mycenaean times has hitherto been underestimated. Deshayes, for example, has shown this to be true for sites like Argos[71]; but more examples continue to come to light[72]. The most plausible way to interpret the evidence is to see in Submycenaean cist burial a continuation of primarily Mycenaean forms unaffected by outside influence. In essence the same conclusion might suggest itself in the case of cremation which in Attica at any rate became the exclusive burial mode during Protogeometric.

This surprisingly uniform habit at the conclusion of the Bronze Age was wont to be connected with the Dorian arrival in Greece, and generally provided the strongest argument in favour of the intrusion of foreign elements. Unjustly so, however, for cremation, too, "was not a sudden change of burial custom but a progressive one"[73]. This conclusion applies also to Attica, as becomes apparent from Styrenius' diagram of the distribution of Attic grave forms in Submycenaean and Protogeometric[74]. Before Submycenaean, too, cremation occurred sporadically in the Mycenaean period in Pylos, Leukas, Argos, Rhodes and Attica, as well as at Knossos in Troy, and at certain L.H. III B Carian sites[75]. It is worth noting that cremation (for adults) in Protogeometric was almost universal in Athens and possibly the rest of Attica. It was also universal at Lefkandi, and at Medeon in Phocis, and wide-spread in central Greece. But inhumation

---

[68] E:g. B.S.A. 25 (1921/3) Pl. 53 f.; 60.
[69] A. J. B. Wace, *Chamber Tombs at Mycenae*, 38, fig. 19. See also F. Schachermeyr, *A. kl. A.* 19 (1966) 30.
[70] Cf. O. Frödin–A. W. Persson, *Asine* 355.
[71] Deshayes, *Argos* 24 ff.
[72] E.g. at Athens and Perati, Styren., *Sub. St.* 162. According to the excavator, the Perati graves had to be built this way because of the hard ground. I owe this information to Mr. Desborough.
[73] Styren., *Sub. St.* 154.
[74] *Op. cit.* 153, diagr. 14.
[75] H. L. Lorimer, *Homer and the Monuments*, 104 f.; *J.H.S.* 76 (1956) Arch. Suppl. 7; 16; 32. Styren., *Sub. St.* 154 f., cites further examples from Prosymna Tomb XLI and Perati, on the east coast of Attica, belonging to L.H. III B & C. See also Desb., *L.M.* 71; Deshayes, *Argos* 246 and n. 5. For Caria see Boysal, *T.A.D.* 13, 2 (1964) 82 (with Mycen. pottery).

continued as a fairly common practice in other parts of Greece[76]. The reason for the confining of cremation to a relatively few principal areas is not at all clear, but at least one modern scholar has reasonably suggested that the practice was due to overcrowding in Attica at the time[77]. As proof of a novel mode of burial, introduced by newcomers, cremation must fall away. And it matters little in this connection whether cremation had ultimately been brought to Greece from Cyprus or Syria, as Desborough maintains[78], or whether the custom came from Asia Minor[79].

Certain types of dress-pins and fibulae, apart from weapons and other dress ornaments like rings, were very commonly associated with Submycenaean graves. These artefacts at the beginning of the period were generally made of bronze, while iron tended to be used exclusively for the manufacture of such articles at the end of Submyc. and in Protogeom.[80]. With some, perhaps significant, exceptions[81] the ability to work this metal was learnt only in Protogeom. Desborough believes[82] that this new skill was imported from the east. Mediterranean, which does not necessarily argue the presence of foreign craftsmen[83]. Certain types of jewellery, pins and fibulae, which made their appearance in considerable numbers in Submycenaean, particularly the long dress pin and arched fibulae, archaeologists have thought to be introductions by invaders from the north[84]. But the case is not at all clear[84a]: Desborough feels bound to admit that the forms of these ornaments

---

[76] Styren., *Sub. St.* 153 n. 3, cites some examples. See also Desb., *Proc. PS* 1965, 216 ff.

[77] Webster, *Myc. to Hom.* 140; 290.

[78] *L.M.* 71.

[79] A. J. B. Wace–F. H. Stubbings (ed.), *A Companion to Homer*^{2}, 487; Lorimer, *op. cit.* 107; E. Vermeule, *Greece in the Bronze Age*, 301; Styrenius, *Sub. St.* 154; Andronikos, *II Cr. Con.* 115–19; see also C. Mavriyannaki, *A.S.I.* 29/30 (1967/8) 167–79.

[80] Desborough, *L.M.* 70; Styrenius, *Sub. St.* 156 f. Iron could not have been introduced to the south by the Dorians, P. Demargne, *Aegean Art* 283.

[81] E.g. the iron pins in a Submycenaean tomb in the Kerameikos, *Hesp.* 30, 175 f.; Desborough, *L.M.* 70 n. 2.

[82] *Ibid.*

[83] Cf. Dow, "The Greeks in the Bronze Age", 165 n. 2.

[84] Desb., *L.M.* 71; cf. Styrenius, *Sub. St.* 163.

[84a] In Attica, for instance, while the multitude of Cypriote gold ornaments in Perati tombs probably came from Mycenaean settlers in Cyprus, new jewellery forms at that time in the Kerameikos could have been connected with northern elements like the Lausitz Culture. But older Mycenaean traditions usually also continued, albeit in debased form, e.g. Higgins, *B.S.A.* 64 (1969) 144.

might have been evolved by the Mycenaeans without external interference[85]. Deshayes, too, states quite plainly that there is no convincing proof of the northern origin of these objects[86].

The scene appears to shift. Archaeological remains, which at first were thought to constitute the strongest source in defence of cultural change at the end of the Bronze Age, actually tell no conclusive story. The substance of the archaeological arguments is elusive: it seems to dissolve when rigorously considered. There is nothing, no new artefact, no mode of burial, which cannot be interpreted as an essentially internal development. In the face of such possible conclusions the Dorians, as destroyers of Bronze Age culture, retreat in significance. These northern invaders become somewhat shadowy unless we are to put all our faith in the oral tradition. But what we read there most likely is part fictitious and part exaggeration of historical fact on a scale comparable perhaps with the Homeric description of Agamemnon's expedition against Troy. This is not to deny that infiltration occurred into the Mycenaean world, that new peoples arrived in the south. What is debatable, however, concerns the period of time involved during which such newcomers arrived on the scene, and their impact on cultural and religious life. After all, even in oral tradition Heracles' association with outsiders antedates the Trojan War and involves his descendants over more than one generation.

The tenor of all the available evidence is that the Mycenaean world was not disrupted at one stroke but received new elements which over a considerable period of time it integrated with itself. Political changes are no satisfactory indication of cultural and religious discontinuity. There are, of course, worlds of difference between the Mycenaean bureaucratic palace administration and the government of the later Greek *polis*. Who is to say, however, that the impetus for this kind of innovation did not come largely from within? What is more to the point for our purposes, is that the new era, the change from the Bronze to the Iron Age, far from being rung in abruptly, was the result of an organic development of preceding forms. In other words, there is no need to look for signs of foreign culture or of an irrevocable break in inherited religious tradition, despite some apparent interruptions in the archaeological picture of the time.

[85] *L.M.* 71.
[86] *Argos* 249.

Desborough speaks of the disappearance of the "typical 'goddess' figurine" from post L.H. III C Mycenaean graves[87]. But is this a real break or just a gap in our knowledge? The latter seems more likely in view of what is known already concerning the continuing tradition of terracotta idols of the goddess and her animals, notably the bull, in Crete, Cyprus, on the mainland of Greece, as in Attica, and in parts of East Greece, like Samos[88]. If such a sequence cannot yet be established for all parts of Greece, this may be due to the accident of survival, but should not be read as negative evidence against persistence of cult. For a time in the Dark Age the Greek worshipper modelled his goddess in a more perishable material, but her nature, power and functions remained the same[88a]. It need occasion no surprise, then, that by the eighth cent. the small votive terracottas of the goddess had "reappeared" throughout Greece. She, as also her larger wheel-made likeness, was fashioned then in the old technique and dedicated at sanctuaries ranging from Samos to Rhodes, Boeotia, and even non-Greek Lemnos. On numerous statuettes of the seventh century the goddess is shown in the familiar attitude of the "Segensgestus," with raised arms, and her small handmade votives, at least in Athens, were almost as common for a time as they had ever been in the B.A.[89]. But other mainland and Cretan sites, like Sparta and Gortyn, also remembered the Mycenaean way of portraying the goddess[90]. Of great interest in this connection are the discoveries which prove that the practice of making large and even life-size cult images was also known to the B.A. already. Examples are the sixteenth cent. statues from the temple at Hagia Eirene on Keos[90a], and the hand from a life-size statue in the Herakleion Museum[90b]. Recently Lord William Taylour uncovered a number of two-feet high idols from a thirteenth cent. shrine at Mycenae[90c]. This kind of evidence seems to suggest that religious

---

[87] *L.M.* 231.

[88] See R. V. Nicholls, *Auck. Cl. Ess.* 8 ff.

[88a] Cf. Nicholls, *op. cit.* 21 f.

[89] Nicholls, *op. cit.* 17 f.

[90] D. Levi, "Gli Scavi del 1954 sull'Acropoli di Gortina", *A.S.I.* 33/34 (N.S. 17/18) (1955/6) 281, cf. fig. 37 b, see also R. M. Dawkins, *The Sanctuary of Artemis Orthia at Sparta*, London 1929, 155 ff., Pl. XL, cited by Levi; G. Rizza – V. S. M. Scrinari, *Il Santuario sull' Acropoli di Gortina*, Pl. VII, 28; 32; 33; IX, 51; 54; X, 53; 55; 56; 58; XI, 59. Cf. below p. 218.

[90a] E.g. Vermeule, *Gr. in the B.A.* 217.

[90b] Cited by Nicholls, *op. cit.* n. 25.

[90c] *Ant.* 43 (1969) 91 ff., Pl. XII, XIII.

continuity was not confined to a few disgruntled conservatives unwilling to surrender established beliefs in a new world. The religious historian will find traces of innovation and change not in political upheaval but in altered artistic and cultural patterns. Continuity of divine names, functions and possibly mythology, which connect the B.A. with Greek Archaic times, suggests continuity of cult.

To penetrate the darkness surrounding the many years from the end of the millennium until Geometric and later one looks for signs of survival and continuity at some of the old cultural centres. It is indeed surprising to realize how much did endure in a disturbed world. New sites are being discovered in a growing number of centres where Mycenaean tradition persevered and eventually found its place in the historical Greek world. It seems that the earlier picture of a largely desolate and deserted Peloponnese in the wake of the northern onslaught was too gloomy. More was left than one could at first suspect. The most recent archaeological work provides a fairly broad map of settlement in Greece, on the islands and in the Near East, which continued across the crucial period from Mycenaean to Geometric.

Before the more detailed discussion of this part of the evidence, it is important to make clear a few points regarding the nature of the archaeological material and its usefulness in establishing continuity of settlement and/or of cult. Obviously evidence from this kind of source is often fragmentary and subject to constant correction in the light of new excavations. A number of the sites mentioned below have only a few Submyc. and Protog. remains which make it extremely difficult to argue strongly for continuity of settlement, and it will inevitably appear that at times the case for persistence of occupation or cult on archaeological grounds has been overstated. Conversely there are a good many mainland areas where incomplete excavation, or the physical destruction of remains, have made the detection of settlement survival impossible, so that our picture can never be complete and we should be warned against arguing from negative evidence. However, it is right and proper to examine what archaeological evidence there is, because it will lead to a good deal of positive knowledge despite the reservations regarding the value of this particular source. There is one rather cheering thought to accompany us through the following discussion, and that is that the archaeological material cannot be used to disprove continuity which has been established on other grounds.

A brief list[91] will give some indication of the extent of survival and persistence of settlement. Achaea and Arcadia still await full exploration, and in consequence the information from these areas is rather thin. In Achaea most of the finds come from tombs[92], and they are examined in detail by Alin[93]. At least some of these tombs, however, must have been associated with settlements – especially in the case of the extensive necropolis at Prostovitsa – which have now disappeared entirely[94]. The majority of finds from Achaean sites belong to III C[95], so that some scholars believe Achaea to have been the home of refugees during this time of crisis[96]. Some sites, however, must have been inhabited by III A and B[97]. More important, continuity into Submyc. can be shown at Chalandritsa and Prostovitsa[98], and is likely at other sites for later times but has not yet been established[99].

Arcadia is even less well known. There may be some Submycenaean remains from tombs at Palaeocastro[100], but there is nothing to prove continuity beyond Mycenaean[101].

From Attica the evidence is considerably stronger, certainly for Athens. Actual Mycen. structural remains in Athens are sparse, because of great subsequent building activity there. But there is every indication of a significant Mycen. settlement on the acropolis, and probably in the later agora, and about the Kerameikos cemetery north-west of the acropolis on the road to Eleusis[102]. Habitation endured there, perhaps in the Kerameikos area from L.H. III C, through the transitional period into Protogeom. and eventually

---

[91] Cf. the careful discussion by R. Hagg, "Myken. Kultstätten im arch. Material" *Op. Ath.* 8 (1968) 39–60.

[92] See esp. Vermeule, *A.J.A.* 64 (1960) 1–21; Alin, *Ende* 63 ff.; Desb., *L.M.* 97 ff.

[93] *Ibid.*; cf. P. Aström, "Mycen. Pottery from the Region of Aigion", *Op. Ath.* 5 (1965) 89–110.

[94] Desb., *L.M.* 98.

[95] Desb., *ibid.*

[96] Desb., *L.M.* 100.

[97] Aström, *op. cit.* 96; Styren., *Sub. St.* 125.

[98] Styren., *ibid.*

[99] See e.g. the question mark in Vermeule's list, *Gr. in B.A*, App. III, 324. In *A.J.A.* (1960) 1 f., Vermeule mentions Protogeom. finds from Achaea. Continuity is probable therefore, cf. Alin, *Ende* 68. Desborough, on the other hand, *L.M.* 101, posits a complete break in Achaea at the end of the Mycen. period.

[100] Alin, *Ende* 73; Styren., *Sub. St.* 126.

[101] Alin, *Ende* 75. Cf. R. Hope Simpson, *A Gazetteer & Atlas of Mycen. Sites*, 37 ff.

[102] Alin, *Ende* 99; 101; 103; H. Simpson, *op. cit.* 101.

classical times[103]. The tombs in the Kerameikos cemetery in particular tell a story of uninterrupted use from the end of the Helladic Age[104].

The most recent archaeological discoveries at Salamis, outside Athens, brought to light evidence of settlement in Submyc. But, although Mrs. Vermeule believes in continuity of occupation of the island[105], there was probably a break during III B, while there is no evidence yet for continuity after Submycen.[106]. Possibly more will be known in the future about affairs in Salamis after III C, but here, as indeed in Athens, continuity of settlement, after what has been said above, implies continuity of predominantly Mycen. elements rather than the arrival of new cultural and religious forces[107].

In Eleusis the picture is clearer. Settlement endured on that site from E.H. throughout all periods of the B.A. and continued into classical times[108]. Admittedly our evidence for Protogeom. is thin, but it exists[109] and points to uninterrupted use of this important cult site[110], and there is no trace of destruction between Submycen. and the richly documented Geometric period[111].

A similar continuity of occupation in Attica can be attested fairly certainly for Marathon and Aegina[112]. The Argolid, too, thanks to the most recent excavation, retains numerous traces of a smooth flow from Mycen. to Protogeom. The latest finds from this period suggest the need to modify first impressions of an almost total desolation of the area at the end of the B.A. Alin, in his discussion and list[113], assigns certain continuity in the Argolid to Mycenae, Tiryns, Argos, and Asine, while he believes continuity to have been probable or possible in Dendra, Nauplion, and Candia. To this group Mrs. Vermeule added Epidaurus, at the same time establishing

---

[103] Alin, *Ende* 103; Styren., *Sub. St.* ch. I, with a description of the finds.
[104] A good description of the importance of this necropolis, with the references to excavation reports and discussions, in Starr, *Origins* 84 ff.
[105] *Gr. in the B.A.* 324.
[106] Alin, *Ende* 114; Desb., *L.M.* 115.
[107] The last is Desb.'s view, *L.M.* 37. "The main centre (of prehist. settlement) seems to lie not far from the hist. centre of Salamis", H. Simps., *Gazett.* 111.
[108] Alin, *Ende* 112 f.
[109] Desborough, *Protogeometric Pottery,* 316; Styren., *Sub. St.* 88.
[110] Desb., *L.M.* 115, believes in a break of *occupation* after IIIC.
[111] Alin, *op. cit.* 113.
[112] Alin, *op.cit.* 110; 115. In Aegina there may have been a regression of occupation during IIIB, but no complete break. But see Desb., *L.M.* e.g. 119.
[113] *Op. cit.* 10 ff.; 53. But see H. Simps., *Gazett.* e.g. 15; 16 f.

(in 1964) certain continuity also for Nauplion and Dendra[114]. Desborough, however[115], believes that a break in occupation at Argos after L.H. III C is probable, and possible at Mycenae[116]. Tiryns, he maintains[117], may also have been deserted between III B and the end of III C, while Mycenaean occupation of Asine "fades out" after III C[118].

Much of this interpretation, however, hinges on identification of vase finds from these areas as III C, Submycenaean or Protogeometric. Yet the three styles, particularly Submycenaean and Protogeometric, are closely related, so that the archaeologist's task becomes very difficult indeed. Recent work, too, has helped to fill the gap between Mycenaean and Protogeometric in the Argolid with the result that a clearer picture of continuity in the Argolid is beginning to emerge[119]. Vases belonging to Submycenaean, or the transitional period between Submycenaean and Protogeometric, have now been found in Argos, Asine, Mycenae, Nauplion, and Tiryns[120], assuring continuity of occupation at least in these centres.

Boeotia has not yet been explored sufficiently to provide a full impression of the state of affairs in Submycenaean and of the immediately subsequent history. However, evidence of Submycenaean has come from Orchomenus and Thebes[121], bearing witness to continuity at least in those two cities. A few finds, mostly sherds, from Old Corinth and Isthmia speak for settlement in the transitional period into Protogeometric in Corinthia[122]. The evidence is not strong, however, and Desborough believes in a break before Protogeometric[123].

---

[114] *Op. cit.* 323. Vermeule does, however, take Candia off the list.
[115] *L.M.* 81; 82.
[116] *L.M.* 75.
[117] *L.M.* 79.
[118] *L.M.* 83.
[119] See especially N. M. Verdelis, "Neue geometrische Gräber in Tiryns", *A.M.* 78 (1963) 1–62; *J.H.S.* Arch. Rep. 1964/5, 10 (Mycenae); Deshayes, *Argos*.
[120] For lists and references see Styrenius, *Sub. St.* 128 ff. The case for Dendra is too uncertain, since the amphoriskos, found in the tholos tomb there and identified as Submycenaean by A. W. Persson, *The Royal Tombs at Dendra near Midea*, 66 f., fig. 47, may still be Mycenaean, Styrenius, *Sub. St.* 133.
[121] See already S. Wide, "Gräberfunde aus Salamis", *A.M.* 35 (1910) 17–36; A. Keramopoullos, "Thebaika", *Deltion* 3 (1917) 25 ff.; H. Simps., *Gazett.* 113 f.; 121 f.; Styrenius, Sub. St. 137 f. Following his argument concerning Salamis, Desborough, *L.M.* 122, believes that the use of cist tombs in Thebes in IIIC announced the arrival of new people.
[122] Styrenius, *Sub. St.* 138 f.
[123] *L.M.* 85; cf. Vermeule, *op. cit.* 324.

In ancient Elis fourteen earth-cut graves, discovered recently, have yielded vases from Submycenaean and the transitional period to Protogeometric[124]. Other sites in Elis, which can be shown to have enjoyed continuity of occupation, are Ayios Andreas, Ayios Elias, and Koutsochira[125].

The most interesting site in Laconia, whose Submycenaean period is otherwise imperfectly documented, is the B.A. sanctuary at Amyclae which most likely continued in use after III C into historical times, despite the present evidence of an "archaeological break" at the site[126]. Messenian sites which survived into Protogeom. include Tragana, Kato Englianos, Kaphirio, Kokkinochomata, Malthi, and Nichoria[127].

Of the four Phocian sites, where Submycenaean vases have come to light – Itea, Galaxidi, Medeon, and Delphi –, the last is by far the most important[128]. Delphi, like Amyclae, was a cult site, and its continued use argues in favour of survival of at least a portion of traditional religious belief[129].

Further north on the mainland Submycenaean finds become scarce. The only site of note in this respect is Iolkos (Volos) in Thessaly, the home of the Argonauts. The Mycenaean palace there was destroyed about the end of III B[130], or early in III C, about 1200 B.C.[131]. Near the area, however, and round about it remains, representative of all periods, were found from E.H. to Geometric with the possible exception of Submycenaean[132], so that settlement in Iolkos, albeit on a reduced scale, continued after the end of the Bronze Age palace.

[124] N. Yalouris – V. Leon, Öst. Jahr. 46 (1961–3), Beiblatt 33 ff.; Ergon (1963) 117 ff.; Deltion 19 (1964) 181, Pl. 198 ff.
[125] W. McDonald – R. Hope Simpson, "Prehistoric Habitation in Southwestern Peloponnese", A.J.A. 65 (1961) 224; 229; cf. Alin, op. cit. 69 f.; 71.
[126] Vermeule, Gr. in the N.B.A. 270; 323; Styrenius, Sub. St. 143. Desborough says, however, L.M. 88, that the site was probably not used as a sanctuary in Protogeometric and Geometric times.
[127] Styrenius, Sub. St. 143 f. Continued settlement in Malthi, after IIIC, might have been on a smaller scale, Alin, op. cit. 78; Desb., L.M. 94.
[128] See Styrenius, Sub. St. 144 ff., with references and discussion.
[129] Desborough again, L.M. 123, believes that some sort of break occurred at Delphi between IIIC and Late Geometric.
[130] Alin, op. cit. 143.
[131] Theocharis in Ergon (1960) 57.
[132] Alin, op. cit. 143 f.

Because Submycenaean as a temporal subdivision has hitherto been rather ill defined[133], scholars tend to find themselves speaking in defence of two diametrically opposed camps, of which the first firmly believes in a break in occupation at the end of the Bronze Age[134], and the other is equally convinced of continuity of settlement after that period[135]. In Crete Bronze Age custom, and presumably cult practice, also continued into Protogeometric and later at a number of sites. Furthermore, despite new features in pottery decoration, architectural design, dress ornaments and the introduction of iron to replace bronze, there is no convincing proof that strong intrusive elements arrived on the island during the transitional period between Minoan and Protogeometric[136]. One well-known Subminoan site is the Underground Spring Chamber at Knossos with its famous hut urn containing the figure of a Minoan goddess[137]. At Phaestos occupation continued even after the destruction of the palace, and was strengthened (perhaps late in III B or early in III C) by buildings, traces of which were discovered by Doro Levi[138]. This settlement survived into Geometric[139]. Similar continuity can be attested for Gortyn[140], and, of course, for the well-known settlement at Karphi[141]. The harbour town of Amnisos, near Knossos, also survived throughout Cretan history[142].

In the eastern Aegean and Asia Minor the fate of Mycenaean settlements has not been clearly determined in many instances, although fresh evidence is continually appearing. It is not always easy to decide what settlements, as in Lesbos, Aeolis, and in Ephesus, owe their existence to the migrations from the Greek mainland after the collapse of the Bronze Age, and how many had been established earlier and continued into Protogeometric. Mycenaean occupation may, for example, have survived on Samos and at Miletus[143], while a break was likely in Chios, Kolophon, Rhodes, and Kos[144]

---

[133] See Styren., *Sub. St.* 147, for possible examples of Submyc. or transitional.
[134] Desb., *L.M.* 136; Alin, *op. cit.* 144, also inclines to that belief.
[135] Vermeule, *op cit.* 270; cf. Webster, *Myc. to Homer*^{2} 139.
[136] Cf. Desb., *L.M.* 193.
[137] Evans, *P.M. II*, 128 ff.; Desb., *L.M.* 180.
[138] *A.S.I.* 19/20 N.S. (1957/8) 255 ff.
[139] Desb., *L.M.* 182.
[140] Doro Levi, *A.S.I.* 17/18 N.S. 215 ff.
[141] See above e.g. p. 137.
[142] J. D. S. Pendlebury, *The Archaeology of Crete*, 305; Desb., *L.M.* 169.
[143] Cf. Webster, *Myc. to Homer*^{2} 147; H. Simps., *Gazett.* 193; Desborough, however, states that the excavation indicates a gap in Miletus after the IIIC destruction.
[144] E.g. Desborough, *Protog. Pottery* 222; 232; *L.M.* 233.

before Protogeometric. Again Mycenaean survival may be assumed in the Carian cities of Iasos and Halikarnassos, on the grounds of Mycenaean, Submycenaean, and Protogeometric finds there[145].

Before we leave the eastern Aegean it is worth noting at this stage that a break in settlement during the crucial Submycenaean period does not necessarily imply the end of a well established sanctuary or cult. A case in point is Apollo's ancient oracle at Klaros[146] which endured into historic times despite the apparent break in the settlement at Kolophon[147]. At Ephesus the sanctuary existed before the arrival of the Greek migrants and continued throughout Greek history, although Artemis was identified with, and absorbed, the earlier local deity. The oracle and cult at Didyma, near Miletus, was old, too[148], and survived without interruption even if we assume with Desborough that there was break in settlement at Miletus before Protogeometric.

A strong case for survival from Mycenaean into historical times can be made out for the two islands in the Ionian Sea Kephallenia and Ithaka. In Kephallenia the evidence almost exclusively comes from finds made in the cemeteries[149] which prove uninterrupted occupation of the site from at least III C. The story is the same for the two settlements Polis and Aetos in Ithaka[150]. Of special note is the cave sanctuary at Polis which probably served cult purposes from Mycenaean onward[151].

Three major areas remain where continuity of settlement or cult can be proved from Mycenaean to Geometric times or later. All three are Cycladic islands in the central Aegean. A series of superimposed structures, including a megaron-type Protogeometric building, was discovered at Grotta on Naxos[152]. Also on Naxos finds from tombs on the Aplomata

---

[145] *A.S.I.* 39/40 (1961/2) 537; *A.J.A.* 67 (1963) 185; 352. On the Dodecanese see also *B.S.A.* 57 (1962) 154. Vermeule adds Tarsus, on the Cilician coast, and Enkomi, in Cyprus, to the list of Mycen. survivals, *Bronze Age* 270. According to Desborough, however, Tarsus was deserted before the Iron Age, and Enkomi suffered a similar fate at the end of IIIB, *L.M.* 206; 198.

[146] Paus. VII, 3, 1.

[147] Cf. Webster, *Myc. to Homer*² 150.

[148] Paus. VII, 2, 6.

[149] Desb., *L.M.* 103 ff.

[150] H. Simps., *Gazett.* 95; 96; Desborough, *L.M.* 109 f., states that there may have been a break at Polis at the end of the Mycenaean period.

[151] S. Benton, *B.S.A.* 35 (1935) 31 ff.; 40 (1945) 9 f. Desb., *L.M.* 108, with reservations.

[152] N. M. Condoleon, *Praktika* (1949) 112 ff.; (1950) 269 ff.; (1951) 214 ff.

coastal ridge probably prove uninterrupted occupation from III C across Protogeometric into Archaic times[153].

Recently Caskey excavated a long and narrow temple, probably first constructed in M.H., at Hagia Eirene on Keos[154]. This site remained sacred until late classical times, because new temples or sanctuaries were built on the ruins of the first building. Significant, too, is the discovery on Delos of three cult buildings one of which lies directly beneath the Archaic Artemision[155]. Continuity of cult on Delos, as on Keos, may imply continuity of settlement[156]. Occasionally a well established cult survived a temporary break in settlement, as we have observed at Miletus, Klaros, and Ephesus. In the last city a famous premigration shrine was taken over by newcomers at the turn of the Bronze Age: the goddess there changed her name to Artemis, but her nature and functions remained the same[157].

The almost extreme religious conservatism in Crete during the Dark Age is well known. Small refugee colonies, like the community at Karphi, might desert their habitations on the plains in time of danger during Late Minoan and retire to mountain strongholds but they revered the same type of goddess that had watched over them throughout the Bronze Age and before. The persistence of traditional religious material in Crete is well illustrated by the history of continued production of the goddess and her animals, especially the bull throughout the Dark Age. Examples from East Crete, with the exception of Vrokastro, Kavousi, and Praisos, are few only, but the rest of the island, particularly in the Achaean and Dorian areas, preserved a good deal of evidence that the typical hand and wheel-made votary figures of the goddess and her animals endured from the eleventh to the eighth century at sites like Hagia Triada, the Dictaean Cave, Gortyn, Arkades, and Anavlochos[158]. The goddess often continued

---

[153] Condoleon, *Ergon* for 1960, 185 ff.; for 1961, 199 f.; H. Simps., *Gazett.* 181; Desb., *L.M.* 152, leaves open the possibility that there was some "dislocation" of settlement at Grotta, and that intruders may have arrived there at the end of IIIC. But, he says, "there may well, from the evidence of some continuity in the ceramic tradition, have been a fusion with the existing inhabitants." Mr. Desborough privately informed me that the type of tomb changed at Aplomata after IIIC.

[154] J. L. Caskey, *A.J.A.* 66 (1962) 195; *Hesp.* 31 (1962) 263–83; 33 (1964) 326 ff.; 35 (1965) 367 ff.; *Arch.* 16 (1963) 284. Cf. above p. 140.

[155] H. Gallet de Santerre, *Délos Primitive;* cf. above p. 139.

[156] Cf. Desborough, *L.M.* 149.

[157] See Webster, *Myc. to Hom.* 149; 150.

[158] R. A. Higgins, *Greek Terracottas,* 17 f. For Gortyn see Rizza, *Santuario* Pl. X, 53; 55; 56; 58; XI, 59. Cf. Levi, *A.S.I.* 17/18 (N.S.) (1955/6) 281. For Greece see p. 210 f.

in the shape of the cylindrical idol, so familiar from Subminoan shrines like Gazi, a good ninth century example of which has been found at Phaistos[159]. At Vrokastro, too, three fragmentary goddess statuettes illustrate the smooth continuity of the type through the Dark Age, for one of the figures is Subminoan and the other two show the schematization of the eighth century votaries[160]. Beside the goddess the figure of the bull, modelled in clay or bronze, also survived in Crete at cult sites like the Patsos and Dictaean Caves, Tylissos, Prinias, Kavousi, Vrokastro, etc.[161].

An interesting and most instructive cult locality is that at Gortyn, a few miles north-east of Phaestos. This area was inhabited and saw some form of cult from Neolithic times[162]. During L.M. III C, or Subminoan, there was a village on the acropolis and the surrounding slopes of the hill[163]. The cult of the community was conservative, continuing older tradition, and concerned the type of goddess who was destined to become the classical city goddess[164]. The remarkable fact is that, from at least the end of the Bronze Age, cult continued in a line probably uninterrupted until Roman times[165]. On the same acropolis the first temple, which Levi calls pre-Hellenic, was built after the houses of the settlement had been moved to make way for the new structure[166]. The same area, however, yielded vase fragments belonging to Early and Middle Minoan, as well as Subminoan[167], which, together with the Geometric sherds there, suggests a continuous B.A. occupation.

Gortyn may well become a textbook of religious development from the Bronze to the Classical Age. Religious sculpture at Gortyn, for example, provides an almost unbroken series from Subminoan to Geometric and across the so-called Dedalic period to Archaic times[168]. What is more,

---

[159] Higgins, *op. cit.* 17, fig. 10.

[160] E. H. Hall, *Excavations in Eastern Crete, Vrokastro*, Philadelphia 1914, 101, No. 1, figs. 55 b; 108, No. 1; 111 f., No. 3, figs. 55 a; 63. *Jahrb.* 79 (1964) 15, fig. 14; Nicholls, *Auck. Cl. Ess.* 12.

[161] Nicholls, *op. cit.* 12.

[162] Levi, "Il Palladio di Gortina", *P. d. P.* 11 (1956) 285.

[163] Levi, *A.S.I.* (1955/6) 216; cf. Desb., *L. M.* 183.

[164] A clay head or mask, for example, discovered at the Gortyn site, Levi, *A.S.I.* (1955/6) fig. 38 a, immediately recalls the many Karphi terracottas. Cf. *P.d.P.* 11 (1956) 285 ff.; Rizza, *Santuario* 250.

[165] Levi, *P.d.P.* (1956) 290; Rizza, *op. cit.* ch. I–III.

[166] *A.S.I.* (1955/6) 216.

[167] *Ibid.*

[168] Levi, *A.S.I.* (1955/6) 277; 297; 280 ff.; J. Boardman, *Pre-Classical*, 107.

artistic and religious links join a number of Gortynian cultic statuettes with religious centres on the mainland like Perachora, and Artemis Orthia's sanctuary at Sparta. Particularly interesting, and most revealing with respect to the conservatism of religious practice, is a Submycenaean statuette from Gortyn[169] which is related to a cylindrical goddess figurine from Perachora[170] of the sixth century[171]. Finally, the close family resemblance, especially between Cretan and Dedalic figures, is evident from Gortynian examples[172] when compared, for instance, with the ivy statuettes found in a grave near the Athenian Dipylon[173].

Crete may be a special case, of course. The island mentality of its inhabitants was rather more impervious to change: the people more tenaciously than elsewhere in the Aegean world clung to their Bronze Age religious traditions, so that we should not look to Crete for examples of religious development in the Dark Age[174]. But two considerations greatly weaken this objection. Firstly, Crete was never entirely cut off from the outside world. Gortyn, for example, maintained its relations with Cyprus and the East even after the end of the Bronze Age[175]. Secondly, it is unlikely that in matters of cult the close connection between Crete and the mainland, which we observed in the previous chapter, was broken by the events of c. 1200 B.C. The part played by Cretan sculpture in the development of Greek forms is an argument against such a break[176]. Apart from the examples already given, we may cite other votive remains, particularly of the bull and other animals, which firmly link Cretan sanctuaries, like Hagia Triada, with mainland cult sites well into the Dark Age. Eileithyia's cave at Amnisos was the scene of worship until historical times[178]. Mycenaean interest in this cult is obvious from the part played in it by Poseidon

---

[169] Levi, *A.S.I.* (1955/6) 281, fig. 37 d.
[170] *Ibid.* and n.l.
[171] Levi, *op. cit.* 245; 281 and n. 1 & 2; Rizza, *Santuario* 250; Cf./Dawkins, *Sanct. of Artemis Orthia.* For early Archaic *vis-à-vis* the xoanon type sculpture see F. R. Grace, *Archaic Sculpture in Boeotia*, 1939, fig. 14 and compare with Levi, *op. cit.* 283, fig. 38 d.
[172] Levi, *op. cit.* 277 ff.
[173] G. M. A. Richter, *Korai, Archaic Greek Maidens*, London 1968, figs. 16–19.
[174] See e.g. Starr, *Origins* 83.
[175] S. Mollard-Besques, *Les Terres Cuites Grecques*, Paris 1963, 49.
[176] Cf. Levi, *A.S.I.* (1955/6) 277. Rizza, *Santuario* 264. For a discussion of the parallel development of plastic art in Crete and on the Mycen. mainland see Levi, "Gleanings from Crete", *A.J.A.* 49 (1945) 290.
[178] See above p. 78; 87 f.

(Enesidaon) who is recorded on one of the Linear B tablets as receiving offerings within the cave[179].

Evidently what we know of the continuing religious tradition in Protogeometric Crete of the tenth and ninth centuries should not be regarded in isolation as reflecting only island cultic practice, but this knowledge should also be applied to those mainland areas where cult survived the end of the Bronze Age. We noticed above that the fashion of modelling their goddess in the primitive style never quite fell out of vogue in Crete and Greece during the Dark Age. The cylindrical idol, like the ninth century examples from Phaistos[180], and the famous wheelmade head from Kalokhorio, in the Pedhiadha Plain[181], may have been produced in a peculiarly Cretan style, but such figures "expressed the beliefs of a rather mixed population, part native and part Achaean"[182].

The large wheelmade terracotta statuette of the goddess' bull splendidly illustrates this interdependence and interplay between Crete and the mainland which endured through the Dark Age. The figure of the bull beside the goddess was a common Aegean association. But the typical thirteenth/ twelfth cent. Mycen. votive terracotta directly derived from the Minoan bull rhyta. The Mycen. form found favour eventually in Crete in the twelfth cent. and survived there until the eighth cent. Artistically it developed along different lines in Greece, but in the sphere of religious cult the significance was the same in both centres[183]. There is one particularly striking illustration of this remarkable religious conservatism which emerges from a history of the Greek votive terracottas: in the B.A. sanctuary at Hagia Eirene, on Keos, the head from a sixteenth cent. statue was fixed on a makeshift base and still served as a cult image in eighth cent. Greek worship[184].

Outside Crete, on the mainland and on some of the islands, there are some persuasive examples of the persistence of cult localities. Beyond the few instances, which can be controlled with archaeological evidence, there

---

[179] KN Ma 719
[180] Higgins, *Grk. Terrac.* 17, fig. 10; *A.S.I.* N.S. 23/4 (1961/2) 407, fig. 52; 501, fig. 193.
[181] *K. Ch.* 5 (1951) 98; 12 (1958) 214, Pl. 10, 3.
[182] Nicholls, *Auck. Cl. Ess.* 6.
[183] On this history see Nicholls, *Auck. Cl. Ess.* e.g. 8 ff.; II, 12; 21; Higgins, *op. cit.* 13, with some reservations on mainland continuity.
[184] *Hesp.* 33 (1964) 330 f.; Pl. 60 e–g; Nicholls, *Auck. Cl. Ess.* The original torso was also recovered from the floor deposit of the B.A. room below the head, cf. *Hesp.* (1964) Pl. 61 a–c.

are a good many sites where one may plausibly expect a continuity of Mycenaean religious practices. Such sites include the area of Helen's temple in Therapnae, near Sparta[185], that of Athena Alea in Tegea[186], and that of Athena Kranaia in Elateia[187], in each of which Mycenaean sherds have been discovered[188]. We may be more certain of our evidence in the case of Apollo's Archaic temple in Thermos which was built apparently over a structure that may have served as a sanctuary from Mycenaean times[189]. Aetolian Thermos was settled from at least L.H. II, and although remains from III C are few only, many Geometric finds have been made, and there is no evidence of interruption at the end of the Bronze Age[190].

Of considerable interest is the temple of Apollo Maleatas at Epidaurus, for this precise area had been a cult locality from as early as E.H.[191]. Rich deposits of votive Mycenaean human and animal figurines, together with Geometric and Archaic finds, show the sacredness of the locality which endured throughout the stages of Late Helladic and beyond the end of the Bronze Age[192].

The sanctuary of Apollo-Hyacinthus at Amyclae, south of Sparta, pretty certainly had a similar history of cultic continuity from the Bronze Age into historical times. No Mycenaean buildings were associated with this Laconian site[193], which suggests that Amyclae may have been nothing but a cult centre[194]. Apollo's Archaic temple there covered the traditional sacred

---

[185] *B.S.A.* 15 (1908/9) 108 ff.

[186] *B.C.H.* 25 (1901) 256; 45 (1921) 403; H. Simps., *Gazett.* 40 (cult cont. was possible).

[187] P. Paris, "Elatée" *Bibl. ecol. franc.* 60 (1891) 283.

[188] Cf. M. P. Nilsson, *Gesch.*, I, 341.

[189] Rhomaios in *Deltion* I (1915) 225 ff.; II (1916) 179 ff.; cf. Nilsson, *Gesch.* I, 342; H. Simps., *Gazett.* 91 f.

[190] See Alin, *Ende d. Fundst.* 136.

[191] Papademetriou, in *Praktika* (1948) 90 ff.; (1949) 91 ff.; (1950) 194 ff.; (1951) 204 ff. There seems to be an "archaeological" gap at this site between IIIB and Geometric, H. Simps., *Gazett.* 20.

[192] Cf. Desb., *L.M.* 43, "There seems no reasonable doubt that the memory of the area as being sacred survived the fall of the Mycenaean civilization." On p. 78 Desborough is rather more sceptical. Cf. Alin, *Ende* 51, "Direkte Beweise für eine Kontinuität bis in die historische Zeit fehlen anscheinend, ein gewisses Weiterleben von Kultvorstellungen ist aber anzunehmen."

[193] Desb., *L.M.* 42.

[194] V. Ehrenberg, *From Solon to Socrates*, 29 f., believes that Amyclae was the pre-Dorian settlement centre of the Achaeans. An interesting connection between the Laconian site and Crete is the name Amyklaion which occurs at Gortyn, Ehrenberg, *op. cit.* 382 n. 8. The presence of an Amyklaion at Gortyn does not necessarily hint

area which contained a great many of the usual Mycenaean human and animal figurines[195], while Protogeometric and Geometric remains serve to prove continuity of cultic use beyond the end of the Bronze Age[196].

Of the three great classical cult sites on the mainland, Delphi, Eleusis, Olympia, at least the first two have strong ties with the Mycenaean Age. The case for Olympia, however, is uncertain. The general area surely saw Mycenaean settlement[197], but probably not in, or immediately near, the Altis. It is, of course, possible that the latter and the adjacent stadium area in Mycenaean times had, like Amyclae, merely served for cultic purposes. But the few Mycenaean sherds found there, and under the Heraion, hardly constitute sufficient proof of that, while the absence of Protogeometric and Geometric material at present is no argument for cult continuity[198]. The great importance of the games in classical times tended to overshadow the original significance of the locality as an oracle[199]. But the debate still continues whether Zeus' oracle was the first there, and indeed how far back oracular activity can be traced in Olympia. This problem cannot detain us now. In the meantime it is worth noting that Middle Helladic buildings, which may have been sanctuaries, were recently discovered on the Kronion hill flanking the Altis[200]. Perhaps, like Delphi, Olympia saw a transference of cult at the end of Helladic. It is possible that a sanctuary or shrine was moved then from the Kronion hill to the Altis. But this must remain conjectural at present.

The picture is considerably clearer at Delphi. A Mycenaean settlement was well established there by L.H. III in the area between Castalia and the temple of Apollo[201]. This temple was built on what must have been the site

at a pre-Dorian settlement there from Amyclae. The more likely explanation is that the name signified a certain type of cult or cult locality. But, in the absence of other examples, this must remain conjecture.

[195] Desb., *L.M.* 42.
[196] Desb., *L.M.* 42; 88, is inclined to doubt continuity on the ground that, as he claims, "there is no ceramic link between the last Mycen. pottery and the Protogeometric material"..."Nevertheless it does seem possible that in this instance the memory at least of the spot's being sacred survived." Vermeule, *Bronze Age* 270; 323, is rather more optimistic when she confirms continuity between twelfth century wares and Protogeometric remains. Cf. Styrenius, *Sub. St.* 143; H. Simps., *Gazett.* 42.
[197] Desb., *L.M.* 91; Alin, *Ende* 69.
[198] Cf. Alin, *ibid.*
[199] See H. W. Parke, *The Oracles of Zeus*, Oxford 1967, 180 ff.
[200] See *J.H.S.* Arch. Rep. 1960/1, 14; Wiesner, *Olymp.* 145 f.; H. Simps., *Gazett.* 79.
[201] Alin, *Ende* 129 f.

of a Mycenaean sanctuary, because of the number of idols found there in the earth which was richly mixed with remains of offerings and sacrifice[202]. Amongst the many votive offerings a rhyton was found in the shape of a lioness' head of Minoan type which may point to a connection between Delphi and Cretan cult[203]. Whatever the truth of this may be, and there is some literary supporting evidence, a Mycenaean sanctuary preceded Apollo's temple on the same site.

Again it is possible that during the Mycenaean period such a sanctuary was transferred a little way off to Marmaria, for there beneath the foundations of the Archaic temple of Athena Pronaia an even greater number of goddess idols has come to light pointing to strong cultic activity. This last find was not associated with any buildings, so that one could suppose the deposit to have been no more than a collection of offerings buried to consecrate Athena's Archaic temple at the time of its construction[204]. Instances, however, of isolated Mycenaean sanctuaries, as at Amyclae for example, seem to contradict such a supposition. Furthermore material found under the temple, from later periods like Geometric, disturbed or not in their context, argue for continuity of sacred ritual[205], and Delphi and the immediate neighbourhood was a religious site of some consequence from Mycenaean times. The settlement may have suffered a natural catastrophe in L.H. III C[206], but life continued there across Submycenaean into Geometric and later[207]. In view of this persistence of settlement at Delphi, a continuous flow of cult, certainly at Marmaria, is more likely than a temporary interruption at the finish of the Bronze Age which was followed by reinstitution of cult sometime during the Archaic Age[208].

At Eleusis, too, there was, according to Desborough, a "cessation of worship" at the end of Helladic[209]. But what evidence there is seems to point

---

[202] Cf. Nilsson, *Gesch.* I, 339.
[203] This find is unique and may, of course, be an accidental import, cf. Parke, *Greek Oracles*, London 1967, 33.
[204] Cf. Desb., *L.M.* 44.
[205] See also P. Amandry, *La Mantique Apollinienne à Delphes*, Paris 1950, 231; Nilsson, *H.* 7 (1958) 240.
[206] Alin, *Ende* 130.
[207] Cf. Styrenius, *Sub. St.* 144 f.
[208] W. G. Forrest, "Colonization and the Rise of Delphi", *H.* 6 (1957) 171, mentions the absence of archaeological evidence for Protogeometric and Geometric in support of unbroken cult which, however, he admits as being possible. Cf. Desb., *L.M.* 125.
[209] *L.M.* 47; 115.

to another conclusion. The sixth century Peisistratean telesterion at Eleusis marked the area which had been sacred from at least the time of the Mycenaean Megaron B[210]. Here cult was continually observed into historic times, sometimes even at the cost of considerable hardship on the part of the generations of worshippers[211].

Cult continuity in the Aegean islands is well established at least in Aegina, Keos and Delos. The case for Samos in the eastern Aegean is rather more difficult. Mrs. Vermeule believes that continuity there between twelfth-century and Protogeometric ware is affirmed[212]. The evidence is fairly thin[213], but there probably was a Mycenaean settlement in L.H. III associated with the Heraeum near the mouth of the Imbrasos river. Because of the difficult conditions the area beneath, and in the vicinity of the temple, has not yet been fully explored. The first sanctuary of Hera was probably built there at the beginning of the first millennium B.C. on the same site as the cult locality of an Aegean goddess of nature[214]. It is possible, however, that there was a break in occupation of the area between the Bronze and Dark Age. Nevertheless, as at Ephesus, the type of cult practised most likely remained the same in Samos.

A useful indication of this continuity is furnished by the persistence of the typical Bronze Age votive terracottas of the bull found in the open-air sanctuaries and the earliest of the great temples[215]. These statuettes were part of the same cult throughout the Dark Age[216], in honour of the same goddess whose classical name of Hera may have come to Samos with the Ionian immigrants from the Argolid. Witness to Hera's function in Samos as a nature goddess are the rites of the Tonaia festival and her *hieros gamos* with Zeus on the island[217].

---

[210] See above p. 140; cf. H. Simps., *Gazett.* 110.
[211] Mylonas, *Eleusis* 44; cf. Nilsson, *Gesch.* I, 340; Webster, *Myc. to Homer* 139.
[212] *Br. Age* 270. But see her list on p. 325.
[213] See Desb., *L.M.* 158.
[214] Cf. Wiesner, *Olympos* 248.
[215] *A.M.* 55 (1930) 1–20; 58 (1933) 146–73.
[216] D. Ohli, *A.M.* 65 (1940) 57–102; cf. 72 (1957) 36 ff.; *Anz.* (1964) 220–31; B. Fryer-Schauenburg, *Elfenbeine aus dem samischen Heraion*, Hamburg 1966, 117; Nicholls, *Auck. Cl. Ess.* 15. The excavators' conclusions have been contested by J. Boardman, *Excavations in Chios 1952-55. Greek Emporio (B.S.A.* Suppl. paper VI), London 1967, 188, and by Higgins, *Greek Terrac.* 18.
[217] This aspect of Hera is therefore somewhat in contrast with her position as palace goddess in Greece as defined by Nilsson, *Gesch.* I, 429 f.

On Aegina the temple of Artemis Aphaea marks the site of an older cult which had endured from at least L.H. III B[218]. We have already touched on the startling evidence from the islands of Delos and Keos[219]. A later sanctuary constructed at Hagia Eirene within the ruins of the B.A. temple, and dedicated to Dionysus[220], graphically confirms the persistence of cult, as does the curious cult image there[221].

Here then we are confronted with a fairly extensive list of sites whose continuous use as sacred localities is pretty certain. Their number may well grow as the result of current and future excavation. The sites covered a major portion of the Mycenaean world in the East, on the islands in the Aegean, in Crete, and on the mainland. It would seem that the localities mentioned and examined above, where occupation and cult persisted even through the crucial years of the Dark Age, offer us a model of what obtained in the Aegean lands. It is really difficult to believe that Gortyn, Amnisos, Epidaurus, Delphi, Eleusis, Delos, and Keos and the other sites were exceptions to common religious practice in that part of the world: that all religious faith and ritual were swept aside together with the Mycenaean palaces and their attendant bureaucracy.

Desborough's conclusion that only Delos and perhaps Keos enjoyed religious continuity is unduly pessimistic[222]. Even less likely appears to be the claim occasionally made that cult instituted at older sites in the Archaic Age was new in form and content due to the influence of Homeric epic[223], for Homer himself is far from definite regarding the Mycenaean world and cannot be used as a textbook for the period[224]. It remains a fair axiom that uninterrupted settlement presupposes enduring cult, especially where a sanctuary, however small, continued in use. Therefore, as Nilsson has already pointed out, we can confidently claim continuity of cult for the site where a classical temple was constructed over the area of the old Myce-

---

[218] See above p. 157. H. Simps., *Gazett.* 113, believes the remains are too few to establish Mycenaean cult with certainty.

[219] Above p. 139; 140 f.; 218.

[220] *Hesp.* 31 (1962) 278 ff.; 33 (1964) 326 ff.; 35 (1966) 367 ff.

[221] See above p. 221.

[222] *C.A.H.*² II, ch. 36 (1962); *L.M.* 244.

[223] "The Greeks of the end of the eighth century had a clear knowledge, not only of where the tombs of their long dead heroes were, but also of the location of their places of worship." Desb., *L.M.* 46. Desborough suggests that the Greeks had "continuity of memory, even if not of worship."

[224] Cf. e.g. A. Andrewes, *The Greeks*, 28.

naean palace as at Mycenae, Tiryns, Athens, and so on[225]. It has occasionally been argued, falsely we believe, that in these last cases the prominent position of the old acropolis attracted the classical temple builders, rather than the sacred associations of the old palace site[226]. The factor determining the selection of the temple area was not geographical chance, but in every case the locality's former sacredness, for the simple reason that the goddess inhabiting the new temple, the city goddess, kept her old home which she had in the palace at an earlier stage of her history.

We have, of course, no means of knowing precisely what ritual was practised at the Bronze Age sanctuaries. Our knowledge is confined to an understanding of the broad outlines of the nature of the cult. This should be clear from what has been said in previous chapters. However, the same difficulty attaches to the exact interpretation of cultic performance in classical times. Figures like Demeter, Athena, and Artemis had lost themselves in a multiplicity of functions of which the older features are barely discernible to the religious historian. Yet even the national cults of Athena and Artemis on the Athenian acropolis contained many ancient, traditional, parts in their ritual whose original significance was incomprehensible to the worshipper. Accordingly, a fifth century theologian and thinker, like Euripides, felt free to invent plausible histories of cult foundations in Athens, Attica, and further afield. Aetiological fabrication and myth-making were rife throughout historical times, in order to account for divine functions and cult practice which reached back into the second millennium B.C.

With our greater understanding of the Mycenaean world we most certainly have the advantage of isolating traditional features which were destined to survive into classical times. These features consisted not merely in the divine names that continued unbroken from the thirteenth century, and earlier, throughout Greek history, but in the cult localities where these deities were revered. The type of cult, like the deity associated with it, one might suppose, was as closely bound to a locality as hero cult in historic times centred about a tomb. This rule, if true, helps to throw light on the religious history of important cultic sites in classical Greece. In other words, oracular activity in Delphi, Dodona, or Olympia, for example, should in some form have naturally arisen from cult observance and practice which obtained there in the Bronze Age, if, that is, continuity of cult can reasonably be assumed for these places. To this very difficult

---

[225] Nilsson, *Gesch.* I, 345 f.; cf. U. Bianchi, *La Religione Greca*, 426.
[226] E.g. Starr, *Origins* 174 and n. 8.

point we shall have to return another time, because it connects with problems arising from the possible change of divine government at a given locality in the course of its history, such as Apollo's usurpation of the oracular seat at Delphi.

As far as the cult localities are concerned which have been discussed as continuing from Mycenaean until classical times, it is safe to assume that the fundamental beliefs attached to the area also endured. There is no precise evidence to confirm this assumption – precise evidence does not exist for any aspect of this period in Greek history –, but proof lies in the nature, function and probable history of the deities associated with the continuing cult sites. They are figures in common vogue in Crete and on the mainland in Mycenaean times, such as Eileithyia in Amnisos, Aphaea on Aegina, Hera, Athena, Artemis, and Poseidon[227] and Apollo, although the last, apart from his obvious Eastern and Cretan ties, has successfully hidden his earlier history. In the East, Mycenaean settlers who had taken their gods with them, and also immigrants from the West at the beginning of the Dark Age who continued Mycenaean tradition, came to terms with the already established Eastern cults as at Samos, in Ephesus, probably in Miletus, and at other Ionian sites[228]. Hera, Artemis, Poseidon, and perhaps Apollo became the new names at often older Eastern cult sites; but the nature of the cult remained basically unchanged: the new Hera in Samos, or Artemis at Ephesus, held functions no more incompatible with her nature than those of Artemis and Aphaea, or Eileithyia, in Aegina and Crete.

If the same type of deity remained connected with an ancient cult site until classical times, then surely we are entitled to assume continuity of cult form at that site through the Dark Age, provided, of course, that settlement and/or worship continued there unbroken from the Mycenaean period. It is worth repeating, therefore, that one should not equate the lack of satisfactory monumental or any other kind of evidence for the period with an actual void in the history of Greece[229].

There are three features of the Greek scene which are usually cited as causes and results of an absolute cultural break at the end of the Mycenaean Age. These causes and effects are ethnographic, political, and architectural. The Dorians have been held to account for much of the damage.

---

[227] Cf. above p. 154 f.
[228] Cf. Webster, *Myc. to Homer* 145 ff.
[229] Cf. C. Vatin on Desborough's disbelief in religious continuity on Delos, "Les doutes peuvent êtres jugés excessifs", *B.C.H.* 89 (1965) 229 f. n. 3.

One may hope, though, that what has been said above will go some way towards absolving these barbarians from their guilt. If new popular elements penetrated south at the end of the second millennium, they did not come at once in overwhelming strength, nor did their arrival materially affect the development of mainland culture. It is interesting to observe in this context that even those scholars who firmly believe in large scale invasion are often prepared to admit that there is no noticeable distinction in religious custom between the so-called Dorian and non-Dorian areas in Greece[230].

Whatever the exact history of local government may have been in individual Greek communities, and we shall never know the personalities and struggles involved, the evolution of the classical *polis* was marked by a variety of political changes. The political power of the wanax declined with the disappearance of his palace. The king, with his close association with the palace goddess, becomes an object of cult, while secular power devolved on to the shoulders of a local noble, the basileus, and his aristocratic supporters until, with the advent of the archonship, the basileus, too, is no more than a mere religious functionary. This progression of events from monarchy via aristocratic rule to democracy is mapped for Athens by Aristotle in five stages[231] which basically seem a plausible reconstruction of Athenian history during the Dark Age.

What occurred in Athens quite likely reflects the history of many areas of the Greek world. Recent archaeological discovery at Emporio on Chios, for example[232], illustrates the evolution that took place there over the centuries. Political government and cult, in the hands of an aristocratic ruling class, still centred about the acropolis in c. 800 B.C., while within two-hundred years a new Chian constitution incorporated separate magistracies and a *demarchos*. The dates for such political reorganization no doubt varied over a large time-span, but they all fell within the so-called Dark Age from its early years to the end, for the Homeric Scheria already pos-

---

[230] Cf. Nilsson, *Gesch.* I, 339, "Die griechische Religion ist im wesentlichen dieselbe in den von den Dorern besetzten und in den von ihnen nicht berührten Landschaften, und das beruht keineswegs auf nachträglicher Ausgleichung unter Einwirkung von Homers allgegenwärtigen Einfluß, sondern auf ursprünglicher Wesensgleichheit."

[231] *Ath. Pol.* 3. Cf. the discussion in Webster, *op cit.* 142 ff. It is, however, more difficult to agree with Webster on the divinity of the early king.

[232] J. Boardman, *J.H.S.* 75 (1955), Suppl. 45; 76 (1956) 35; Webster, *op. cit.* 157.

sessed the vital features of the classical *polis*: the central walled agora containing cult and government[233].

What effect did these political changes have on inherited religious belief, or on cultural and artistic tradition? There is, of course, no detailed source one could consult for an answer. Let us consider, however, that these changes occurred from within. They were the result of contests between the wanax, the basileis, possibly the lawagetas, and the nobility of a community, not, though, of the advent of the Dorians who might have imposed their government, their gods and cults, on the older settlements. Intruders from outside can hardly be held directly responsible for political events in Greece, when no part of the mainland was exempt from the movement to the new *polis*, including thoses areas and cities, like Athens, which traditionally escaped the onslaught of the legendary Sons of Heracles and, for all the upheavals, kept her gods and cults. No foreign invader dictated an alien religion to a vanquished people.

True, with the end of palace administration and the political power of the wanax there disappeared the close relationship of the king with the goddess who was revered within the palace. Her position and functions did not materially alter, however, so much as develop and extend. Her temple replaced the palace, because the divine house served the entire new city and within it she now received the old king as Athena, according to myth, received Erechtheus. The wanax survived, but now as the title of a truly divine figure, the object of cult.

We need not suppose that the rise of an aristocratic government affected traditional religious beliefs more than outwardly. The administration of cult passed into the control of a few chosen noble families who justified their position by claiming divine origin. The Mycenaean world with its numerous strongholds and its excellent communication declined and eventually disappeared. It was a relatively lengthy process which began at about 1300 B.C. and continued for some two-hundred years. Artistic styles and culture remained, but they deteriorated, became stiff or decadent perhaps, and they were no longer part of a *koine*. Gradually individual styles became noticeable[234], for the simple reason that the people of the mainland grew more isolated from one another.

To what extent is it possible to assume that the evolution in temple architecture reflected a break between the old and classical times? The

[233] Homer, *Od.* 6, 9; 266.
[234] Cf. Vermeule, *Gr. in the B.A.* 220.

answer to this question is, like so much of the evidence from this period, inconclusive. Noteworthy, however, is that the architectural order of the megaron for religious structures remained from the Mycenaean palace to the classical Greek temple. The shrines or temples erected by the communities of the Dark Age were, as one might expect, puny and ephemeral. Nothing identifiable now survives. But from the ground plan of the houses of the period, one may form an idea of the religious structures. The shape was rectangular, the megaron, and therefore familiar to the Mycenaean architect.

The other common form of building in the Dark Age was apsidal[235], an order which, as is well known, was not only fashionable in Middle Helladic but continued to be used for temples in Geometric times[236]. Excellent examples of this order are the apsidal temple beneath the Telesteria at Eleusis, and Apollo's temple at Thermos[237]. Also a few clay models of temples from Perachora and the Argive Heraeum illustrate the primitive but traditional architecture of the Dark Age[238]. Despite the very useful evidence of continuing fashions in building, the remains of this from the Dark Age are, not surprisingly, scanty. It is quite reasonable to say that "architecture was reduced to cottage terms"[239], for the simple structures soon collapsed and perished. That was part of the recession of the age.

The lack of architectural glamour, however, has no bearing on the nature of the cult celebrated within the primitive sanctuary. Rather more significant is the fact that these temples, as the models illustrate, were separate buildings, not part of larger dwellings also used for domestic purposes like the shrine within the Mycenaean palace. This divorce of the divine from the secular some modern historians commonly cite as proof of the religious break in the first millennium away from Mycenaean custom. The generally accepted account of the development of Greek sacred architecture begins with the simple chapel, like the Perachora models, which appeared about the ninth century in association with the earlier free-standing altar as the site

---

[235] See e.g. Starr, *Origins* 247 f. For a good account of Greek architecture in Geometric times see now H. Drerup, *Griechische Baukunst in geometrischer Zeit (Arch. Hom.)*, Göttingen 1969.

[236] Absent, however, in Late Helladic.

[237] Mylonas, *Eleusis* 57 f.; cf. P. Demargne, *Aegean Art*, 315, fig. 412 f. (Samos).

[238] These belong to the ninth cent. at the latest, *Perachora* I, 34–41; K. Müller, *A.M.* 48 (1923) 52–68; Starr, *Orig.* 249. See above p. 142 on the D. A. and 12/11th cent. terracotta models of round & rectang. shrines from Crete and Greece.

[239] Andrewes, *Greeks* 48.

of worship. Larger temples, like the Heraeum on Samos, replaced such structures in the course of the eighth century.

Therefore separate temples, which rose at this time not only on the islands but in the East and on the mainland at Corinth, Sparta, in the Argolid, and so on, are assumed to be a purely Greek feature with no ties binding them to Mycenaean custom beyond the use of the megaron plan. Such beginnings, whose roots lie buried in the history of the Dark Age, led in the seventh century to a veritable revolution in temple building when combined with a new Greek awareness of Oriental, and particularly Egyptian, styles in monumental architecture and sculpture. The new stone edifice, the father of the classical temple, which soared to the sky isolated from, and dwarfing, the miserable houses of mudbrick of the mortal worshipper must then represent a fresh, enlightened, and entirely changed epoch of Greek religious faith[240].

A new epoch was undoubtedly born after the gloomy recession of the many Dark Age generations, when the seventh century heralded a fantastic spurt in building activity, but hardly a change of religious faith. To begin with, the Egyptian contribution to Greek building and sculptural concepts in this and subsequent ages has consistently been overrated[241]. The Greeks probably owed the habit of building their temples in stone to Egypt, but neither the Doric nor the Ionic order, which after all "was evolved in the islands and Ionia," was the direct product of Egyptian influence. The Doric style, in fact, merely continued earlier mainland architectural habits: it "is a sophisticated version in stone of the sort of timber-work which went before"[242].

Nothing but local pride lies at the bottom of the upsurge in the building of imposing and costly temples, when the settlements, growing in strength, vied with one another in doing honour to the gods[243]. What is more important to the religious historian is the isolation of the temple from the secular houses. The divinity who is no longer in intimate contact with the worshipper in his private house, or in the palace chapel, or even at a simple

---

[240] See e.g. Starr, *Orig.* 247 ff.

[241] See still Richter, *Korai* 4. For Egyptian influence on Greek sculpture see *ibid.*, where Miss Richt. remarks on the import from Egypt of "the arch-like openings at the bottoms of the garments". Her examples are not very illuminating, see Pl. I c–f. Furthermore this feature was not unknown on the Minoan idols, cf. e.g. the idol from Karphi, repr. in Nilsson, *M.M.R.* fig. 26 – double arch.

[242] J. Boardman, *Pre-Classical* 126.

[243] Cf. *op. cit.* 134.

country altar or shrine[244], it may be argued, must have changed his or her nature.

If such arguments were still possible a few years ago, they do exemplify the considerable risk of reaching firm conclusions without sufficient archaeological or other data. Until recently there was little in the way of monumental remains from the Mycenaean world to testify in support of the use of separate cult buildings unattached to some form of domestic dwelling. The immediate deduction seemed obvious that Mycenaean, like Minoan, cult essentially belonged in the home or palace or, by the end of the Bronze Age, in open-air sanctuaries[245], whereas worship in isolated temples signified a Greek departure from former practice. This opinion will have to be revised, however, in the light of the latest discoveries. In fact, it is possible that the Greek temple developed from the sacred building often associated with open-air sanctuaries, like e.g. the twelfth century megaron-type structure at Hagia Triada[246], which may have served the purpose of holding the cult image[247]. In any case, such isolated buildings were known to the Bronze Age and could assume the grand proportions of a temple.

At Eleusis, on the east slope of the acropolis, the remains of the Telesteria mark the site of free-standing temple structures which were erected there probably from L.H. II, until classical times[248]. Moreover what could be proved for Eleusis should be strongly suspected of other sites, like Amyclae or Delphi, either in the area of Athena's temple at Marmaria, or possibly in the precinct of Apollo's temple[249]. Suspicion becomes certainty with the evidence of a Helladic temple on Keos, and with the discovery of the pre-Artemision below the later temple of Artemis on Delos[250].

Neither artistic evolution, provided its roots lie firmly embedded in traditional concepts, nor political development should of necessity reflect a break in conservative religious beliefs. The bald truth is that with our

---

[244] See above ch. 2.
[245] See L. Banti, *A.S.I.* 3–5 N.S. (1941–3) 40 ff., for an account of these sanctuaries in Greece, Crete, and the islands.
[246] Mylonas, *Eleusis* 37.
[247] Cf. Nicholls, *Auck. Cl. Ess.* 8; 21.
[248] Mylonas, *Eleusis* 37.
[249] Mylonas, *Mycenae* 148.
[250] See above p. 139 f. A succinct account of the plan of these structures can now be found in Mylonas, *Mycenae* 146 ff. Cf. Lord William Taylour, *The Mycenaeans*, 69; Webster, *Myc. to Homer* 319 n. 49; and in *L.* 11 (1966) 7; Mylonas, *Mycenae* 148, "We may, however, on the evidence of Keos and Eleusis, maintain that separate buildings serving as temples ... did exist in Mycenaean times."

poor understanding of the critical early centuries of the first millennium we cannot argue with any kind of optimistic dogmatism. Any deductions made remain pretty well empirical and open to revision in the light of further evidence. Archaeology is, of course, an extremely valuable science which constitutes our only real aid to the understanding of the Dark Age. However, archaeological discoveries, too, are comparatively unrewarding, and the reason for that lies partly in the nature of an impoverished age unused to monumental building. Therefore the danger of misinterpreting what there is is obvious.

Accounts of the Dark Age have emphasized the impersonality and symmetry of the evolving Geometric style of pottery decoration, the absence in the beginning of human and animal figures or plant life, in order to draw certain conclusions about the nature of contemporary society and belief[251]. This method is unsatisfactory, however, since the artistic fashions of a particular period rarely reveal much about the contemporary cultural and social institutions. This is certainly true of the Geometric style which at most betrays the history of its development from Protogeometric and ultimately Bronze Age forms. It seems wrong, therefore, to speak of a "geometric outlook...rising out of parallel political and social simplification," or to call on the many monsters in Late Geometric and Orientalizing art as witnesses to the human fear which was a sign of the times"[252]. These points may have substance but they cannot be deduced from artistic styles alone. Again, human or divine and animal representations for a time ceased to be painted on vases[253]. But this temporary change of fashion is of no consequence to the history of religious belief[254]. Altogether the vase material is difficult to work with from the point of view of the historian of the eighth century, and the vase designs are unreliable evidence for cult practice. In terms of source material this is a costly argument which ought, however, to be fairly rigorously observed.

---

[251] See e.g. Starr, *Origins* ch. 4.
[252] Starr, *op. cit.* 142; 280.
[253] Cf. Boardman, *Pre-Class.* 58, figs. 30–37.
[254] The first human figure found on a Greek vase is that of a female mourner painted above the handle of a krater from the Kerameikos. The date of the vase is the second half of the ninth century, Middle Geometric, J. N. Coldstream, *Greek Geometric Pottery*, London 1968, 21. By the eighth century definite scene composition begins to replace such isolated figures. Not surprisingly, since these were funerary vases, the most popular representation is that of a burial, the laying out of the dead together with attendant mourners and ritual (Coldstream, *op. cit.* 350).

In this period of swirling uncertainty let us hold on to two important facts: a) the continuity of cult sites, and b) the continuity of divine nomenclature. Furthermore we may assume with reason that the relatively few sites, discussed above, which have left archaeological traces of probably uninterrupted use are merely representative of what went on over a wide area of the Greek world throughout the dark years. This is surely a tenable position despite the excessive caution of the archaeologists. Consider, too, that, however resplendent the temples that began to rise up in the Archaic Age, the gods and goddesses residing in them were no fresh creations or recent imports from the East.

Zeus was known to Cretans and Mycenaeans in the Bronze Age; Poseidon was known, and Hermes, Dionysus. Equally familiar to worshippers of the time were Athena, Hera, Artemis, perhaps Demeter, Eileithyia and others. Fortunately these names have safely come down to us by means of the Late Helladic Linear script. From the same source we gather that the Mycenaeans already possessed the concept of the individual deity (*theos*) and of the collective gods (*pantes theoi*). Here are the parts and essence of a pantheon which would not have come as a surprise to the classical Greek. We also noticed that the gods and goddesses, whom we can identify from the Linear tablets, were compatible in the sense of conforming to the image we had formed of a goddess of nature in all her aspects associated with a male figure[255].

The latter was chthonic, often a lesser companion, or paredros, of the goddess, and he was connected with the annual vegetation cycle[256]. The male figure enjoyed a close relationship with the Mycenaean king, the wanax, to the point even of becoming interchangeable with him[257], while both god and goddess had a curious affinity to particular animals, like the bird, bull, snake, and goat, and consequently could appear in zoomorphic or human shape[258]. Such features belong to an earlier stage of religious development whose progress, however, moved along to classical times on a fairly predictable path. Traces of older religious custom survived in myth, in cult, and even in state religious practice, but usually in mutilated form[259].

---

[255] Cf. L. Séchan – P. Lévêque, *Les Grandes Divinités de la Grèce*, 184, "Il n'y a guère de divinité féminine, en Grèce, qui ne soit l'héritière des Mères préhelléniques."
[256] Above p. 158; 177 ff.
[257] 172.
[258] 171.
[259] E.g. 173 f.

The line of progress is really quite clear at least in broad outline. Many of the major Greek deities still betray their connection with nature cult, including Zeus, Athena, Hera, and Poseidon. They may ultimately be traced back to a nucleus, in the Bronze Age, of a goddess and male associate concerned with all aspects of birth and death and fertile nature. Perhaps one could speak of a governing divine duality, but the term is not particularly significant since the goddess, and most likely the male figure too, already in Minoan and Mycenaean times had assumed a number of aspects connected with rather more specialized functions. She became a goddess of birth as Eileithyia in one aspect, a palace goddess who developed into the later figure of Athena, or she was concerned with the wild, and with animal life when, perhaps, she resided on mountains tops, and we meet her again in the goddess Artemis.

These were all aspects of one central divinity and her associate[260], aspects which can be presumed to have crystallized into separate identities. A Minoan and Mycenaean custom, indicating incidentally the relationship between all these aspects and reflecting a stage prior to the formation of separate figures, was to call on the divine power under various invocatory titles such as "The Sweet One," "The Mistress," "The Holy One," "The Lord or Lady"[261]. That this habit survived until the end of the Mycenaean Age we learn from the use of Wanax and Potnia on the Linear B tablets. But even after that age, outside literary usage, the Anakes and Potniae endured in cult, albeit in shadowy form[262].

The invocatory title suggests that the divinity was expected to appear in an epiphany in bodily form, like the figures we see floating down from above on so many Cretan seals, but it also hints at a stage of evolution when the various aspects had not yet become separate individual figures. Such individualization must have occurred when particular divine aspects became closely concerned with particular functions, that is to say independent divinities began to isolate themselves into, for example, a domestic or palace goddess, a goddess of birth and death, a goddess of the wild, a goddess of fertility and growth of nature, and so on. The male figure suffered a similar experience: we meet perhaps a Master of Animals and, of course, the god closely concerned with the protection and safety of a settlement, like Poseidon at Pylos.

---

[260] Cf. above p. 171 f.; 174.
[261] Above e.g. p. 180.
[262] Cf. the use of Potnia in the hierophant's cry at Eleusis, above p. 167.

Isolation of function implies separate ritual and cult locality which ranged from shrines in the house or palace, the ancestor of the city deity's temple on the acropolis, to cave sanctuaries that continued in use[263]. More significantly departmentalization of particular divine aspects led to the emergence of individually named deities with well defined spheres of influence. The highest form of this development we meet with in the classical pantheon where each god has found his home and function. Quite evidently shifts and changes in divine stature occurred during the centuries prior to the classical period, and no doubt in part we have to thank Homer and subsequent literature for a closer delineation of the gods' functions.

Partly, though, the Dark and Archaic Ages helped to strip the earlier gods of much of their originally chthonic nature. They came to be largely purified, as it were, of their former narrow association with animals and with the perennial vegetation cycle before being admitted to state cult which had no place for the traditional attributes of snake, bird, or bull[264]. Also the curiously close relationship between man and gods, exemplified by the divine form of epiphany, fell by the way, as did the intimate, almost mystic, association between goddess and secular ruler, the wanax. But religious values had remained fundamentally the same even from the end of the previous millennium. What changes there were could perhaps best be described as ethical or moral, if one may use that word in this context. The new official cult had less depth, but more light and beauty and reason[265].

It seems to follow, then, that the pantheon of a classical *polis* represented a more or less tidy, coordinated and unified, picture of gods and cult which already existed in the Dark Age, even if in a locally scattered form throughout many separate communities. There are two extremely important points that arise from our observations on the continuous evolution

---

[263] The chronological sequence of the use of particular cult localities is impossible to establish beyond the broadest outline. In Crete, of course, see Appendix, peak sanctuaries generally were confined to Middle Minoan – see also my article in *H.* 18 (1969) 257 ff. –, while domestic sanctuaries did not begin before M.M. Furthermore cave cult continued in vogue at all periods. All these cults, however, particularly cave and domestic cult, shared basic features – see ch. 2 – which betray a common denominator of religious belief.

[264] Cf. above p. 171.

[265] Cf. the lines of R. Pettazzoni, *La Religione nella Grecia antica*, 53, "Non fu (l'ordine nuovo) una riforma religiosa. Non fu protesta contro le forme tramandate, in nome di un nuovo principio bandito da un verbo rivelature. Forse, anzi, si può dire che vinse una più superficiale religiosità – ma più bella – sopra una più profonda."

of Greek religion. The first one is in the way of confirmation that our belief in the travel of religious tradition across the gap of the Dark Age is substantially correct. The confirmatory evidence is contained in the linear texts, where, as has been remarked before, a number of names of the classical Greek gods are cited. The lesson to be learnt from the occurrence in Mycenaean writing of Zeus, Hera, Athena, Artemis, Hermes and others seems fairly obvious with reference to such gods' continued government of Greek cults[266].

A further conclusion that may be drawn from the Greek gods in Mycenaean dress is that evidently the move towards departmentalization of individual divine aspects, to which we alluded above, had already progressed some way by the Late Mycenaean Age. Yet beside these gods with presumably defined functions the linear tablets record not only what should be zoomorphic figures like a Dove Goddess and a Horse God, but also the old invocatory titles of e.g. Wanax, Wanassa, and Potnia. We now have no means of telling to what extent such titles were still considered interchangeable with particular gods, in the sense that Artemis, or Athena for example, could be addressed as Potnia, although there is some indication that this may have been so. The main point is that name and title existed side by side. Neither disappeared in the storms of the Dark Age, there was never at any time a general jettison of invocatory titles, but only the former was acceptable to state cult. Therefore we cannot speak of a new religious order in later times, merely of the development into a clearer division, for the old Potnia, Wanax, etc., passed into another form of cult which lived below the level of the officially sponsored one.

The second point which requires comment is of a somewhat different order. It was noticed above that the nature of the gods and goddesses occurring in Linear B was compatible[267], in that all of them could be derived from the figures of a central goddess and a chthonic male associate. This applied equally to Hera, Artemis, Athena, and to Zeus, Poseidon, Dionysus, and probably to Hermes[268]. The gods could be identified with the Minoan

---

[266] This is meant as a statement of general truth. The Mycenaean written evidence is still too ambiguous regarding exact ritual – cult practice. Nor can we at present take into account the influence exerted on the nature of major gods, like Poseidon and Apollo, by Homeric epic and late literature.

[267] P. 177 f.

[268] On Hermes' probable function as paredros cf. O. Pestalozza, *L'éternel féminin dans la Religion Méditerranéenne* (Coll. Latomus 79), Brussels 1965, 31. On Poseidon's connection with Dionysus, their bull shape and association with the Divine Child see

and Mycenaean figure of the "Divine Child," usually the youthful paredros of the goddess[269]. The young Zeus, with the epithet of Velchanos as he is occasionally depicted on coins, fitted the same pattern. This was the Zeus Kretagenes whose myth transmitted the story of his annual birth and death. The god had little in common, however, with another Zeus, the Sky God, who ruled supreme on the classical Olympus. The clash was evident, even in antiquity, and the myth of Kretagenes' apparent mortality outraged the feelings of a later age which was ignorant of the religious significance of the paredros figure[270].

Zeus' history in the Greek world is unmistakable evidence of a conflict of two religious concepts. Stories of Zeus' birth and death, of his association with a goddess of nature, which lingered on in myth throughout historic times, illustrate the unsuccessful attempts made in order to come to terms with the contradictions that lay between the supreme functions of the Indo-European god and those of the Aegean and Cretan male figure whose province Zeus had invaded after his arrival in Greece. Yet a certain amount of assimilation was inevitable in the meeting of these two important, but culturally diverse, gods: Zeus absorbed Velchanos' cult and became involved in the myths, functions, cult, and ritual of the paredros, so that there arose a dichotomy between his now essentially chthonic and often zoomorphic aspects, also destined to survive in some form in what we might call popular Greek cult as e.g. Ktesios and Meilichios, and the lofty Olympian figure.

This kind of history suggests that Mycenaean religion was composite, a kind of "Sammelbecken" in which were gathered three or four main streams. Such streams, in general outline, consisted of Aegean, Oriental, and Cretan religious material together with an "urgriechisches" element contributed by the Indo-European Greek speaking people of the mainland[271]. For example, beside the descriptive and invocatory titles, the names of gods and goddesses current in Mycenaean society assuredly could not all have derived from one local source, but they must have come together from a variety of regions, from the East, from the islands perhaps, and Crete, and, no doubt, from the mainland of Greece itself. But precisely when and

---

now also G. A. Privitera, "I Rapporti di Dioniso con Posidone in Età Micenea", *St. Urb.* 39 (1965) 180–238.

[269] See above 11 ff.; 88 ff.; 116; n. 285; 172 f.
[270] Callimachus, *Jupp.* 8.
[271] Cf. Nilsson, *Gesch.* I, 336.

where remains a mystery. Neither archaeological records nor etymological ingenuity can now take us beyond supposition and shrewd guess. Contrast, for example, the purely Greek word Demeter (*Ge meter*), Earth Mother, with the perhaps partly Greek partly Aegean "Husband of Earth" (*Posis Da*), Poseidon[272], or the possibly Greek names of Hera and Hermes[273] with the Aegean, non-Greek, Athena[274], or with the as yet incomprehensible Artemis and Apollo[275].

While archaeological remains make it possible in broad outline to isolate Aegean and Cretan belief revolving about a central goddess and her male associate, the early Greek divine figures are less easy to define from the mists of Middle Helladic history. The first Indo-European Greek speaking peoples, since Schliemann's days sometimes called Minyans, may have arrived south in the Greek peninsula during a span of time covering the end of the third and the beginning of the second millennium B.C. Their presence and cultural habits, so far only archaeologically identifiable, marked the beginning of Middle Helladic[276]. From the point of view of religion, with one certain and one possible exception, next to nothing can be said about the gods and goddesses introduced into the south by the Greeks. In

[272] Dietrich, *Death, Fate and the Gods*, 130 n.l. "*DA* ist Lallname", Schachermeyr, *Poseidon* 13 n.l.
[273] Hera's etymology is still under debate and some fanciful ideas have been produced, see Séchan–Lévêque, *Les Gr. Div.* 177 f. and n. 55. On Hermes see Nilsson, *Gesch.* I, 501 ff. On the possible effect of the Lin. B spelling on earlier etymologies see J. Chadwick – L. Baumbach, *G.* 41 (1963) 194.
[274] E. g. F. Schachermeyr, *D. minoische Kultur des alten Kreta*, 142; see also A. Carnoy, *Dict. Etym. d. l. Mythol. Gréco-Romaine*, Paris 1957, 29.
[275] Nilsson, *Gesch.* I, 309 (Artemis); 567 (Dionysus). Nothing really convincing has been proposed in the case of Apollo, Nilsson's thesis can be found, *op. cit.* 555 f.
[276] Obviously no detailed history of this period yet exists. Most modern accounts tend to hasten through this vital era with relatively few words. However, scholars seem to agree on the general time of arrival of the Greeks which may arbitrarily be fixed at c. 1900 B.C. Amongst the most recent work see Vermeule, *Gr. in the B.A.* 72 ff.; Andrewes, *Greeks* 18; Starr, *Orig.* 32; Ehrenberg, *Solon* 3. Cf. Schachermeyr's work in this field e.g. *Poseidon*, 6, and later work. It should be said, however, that this subject cannot be regarded as closed, cf. the various papers read at the Sheffield Mycen. Congress (March 1970) by D. H. French, "Migrations and 'Minyan' Pottery in W. Anatolia and the Aegean"; J. D. Evans, "The arch. evidence and its interpretation: some suggested approaches to the problem of the Aegean B.A."; C. Renfrew "Difficulties in General Correlation of Arch. and Linguistic Strata in Greece". Contrast with M. S. F. Hood, "Northern Penetration of Greece at the End of E. H. III", and R. J. Howell, "The Origins of the M. H. Culture". These papers will shortly be published. Cf. above p. 2 ff.

fact, the Indo-European Sky and Weather God, the *Dyaus Pitar*, is the one proven import in Middle Helladic, the god whom the Greeks called Zeus[277]. The other Indo-European divine arrival in the Aegean area might have been Hestia. The etymology of the goddess' name is uncertain and does not help to confirm the usual history of her origin, but Hestia could have been the "Queen of the Megaron" with its central hearth.

The impression we have gained of the Late Mycenaean pantheon is one of a more or less harmonious group of divinities. Individual members of the pantheon, even though of widely differing provenance, by this time had come together to constitute a workable and probably uniform system. To what extent they had by then forgotten their origins remains a moot point. Apollo, for example, who most likely found his way into Minoan and Mycenaean religion before the end of the Bronze Age, although the exact name has not yet been read on the tablets, obviously had strong Eastern ties[278] which are discernible through his Minoan associations[279].

The moral to be drawn from the immediately preceding discussion is twofold. Firstly the complex of basic Greek religious beliefs had already been established in the Mycenaean world by the end of Helladic, and no political or other factor can be assumed to have fundamentally altered such earlier beliefs. Secondly, if we look for changes in the religious scene the logical time would seem to be the beginning of Middle Helladic rather than the end of the Bronze Age. In this light we must understand the remarkable persistence of Mycenaean cult sites and divine nomenclature as supporting evidence of such a sequence of events, and indeed as direct confirmation that the nucleus of Late Mycenaean religious belief endured across the gap of the Dark Age. Nor need we disturb ourselves unduly over the probably temporary severance of contact, if it occurred at all, between Greece and the outside world and particularly the East, at the beginning of the new millennium, for significant Oriental religious concepts, such as the theogonic material discussed in the first chapter, had already arrived and been absorbed in the course of the second millennium[280]. In the East itself, and on some of the islands, Mycenaean traditions were kept alive by the settlers

---

[277] Nilsson, *Gesch.* I, 336 f.
[278] Nilsson, *Gesch.* I, 559 ff.
[279] These associations and Apollo's impact on the Cretan religious scene one gathers from the Hom. Hymn in his honour, and from his later multiple cults on the island, see e.g. R. F. Willetts, *Cretan Cults and Festivals*, 256 ff.
[280] See also F. Schachermeyr, *Ägäis und Orient*, ch. 4 and p. 69.

who migrated across the Aegean in order to escape the rigours of a declining mainland culture[281].

Those who stayed at home were faced with a long period of hardship and poverty. Pettazzoni, perhaps in unnecessarily gloomy terms, speaks of a time when one by one the hearths of Mycenaean civilization flickered out in Greece[282]. Life contracted, it became cantonal[283], and people congregated in what Thucydides called village communities[284], no longer bound together into a kind of common realm as were in all likelihood the Mycenaean strongholds. Physically such communities were no doubt weak, mere shadows of their ancestors of even a few generations previously[285]. An age of misery, in fact, which gave birth to the belief voiced by Herodotus so many centuries later that "Hellas hath ever had poverty for her companion"[286] descended on the mainland peoples. Some groups may well have become briefly nomadic in their habits[287], but the majority of those who did not migrate to the East remained attached to their settlements if we are to believe the archaeological evidence discussed above. It may be correct to define these groups as tribes and clans so long as we do not insist that their common factor was one of kinship.

These Dark Age communities may have been insignificant, leaving no trace of their existence outside some tombs and sherds, nonetheless they were the instrument of transmission of basic religious belief across the gap into historical times[288]. What must be remembered is that they had a foot in both camps, the Mycenaean and classical, in that they did not consist of an amalgam of a few scattered refugees and predominantly invading peoples with novel cultural habits[289], so that direct continuity from Bronze Age tradition would have been broken. Furthermore it was these village communities that gave birth eventually to the classical *polis*[290] which

---

[281] Cf. Pettazzoni, *Rel. Greca* 40, "Da quel momento (the end of Helladic) su le due rivo dell'Egeo vibrò di duplice vita l'anima greca."
[282] *Ibid.* "Ché della civiltà micenea si spegnevano, intanto, i fuochi ad uno ad uno nella Grecia propria."
[283] Nilsson, *Homer and Mycenae,* 240.
[284] 1, 5.
[285] Cf. Mylonas, *Mycenae* 233.
[286] 7, 102; Mylonas, *ibid.*
[287] Cf. Starr, *Origins* 80.
[288] Cf. Starr, *Orig.* 174, who is aware of the religious function of these groups.
[289] Andrewes, *Greeks* 34, believes that the tribal system was a Dorian import.
[290] Cf. Nilsson, *Homer and Mycen.* 246.

throughout Greece was constructed on the same political and religious pattern.

This last important feature again presupposes a reasonable state of communication between individual communities in addition to a commonly shared heritage naturally explained by the universally enjoyed Mycenaean origins[291]. The one, single, and comprehensive factor to impose unity on all the communities, and to see them through to the eventually walled *polis*, was religious tradition and common religious practice[292]. Therefore it was entirely natural for the *komai* of the Dark Age in "fairly large districts, such as Attica-Boeotia and Corinthia-Argolid" to join in common worship in leagues or amphictyonies[293]. The exact date, when such leagues were first officially constituted, escapes us, but many must have been early, and they include, for example, the Calaurian Amphictyony which was formed at least in the ninth century[294], while the first contacts between Athens and Delphi might have come about a hundred years earlier[295]. This situation, which was natural and predictable under the existing circumstances, did, however, prove a fertile ground for a kind of power politics. A community shrewd enough to sense the possibilities of the situation, and above all blessed with a sufficiently strong claim as a traditional cult locality of some consequence, might and, in the case of e.g. Delphi, did lever itself up into prominence by virtue of its pre-eminent religious position[296].

This type of selfassertion by distinguished centres on political and primarily religious grounds belonged, of course, to the centuries of the Dark Age. Of more immediate concern is the effect of this curious community structure on the shape and form of the official classical state cult. Since this cult continued fundamentally traditional religious material, it was bound in some form to reflect the dispersal of a relatively few major Mycenaean centres into multiple small communities often attached to a partic-

---

[291] Nilsson, *op. cit.* 247; 269, defines the common bonds which reached back into Mycen. times and united the *poleis* as consisting of 1) the language of epic, 2) the world of gods – the Olymp. family under Zeus the father of men and gods having been devised by the Mycen. –, 3) heroic mythology which, too, according to him, was born in the Mycen. world. Cf. his book *The Mycenaean Origin of Grk. Mythology*, and W. K. C. Guthrie, "The Religion and Mythology of the Greeks", *C.A.H.*² II, fasc. 40 (1961) 32.

[292] Cf. Pettazzoni, *Rel. Greca* 58.

[293] Starr, *Origins* 338.

[294] Coldstream, *Grk. Geom. Pottery* 342 f.

[295] Coldstream, *op. cit.* 353.

[296] Cf. e.g. Pettazzoni, *ibid.*

ular cult locality. Yet these many communities were joined together, as it were, by their common religious heritage; their worship conformed to a shared pattern and was celebrated in honour of gods who not only carried the same names, but also possessed the same nature and functions. Consequently the renewed expansion by virtue of the Dark Age leagues paved the way for the founding of the *polis* which was held together eventually by ties of political convenience.

To these *poleis* now the older and smaller communities transferred their individual gods, so that in effect a city's acropolis became the site of a universal cult which had grown out of the many rather more strictly localized versions[297]. The result of this process of unification, or perhaps a happier word would be centralization, was a somewhat bewildering array of community and protecting deities who had been uprooted from their home and collected together, like a band of recruits, in one larger *polis*. There is no mistaking the consequence of such a development on the polytheism crowding out the acropolis of a classical city – state. Neither literature nor myth was quite successful enough to create more than an uneasy family of Olympians composed of members with so many diverse local roots. Like the seemingly countless members of the modern Smith or Jones clan this divine family always remained faintly bellicose and very large, despite the fact that some major deities eliminated a host of lesser figures by swallowing up their names and cults.

Of the many figures from various communities Athena, for example, became the city goddess *par excellence*, or Artemis embraced a variety of divinities whose sphere of influence involved birth, death, animal life, and the wilds. This process of unification, essential to the more centralized *polis*, in which a few major deities absorb or swallow other, more localized, gods with related functions, can still be observed from the numerous cult epithets of the important Olympians. Witness to this fact are titles like Artemis Aphaea, Eileithyia, and others[298]. The best illustration of this unification by absorption comes from the history of the city goddess, the protectress of the classical *polis*. The title of Polias was preeminently associated with Athena who gathered in her province the cults of a great many localized city goddesses throughout the Greek world. As a mark of this assimilation Athena was endowed with a variety of toponyms as *epikleseis*,

---

[297] Cf. G. Thomson, *Studies in Ancient Greek Society*, 123, whose views on this point are entirely plausible despite his now untenable belief in Greek totemism.
[298] Cf. above p. 154.

and such names indicate the localities or communities where she asserted her unifying power. Therefore examples like Athena Lindia on Rhodes, Magarsia in Cilicia, Samonia, Oleria, Cydonia in Crete, and Gygnia in the Troad, not only prove the existence in pre-Greek times of such a cult of a community goddess but also the cult's continuation under the unifying aegis of Athena[299].

It would seem that the community system which obtained in the Dark Age played a large part in shaping classical Greek state religion: it helped to determine the type and number of gods and their cult. Homeric epic, of course, contributed much to this development. The language of the epic and the beginnings of its mythology reached back into Mycenaean times[300], so that this literary organ of transmission served as a strong connecting link in religious matters between the Mycenaean and classical periods. Let us also be sure to remember that the epic tradition which, after the collapse of Mycenaean political power, continued in the East – in Ionia probably[301] or possibly in Cyprus[302] – was associated with, and found its form in, the typically post-Mycenaean community and therefore was bound to reflect the latter's custom and beliefs.

These communities, then, their structure, composition etc., are of considerable significance to an understanding of the Greek Dark Age, and it will repay the trouble to have a closer look at some of their salient features in the light of the available evidence. Compared with what had preceded and what was to follow they were primitive, devoid of ostentation and the material resources which would have made any kind of show possible. Therefore archaeologically these settlements practically left no trace,

---

[299] See U. Bianchi, "La Dea di Lindos", *Epig.* 19 (1957) 10 f.; 12 and n. 3. A similar story can, of course, be told of the city's protecting god, the Polias, Poliaios or Poliouchos, a title which in classical times normally was associated with Zeus. If Nilsson is right – *Gesch.* I, 345; 417 f. – Zeus achieved the position of Polieus from the somewhat narrower province of special protector of a pre-Greek community's king. However, in Homer, and in the *polis*, Zeus possessed a more universal status which could not be narrowly confined to a specific set of functions. Pettazzoni neatly compares the *polis'* "civico polieus" with the "dio patrio" of the preceding communities, *Rel. Grec.* 62.

[300] Nilsson, *Hom. & Myc.* 277 f.; Severyns, *Grèce et Pr. Or.* 202; 204; D. Page, *History and the Homeric Iliad,* 254; 259; Webster, *Myc. to Hom.* 174 ff.; 182.

[301] E.g. Page, *op. cit.* 259.

[302] Plausibly proposed by Severyns, *op. cit.* 205, who maintains that Ionia was too weak between 1200 and 1000 B.C. to "preserve intact the Achaean patrimony."

although enough remains to prove continuity from Mycenaean times of e.g. architectural features like the megaron.

The one signal aspect, apart from size and splendour, to distinguish the early community from the *polis* was the differing composition of the two. The former was defined by ties of tribal and clan association[303] which, in view of their small size, could have been in the nature of kinship, while the *polis* was held together by local or geographical bonds and by those of political convenience. Two factors manage to confuse the picture. Both are interrelated, consisting of the ogre of the Dorian invasion and the introduction into Greece of the tribal system by these invaders. The scene enormously complicates itself if we are prepared to accept these two features unchallenged. The immediate consequence would be, and has been for many scholars, that, however evident the evolution from Dark Age community to classical *polis*, communication with Helladic culture was absolutely severed by the Dorians who had brought with them their tribal system for the new type of settlement.

In fact we would be where we started: helpless to explain the strongly enduring Mycenaean tradition. But events need not have conformed to such a programme which in any case must remain suspect while the Dorians continue to be the shadowy figures we have found them above. Our main concern is to trace the development of Greek religious ideas. Such development did not come to a sudden halt some time about 1100 B.C. after which religious concepts travelled in a new direction, but it was allowed to progress uninterrupted in a more or less straight line at least since Middle Helladic.

In order to illustrate this thesis it is important to recognize that the arrangement of the settlements, like other facets of the Dark Age, fundamentally reflected customs which had already obtained in the Mycenaean Bronze Age. The sources again for this are far from full but perhaps sufficient to back our argument and to persuade the historian that there is no need to invoke a momentous cultural irruption at the beginning of the first millennium in order to explain Greek beliefs in the Classical Age. In fact, the functions and import of e.g. Zeus, Poseidon, and Athena did not alter fundamentally between the eleventh and eighth centuries. This conclusion becomes acceptable if one takes the trouble to understand some basic traditional features of the developing Greek religion. It is a fact that all gods in the Mycenaean city, as well as in classical Athens, had a special place and

---

[303] Cf. Thomson, *op. cit.* 123; Starr, *Origins* 174.

sphere of influence in the community structure of the city. That is to say, the political unity of, for example, Nestor's Pylos would have been unthinkable without Poseidon, or without the palace goddess, in their appropriate hierarchical position and receiving their special worship, which was administered by particular representatives of the community on the appointed days.

The same was true of the historical period when the cult of the gods was integrated in the political organization of the *polis* and administered by a chosen group of priests who cherished their rights like the Eteobutadae who were in charge of the cult of Poseidon and Athena Polias. The fact that, by and large, the same divine names were shared by Greek cities shows not only the excellent communications between them but above all that the community structures, like the divine hierarchies, were shared. These are weighty claims to make for the generations of the Dark Age which are not subject to written proof. But is it possible to assume that, for example, Athena was likely to retain her prominent position, and develop from the goddess of the palace, the centre of the old city, to the protectress of the classical *polis*, unless the religious concepts surrounding her had persisted, together with the structure of the city society administering the religious cult?

The religious practice of Dark Age communities was not likely to have signally differed, whether they had taken refuge in the more inaccessible reaches of the Peloponnese like Arcadia, or whether they continued to worship e.g. at Eleusis or Amyclae. Yet one thing is clear: with the major gods and their cults there must have survived the community, or group organization, which was associated with them. And it does not really matter whether the ties that bound these groups together were those of kinship or whether they were more military in nature and designed for common defence or attack.

To follow this line of argument involves the acceptance of three consequences. Firstly we will be compelled to revise the notion[304] that the curious tribal arrangement (with their various subdivisions into *phratry* and *genos*), found in Greek cities on the mainland and overseas, had its origin at the end of the Dark Age, or at any rate not much earlier. Secondly we will seek in such group organization within a community the decisive organ, as it were, which transmitted religious ideas through the dark into the historical age. Finally it is obviously important to find at least a trace

---

[304] Most recently in Andrewes, *Greeks* e.g. 80.

in the extant Mycenaean records of communal organizations, call them *genos*, *oikos*, *demos* or what you will, which played a significant part in the city, however much the latter might have politically differed from the *polis*.

The first point is reasonably easy to establish, because Andrewes' proposal, in the absence of firm evidence, consists of an enlightened conjecture based on the ideas of the decline in the Dark Age of the wanax' position and the relative growth in importance of the basileus and the beginning of an aristocracy[305]. The chain of events which led to the establishment of communal groups could well have been earlier, for already in the Dark Age these groups not only continued their religious heritage[306], but managed to combine into amphictyonies[307].

The task of identifying and naming such communal units, and of integrating them in the structure of the city, alas, is quite impossible for all but the historical period. After the fifth century, indeed, inscriptional and literary evidence, mainly from the orators, is plentiful but tells us very little about earlier tradition and history. What we known of Cleisthenes' reorganization of Attica into ten tribes and thirty *trittyes*[308] does not materially help, because this system was based on political motivation. Nor do we learn more from the notice in Aristotle that this system superseded an older arrangement in Attica of four tribes divided into twelve *phratries* and thirty clans[309]. This neat arrangement, which represented in turn the four seasons of the year, the twelve months and thirty days of the month, was an invention of the fourth century and recalls the equally late similar arrangement of a Greek city in Egypt where tribes, *phratries* and *demes* were divided to fit the local year[310]. All we may gather from such political innovation is that older established community groups, whether they were bound together by local or kinship bonds, represented so firmly entrenched a custom that still in the sixth and later centuries they provided a convenient basis on which the political system and franchise of a city could be designed.

Three group names in particular stand out. These were the *phyle*, the *phratry*, and the *genos*. In historic times these, as we have seen, were inte-

---

[305] Cf. Webster, *Myc. to Hom.* 142 f.; 155.
[306] Cf. Starr, *op. cit.* 174.
[307] See above p. 243.
[308] Herod. 5, 66; 69. Cf. the similar arrangement in Sicyon, Her. 5, 68.
[309] Aristotle, *Ath. Pol.* frg. 5.
[310] See K. Latte, "Phratrie", *P.-W.* 20, 1 (1941) 748.

grated into a system according to which the *phyle* was the largest unit subdivided and, at that time, interdependent with the *phratry* and *genos* in this order. However, scholars have debated for a long time, and still continue to debate, whether such an arrangement was of old standing or imposed on three essentially unrelated groups. This argument we cannot now join, but content ourselves with citing some of the important literature where the various views are put forward and discussed[311]. Another problem surrounding these groups is their age, that is to say the question whether they were new historical foundations or had substantially survived from earlier times. And, if the latter, what was the period of their origin. Prior to the sixth century we possess few accurate data and none of them can conclusively answer the problem. What evidence there is, particularly from the classical period, is all too easily manipulated to suit particular theories. This we shall try to avoid but confine ourselves to isolating some general points which have a bearing on prehistoric practice. A part of the difficulty of this subject is due to the changes which must have occurred in the nomenclature of communal groups and their structure in the course of the Dark Age. This period saw the decline of kingship and the strenghtening, rather than fresh emergence, of aristocratic rule by a few families that arrogated political power and possibly also the exclusive administration of communal cults. To this point we shall return below.

The origin of the *phyle* as a communal institution is obscure. Traditional literary evidence dealing with events of the Late Bronze Age is explicit only about the Dorians with regard to a system of *phylai*[312]. The three Dorian tribes, the Hylleis, Pamphyli, and Dymanes, acted together as military units without obvious kinship bonds[313]. A line from a Tyrtaios fragment still alludes to the arrangement at Sparta of the Dorian army according

---

[311] G. Glotz, *La Solidarité de la famille dans le droit criminel en Grèce*, Paris 1904; G. Busolt–H. Swoboda, *Griech. Staatskunde*, Munich 1920, 26; E. A. Gardner, M. Cary, F. A. Adcock in *C.A.H.* III (1925) 582 ff.; 688; W. S. Ferguson, "The Athenian Phratries", *C. Ph.* 5 (1910) 257–84; "The Attic Orgeones", *H.T.R.* 37 (1944) 61–140; M. Guarducci, "L'Istituzione della fratria", *Mem. L.* VI, 6 (1937); K. Latte, the following articles in *P.-W.* 20, 1 (1941): "Phyle", "Phylobasileis, "Phratrie", "Phratrioi Theoi"; C. Hignett, *Hist. of the Athen. Constitution*, Oxford 1952; H. T. Wade-Gery, *Essays in Greek History*, Oxford 1958, esp. 150–4; G. Thomson, *Prehist. Aeg.*[2], esp. 106–146; Andrewes, "Phratries in Homer" *He.* 89 (1961) 129–40; "Philochorus on Phratries", *J.H.S.* 81, (1961) 1–15; *Greeks* esp. ch. 5.

[312] On these traditions see esp. Hammond, *C.A.H.*[2] II, 36, 25 ff.

[313] The Heracles – Hylleis connection is a special issue which we cannot discuss here.

to the three tribes[314]. During the migrations these three tribes continued as units which either individually founded settlements, as in Crete, or lived side by side in one city[315]. This *phylai* system seemed to have been peculiar to the Dorians. Doric *phylai* obviously were known to the poet of the Homeric Catalogue[316], but otherwise clashed with the common Homeric usage of *phylon*[317]. Outside Dorian custom there is no evidence that *phyle* was an early denomination of communities among the n.w. Greeks, Ionians, Aeolians, Boeotians, Thessalians, or elsewhere in Greece[318].

The history of the *phratry* presents an equally sticky problem. The word is an old and common Indo-European term which should consequently indicate the antiquity of the *phratry*. But, apart from Ionic dialect[319], *phrater* = "brother" did not survive in Greek but was replaced by words like *adelphos, kasignetos*[320]. The *phratry* as a designation of a communal unit was, with the exception of Cos and Argos, unknown to Doric states which presumably called similar groups *hetaireiai*[321]. Again there is no proof that *phratries* were homogeneous groups by virtue of kinship. It can reasonably be argued that *pratries,* and indeed *gene,* at some date in the Archaic period had a common ancestor imposed on them who is reflected in the patronymics which, with the suffix -idae, gives us the names Achniadae, Clytidae, Labyadae, and of course, the Alcmaeonidae, Boutadae, and so on[322]. By the sixth century *phratries* had become purely territorial units, convenient organizations for administrative purposes[323]. Despite their decline into political bodies *phylai* and *phratries* always retained a number of features and rights which belonged to them from the beginning. Some of these we shall mention in a moment. But first we should raise one other point. The subdivision of tribes into *phratries* and clans, as we find it in Aristotle, is an artificial one which could not have been very old[324]. *Phra-*

[314] Frg. 1 A 12 (Diehl).
[315] For sources and discussion see Latte, *P.-W.* "Phyle" 997 f.; Andrewes, *He.* 89, 132.
[316] Where Tlepolemus is said to have colonized Rhodes *trichtha kataphyladon Il.* 2, 655; 668. Cf. the *Doriees . . . trichaikes* in Crete, *Od.* 19, 177.
[317] Andrewes, *ibid.*
[318] Latte, "Phyle" 995; 1000.
[319] Cf. the Hesychius gloss *phreter; adelphos.*
[320] See Latte, "Phratrie", 746; Andrewes, *He.* 89, 137.
[321] Latte, "Phratrie", 746; *C.A.H.* III, 582.
[322] Cf. Andrewes, *Greeks* 81; *C.A.H.* III, 582 f.; Latte, "Phratrie", 746.
[323] For *Phratries* = *demes* see Andrewes, *Greeks* 83.
[324] *C.A.H.* III, 582, speaks of this event as occurring in Attica after synoecism. But the dates for this, p. 580, are made very wide: between 1000 and 700 B.C.

tries and tribes, and certainly *phratries* and clans, shared certain features like land tenure, property rights, the administration of cults, which may well suggest that each group was originally independent[325]. *Phratries*, already in Homer, also served as military units and above all as communities from which sinners could be excluded as from the family hearth. As community groups *phratries* again could have been as old as the *phylai*[326], although lacking proof we must leave this an open question. The fact remains that as late as the sixth century our sources are not very clear in their distinctions between *phratry* and clan, or *genos*, in Attica[327], nor about the distinction between the *genos* and a number of other groups which basically seem to have been similar units[328].

These blurred divisions are due quite probably to our own inadequate understanding of all the contemporary social conditions involved. This should not, however, alter the fact that we are confronted with a great many community groups which need not originally have stood in any close relationship to one another, but which transmitted some features of religious cult as well as continued certain rights vested in the community. These latter included legal rights, especially those concerning murder, or blood guilt, within the community[329], and the common ownership of property

---

[325] A case could perhaps be made out that *phylai* were peculiarly Doric and *phratries* Ionic, or at least non-Doric, institutions which came together only after the end of the Bronze Age. *Il.* 2, 362 f., however, is a potent argument against such a supposition unless we assume that Nestor's *phyla* differed from the Doric *phylai*.

[326] *Il.* 2, 362 f.; 9, 63. Andrewes, *He.* 89, 132; 139 f., argues that Nestor's adive in *Il.* 2 falls out of context and differs from the usual mode of Homeric fighting. The reason for this, he believes, is that *phratries* were instituted as late as 9th/8th century when loyal followers of competing aristocratic leaders banded together. He does admit, however, *ibid.*, that *phratries* might have come to the mainland with the first Greeks but then subsequently disappeared.

[327] To give two examples: a *phratry* and *genos* may have the same law and carry a common membership register, Isaeus 7, 15–17. In the famous Demotionid decrees (*IG* II² 1237) the *oikos* of the Dekeleies is understood as a *phratry*, although the former is usually counted as a subdivision of a *phratry*. On the law and decrees see Andrewes, *J.H.S.* 81, 5.

[328] Groups parallel to the *genos* appear to be *oikos*, *patra*, *patria*, *homogalaktes*, *orgeones* and *demes*, cf. Latte, "Phratrie" 747. Some of these do not, however, seem to have enjoyed equal standing, as witness the law (7th/6th cent.) cited by Philochorus (Phot., Sud. s.v. *orgeones*) which compelled *phratries* to admit to their ranks *orgeones* and *homogalaktes* = *gennetes*.

[329] Latte, "Phratrie" 753; Andrewes, *Greeks* 85. Cf. Draco's Law on this point *IG* I² 117, 18.

as well as land tenure[330]. Religious cults were originally in the hands of the king or leader of the community like the *phylobasileus*[331], as must have been the administration of the land. In the course of the Dark Age, and sometimes later, these rights were generally usurped by individual aristocratic families (whose members earlier on had obviously provided the basileus) which henceforth, like a "Priesteradel", exercised sole control of the great cults and festivals. Thus the Eumolpidae were in charge of the Eleusinian Mysteries, the Lycomidae of those in Phyla, the Phytalidae and the Poimenidae supervised a cult of Demeter each, while the Hesychidae had a cult of the Semnae.

Nevertheless, whatever the eventual internal adjustments within a group, it is quite plain that cult could not have been transmitted across the ages if it had not been preserved and continued by community organization. This does not mean to say that each larger group, perhaps representing a settlement, was concerned with the worship of only one major deity destined after synoecism to join the gods of other tribes or *phratries*. Already the Mycenaean city had contained the various cults of both major and minor gods who could have been accommodated in the worship of one community. Quite possibly, though, family or *genos* or *oikos* divisions within a larger group contributed, as it were, to the latter those divine figures that had been in their particular care. These points can be illustrated from the classical and post-classical cult practice of *phratries*. From this it appears that the major gods, as city gods, like Zeus, Poseidon, Artemis, and Athena received cults which were shared by all *phratries*. Beside these, however, we find the collective *phratrioi theoi, phretores theoi* which, in certain circumstances, could evidently refer to any or all Hellenic gods[332]. *Phratry* cult also included figures like the *Tritopatreis*[333], that is "Ahnengeister" who, in the beginning, had more naturally belonged to units smaller than the classical *phratry*[334]. The last figures in particular suggest that cults of family groups might at one time have been transferred to larger units, as happened, in fact, in Chios as late as the fourth century[335]. Despite the considerable body of evidence on this question it is still impos-

---

[330] Latte, "Phyle" 1010 with sources; "Phratrie" 753; Andrewes, *ibid.*
[331] Pollux VIII, 111.
[332] Cf. *IG* XIV, 721 (Naples), but very late (empire).
[333] Zacyadae in Athens *IG* II² 2615.
[334] See also below.
[335] *Syll.*³ 987.

THE PROBLEM OF CONTINUITY IN THE DARK AGE   253

sible to construct a historical sequence of cult development within a *phratry* or similar group, in view of the enormous accretion of new cults which must have found their way into the ranks of a *phratry* at comparatively late dates[336].

Here we are not aiming at a comprehensive outline of historical Greek tribal organization. What has so far been said should, however, establish a) the vagueness in the relationship between individual groups, b) the great age of some of them, c) their function as organs transmitting from perhaps prehistoric times not only religious cult but also old community rights concerning law, property ownership, and land tenure. With these points in mind it will be useful to consider the Mycenaean written evidence for some record of a Bronze Age community organization which might, as we could expect, bear comparison with the historic tribes, *phratries*, and *gene*. It is as well to say at the outset of the search that, however likely a kindship basis was at least in what seemed to be the smallest units like *genos*, *oikos*, *orgeones* and *homogalaktes*, we cannot hope to establish its precise nature or degree, and therefore had best leave this problem to one side. Much less can we expect to make any anthropological deductions about the nature of the early societies in Greece, that is to say, we may not lightly describe the social structure of individual communities as matrilineal, patrilineal, or even originally totemistic[337]. In addition to the use of patronymics, establishing in good Homeric fashion the descent of individual persons, some other evidence for kinship groups does exist on the linear tablets, but it is weak as we shall see. What does emerge strongly, however, from the extremely difficult evidence of the Mycenaean script is the existence in the social structure of the city of one or more communal groups with apparently clearly defined rights of property and the administration of religious cult. These recall, indeed, historic practice.

The most valuable evidence in this connection derives from a series of tablets (the E series) discovered in the Archive room at Pylos and dealing

---

[336] E.g. Leto, worshipped by the Demotionidae at Athens – *Syll.*³ 921; 125; Apollo Hebdomaeus who received cult from the Achniadae, also in Athens – *Syll.*³ 923.

[337] On these identifications see Thomson, *Preh. Aeg.* ch. IV. Prof. Hammond – Tooke has kindly pointed out to me that matrilineal descent is purely a matter of inheritance (from mother's brother) and not of terminology. Thus to call members of a group *homogalaktes* ("of the same milk") is no indication that that group must have been matrilineally oriented. The subject of totemism is so little understood that it might well be thought fruitless to apply the description to any society, least of all the Greek.

with land tenure. These documents naturally describe the conditions of social organization in Pylos and the outlying districts, but they are also a fair reflection on similar arrangements which obtained at other Mycenaean centres, because the latter shared some technical terms[338]. The Pylian records are full in their way but, like many of our later sources on the same subject, they assume a familiarity with the system which we do not possess, so that the material is liable to become obscure and the interpretation hazardous. A detailed analysis here would take us too far afield, and we may be content with a reference to a few modern discussions of the subject while picking out particular features of special interest to this topic[339].

In general Pylian land fell into two major categories, the *kotona kitimena* and the *kotona kekemena*[340]: the former probably being privately owned and "leased" land and the latter consisting of "common" land. Beside these two larger divisions there were also the private *temena* of the wanax and *lawagetas*. It is, however, not entirely clear whether the *kitimena* were the exclusive property of one single individual rather than of a group, however small, and whether the *temena* of the highest officers of the community were not, rather than separate property, portions of land integrated in, or part of, a larger estate which belonged to the perquisite of the king together with special religious functions. These kinds of *temenea* king Battos possessed in Cyrene[341], Alcinous in Scheria, and Odysseus in Ithaka[342]. The relationship between private and common land is uncertain, although there does appear to be a clear distinction between the *kitimena* and the *kekemena*. The former, the private land, it seems, could be held by any person who, however, even when he "leased" the land to another, carried the technical title of *tereta*. Public land, on the other hand,

---

[338] E.g. *korete* and *tereta* at Knossos and Pylos.
[339] See especially M. Ventris–J. Chadwick, *Documents in Mycenaean Greek*, 232–74; W. E. Brown, "Land Tenure in Mycenaean Pylos" *H.* 5 (1956) 385–400; L. R. Palmer, *The Interpretation of Mycenaean Greek Texts*, 186–224; *Mycenaeans and Minoans*², esp. 97–108; L. A. Stella, *La civiltà Micenea* 47 ff.; 129 ff. All these authors also have full bibliographies of the great number of modern discussions of all aspects of the subject. A useful guide to references and etymologies of individual Mycenaean terms in Chadwick–Baumbach, *G.* 41, 157–271.
[340] For the morphology of these words see Palmer, *Interpret.* 186 ff.
[341] Herod. 4, 161.
[342] *Od.* 6, 293, near a sacred grove of Athena. *Od.* 11, 185, Telemachus administers the royal *temenea* in Ithaca during Odysseus' absence.

was exclusively administered by the *damos*, the people, in this sort of context also evidently a technical term for a "commune"[343]. Now an interesting fact is that the Pylian register also describes as *tereta* a person holding land from the *damos*, thereby in some, as yet inexplicable, way relating the socalled common and private land. To the *tereta* we shall return immediately below.

The land thus "leased" from the *damos* is called *ktoina* – land (*kotona*) by the records, and the *tereta*, in charge of *damos* land, becomes a holder of *ktoina* – *kotonooko* or *kotoneta*[344]. The difference, if any, between the last two terms is not obvious[345]: both are holders of common land, and it is within the bounds of possibility, though this cannot in any way be proved, that the *kotoneta* were associated by ties of kinship[346]. That kinship should have played a part in this context is not, however, of vital concern to our purposes. In any case the degree of kinship underlying any communal group is an elusive problem for most periods of Greek history. We can learn much more from the term *ktoinetai* itself, if indeed our reading is correct, because it survived in some form in inscriptions of historical times primarily in Rhodes (Syme). The word, as we saw, described a person in Pylos who held public land from the *damos*. Therefore we may suggest, although again there can be as yet no certainty, that the same person stood in some relationship to, or perhaps was a member of, the Pylian community which was the *damos*. For it is in this sense that the word *ktoine(a)tes* appears in Rhodian inscriptions, designating a "member of a *ktoina*"[347]. The *ktoina* in Rhodes was a localized community, very much like the Attic *demos* and, we suspect, not very dissimilar from the Pylian *damos*[348]. This feature also appears from a gloss in Hesychius who probably further alludes to the sacral rights of such a community[349]. If, therefore, we are moving

---

[343] On the *kama*, another uncertain kind of land, and the *kamaewes* ("Holders of *kama*"), see e.g. Brown, *H*. 5, 400; Ventr.–Chadw., *Docs.* 261; Palmer, *Interpret.* 190; 194; 202, etc.; *Myc. Min.* 104.

[344] Cf. the *kotonewe*, for refs. see Chadw.–Baumb., *G.* 41, 214.

[345] Ventr.–Chadw., *Docs.* 264, for some reason deny that these words are synonymous.

[346] The second part of *ktoin etai* recalls the Homeric *etai* = "kinsmen and dependents of a great house", e.g. *Il.* 6, 239; *Od.* 15, 273; *Il.* 9, 464. Subsequently *etes* came to designate a special kind of citizen, cf. the inscr. (6th cent.) from Olympia, *S.I.G.*³ 9. 8. Still enigmatic is the Pylian *etonijo* describing a particular kind of land holding and probably containing the same root *eta*, cf. Brown, *H*. 5, 397.

[347] *IG* XII (1). 694. 14; 157. 9; XII (3). 1270 A 13 (Syme).

[348] *IG* XII (1). 694, 1033 etc.

[349] Hesych. s. v. κτοῖναι· χωρήσεις προγονικῶν ἱερείων (ἱερειῶν), ἢ δῆμος μεμερισμένος.

on the right path, there is every indication that already in Pylos the *ktoinetes* was the equivalent of the *demotes* or *phyletes*, that is a member of a community with all that entails[350]. This must, however, remain a suggestion, for the Mycenaean Greek evidence is anything but conclusive, and we can do no more than surmise that *kotoneta* and *kotonooko*, though perhaps not synonymous terms, in principle describe members of the same group. It is also well to remember that so far *kotoneta* occurs only once, so that we cannot accurately control the proposal that these persons were the same as the historical *ktoinetai*[351]. For all that, however strong our caution and reserve in interpreting the Mycenaean material, the collective weight of the Pylian land tablets creates the overwhelming impression that in Pylos, and by implication in other cities, communal groups either separately or as integrated units played a vital part in the structure of the city.

Two words which particularly strengthen this impression are the Mycenaean *tereta* and *damos*. *Tereta*, we noticed, described persons holding both *kitimena* and *kekemena* (under certain circumstances), that is "private" land and land of the *damos*. What does *tereta* mean? In Mycenaean *tereta* is always associated with the holding of land, and the title in Palmer's words "is a tenure bound status word"[352]. Generally it is equated with the Greek *telesta*, *telestes* (cf. *teletes*, *telester*) which occurs with two chief meanings: 1) "initiation priest", or "the person initiated", 2) a special class of citizen or possibly official as distinct from the *etas*[353]. Therefore Brown and Chadwick agree on the interpretation of the Mycenaean *telestas* as "initiation priest"[354]. Whether this technical term, on analogy with Hittite practice, also described a member of the nobility can, though likely, quite frankly no longer be determined[355]. What is important, however, is that the office of priest and membership of a particular group of citizens are compatible terms precisely in the context of organized communal groups which, together with certain legal rights and rights of land tenure, continued sacral functions that had always been in their care. Although, in their brevity, even historical inscriptions may leave the door open to a variety

---

[350] Cf. Brown, *H.* 5, 396; C. D. Buck–W. Peterson, *A Reverse Index of Greek Nouns and Adjectives*, Chicago 1944, 545; Ventr.–Chadw., *Docs*, 264.

[351] Cf. Brown, *ibid*.

[352] *Myc. Min.* 103.

[353] *L. & Sc. J.* q.v.

[354] Brown, *H.* 5, 395; J. Chadwick, "Potnia", *M.* 5 (1957) 126 ff. Palmer, *Interpret.* 193, rejects this identification, but see below.

[355] On this point see Palmer, *Interp.* 192; *Myc. Min.* 105.

of interpretation, there is little doubt that the sixth century Elean record, which divides the citizen body into *etas, telestas* and *damos*[356], is describing communal organizations whose names were "evidently of great antiquity"[357]. Accordingly it is eminently reasonable to argue that the Mycenaean *telestas* already possessed the two signal rights of a community like the tribe, *genos* or *phratry* member, namely those concerned with sacral office and land tenure. Perhaps we should also learn something from the interesting correspondence between Mycenaean and later Greek practice of including particular occupations, or their representatives, within these communities[358], although it may be too early to draw definite conclusions from the Mycenaean evidence.

However this may be, the Pylian *telestai* clearly alluded to the kind of community organization which we hoped to find mentioned in the Mycenaean archives and which could have served as one transmitting organ of, among other features, religious material. And it matters little in this respect whether the precise nomenclature of this group survived outside the conservative religious strongholds of Elis and possibly Arcadia. Finally the exact relationship of the *telestai* to the *damos* cannot be defined, but the former may have been a group in its own right which at least in one text (PY Un 718) appears "to be equated with the *damos*"[359].

In the Mycenaean *damos* we recognize inevitably the closest parallel to later communal groups like the *phyle*. *Damos* was not a loose description of the inhabitants of a city but a technical term which described "both the land and the community attached to it"[360]. The leader of a *damos* was styled *korete* or *damokoro*[361], titles which most likely were equivalent to that of

---

[356] *S.I.G.*³ 9 (Olympia).
[357] Palmer, *Interp.* 191. *etas* in a similar context also occurred in an Arcadian inscr. – *IG* 5 (2). 20. The question of kinship, again, regarding *etas* outside Homer is unanswerable.
[358] The *telestai* included shepherds, fullers, potters – Palmer, *Myc. Min.* 102 f.; Webster, *Myc. to Homer* 16; just like some *phylai* which, as in Philadelphia, counted among their number weavers of wool, cobblers, etc. – see Latte, "Phyle" 1004 for sources – in a practice which, of course, recurs among the names of Attic *phratries* and *gene*: e.g. Buzygae, Kerykes, etc. Gardner and Cary, however, *C.A.H.* III, 585, maintain that the latter were merely fancy names. But on occupational and craft clans see Thomson, *Preh. Aeg.* 332 f.
[359] Ventr.–Chadw., *Docs.* 121.
[360] Palmer, *Interp.* 188; cf. the etymology of the word "division, part" ("Abteilung", "Teil") – H. Frisk, *Griechisches Etymologisches Wörterbuch*, 1954 –, q.v.
[361] *Contra* Palmer, *Interp.* 340 f.; 354 f., who identifies *damokoro* as a proper name.

basileus[362] and which can be compared, if not identified, with the later *phylobasileus*[363]. As a collective body the *damos*, like the historical *phyle*, *phratry* etc., exercised some apparently well defined juridical (land tenure disputes) and religious functions[364]. It has been remarked that the majority of references to the *damos* on Pylian tablets do not apply to the city centre, but to *Pakija*, one of the nine outlying districts which altogether represented the loosely knit city of Pylos[365]. This kind of loose arrangement survived through the Dark Age until synoecism, and was still well remembered by Thucydides[366]. Such a village system, which, we can now see, existed in the Bronze Age already, would have represented a federation, as it were, of *damoi* communities with their worship, land, and rights. These features persisted into the classical *polis*, although the primitive unwalled villages themselves perished without a trace. This *damos*, then, at such an early date was a social unit with apparently a particular topographic location[367].

The *damos* most frequently referred to on the Pylos tablets was at *Pakija*. This name, however, is generally spelled in a nominative plural form (*Pakijanes*) "which looks more like a clan or tribal name than primarily a place name"[368] and recalls the forms Hellanes or Acarnanes. Locality and community names were not incompatible and may be paralleled, albeit very much later, by e.g. the Amyklaieis *phyle* outside Sparta[369]. Much more significant, however, is that the Pylian evidence most elegantly ties up with Homer's division of Pylos into nine *demoi*. The passage (*Od.* 3,5–8) is fully discussed by Thomson[370] who shows that, on the occasion of a sacrifice to Poseidon, Nestor's Pylos was divided into nine *hedrai*, or separate areas, "marked out for the nine groups into which the people were divided." The groups Thomson calls *demoi* and equates them with clan groups. Homer's memory served him well, for he not only recalled the nine

---

[362] Cf. Ventr.–Chadw., *Docs*. 175; 296.
[363] Cf. G. P. Carratelli, "Nuovi Studi sui Testi Micenei", *P.d.P.* 36 (1954) 217.
[364] Palmer, *Myc. Min.* 103 f.
[365] Ventr.–Chadw., *Docs*. 235.
[366] I, 52 ... πόλεσιν ἀτειχίστοις καὶ κατὰ κώμας οἰκουμέναις, cf. I, 10.
[367] This last point, however, is doubted by Chadw.–Baumb., G. 41, 184.
[368] Ventr.–Chadw., *Docs*. 235
[369] *IG* V (1). 680; 683. Cf. the gloss in Hesych. Δύμη· ἐν Σπάρτῃ φύλη, καὶ τόπος. The last quotation does, however, suggest a secondary development after the Dorian (Dymanes) settlement of this area.
[370] *Preh. Aeg.* 361 f.

Pylian districts but also Poseidon, one of the chief gods of the Bronze Age city who is possibly the same god as the *theos* of a number of *Pakija* records[371].

Despite this clear evidence of community survival there are arguments, put forward by Gardner, Cary, and Andrewes[372], according to which e.g. the historic Attic *phratries*, *gene* etc. descended directly from military organizations formed during the tenth, ninth, or eighth century, a period of unrest when the king's power declined and individual aristocrats formed companies of loyal followers or *hetairoi*. This picture is said to be reflected in the system of fighting in the *Iliad*. A feature of these *hetairoi* groups in classical times was that they drew their members from the aristocracy – *aristinden* – and that many of them had an eponymous ancestor imposed on them whose kinship relationship with the other *hetairoi* might have been fictitious, but whose origin was also aristocratic. There is much in this thesis[373] which is plausible in the light of some of the Homeric evidence and later Greek practice. Furthermore the primarily military and aristocratic character of these groups is seemingly at variance with the bureaucratic arrangement of the Mycenaean army as set out in the Linear B tablets. Considering the general historical vacuum of the Dark Age, we will not quarrel with the belief that communities, tribes or *gene*, possessed important military functions. The tradition concerning the Doric tribes is sufficient evidence for that. What does seem unlikely, however, is that this was a new feature imported after the end of Helladic.

The Mycenaean tablets also record traces of figures and conditions which appear to contradict the suggestion described. The strongest indication that the *hetairoi*, as noblemen who rendered military service to a local aristocrat or basileus, were not a phenomenon thought up in the Dark Age comes from the Mycenaean term *eqeta*. The word is translated as *hepetes* which Palmer equates with the Homeric *hetairos* "companion of the king" (Lat. *comes*, "count"), precisely the sort of figure that is thought to belong to the Dark Age[374]. Concerning this *eqeta* there are two other major points of interest. Firstly he was a nobleman, as well as a military official, who quite likely stood in some sort of relationship to the *damos* as holder of

---

[371] On this *theos* see Ventr.–Chadw., *Docs.* 235.
[372] *C.A.H.* III, 585; cf. 688 (F. E. Adcock); Andrewes, *He.* 89, 138 ff.; *J.H.S.* 81, 14 f.
[373] For a diametrically opposed view see e.g. Thomson, *Preh. Aeg.* 106 ff.
[374] Palmer, "Mycenaean Greek Texts from Pylos", *T. Ph. Soc.* (1954) 51; cf. Ventr.–Chadw., *Docs.* 121; Chadw.–Baumb., *G.* 41, 192.

land[375], and secondly the *eqeta* had important religious functions[376]. This *hetairos* prominently figured on the so-called Pylian military tablets as a commander of contingents of military personnel who are guarding the coast[377]. These contingents could conceivably have represented localized *damoi*, for some of them are given ethnic names or are associated with a particular place[378]. The *hetairos*' aristocratic status is evident from his Homeric type patronymic, a distinction altogether uncommon on other Mycenaean records[379]. Although the present information does not allow us to assign the *eqeta* a definite station in a Mycenaean community, he does appear to fulfil the important requirements of a high official in a clan or tribal group in his capacity as a military officer and priest and in his relation to a basileus. He also seems to prove that the question regarding the date and circumstances of the formation of aristocratic clan and *phratry* groups must still remain open.

However, our prime concern is to give some substance to the belief that the reason for the survival of certain major gods, like Athena, Artemis, or Poseidon, and of religious concepts and cult, as at Eleusis, can be found not only in the continuity of cult sites but also in that of the communities administering the cults. No doubt the system of communal groups declined eventually into a political tool of administration. Yet at no stage of their life did these groups lose all trace of their principal concern with property, juridical, and especially religious, matter. The Greek system of these closely knit societies goes back to Mycenaean times. The Pylian *damos* is proof of that as well as the figure of *telestas* and, to a certain extent, that of *hepetes*. We must remember, too, that these are only the most obvious examples gathered from a peculiarly difficult source. More material and further work will inevitably bring to light fresh evidence. Of this we already have some indication from Mycenaean words like *trisheros*, "Clan Ancestor", the typical figure of a clan hero[380], *worokijonejo* which may be = *orgeoni-*

---

[375] Although he is never expressly said to hold *kekemena*.
[376] Brown, *H.* 5, 396; Palmer, *Interp.* 152; *Myc. Min.* 144.
[377] Ventr.–Chadw., *Docs.* 188 ff.
[378] Cf. Webster, *Myc. to Hom.* 21.
[379] Ventr.–Chadw., *Docs.* 121; Palmer, *Myc. Min.* 144. The patronymic suffix -das, -dai, common in the names of historic *phratries* and clans, is almost totally absent from Linear B, Ventr.–Chadw., *Docs.* 94; Webster, *op. cit.* 156, 163. Other patronymic forms do occasionally occur like the "splendid figure" Alectryon, son of Eteocles, Palmer, *Myc. Min.* 105; Ventr.–Chadw., *Docs.* 92; 418.
[380] Occurs on the "Oil" tablets of Pylos, Fr 1204; Tn 316, Ventr.–Chadw., *Docs.* 289; Palmer, *Interp.* 263. On the *trisheros* see esp. B. Hemberg, "TRIPATOR und TRI-

kos from *orgeones*[381], *dopota* (on the same tablet as *tiriseroe*) = *dospotai* "Herr des Hauses"[382], and the house or *oikos* itself as a kinship, or at least clan, unit[383].

There is much in the Mycenaean evidence which must remain open to correction in detail, nor is it prudent to exclude the possibility of the occasional misreading or misinterpretation of the difficult linear script. In general outline, however, the tablets contain ample confirmation of the existence of community groups in Mycenaean times which might have been governed partly by local, partly by military, and partly perhaps by pseudo or real kinship bonds. In other words, there is no single feature in the composition and arrangement of the Greek community groups which must needs be directly attributable either to a cultural break during the Dark Age or to specific post-Bronze developments. Thus, for example, the military tribal or community arrangement need not have been a Dorian invention imported into Greece at the end of the millennium, but traces of similar organizations survive on the tablets even if in vague form.

This conclusion is in direct contrast with general modern opinion as it is expressed by the scholars cited above. It will be useful, therefore, to digress and make plain the results of our examination of the evidence. How is it possible to reconcile this finding of continuing community organization with the close association of the *phylai* with the Dorians, if the latter in fact arrived on the scene at the end of the second millennium? We noticed that in literary tradition the term *phylai* was connected with the three Dorian tribes probably as military units. Therefore the *phylai* system with its neat subdivision into *phratries* and *gene* should have been the product of the Dark Age[384].

SHEROS", *Er.* 52 (1954) 172–90. Cf. the cult of the *Tritopatreis* worshipped by the Zacyadae *phratry* in Athens, sources in Hemberg, *op. cit.* 174 n. 11.

[381] E.g. Ventr.–Chadw., *Docs.* 265; Stella, *Civ. Micen.* 265 ff., who does, indeed, connect the word with the Mysteries. This identification with the *orgeones* community is rejected by Palmer, *Interp.* 214.

[382] Hemberg, *op. cit.* 179 f.

[383] *woikode* = "to the house of ... neus" (KN As 1519), Ventr.–Chadw., *Docs.* 412. This tablet introduces the summation of a list of ten men who might have belonged to the same *oikos*, *anchisteia* ("household") community, see Thomson, *Preh. Aeg.* 109 ff.; on *oikos* as a subdivision of *phratry* see Latte, "Phratrie" 747 and bibliography in n. 311 above.

[384] E.g. Adrewes, *Greeks* 80. We cannot here discuss the interesting proposals of S. Hood, *The Home of the Heroes*, 66; 126, etc. that Greek speaking peoples did not arrive on the mainland before the end of the thirteenth century, and that the invaders in

It seems a pity to disturb such a tidy sequence of events, but there are several difficulties which cast doubt on this reconstruction. While the *phylai* apparently were peculiarly Doric institutions, *phratries* were not. If anything this ancient Indo-European term came to be attached to Ionic popular groups[385]. However, *phylai* and *phratries*, as well as *gene*, most likely were originally independent organizations which may, of course, have come together in the Dark Age, but Nestor's advice in *Iliad* 2,362 f. hints at a pre-Dark Age combination of at least the first two units. The leader of each *phyle* was the king, *phylobasileus*, and Hammond convincingly argues that this was the title of the chief of the three Dorian tribes which tradition says attacked the Mycenaean world[386]. The basileus, however, was a well established functionary in the Mycenaean hierarchy, so that, unless we suppose the extraneous Dorians to have independently coined the title, its use to describe the community leader presupposes prior acquaintance between Dorians and Mycenaeans.

Homer does little or nothing to resolve the problem. The Dorians are mentioned only once as living in Crete[387]. This seems odd, for, although Nilsson concludes from Homer's disinterest that the poem represented conditions prior to the Dorian invasion[388], we know that epic composition was continuous from Mycenaean times and included at least Dark Age customs[389]. Therefore, if the Dorians dramatically crushed the Mycenaean world some two or three generations after the Trojan War, one might expect the event to be rather more clearly reflected in epic tradition. As it is, the Dorians are ignored by the Achaean Catalogue. Yet in the same Catalogue we hear of the Heraclid Tlepolemus who brought his contingent of nine ships from Rhodes to join the Achaean fleet[390].

Literary tradition, of course, connected the Heraclidae with the Dorians from well before the Trojan War[391], so that we are not surprised to read in Homer that Tlepolemus, one of Heracles' sons, had settled Rhodes

---

Middle Helladic were of Anatolian origin. Cf. the review by A. M. Snodgrass in *J.H.S.* 88 (1968) 213 f.

[385] See above p. 250.
[386] *C.A.H.*² II, ch. XXXVI (1962) 38.
[387] *Od.* 19, 177.
[388] *Homer and Mycen.* 157.
[389] E.g. Page, *Hist. and the Hom. Iliad* 254; 259.
[390] *Il.* 2, 653 ff.
[391] Hammond, *op. cit.* 27 f.

THE PROBLEM OF CONTINUITY IN THE DARK AGE 263

according to the known system of the Dorian three *phylai*[392]. This notice, together with *Il.* 2,362 f. and the reference to Dorians in Crete in the *Odyssey*, suggests plainly the conclusion that the Homeric audience was familiar with the Dorians and their customs in the Mycenaean world as a presence which required no special mention.

Their absence, like that of the Heraclidae, from the Catalogue Hammond explains by supposing the list to have covered an area whose northernmost point bordered on Leucas and therefore excluded Epirus and part Thessaly which then harboured most of the Dorians[393]. But we know now that both Thessaly and Epirus, especially Dodona, had been in contact with Mycenaean culture, so that a line south of Leucas might well be thought an arbitrary division[394]. Is it not possible that in the thirteenth century the Heraclidae and the Dorians did not, as a clan and a race, send men to join the expedition against Troy and therefore hardly merited separate mention? The Dorians may have been a disruptive force in Late Mycenaean, but newcomers they were not[395]. Nor does this conclusion, with the possible exception of an established Dorian presence in the Argolid, really conflict with the literary tradition, for Dorian tribes had been in the orbit of the Mycenaean world for anything up to six generations before the Trojan War[396]. They were a race of wanderers, criss-crossing Thessaly and central Greece during the second half of the millennium, in continuous contact, one must suppose, with the Mycenaeans. In fact, when Herodotus[397] constructs the royal Dorian genealogy of Deucalion – Hellen – Dorus, he does not so much describe historical figures as establish the rightful place of these tribes in the Mycenaean world from the earliest days of Greek prehistory[398].

---

[392] *trichtha ... kataphyladon, Il.* 2, 668.
[393] *Op. cit.* 28.
[394] On Dodona see now the report of S. Dakaris' most recent Mycenaean finds (III C) beneath and about the sanctuary, in *J.H.S.* Arch. Rep. for 1967/8, 13 f. Contrast with this Parke, *Oracles of Zeus* 20 and n. 1, where he cites Nilsson, *Gesch.* I, 280 ff. More relevant is p. 427 where Nilsson leaves the question open, "Sei es, dass der Zeuskult in Dodona ein Relikt aus der griechischen Vorzeit ist, sei es, dass er ein fremder ... ist."
[395] Nixon, *Rise of the Dorians* 102, calls the Dorians "fringe Mycenaeans" and believes that both were "Minyan in derivation".
[396] Cf. the conclusion Hammond draws from Herodotus 5, 59, *op. cit.* 26.
[397] 1, 56.
[398] Cf. Hammond, *ibid.*

One now begins to suspect that by the end of the second millennium the Dorians, as far as culture and beliefs are concerned, were part of the Mycenaean world. "The Dorians regarded Zeus as their special god... Their other special god was Apollo of Pytho[399]". But we learn from the Linear B documents that both these deities already belonged to the Mycenaean pantheon long before the Dorians are supposed to have ended Mycenaean civilization. The Indo-European Zeus, in fact, had come to Greece at the beginning of Middle Helladic[400].

Let us then try to lay to rest the concept of the Dorians as primitive destroyers of Late Mycenaean culture. Their presence seems not to have affected the survival of fundamental ideas of gods and cult. The vehicle of transmission for such ideas was the communities which preserved inherited religious material. The structure of the communities was basically simple: the military and religious leader was the basileus. He had been a minor local Mycenaean functionary who remained the chief of the splinter groups which therefore quite possibly might have originally constituted components of a larger Mycenaean settlement or political entity.

The basileus could hardly have been a grand king holding "great power and wide estate"[401]. Perhaps a *primus inter pares* rather than an absolute ruler, he maintained a precarious position by virtue of his personal ability, but even so eventually was compelled to relinquish the reins of government to his fellow noblemen in the community's leading families. Occasionally, however, the single basileus lost merely his political power but retained the administration of cult and of his own land (*temenea*), as was the case with Battus in Cyrene[402]. Precisely when these events occurred escapes us, nor can we overlook the possibility that an aristocratic vassal and his family could have been in charge of a community cult from before the social revolution. In any case the movement away from monarchy must have come early, for Homeric epic already was fully aware of political forces like the *demos*, *agora*, and *boule*, while it was not the king but the town-elders who decided the famous law-suit modelled on Achilles' shield[403].

---

[399] Hammond, *op. cit.* 40, who suggests that the Dorians might have "brought the worship of Zeus from Dodona", since Epirus was one of their strongholds.
[400] Above p. 241.
[401] Starr, *Origins* 125.
[402] Herod. 4, 161.
[403] *Il.* 18, 497. On these points see Starr, *Orig.* 123 ff. with the relevant references to modern literature.

The most significant feature of these communities, however, was their composition of tribes, clans, families. The basileus was a tribal king who derived his authority direct from the protecting community deity[404], from whom he claimed descent and whose cult he was in charge of. This kind of arrangement where the king, through his religious authority, contained and held together his subjects, who in turn were bound together by their tribal and clan associations, was typical of the early Greek communities and left its mark on the later *polis*. It was ingrained so deeply that the aristocratic families, who replaced the basileus, observed precisely the same system: they justified their government through divine descent and arrogated the right to administer city cult.

Eventually, as in Athens, synoecism brought the family and community gods together in one *polis*. The curious Greek community structure, with its roots anchored in the Mycenaean world[405], gained strength as a force of religious conservatism during the centuries following the Mycenaean political disaster into Archaic times. The fresh impact of Eastern thought on the Greek scene from the eighth century did not essentially harm mainland tradition so much as contribute its share to the developing Greek religion. This point we shall touch on again. Again, political changes in Archaic times – the establishment of the *polis* structure – did not greatly affect inherited cult and beliefs, in the sense that the close ties between clan, community, and their special gods might have been broken.

Throughout its history, and most likely in Mycenaean times already, Greek religion was a family or group matter in which the state and church, as it were, meant one and the same thing[406]. We may describe this phenomenon as a "Gesellschaftsreligion" where tension or even open strife between secular and religious government, along the lines of Henry II's or Frederic II's contest with the church in 12th–14th century England and Germany, would have been unthinkable. The intimate relationship between the Mycenaean wanax and his goddess may strike the classicist as un-Greek, but only until he appreciates that very little had changed between the clan and its tie with a protecting deity.

---

[404] Cf. Starr, *Orig.* 174, who speaks of the Zeus-sprung and Zeus-nurtured basileus.
[405] Cf. Mabel Lang's interesting discussion in L. R. Palmer–J. Chadwick, *Proc. Myc. St.* From the study of some Pylian tablets (Tn 316 in particular) she concludes that the Pylian realm was composed of fourteen tribal communities, each one with its own tutelary deity. I have taken this information from J. B. Hainsworth's review of the collection of papers in *C.R.* 18 (1968) 70.
[406] Cf. Nilsson, *Gesch.* I, 708.

The god's cult was no longer administered by the wanax, but by the basileus of the community[407], and eventually by chosen aristocratic families and the *archon basileus*. A god belonged to his community which he protected and from which he in turn received worship. The bond was close and permeated the structure of Greek society so strongly that a person's group ties could be seen from the particular god revered by his clan[408]. Below the chief deity of a community no doubt a host of lesser divine figures was attached to particular families or clans, but it was the overall god, Poseidon, Zeus, Athena, or other major figure, who, as it were, represented his tribe or community when the latter joined together with similar groups in Archaic times to found the new city.

The *polis*, therefore, although really an artificial political creation, nevertheless preserved the clannish flavour of the old community, for the former hearth, the centre of the family group, became the common city's hearth which served as the religious symbol binding the people together, and from which colonists took a brand destined to keep alive the tie between any new foundation and the mother city[409]. What is particularly important is the fact that the gods and their cult in the *polis* represented a cross-section of the earlier communal practices. The drawing together into *poleis* of the scattered communities, together with their chief gods, directly resulted in the many gods crowding out the acropolis of a Greek city[410], and in the variety of noble families attached to a *polis* who had retained the administration of particular major cults.

Attica again provides the best example of this development. In Athens, for instance, the Eteobutadae remained responsible for Poseidon's cult in the Erechtheum, the Praxiergidae were primarily concerned with the worship of Athena Polias, while the Buzygae cared for particular Zeus cults as well as looked after the annual sacred ploughing beneath the acropolis[411]. The canon of the twelve Olympian gods, to whom Peisistratus' son Hippias dedicated the altar in Athens in 525 B.C.[412], was born from the

---

[407] Cf. Webster, *op. cit.* 155. Mylonas, *Mycenae* 206, is inclined to doubt that the wanax ever was a religious functionary.

[408] Cf. Herodotus' story, 5, 66, of Isagoras whose background the historian does not know except that the man's clan made sacrifice to Zeus Karios.

[409] Cf. Nilsson, *Gesch.* I, 709.

[410] On the advent of democracy the many cults were cut down in number and thrown open to the people, Arist., *Pol.* 1319 b 19.

[411] Cf. Nilsson, *ibid.*

[412] Thuc. 6, 54, 6.

number of twelve Attic *poleis* which corresponded with the local subdivision of *phylai* into twelve *trittyes* described by Aristotle[413].

The state religion of Greek classical times arose from what can be described as family religion associated with clans and tribes of our much discussed communities. Outstanding names, therefore, in a city's pantheon would be the *Polieus* or *Polias*, Zeus, for example, Hera and Athena whose function as protecting deities of a community date back to Mycenaean times. A few historical factors, however, tended to complicate what might otherwise have been a regular progression from community to *polis* cult. Political innovation, for example, during the Archaic period broke through the narrow clan ties of cult which became generally accessible to all citizens of the new *polis*. Cleisthenes' Attic reforms substituted ten *phylai* for the traditional four, and purely localized demes replaced the family associations of the old *phratries*.

The effect of these reforms on the substance of cult was minimal, however: the narrow *phratry* groups certainly retained some cultic functions, but the worship of the original community gods became universal among the new and larger body of citizens. In fact inherited religious tradition proved so strong that it could be used in support of calculated political moves. This is not meant to refer to the squabbles, which still marred the fifth century, concerning claims to land on mythological grounds, but to the concessions made to cult by an influential *polis* wishing to expand its borders.

Two examples will illustrate this process. When Athens, perhaps late in the Archaic Age, annexed the important religious centre of Eleusis, the city agreed to import the cult of Demeter and Kore. An Eleusinium was built beneath the acropolis, and there the ἱερά were kept during the days preceding the great procession to the home of the Eleusinian Mysteries. The Brauronian Artemis, too, was honoured by a temple on the Athenian acropolis, whence every four years a sacred procession set out to Brauron[414].

A powerful determining factor in the actual standing of a major god and his cult consisted in his continuing suitability as the predominant figure

---

[413] *Ath. Pol.* 8, 3. See also Ehrenberg, *Solon* 53. For the importance of the event in Greek art see Boardman, *PreClass.* 137.

[414] Arist., *Ath. Pol.* 54; Aristoph., *Peace* 873 f.; cf. Nilsson, *Gesch.* I, 712. The date of Eleusis' annexation by Athens is uncertain, but most probably belongs to the time of Solon or slightly earlier, cf. Mylonas, *Eleusis* 63.

in the official religion of the *polis*. In other words, from what we might call a power struggle among gods for the chief position within a city a few divinities appeared to emerge victorious in classical times, such as Zeus, Athena, and Hera. One significant casualty in this context seems to have been Poseidon, a leading community god in Mycenaean times at least in Messenian Pylos. His earlier prominent position declined, his functions changed to those we know from literature. Homer, in Poseidon's quarrel with Zeus, retains only a faint memory of the chthonic god's ancient glory. In mythology, about the Argolid and Saronic Gulf, Poseidon is often described as fighting for the possession of a city, and he invariably loses: to Hera in the Argolid, to Helios, and eventually Athena, in Corinth, who also defeats him in Athens and in Troezen, and to Zeus on Aegina[415].

The *Polias* or *Polieus* was at the head of the Greek *polis*. He, or she, was not an absolute divine monarch, like the supreme god in a theocracy, but formed an integral part of the city-state's political life. His original function as the protector of an individual community had expanded to include the welfare of a group of communities united by bonds of political convenience. The end-result of this change is reflected in classical Greek literature. The great city gods like Zeus, Athena, Hera, became the universal luminous figures of Greek belief[416]. Therefore the *Polias* or *Polieus* was primarily a political figure in that he represented the centre of state cult, that is, one aspect of the city's political life. Beside him on the acropolis were ranged the other deities whom synoecism had brought together. It is important to understand in this context that, although these figures carried along with them their unaltered cultic nature and ritual, they were separated from their localized roots and, like the *Polieus*, integrated in state cult. In this way the gods of the *polis* lost much of their intimate connection with the earlier tribal communities. Their new cult, as we mentioned, formed a part of the city's political organization.

The nature of the *polis* gods, however, remained basically unchanged by synoecism, so that we need not detect significant religious breaks accompanying political revolutions of the late Dark Age. Cults were moved into the new *polis*, bodily, stone by stone, as it were, or even duplicated, as we noticed in the case of Demeter's Mysteries in Athens, or of Artemis' Brauronian cult.

---

[415] See also Schachermeyr, *Poseidon* 23; Wiesner, *Olympos* 67; 119 f.; 123, etc.

[416] Apollo belonged to this group, too, for by Archaic times his position as major city god, as in Corinth, was firmly established, see e.g. Wiesner, *Olympos* 120.

A good example of this procedure is still extant from the later historical founding of the Arcadian Megalopolis. The first half of the fourth century B.C. saw the founding of the Great City, Megalopolis, in Arcadia[417]. This was the result of synoecism of a number of communities in western Arcadia into one large city. The event is fairly well documented but late for our purposes. But it is fair to assume that the Megalopolis example followed a well-established pattern and therefore represents a reasonable model of the founding of the earlier Greek *polis*. The arrangement in the case of Megalopolis, like other *poleis* arising out of synoecism, was one of political convenience. Our more immediate concern is the fortune of the cults and deities closely attached to the lesser communities which were brought together into one new city. And in this instance we may perhaps see a working example of what occurred in the Dark Age of Greece.

Some of the cults were physically transferred to the new centre. This is true of the cults of Pan Sinoeis and Skoleitas[418]. The cult of the Great Goddesses, however, that is Demeter and Kore, or Despoina, which in Arcadia was almost ubiquitous, could not be confined in the one *polis*. In this case Megalopolis probably became the centre of worship of these two figures, while other localities, like Andania and Lycosoura, retained their rites[419]. The cult of Demeter and Despoina at Lycosoura, in fact, had acquired such importance by the fourth century that the people there successfully resisted the religious synoecism. In a way, therefore, Demeter's and Kore's Mysteries formed a kind of exception to complete synoecism, in the sense that the prestige of this particular worship kept it alive at sites other than the new *polis*. But the fact remains that henceforward Megalopolis took precedence in the celebration of this cult[420].

Perhaps more in the pattern of old established practice was the transference into the new city of major cults which, unlike the lesser forms of Pan, were less easily moved to the new site. In such cases the cult was either duplicated or moved symbolically to the new city, although the

---

[417] See Paus. VIII, 26. This brief description of the historical synoecism depends on Nilsson's discussion in *Cults, Myths, Oracles*, 18 ff.

[418] Paus. VIII, 30, 3; 7.

[419] The actual form of the worship of the Arcadian Great Goddesses is of less concern at the moment, or the probability that the Mysteries connected with their cult were heavily under Eleusinian influence. Cf. Nilsson, *Cults* 21.

[420] The transference of the Mysteries to Megalopolis altogether is a difficult problem in which even the date of its institution in the Great City is under dispute. See Nilsson's discussion, *Cults* 19 ff.

ancient locality might keep its sacred memories. Apollo Epikourios, for example, enjoyed an important cult at Bassae where, too, he possessed a splendid temple. This could not be moved, but the citizens brought a statue of the god to Megalopolis and set it up on a site which was named Bassae. Zeus Lycaeus' cult on Mt. Lycaion could also not be transferred, so that at Megalopolis a corresponding sacred precinct, surrounded by a stone wall, was dedicated to the god. In the case of Apollo Parrhasius, who was worshipped on the eastern slopes of Mt. Lycaion, a new ritual was instituted to the god, also called Pythias, in the market place of Megalopolis, and this was connected with the original cult site by an annual sacred procession in the manner of the Eleusinian and Brauronian cults at Athens[421].

Of great interest to the history of synoecism in Megalopolis is the institution at the time of an apparently new cult to Zeus Philios whose temple and cult statue, in the precinct of the Great Goddesses, were the oldest in Greece[422]. Nilsson suggests[423] that Zeus Philios represented "a symbol of the friendship which ought to unite the inhabitants who were drawn from many different, formerly independent, places". If he is right, this is a new custom which, in the present writer's knowledge, had no precedent. The *Polieus* had also become a Philios.

In its general procedure, however, the Megalopolis example sheds light on the practice which obtained in the founding of a Greek *polis* at any time. It is evident that religion and politics were one in the city, a fact which came to serve the tyrants well in the seventh and sixth centuries when they sought popular support for their position. The reason for this close interdependence lies to hand: the various peoples who came together in order to form a *polis* were integral parts of particular community groups which in small settlements had weathered the hardships of the Dark Age. As members of such groups they had naturally been attached to their particular, and localized, protecting deities who even in their new abode continued to dominate the life of their subjects. Gradually, as the kinship bonds of tribe and *phratry* relaxed and gave way to communal ties based on feelings of political unity, administrative and religious affairs came to be centralized in the hands of the governing class.

One example of this can be found in the codification of laws for all citizens, like that for Athens recorded by Draco late in the seventh cen-

---

[421] Paus. VIII, 38, 8.
[422] Paus. VIII, 31, 4.
[423] *Cults* 21 f.

tury. The administration of justice, with few exceptions, such as blood-guilt within a family, was taken away from a particular clan or *phratry* and made universally applicable within the *polis*. The gods, too, who had literally been gathered from the four corners of a wide district, became general city gods. They grew remote, therefore, from all but the members of the nobility administering the cult. It is quite true, of course, that in earlier days only the basileus, or members of the ruling family, were in charge of the community cult, but the distinction lay in the fact that the ties between members of such a community were far closer than those binding the citizens of a *polis*, so that the former must have felt some sense of participation in the worship of what after all were their family gods. In the *polis*, however, a gulf was bound to open between the gods and the lower classes of the city, and such a development was of considerable consequence to later Greek religion.

The virtual isolation, for this is what it came to be, of gods from the majority in the *polis* may well have helped to feed the discontent of the poorer classes already in the seventh century, but it certainly carried the seed of decay for the city gods whose power, and very existence, began to be seriously questioned from the fifth century in a religiously apathetic *polis*. Even more serious for the average citizen in the *polis* of the eighth and seventh century was his forcible separation in the new community from the great variety of deities and cults which had not been found admissable to the city together with the major gods. The Dark Age community, and that of the *polis* no less, was essentially agricultural, ranging from peasant to nobleman with large estates. A great deal, therefore, of inherited religious custom was chthonic in nature and concerned with fertility. But these cults and the divinities involved with them had no official place in the city. When, therefore, the social pressures of the seventh century, the enslavement of the poor by the rich[424], the growing middle class of the lesser landowners, who made up the ranks of the city's new army – the *hoplites*[425] –, created explosive tensions, it took individual men of vision to rise to power on the wave of popular dissatisfaction.

The pattern of political development in many Greek cities repeated itself, for the simple reason that generally the founding of the *polis* occurred along similar lines. The gulf between the ruling nobility, the administrators of official cult, and the lower classes by the seventh century had become

---

[424] See e.g. Arist., *Ath. Pol.* 2; Plutarch, *Solon* 13, 4.
[425] Cf. Nilsson, "Das frühe Griechenland", *H.* 3 (1955) 279 f.; Ehrenberg, *Solon* 20.

seemingly unbridgeable. Nilsson speaks of these unprivileged people as not only being divorced from state cult, but also as possessing no traditional cults of their own[426]. However, despite the new organization of the *polis*, the poorer orders, with little or no landed possessions, did manage to retain their particular cults which were tied to the soil and to their section of the community unit, however small that might have been.

Many such units, independent of the larger tribal and *phratry* structure, must have existed in the Archaic *polis*[427]. We are fortunate enough to have a notice of the so-called law of Philochorus[428] according to which, in the seventh century[429], *phratries* were compelled to admit to their ranks lesser groups like the *orgeones* and *homogalaktes (gennetai)*. The *orgeones*[430], we noticed above, most likely existed as a group in Mycenaean times. They, like the many others that had found their way into the *polis*, concerned themselves with a type of cult which had no place on the Archaic acropolis beside the major city gods. This cult, perhaps including the worship of the ancestor and hero[431], was primarily chthonic in nature, revolving about deities like Demeter and Dionysus who were active in Greek cult in the Bronze Age, but who, like many of the dispossessed people in the *polis*, did not receive full official recognition.

Added to the social wrongs, inflicted on the poor by the landowning nobility, the lack of recognition of a large stratum of deeply rooted religious belief was bound to create those extreme tensions which led to the social crisis of the seventh century. From the point of view of Greek religious development this crisis was of great significance. The contest, insofar as one may speak of a contest in this connection, between the gods of the *polis* and the many divine powers, survivors of the Dark and Bronze Ages, was one between an old and new order, not unlike the struggle between the Aeschylean Erinyes and Apollo in the *Oresteia*.

---

[426] *Gesch.* I, 710.
[427] Cf. Andrewes, *J.H.S.* 81 (1961) 2.
[428] Photius, Suda s.v. *orgeones*, Harpocr., Suda s.v. *gennetai*.
[429] The date of this law is still debated. Scholars variously assign the law to the time of Solon, Cleisthenes, and even Pericles, see Andrewes, *J.H.S.* 81 ff. The seventh century seems the most likely, cf. Nilsson, *Gesch.* I, 710 n. 1.
[430] It must be noted here that Andrewes, *op. cit.* 2, is inclined to think of the *orgeones* as "a fairly small and relatively obscure upper-class minority."
[431] Like the *trisheros* whose cult probably began in Mycen. times, see above and Hemberg, *Er.* 52 (1954) 179. But we cannot enter the debate about the origin of Greek hero cult, whether it was Mycenaean or began only in the Dark Age about the tombs of forgotten Mycenaean heroes.

There was then the danger, which had become acute by the seventh century, that the gods of the leading aristocratic class would sever their ties with the past which, even through the vicissitudes of the Dark Age, had firmly bound the Archaic *polis* with the Bronze Age. These ancient religious traditions were preserved, however, and for that we have to thank the intervention of the tyrants. The generally analogous development of the Greek *polis*, as we observed above, ensured that hardly any city avoided the tension between an oppressive noble oligarchy and the mass of deprived people as well as a rising Middle Class. The political consequence, too, was (almost inevitably) the same in every instance. A single member of the aristocracy, either through motives of personal gain or because of genuine compassion for the poor, rose to dominance in the city.

His title may have been *aesymnetes*, as in Mitylene, or lawgiver, or simply tyrant, his position was the same[432]. His effect, too, on religious continuity was equally dramatic almost everywhere. The tyrant was anxious to retain the popular vote. His energies, therefore, were directed towards the welfare of the people: public works provided employment for the many poor. Theagenes of Megara, for example, built a water supply for Corinth in the seventh century[433]. Even the notorious Polycrates of Samos set his engineers to drive a mighty tunnel through a mountain to provide his people with work and water[434]. More important still were the concessions made by the tyrants to the undercurrents of popular belief in the city. The seventh and sixth centuries were a period of consolidation, of a *rapprochement* between the illustrious city gods and the wide range of chthonic cults and the cults of the deities of the soil, like Demeter and Dionysus, to whom the agrarian society of Greece had been bound since the Bronze Age and before.

The Athenian Peisistratus is a shining example of the contribution made by the tyrants to the religious harmony within the *polis*, and especially to the survival of the age-old chthonic cults. Peisistratus' programme of temple-building on the acropolis is evidence of his deep religious feeling for the *Polias* Athena for whom he also struck the first coin bearing Athena's head on one side, and her bird, the owl, on the reverse[435]. But what interests us here, in addition to Peisistratus' other religious work, is the in-

---

[432] Ehrenberg, *Solon* 23 f.
[433] *A.M.* 25 (1900) 23 ff.; 30 (1905) 49.
[434] *A.M.* 9 (1884) 165 ff. Nilsson, *H.* 3, 281.
[435] Nilsson, *op. cit.* 280; Ehrenberg, *Solon* 81.

troduction into Athens of the cult of Dionysus Eleuthereus in whose honour the dramatic festivals came into being[436]. The cult of Dionysus, in fact, in sixth century Athens became respectable and was observed by all classes in society. The god of the lower orders, as it were, concerned with fertility, orgiastic and mystic rites, had been known to the Homeric poets but was neglected by them. Much of his myth reflected the vigour with which the nobility had resisted the introduction of Dionysiac cult[437]. However, it was the achievement of Peisistratus and his successors that a reconciliation came about between the religious cult of the lower classes and the city gods, the gods of the aristocracy[438]. Dionysus' ascent to the ranks of the Olympians during this period can be judged by the god's becoming the favourite subject of Attic vase painters, and by the temple which was built to Dionysus in Athens in the last years of the sixth century[439].

The rural cults of Demeter, too, who had been spurned by Homeric epic, fared equally well. The centre of Demeter's and Kore's worship was Eleusis, the site which most likely had seen uninterrupted cult from Mycenaean times. Whether or not the Mysteries there had come into being in the second millennium already[440], the cult in Eleusis had always been chthonic, bound up with the annual death and renewal of nature[441]. Therefore the belief underlying the ritual, however elaborate it might have become in later times, agreed well with what we know of Minoan and Mycenaean religious ideas. The celebration of the Mysteries was a community affair even in pre-*polis* times. Accordingly we are not surprised that the administration of the cult remained in the hands of the Eumolpid family, even after Eleusis was annexed by Attica in the seventh century or earlier[442]. Here at Eleusis, on the very spot where, from the time of the Mycenaean Megaron B, the cult had been performed, Peisistratus built the first Telesterion. The tyrant's active support of the Eleusinian Mysteries

---

[436] Nilsson, *ibid.* 281; Ehrenberg, *Solon* 81 f.

[437] See e.g. W. K. C. Guthrie, *The Greeks and their Gods*, 159; 165 ff.

[438] Compare Aristotle's cynical view in *Pol.* V, 1314 B, where the tyrant's god-fearing piety is explained as a calculating move to appease any suspicion of the dictator's injustice.

[439] E. Homannn–Wedeking, *Archaic Greece*, 193 f.

[440] See the arguments in favour of the high antiquity of the Eleusinia in Mylonas, *Eleusis*. Cf. Aristotle in *F.H.G.* II, Frg. 282, who believed that the Mysteries were founded during Pandion's reign at Athens, i.e. c. 14th/13th cent. B.C.

[441] Cf. Nilsson, *Gesch.* I, 470, and modern sources.

[442] See above n. 414.

was of some considerable consequence to the continuity of inherited religious tradition. His religious reforms also created some sort of harmony between what we have called the popular chthonic cults, with all their ramifications, and the burgeoning city gods who, outside their mythological heritage, were cutting themselves adrift from their localized roots and from their connection with nature cult.

At Eleusis, perhaps because of the sanctity of unbroken cult, the two religious streams met, so that, what had always been essentially a vegetation ritual, became acceptable even to the community's ruling nobility. Eleusis, like Delphi, became a religious centre of national importance. But the Mysteries of the agrarian goddess Demeter were also spread to many new sites throughout Greece[443], where the influence of the Eleusinian cult lent respectability to a ritual more at home with the lower classes in society.

The religious confluence of the upper and lower strata of the Greek *polis* may have been short lived, for the common people became disillusioned with their tyrants before the sixth century had ended. But little of what Peisistratus, for example, had achieved could be undone: Dionysus and Demeter joined the city's pantheon. They contributed their vegetation, chthonic fertility, and their orgiastic, rites to the growing complexity of Archaic Greek religion. Their Mystery cult, again, led to new concepts of a kind of "Jenseitsglaube" which went beyond the age-old beliefs in the natural cycle of birth and death[444], but introduced the idea of an existence after death and ultimately the theory of reincarnation. The force of such religious development was considerable, and its impact on the average Greek mind in the Archaic city can be gauged from the religious ferment which marked sixth century Greece and which, producing influential sects like those of the Orphics and Pythagoreans, gave some impetus to the burgeoning of Greek philosophical thought[445].

---

[443] The most notable later sites in Attica were the Marathonian Tetrapolis, Brauron, and Paiania, Nilsson, *Cults* 38 n. 45. These Mysteries had the nature of fertiliy cult. See also *Gesch.* I, 477.

[444] Cf. Dietrich, *H.* 16 (1967) 413.

[445] Cf. Dietrich, *The Semantics of the Soul*, Grahamstown 1964, 16. It is in this context of little consequence whether Orphism was essentially a religion of the upper classes in the *polis,* or whether it belonged to the poor and underprivileged section of society. For the former view see Guthrie, *Greeks & Gods,* 328, and for the latter H. J. Rose, in *C.R.* 49 (1935) 69. On Peisistratus' connection with Orphism see also Nilsson, *Gesch.* I, 721.

In this development a large part was played, of course, by the god Apollo[446], also a city god, as at Corinth, but with Dionysiac traits in his character which appealed to all levels of society. The discussion of Apollo's possible origin does not belong in this context, nor the history of his rise to the position of pan–Hellenic god. But we should not forget that, whether or not he was politically motivated[447], Peisistratus ensured Apollo's status in Athens when the tyrant undertook his famous purification of the god's island Delos[448]. However, Apollo's obscure past, the fact that virtually from the beginning of Greek history his character was universal rather than localized, make him the odd man out in the development of classical Greek religion. In other words, that aspect of Apollo which, in connection chiefly with his oracular seat at Delphi, came to represent enlightenment and reason to the Greeks constituted a separate religious force, or stream, active in the *polis*[448a] beside the city gods and the rising popular religion. The latter commonly found expression in the ecstatic cults, mainly associated with Dionysus, and the vegetation and mystery rites of the agrarian Demeter.

Apollo, Dionysus, and Demeter, in fact, stood for three major elements which Nilsson has shown to have represented the religious structure of the Archaic *polis*. These were the ecstatic Dionysiac, the legalistic Apolline elements, and the more localized mystery cults[449]. These various religious streams, including the prophetic and ecstatic Apolline cult, were essentially in contrast with the cult of the Olympian city gods. The former, and this we touched on before, contributed to the growth of philosophy; but from this primarily non-Olympian religious element there also arose practices and beliefs which became current in the Archaic and classical *polis*, such as the creation of miracle mongers, purveyors of magic, and errant prophets and priests[450].

It should now be clear from the preceding account that any attempt at discovering the presence of two essentially alien cultures in this apparent dichotomy of religious elements is doomed to fail. The view has often been expressed that the dark chthonic forces, relentlessly pushed into the back-

---

[446] See esp. Guthrie, *Greeks & Gods*, ch. VII.
[447] Ehrenberg, *Solon* 81.
[448] Thuc. 3, 104, 1.
[448a] See also Guthrie, *op. cit.* 203.
[449] Nilsson, *Gesch.* I, 611 ff.
[450] These are fully discussed by E. Rohde, *Psyche*[8], transl. by W. B. Hillis, London 1925, ch. 8; esp. pp. 260 ff. Cf. Guthrie, *op. cit.* 194 ff.; Nilsson, *Gesch.* I, 615 ff.

ground in *polis* cult and virtually ignored by the growth of recorded literature, represented the old Mediterranean and Bronze Age religious traditions which were suppressed by intrusive popular elements that eventually imposed their own Olympian divine system on the new Greek community and thus in effect created a neat division in the cults of the *polis*. Only the tyrants' interest in the welfare of the city's lower classes and, of course, their votes, brought about an uneasy truce between the gods of the aristocrats and the earth-bound daemons of the rest of the people. Furthermore without exception the Mycenaean deities, including the palace goddess and community gods, clearly possessed their chthonic traits which are not immediately obvious among the classical figures on Olympus.

The history perhaps began with Herodotus[451] who categorically declared that the Dorian upheaval in the Peloponnese put an end to Demeter's rites on the peninsula. Only the Arcadians, he says, preserved the goddess' cult. This account is taken up and expanded by e.g. Pettazzoni[452] who also firmly believes in the division of "Pelasgian" and Dorian cultic practices. The Arcadians did, indeed, continue a number of ancient cults of Demeter unchanged[453]. But they also by and large avoided building *poleis* along the lines of other Greeks during the Dark and Archaic periods. Therefore the question remains open whether the Arcadians jealously guarded the old from contamination with Dorian beliefs, or whether in their inaccessible mountain reaches they simply remained untouched by the development of the rest of the Greeks.

However, we are not really dealing here with separate sets of religious concepts which distinguished the indigenous population from the alien intruder, along the lines perhaps of the political division of Norman and Saxon in eleventh-century Britain. As we have noticed before, the religion of the Greek *polis* was a religion of the community, a "Gesellschaftsreligion". Therefore a split between two different levels of belief and worship suggests two classes or levels of community. Social divisions, however, do not necessarily imply different gods or cult which is incompatible across the class line. There are, obviously, no longer any accurate means of detecting whether the Bronze Age communities in Mycenaean Greece were governed by a conscious division into upper and

---

[451] II, 171.
[452] R. Pettazzoni, *Essays on the History of Religions*, 78.
[453] See e.g. Dietrich, *Death, Fate, Gods* 118 ff.

lower classes. The strict hierarchical set-up, however, of the Mycenaean settlements, from king and priests to basileus, the various ranks of noble men, like *lawagetas*, down to labourers, male and female slaves, appears to support the existence of such a class system. Evidence of similar import comes from the tablets which we discussed above concerning land holdings and tenure. Finally, and most important of all, it is evident from what has already been said that the Olympian and the chthonic religions did not derive from different sources. Gilbert Murray some time ago had no doubt about the original connection with vegetation religion of every member of the Olympian family. Athena's and Hera's roots as Mycenaean palace goddesses grew from the same soil as those of Demeter and Dionysus. How else could we possibly explain the fact that a number of the major Olympian figures already appeared in the Mycenaean pantheon?

In this history of Dark Age Greek religion, which developed in response to internal social changes alone, there remains one event capable of disturbing this continuity to the Classical Age. The apparently fresh impact on Greece in the eighth and seventh centuries of Eastern, Assyrian-Babylonian and Egyptian, concepts and forms on Greek art might have heralded the arrival of foreign elements on the scene. During that period not only Greek vase painting gives evidence of Eastern influence but also temple architecture, as we already remarked, sculpture, and plastic art in general. It could, accordingly, be said that the Orientalizing style of the seventh century produced a greater effect of a break from tradition than Geometric when compared with Mycenaean. By the eighth and seventh centuries Greece had recovered much of her prosperity, but, it would seem, the people and their beliefs then were more exposed to foreign ideas than at any time during the Dark Age. It is important, therefore, to take issue with the problem as to how far the Eastern factor in Late Geometric and Archaic Greece affected the continuity of Greek religious tradition inherited from the previous millennium.

By the eighth, and following, century Greek art seemed flooded with monsters almost exclusively of Eastern provenance. They were the griffin, sphinx, winged horses, sirens and the like which dominated the scene to such an extent that some scholars cite them as "intriguing evidence of human fears at the time[454]." But such creatures were peculiarly Greek in that they had lost their original dire aspect and become "friendly and elegant, never

---

[454] Starr, *Origins* 280. Cf. Pfister in *P.-W.* Suppl. VI, 162; E. R. Dodds, *The Greeks and the Irrational*, 39; 44.

grotesque⁴⁵⁵", which suggests that Greek craftsmen were aware of Eastern models but used them for their own purposes[456]. Nonetheless the fondness of the Archaic Greek for these monsters, however friendly, might in some measure have reflected his religious outlook especially insofar as the latter was affected by the import of Eastern myths in which such creatures played a predominant part. The prototype, for example, of the myth which tells of Perseus' slaying of the Gorgon was the Assyrian-Babylonian legend of Gilgamesh and Humbaba[457]. The story, too, of Bellerophon who killed the Chimaira with the help of the winged horse Pegasus was of Oriental provenance[458].

The origin of Greek mythology, and its connection with cultic practice, is a sensitive subject, and we cannot digress in order to examine it. What concerns us here is the date of the formation of Greek myth, and to what extent Eastern imports could have given new directions to Greek belief in the Archaic Age. The case was put some time ago by Nilsson that such a date fell in the Mycenaean Age[459]. His arguments are full and convincing, and little of what has been said since in opposition can shake his thesis, despite the dismal poverty of evidence from the years of the Dark Age[460].

We are obliged, therefore, to draw the conclusion that what influence had been brought to bear on Greek ideas of religion and mythology by Eastern imports had been accomplished in the main before the end of the Bronze Age. Greek Archaic art, especially sculpture and vase painting, exhibits two features in particular which caution the historian against discovering evidence of foreign religious importation in the sudden wealth of Eastern motifs. These features are the amazingly rapid absorption of such alien ideas by Greek art which quickly added them to its own repertoire, and the fact that the griffin, sphinx, siren, winged animal, god or goddess, and similar Eastern creations, already were familiar to the Minoan Mycenaean world. In other words, old ideas perhaps found new favour in the Archaic Age and stimulated, or governed, the contemporary artist's

---

[455] Boardman, *Pre-Class.* 75.
[456] Starr, *Orig.* 280 and n. 8, on the various discussions of the figures. Nilsson, *Gesch.* I, 228; Boardman, *op. cit.* 74.
[457] C. Hopkins, "Assyrian Elements in the Perseus-Gorgon Story", *A.J.A.* 38 (1934) 341 ff.; Rizza–Scrinari, *Santuario* 261.
[458] L. Malten, "Bellerophontes", *Jahrb.* 40 (1925) 120 ff.; Rizza–Scrin., *op. cit.* 262.
[459] *Mycen. Origin of Grk. Myth.*; cf. above p. 166.
[460] See Appendix III.
[461] Nilsson, *H.* 3, 277.

choice when he represented religious and other scenes. Nilsson puts this point more bluntly when he says that the Orientalizing Corinthian style of vase decoration was no novel or developed form, but owed its existence to the invention of an individual potter. The resurgence of Asiatic motifs seems to have been determined, therefore, by the whim of the local manufacturer, or rather by the shrewd merchant keen to export a line which would prove fashionable[461].

Most scholars, however, agree that in using foreign models Greek artists were indebted to form rather than content[462]. In any case it was felt to be entirely natural in the sixth century to associate Oriental monsters, like the siren, with deities like Athena, Hera, Artemis, and Apollo[463], precisely because the siren, like other hybrid creatures, had been no stranger to Minoan and Mycenaean religious concepts. An interesting indication of Athena's early connection with the sphinx, for example, can be found in the Gortynian armed goddess, an early form of the classical Athena, whose helmet is of the identical Minoan type[464] as that worn by a sphinx on a piriform aryballos from Fortetsa[465]. The sphinx and the griffin, as well as related monsters, populated Minoan and Mycenaean cult and art from as early as the second millennium, the Palace Period[466], and two examples that come to mind from the end of the millennium are the twelfth century sphinxes from Hagia Triada[467] and the eleventh century examples found in the Spring Chamber at Knossos[468]. Winged horses, too, like Pegasus, and winged male figures or hybrids had also made their appearance in the West by the Late Bronze Age. As examples of their use at that time we have extant from Thebes a few cylinder seals which we may

---

[462] E.g. Starr, *Orig.* 280, who also cites Karo, *Greek Personality*, 34, that Oriental monsters were "promptly imbued with Hellenic spiritual forces, transformed into genuine Greek daimonic personalities." Cf. Boardman, *Pre-Class.* 74; 108.

[463] Cf. J. Pollard, *Seers, Shrines and Sirens*, London 1965, 140.

[464] Rizza–Scrin., *Santuario* 250, Pl. IX, X no. 57, 58.

[465] Doro Levi, *Hellenic Pottery of Crete*, Princeton 1945, Pl. XX, 3.

[466] Schachermeyr, *Ägäis und Orient*, 31 ff. – "Alle Annahmen von einer späteren Entlehnung dieser Ideen, so wie man sie bis vor kurzem anbot, erledigen sich damit von selbst." Cf. Rizza–Scrin., *Santuario* 259 f.

[467] Banti, *A.S.I.* N.S. 3–5 (1941/3) 54 ff.; figs. 43–6; M. Borda, *Arte Cretese-Micenea nel Museo Pigorini di Roma*, Rome 1946, 55 f. no. 1, Pl. 43, 2; Nicholls, *Auck. Cl. Ess.* II; Karageorghis, however, describes these figures as centaurs, *B.C.H.* 87 (1963) 370 ff., fig. 68 a.

[468] Evans, *P.M.* II, 128 ff., fig. 69 k, 1; Desborough, *Protog. Pott.* 236 f.; *L.M.* 180; Nicholls, *Auck. Cl. Ess.* II.

compare with similar contemporary Cretan seals of mixed Minoan-Oriental style. That is, in the latter examples Eastern forms had been absorbed and integrated in Cretan motifs[469].

In addition to monumental sources we may perhaps also possess some written evidence that e.g. the Siren was part of the Mycenaean repertoire in thirteenth century Pylos. On the Ta group of Pylian linear tablets, the word *seremo-* occurs which Mühlstein transliterates as *seiren*[470]. If he is right, such Sirens were not only religious symbols, but, like their counterparts in Archaic Greece, also served for purely ornamental purposes as handles for vases and the like. The Sirens of the Ta tablets apparently were used as furniture decorations[471].

The presence of Eastern artefacts on the Greek mainland in Late Helladic, like the cylinder seals from Crete, the free use and adaptation of Oriental motifs in the West at that time, and above all the evidence of fusion of Western and Eastern religious concepts on a number of seals which we noted from Crete, all these show that Eastern ideas had already become an inseparable part of pre-Greek religion before the end of the Bronze Age. The mixing of the two cultures was so complete that it has become often virtually impossible to separate Eastern from Western motifs, as witness, for example, the many efforts to isolate an Oriental Potnia from her Minoan and Mycenaean counterpart. This early fusion has made it impossible to separate the Minoan cult of the dead from like Oriental or Egyptian practices in scenes like those of the famous Hagia Triada sarcophagus[472].

---

[469] E.g. two L.H. III B Oriental cylinder seals from Thebes with winged men, Schachermeyr, *Äg. & Or.* 54, Pl. LII, no. 184; 186; a cylinder from Knossos with a winged figure, half man half animal, Pl. LII, no. 187; two further cylinders from Crete, one with winged horses, no. 188 (Astrakos), and the other with a winged monster (Hagia Pelagia). How far such winged male figs. were thought to represent the Minoan so-called *Potnios Theron*, who, according to Rizza, *Sant.* 254, is never shown with wings, is of less importance at the moment. From these, and similar, examples it becomes evident that such Oriental motifs had not only appeared in, but been assimilated by, Minoan-Mycen. belief of the second millennium to produce, amongst others, the winged goddess type we meet with in Protoarchaic times in Gortyn and in Artemis Orthia's Spartan sanctuary on the mainland, Rizza, *ibid.*

[470] H. Mühlestein, "Sirenen in Pylos", *G.* 36 (1957/8) 152–6.

[471] On this point cf. M. Lejeune, "Essais de Philologie Mycénienne", *R. Phil.* 32 (1958) 215.

[472] Cf. Séchan-Lévêque, *Grandes Div.* 214, who, in discussing the history of Apollo, emphasize the early fusion of East. and West. religion, and speak of "l'unité de la

The Orientalizing of the Archaic Age should consequently not come as a surprise, especially if we assume, and with reason, that the fruitful contact with the East in the Bronze Age was never entirely broken in the subsequent centuries of economic poverty[473]. There is, on the face of it, no particular difficulty attached to this belief when judged by the prolonged mutual interdependence in commerce and religious tradition of both sides of the Aegean. Were it not for the mysterious "Sea Peoples" who, like the Dorians on the mainland, were, during their activities in the thirteenth/twelfth centuries, blamed for a multitude of sins, and in particular for supposedly cutting adrift the Western Aegean from the East[474], there would be no problem at all. Mylonas, in a recent discussion of the possible intervention by the Peoples of the Sea in East – West communication until the end of the second millennium[475], finds no justification in any claims that the Greek traffic across the Aegean was interrupted. In support of his argument he also cites the relevant archaeological data examined by Desborough, together with his conclusions[476]. At no time, from the Bronze Age to the classical period, could Eastern ideas have been foreign in Greece or Crete.

This knowledge will be extremely useful when we are confronted with Dark Age and Archaic cult in honour of a goddess in multiple form; a goddess, seemingly not of pure Minoan-Mycenaean descent, but one whose image was wrought in mixed Western and Eastern tradition. The best site to illustrate both phenomena is that of Cretan Gortyn. Rizza broadly classified the Gortynian goddess figurines into types of Eastern and primarily Minoan and Mycenaean provenance. The first type was the nude figure, often shown wearing the *polos* and with both arms either alongside the

---

civilis. religieuse qui s'est établie, dès une haute époque, dans le bassin de la Mediterranée orientale et de l'origin asiatique de Crétois."

[473] For the arch. evidence concerning Greek contacts with the East in Geom. times see Rizza, *Sant.* 249; 266 n. 43–51; Coldstream, *Grk. Geom. Pott.* 302 ff. Desb., *L.M.* 227 f., speaks of a "miniature Mycen. *koine*" between East Attica, Cyclades, Dodecanese, Samos, Chios, and Miletus in L.H. III C. There is no real reason why this contact should have been broken in the immediately subsequent periods. See also H. Simps., *Gazett.* 198.

[474] See e.g. J. Vercouttes, *Essai sur les Relations entre Egyptiens et Préhellènes*, Paris 1954, 178; E. T. Vermeule, *Arch.* 13 (1960) 67; 74; cf. *Bronze Age* 208; 269 ff. (in modified form).

[475] *Mycenae* 230 f.

[476] *Op. cit.* 228 f.

flanks, or one hand covering the pubic area[477]. The second type was that of the dressed, and often armed, figure. The gestures and mode of representation differed in both types[478]. But in view of what has been said concerning the early mixing of Minoan, Mycenaean, and Eastern, artistic motifs, we need not attach any special significance to the Eastern aspect of these groups as late as the seventh century. The early stylistic contamination in Gortyn is, in fact, paralleled by similar examples from e.g. Syria and Palestine[479]. Of tremendous importance, however, is the common currency, in the Archaic Age and slightly earlier, of the multiform goddess not only in Crete but on the mainland of Greece, and on some Aegean islands like Rhodes[480].

The mainland type which comes closest to the Gortynian form, can be found at Sparta in the sanctuary of Artemis Orthia[481]. The Spartan examples of the multiform goddess were probably contemporary with the Gortynian and other Greek representations, for there is some strong evidence that the Artemis sanctuary came into being not before seven-hundred B.C.[482]. It is apparent that Greece, and the Aegean world in contact with it, passed through a stage in Archaic times of representing divinities, both male and female, in multiple form. The Gortynian evidence is plain, and so is that of other sanctuaries, notably Sparta, which may have followed the Cretan lead, but obviously only so far as artistic form and style were concerned. Their goddess belonged to the same type of cult and belief as the Gortynian. The proto-Dedalic Athena statuette at Gortyn could not have depicted a goddess substantially different from the divine figure

---

[477] Levi, *A.S.I.* 33/4 e.g. Pl. XXI, 124.
[478] *Santuario* 247 f. Cf. *A.S.I.* 29/30 (1967/8) 293.
[479] Rizza, *op. cit.* 249.
[480] Rizza, *Sant.* 250; Levi, *op. cit.* 281; for Rhodes – group of two seated divinities – see F. W. Winter, *Typen d. figürl. Terrakott.* (cited by Levi, 245). For numerous other examples, includ. the famous 8/7th cent. pendant from the Idaean cave, see Levi, "Gleanings from Crete" 313 ff.; *P.d.P.* 294 ff. T. Hadzisteliou-Price, "Double and Multiple Representations in Greek Art and Religious Thought", *J.H.S.* 91 (1971) 48–69.
[481] Both dressed and undressed, e.g. one pinax of a divine trinity *B.S.A.* 15 (1908/9) 120, fig. 3 no. 32; an ivory & a clay pinax both showing a god flanked by two goddess figs. In the former the figs. are dressed, and nude on the other – Rizza, *Sant.* 252, fig. 346; 347. Cf. Levi, *op. cit.* 243 n. 2.
[482] Boardman, *B.S.A.* 58 (1963) 7, who cites Kirsten for a different conclusion (n. 24). Levi dates the lead figs. from Sparta at 6th cent. *P.d.P.* (1956) 309.

dedicated in the same sanctuary, but perhaps some fifty years later[483]. In the case of these Middle Dedalic multiple figures we are confronted with an artistic representation of a belief which began at least in Minoan times[483a]. Such plural figures were common in the Bronze Age in the East and in Crete, in Archaic times in Greece and again in Crete, as we noticed, but became rare in classical times.

A number of Minoan rings, seals, and seal impressions, show a trinity, or plurality, of similar or identical female figures who are obviously goddesses[484]. If we discard those examples, like the ring from the Candia Museum[485], and the ring from the tomb at Isopata[846], where the goddess is clearly shown with worshippers in an epiphany[487], there remain several seals and sealings with a design most commonly of a trinity of apparently divine figures[488]. Of some significance is the fact that, contrary to Picard and Chapouthier who attribute this feature to Eastern influence, Levi can cite Minoan examples of this type from e.g. Hagia Triada where the figures are both male and female. Such groups usually consist of a female flanked by two male figures[489], in a fashion which becomes increasingly common in our Archaic examples, including the much debated scene on a Boeotian amphora[490]. Therefore the sex of such multiple figures may be uncertain precisely in the same way as that of many of the chthonic beings who, under the title of Megaloi Theoi or Anaktes, continued a precarious existence in classical times.

Ambivalence of sex then was an ancient feature of Mediterranean religious thought[491], and it curiously continued in classical Greek belief in the case of some famous heroes like Heracles[492]. Regarding the multiple figures in Gortyn, and by analogy in other sanctuaries in Greece, like Sparta and the islands such as Rhodes, two prominent features illuminate

---

[483] Rizza, *Sant.* 250, Pl. XI, 59. For largely similar evidence concerning the isolation of a single goddess (Aphrodite) at Axos see Rizza, *A.S.I.* 29/30 (1967/8) 293.

[483a] Cf. G. E. Mylonas, "Seated and Multiple Mycenaean Figurines in the National Museum of Athens, Greece", *Studs. H. Goldman*, New York 1956, 110–121.

[484] But see Levi, *A.S.I.* 33/4, 240.

[485] Nilsson, *M.M.R.* 267, fig. 131; Persson, *Preh. Rel.* 46; 173 no. 7.

[486] Persson, *op. cit.* 47; 137 no. 8 a, b.

[487] Cf. Levi, "Glean. from Crete", 322 f.

[488] Levi, *ibid.*

[489] *Ibid.*, who cites Chapouthier and Picard.

[490] *Ibid.* and 323 n. 251.

[491] Cf. Rizza' derivation from Egypt. custom, *Sant.* 251 f., cf. below n. 513.

[492] Cf. Wiesner, *Olympos* 156 f.

the significance of such representations. First the plural, or dual, image of the goddess did not signify several individual divinities, but a repetition of the same figure in her various forms[493]. Secondly the numerous seventh century reliefs, pinakes or pendants, with scenes of divine dyads or triads, signified a different artistic method, either novel or perhaps rather Eastern-inspired, of portraying the traditional Bronze Age goddess who was invoked in Crete and in the Mycenaean world under different titles.

The goddess so expressed in Dedalic and Archaic sculptural terms had formerly been represented by individual statuettes with perhaps differing attributes pointing to her various functions at the time of the epiphany. Thus we may recognize in a bell-shaped figure of Minoan sculptural tradition at Gortyn one divine hypostasis of the same goddess shown in double or treble form on later reliefs from the same site[494]. Still more persuasive are the numerous goddess statuettes from Subminoan shrines like Gazi and Karphi which often differ only in the various attributes like pomegranates, poppies, horns of consecration, birds or disks that decorate their heads[495]. All these individual figures, it seems, referred to the many epiphanies of the chief nature goddess, as goddess of birth, death, fertility and so on[496], and there is no reason to doubt that the Archaic multiple figures belonged basically to the same type of religious concept.

In other words, the Gortynian, and related, evidence on one hand tends to confirm our belief in the multiple form of the one goddess in the Bronze Age, and on the other shows that the process of individualization of separate divinities with their particular attributes, although begun already in Late Mycenaean as we saw from the Linear B tablets, had not yet in every instance been completed by the end of the eighth century. This progress from the plural to the single city goddess can, once more, be observed from the abundant extant material at Gortyn[497]. The goddess was invoked in her Minoan-type tripartite temple which was as late as proto-Hellenic[498]. Consequently at that time she still possessed her plural form, recalling the many

---

[493] Rizza, *Santuario* 251, "Il fatto che l'immagine della dea appaia ora duplicata, ora triplicata, ci conferma nell'idea che non si tratta, come si potrebbe pensare, di una triade di divinità tra di loro distinte, ma della ripetizione di un'unica divinità nell sue diverse ipostasi."

[494] E.g. Rizza, *Sant.* 250, Pl. IX, 54.

[495] Nilsson, *M.M.R.* figs. 24–26.

[496] Cf. above p. 152.

[497] Levi, *P.d.P.* (1956) 300; Rizza, *Sant.* 250.

[498] Levi, *A.S.I.* 33/4, 239.

epicleseis under which the Minoan-Mycenaean goddess was revered. She also functioned as a single city goddess which she became in classical times[499].

Rizza, working primarily with this local evidence from Gortyn, supposes that full isolation of individual deities had been accomplished between the sixth and fifth centuries. This estimate most likely is too low. A more probable date would be more or less in conjunction with the establishment of the *polis* on the mainland together with the particular developed city gods. In fact seventh century Greek art already reflected the individuality of city gods, and this date should serve as a *terminus ante quem* for such religious development[500].

We must be careful, therefore, not to interpret occasional contemporary scenes of divine pairs, like Zeus and Hera, or Apollo and Artemis, as remnants of an older fashion[501]. In such instances we are probably dealing with later random artistic combinations of gods whose particular spheres and functions had already been clearly defined. More difficult to explain are the several divine triads in Archaic Eastern Greek cities, in e.g. Lesbos, Samos, in Miletus, Cyzicus, and Samothrace, which have individual personalities like Hera, Zeus, Dionysus[502]. It may well be, Oriental artistic influence apart, that such individual names were imposed subsequently on the threefold hypostasis of the traditional divinity. But obviously this must remain conjecture, open to correction in the light of inscriptional evidence.

Athena's plural aspect at Gortyn, mostly trinity or duality, which signified an earlier form, or mode, of representation of the one city goddess, passed into chthonic cult along with the Despoinae, Semnae, Potniae[503], and numerous others who kept their old invocatory titles from Minoan Mycenaean times but, as shadowy chthonic beings, were unacceptable to official Olympian cult and gathered generally in the sphere of Demeter who also, for obvious reasons, could never shed her chthonic associations[504].

The cults of many of these chthonic figures have been carefully examined by Hemberg[505] who traces them back to Minoan and Mycenaean times when, after the fashion of the age, they were identical and invoked by title

---

[499] Inscr. *Athanaia Poliouchos*, cited by Levi, *op. cit.* 246.
[500] Cf. Boardman, *Pre-Class.* 135.
[501] *Ibid.*
[502] Levi, *A.S.I.* 33/4, 240; *P.d.P.* (1956) 294.
[503] Cf. Levi, *A.S.I.* 33/4, 246.
[504] See the discussion in Dietrich, *Death, Fate, Gods*, Part. I.
[505] B. Hemberg, *D. Kabiren; Anax, Anassa und Anakes.*

rather than by name[506]. The individual naming of particular groups was the work of the Dark Age and determined by the geographical location of a cult[507], although, still in classical literature, such figures were often interchangeable and synonymous[508]. Throughout their history these Anaktes and Megaloi Theoi never lost their association with the nature goddess[509] whose cultic home continued in a cave in e.g. Samothrace and on Delos[510].

At times the old chthonic form of cult, by virtue of its continuing eminent position into classical times and later, achieved independent recognition and consequently played a major part in the religious observances even of the *polis*. Such a traditional cult was that of the Eleusinian goddesses whose roots ever remained frankly chthonic, and who therefore did not shed the multiple form of what had been after all one single major goddess identified with Demeter. In the case of the Eleusinian deities the plural became a dual form, a pair of goddesses with the simple title of the Two Goddesses (*to Theo*) in what we might call a partial evolution[511]. Starr and Pestalozza believe that the pair thus crystallized from the beginning manifestly symbolized the maternal and virginal concept of the goddess[512]. This is possible but by no means certain. At all events, behind the Eleusinian and similar twin deities there always lay concealed the one larger Bronze Age figure in her various aspects. This fact accounts for the several historic inscriptions from e.g. Rhodes, Lindos, and Sparta, which refer to the Eleusinian pair not as mother and daughter, but simply as *Damateres* – the Demeters[513].

---

[506] *Kabiren* 297; 300.
[507] *Op. cit.* 298.
[508] *Op. cit.* 272.
[509] *Op. cit.* 82; 85; 290; *Anax* 45.
[510] *Kabiren* 121; 147 ff.
[511] Cf. Levi, *A.S.I.* 33/34, 246.
[512] Starr, *Origins* 178; O. Pestalozza, *L'etern. feminine*, 48; cf. Harrison, *Prolegomena* 274; Nilsson, *Opuscula Selecta* II, 574.
[513] Nilsson, *Op. Sel.*, Lund 1952, II, 552 n. 33; *Gesch.* I, 463 and n. 6. If the two Eleusinian goddesses had always represented the old and the young, the maternal and youthful, or virginal, aspects of the major goddess, then the pair more immediately recalls the figure of the Aegean goddess and her youthful associate, Potnia and Wanax. But we should even then not feel obliged to worry that we are dealing with two rather different religious concepts namely the plural form of the goddess on the one hand, and on the other the goddess and her *paredros*. However, the Eleusinian evidence involves a great many difficulties which we cannot discuss here. Most of the problems are due to the great wealth of myth which grew up about

The others, the many chthonic figures, and nameless Potniae, Anaktes etc. were never discarded by popular belief, but in literature and in myth they formed a world of their own which was partly divine, partly heroic and secular. Two features which they always retained, and by which we may recognize their history, were those of chthonic and plural beings. Therefore let us not confuse the former with funeral cult, or deified spirits of the dead, and the latter with purely Oriental figures[514]. Both theories would be anachronisms. However, the majority of the chthonic spirits had, before the Mysteries involving the central figures of, apart from Demeter, Persephone, Plutos, Pluton, Eubouleus, and Triptolemeus, as well as Iacchos after the political annexation of Eleusis by Athens. These myths, together with the monumental evidence, are discussed in great detail by Nilsson, "Die Eleusinischen Gottheiten", *ARW* 32 (1935) 79–141 = *Op. Sel.* II, 542 ff.; *Gesch.* I, 469 ff., and by Mylonas, *Eleusis, passim*. Miss Harrison, *Proleg.* 274, and Nilsson, still follow Mannhardt's original identification of the divine pair with the symbolic figures of the "Kornmutter" and the "Kornmädchen", whom Nilsson, *Op. Sel.* II, 575, believes to have been imported to Greece by the Helladic Indo-European migrants. Whatever the ultimate source of the nature goddess and her cult, and it now seems more likely to have been the East rather than Northern Europe, the Potnia, in her varied forms, was in the centre of Minoan and Mycenaean cult in the Bronze Age. Her extremely close relationship with her companion, the Wanax probably, we have discussed before, and in the present state of our evidence it need not surprise us if still in historic times he was recognizable from the identical Pluto, Pluton, if not from the Eubouleus, figures. The many multiple figures which yet, under the general title of Anaktes, Anakes, Anaktores, or Megaloi Theoi, haunted the classical world teach us further that the association of goddess with a youthful companion survived from Helladic times. Also these figures were so closely interrelated as to be virtually indistinguishable, and they could be thought of as male and female beings (See esp. the study by Hemberg, *Kabiren*, e.g. 278 f.; 295; cf. Wiesner, *Olympos* 156 f., who points out that the change of sex was commonly associated with life-giving goddesses). In Eleusinian myth, which one may assume to reflect Bronze Age belief, beside the Two Goddesses another pair *Theos* and *Thea*, that is Pluton and Persephone, enjoyed equal prominence. Both pairs were revered at Eleusis, a site, we must remember, which saw uninterrupted cult into historic times (Nilsson, *Gesch.* I, 470; Mylonas, *Eleusis* 198; 238). Admittedly the names cannot be read before the fourth century, to our knowledge, namely on the Lysimachides relief (Nilsson, *Gesch.* I, Pl. 39, 3; cf. the first century Lacratides relief, Pl. 40), but that can hardly be an obstacle to the very early currency of the god and goddess association. What is the original relationship, or perhaps rather the difference, between Pluton and Persephone? If Persephone in fact from the beginning was a youthful aspect of the Potnia concealed behind the Demeter figure, was the Maiden not as close to the Mother as the companion, in this case Pluton, to the goddess? Perhaps a new and full investigation of the Eleusinian evidence will provide some less conjectural answers to these questions.

[514] See e.g. Rizza-Scrin., *Santuario* 252.

the end of the Archaic Age, no further contribution to make to the development of Greek religion, thought, and the young and growing discipline of philosophy. The only aspect of popular belief which played a part in this connection was the Mystery cults; and it is peculiarly satisfying to see that the separated religious streams were bound to come together once more in order to produce some of Greece's noblest and most original ideas.

Appendix I: MINOAN PEAK CULTS IN CRETAN THOUGHT

From the time of the first discovery of peak sanctuaries there have been careful archaeological investigations of individual sites and attempts at interpretation of the material by scholars such as J. L. Myres (Petsophas)[1] and Sir Arthur Evans (Juktas)[2]. In 1951 Platon examined all the then known peak sanctuaries, together with the rock shelters[3]. It was generally believed that this type of sanctuary was relatively scarce, and that usually it was to be found in central Crete and predominantly in the eastern part of the island. Both conclusions are quite natural in view of the two circumstances that western Crete is still imperfectly explored and the millennia of harsh seasons have not dealt kindly with the exposed sites.

Yet it is an error, in the case of the simple rural shrines, whether in the plain or constructed on the mountain top, to argue about the frequency, or otherwise, of their occurrence from the absence of any physically identifiable signs. On the contrary, one would suppose that there were many such open cult localities scattered throughout the island, and, as Schachermeyr puts it, that each larger centre or settlement possessed its own mountain peak sanctuary[4]. In fact, such sanctuaries continue to be discovered, and their known number appears to increase in proportion to the progress of Cretan archaeology. Up to date two only have been discovered in the west, but the overall number of known sanctuaries has grown to over thirty[5]. Most of these are still to be found in the eastern part of Crete.

---

[1] *B. S. A.* 9 (1903) 356 ff.
[2] *J. H. S.* 21 (1901) 121 f.; *Palace of Minos*, I, 154 ff. Cf. A. B. Cook, *Zeus*, Cambridge 1925, II, 2, 939 ff.; J. D. S. Pendlebury, *The Archaeology of Crete*, 102 f.
[3] *K. Ch.* 5 (1951) 96 ff.
[4] F. Schachermeyr, *Die minoische Kultur des alten Kreta*, 158 f.: "Wie heutzutage so ziemlich jeder Ort in der Peloponnes einen eigenen Elias-Berg besitzt, dürfte in minoischer Zeit jeder größere Platz sein eigenes Höhenheiligtum gehabt haben."
[5] Detailed references and discussion in P. Faure, "Sur Trois Sortes De Sanctuaires Crétois", *B. C. H.* 91 (1967) 114–150; "Cultes Populaires Dans La Crète Antique", *B. C. H.* 96 (1972) 389–426.

The two richest and best known sites perhaps are those on Mt. Juktas, south of Knossos, and at Petsophas, on the eastern shore of Crete near Palaikastro. The Juktas sanctuary was excavated by Sir Arthur Evans[6]. The sacred precinct lay on the north peak of the mountain range in such clear view of Knossos, that "it dominates... the whole Central Court of the Palace". The sanctuary itself was surrounded by a massive temenos wall constructed of Cyclopean blocks, in the crevices of which there still are the remains of M.M.I sherds showing that the wall was built before the first palace at Knossos[7]. Of the first sanctuary (M.M.I.), within the precinct, nothing is left. But its site is marked by a stratum of grey ash, immediately overlying the rock, with remains from M.M.I. and II. Above this there is a layer of reddish burnt earth concealing M.M.III pottery fragments and surrounding the foundations of the later sanctuary which perhaps was built as late as L.M.I[8]. The latter was constructed of ashlar blocks and consisted of a rectangular room (BI) whose floor concealed some sacred deposits. This room was flanked on one of its long sides by a small chamber (B2), probably a store room, which in turn was separated by a wall from an inner chamber (C) with white plaster floor, and extending along almost the entire width of the room Bl[9]. The grey ash deposit of the precinct, as well as the burnt reddish earth layer above it, contained, apart from sherds, votive offerings including human-male and female-clay figurines. Figures of oxen and goats were also found, together with clay locks of human hair, a limestone 'ladle', and separate limbs, occasionally with perforations for suspension, of both humans and animals.

The history of the Petsophas sanctuary is very similar to that of Juktas[10]. In the temenos, below a layer of black earth mixed with much ash and charcoal, a stratum of reddish earth also gives evidence of burnt offerings or sacrifice[11]. The black earth layer (M.M.I) itself was covered by a layer of disturbed earth of the same date marking the level of the sanctuary building which matched that of Juktas. One addition to the inner chamber at Petsophas, however, appears to be a plaster bench built against three sides of the room. The earth layers here, again, contained a great many

[6] *P. M.* I, 154 ff.
[7] M. P. Nilsson, *M. M. R.* 71.
[8] Cf. Pendlebury, *Crete* 103.
[9] *P. M.* I, 157, fig. 114.
[10] *B. S. A.* 9 (1903) 356 ff.; cf. Pendlebury, *Crete* 103; Faure, *Fonctions*, 11 n. 4, denies that the Petsophas site served as a sanctuary, but see *B. C. H.* (1967) 116.
[11] Nilsson, *M. M. R.* 69.

votive terracotta figurines which recall those of Juktas and are contemporary with M.M.I[12]. The figures are those of human males and females, of animals, and they include separate limbs. The latter, also occasionally perforated, are composed of severed heads, legs, and arms, or even of bodies "cloven from crown to fork". The animal figures, again, included, apart from oxen, goats, and rams, tortoises, hedgehogs, sometimes "mere vermin" like weasels. Of great interest, too, are examples of bull horns, and one object which looks surprisingly like a part of a stalagmite[13].

An examination of these two, and other, sites reveals that by and large all of them conformed to the same dates of construction and usage, roughly throughout Middle Minoan. The plan of their temenos and sanctuary could vary considerably[14], but in all instances similar offerings were acceptable, including male and female human figurines, and figures of animals, such as goats, oxen, rams, and birds, as well as oxen or bull horns. Among these *ex votos*, common to all Cretan cult localities, two types appear to be unique to peak sanctuaries: the separate limbs and parts of the body from Juktas and Petsophas, and the great range of animal figures including such lowly creatures as pigs and stoats or weasels. It is, of course, impossible to assert with confidence that these two kinds of offerings belonged to the ritual of all peak sanctuaries, because not enough remains of them to reach any conclusion either way. But we should not be surprised if such offerings were not confined to Juktas and Petsophas, but played a part in many of the peak cults. Perhaps the separate terracotta legs, uncovered at the Upper Zakro site, should be counted among this type of offering[15].

The most significant bond which, as it were, unites all peak sanctuaries is the temporal limit of occupation. Cult generally began in M.M. I and extended over the Middle Minoan period[16], occasionally overlapping with L.M. I, when the majority of the sites appear to have been abandoned.

---

[12] Some of these are reproduced also in *P. M.* I, fig. 111.

[13] 'z' in fig. 111 of *P. M.* I.

[14] E.g. K. Branigan, *The Foundations of Palatial Crete*, 104 ff.; fig. 25.

[15] Cf. Nilsson, *M. M. R.* 71. It used to be thought that the naturalistic models of beetles, found in peak sanctuaries, were offerings, peculiar to these sites (Platon, *K. Ch.* [1951] 139). But similar examples have since turned up elsewhere (e.g. Psira, Mallia). Faure, *B. C. H.* (1967) 115, believes them to have been good luck charms. Perhaps they are to be compared with the Egyptian scarabs which were associated with regeneration and renewal of life. E.g. J. Gray, *The Canaanites*, 86.

[16] But see below p. 293, and n. 20.

Thus the last sanctuary on Mt. Juktas may have been built in L.M. I[17], while cult at Petsophas, too, may have endured into the first period of Late Minoan[18]. L.M. pottery from Modhi[19] tells a similar story of a slight overlapping of occupation with Late Minoan, and the same can be said of Kophinas in southern Crete[20]. Exceptions to the rule seem to be the sanctuary at Epano Zakro where, apart from the M.M. figurines, L.M. III A pottery was found[21], and the site at Kumasa with a sanctuary whose second phase Platon dates at L.M. III B[22].

Karphi, too, is a special case, since it probably served as a peak sanctuary during Middle Minoan[23], but much later became a Subminoan settlement, a kind of *Kresphygeton*, or refuge, in troubled times, with its own typically domestic shrine[24] containing a shelf or ledge along one of its walls to hold the offerings[25]. To what extent did the inhabitants in Subminoan utilize the remains of the older sanctuary for their new shrine? Only speculative answers are possible, but the Karphi example suggests two possible conclusions: either, at the end of the Bronze Age, all memory of the spot's sacredness had become extinct, a less than likely theory in view of the subsequent history of e.g. Juktas, or L.M. domestic cult was compatible, so to speak, with M.M. peak cult.

The physical remains on the mountain peaks are too few for a convincing reconstruction of the original building complex. Nor, of course, can we determine the religious function and ritual which occurred within, or in association with, the shrines. The first structures at these sites were possibly earlier than, but certainly contemporary with, the Minoan palace. (e.g. Traostalos, Souvloto Mouri, Maza, Philioremos)[26]. Did their architecture, however, fundamentally differ from that of the subsequent domestic shrines or chapels associated with the palace? Only the extant pictorial

---

[17] Pendlebury, *Crete* 103.
[18] Platon, *K. Ch.* (1951) 120.
[19] Faure, *B. C. H.* 86 (1962) 37; 91 (1967) 118.
[20] *K. Ch.* 9 (1955) 567; 10 (1956) 420; 13 (1959) 387; 14 (1960) 526. There was some cult revival perhaps in class. times, Faure, *B. C. H.* (1967) 125.
[21] *B. S. A.* 33 (1932/3) 99.
[22] *K. Ch.* (1951) 145. For examples of peak cults in class. times see Faure, *B. C. H.* (1967) 129 ff.
[23] *B. S. A.* 38 (1937/8) 97. Cf. R. W. Hutchinson, *Prehistoric Crete,* 320.
[24] Pendlebury, *Crete* 306.
[25] Nilsson, *M. M. R.* 101.
[26] Faure, *B. C. H.* (1967) 116 ff.

representations can answer this question; and those which can definitely be associated with peak sanctuaries are few and occasionally fragmentary. Again, the vessels or seals with figures of peak cult scenes on them belong to the end of Middle Minoan or are as late as L.M. I. But for all that, there is reason to believe the story they tell which may apply to the entire period when this kind of cult was in vogue.

A fragment of an M.M. III/L.M. I rhyton from Gypsadhes[27] shows a steep wooded slope whose peak is crowned by a sanctuary. (Mt. Juktas?)[28]. This consists of a central part, flanked by two lower wings, on a terrace of stone blocks. Horns of consecration surmount the structure which, in fact, resembles a typical Minoan tripartite shrine. In front of the left wing of the building is what looks like a long thin pillar or pole, very much like those painted on the Hagia Triada sarcophagus, and therefore perhaps also crowned with double axes. This cannot, however, be seen from our fragment. The central figure before the shrine is that of a man depositing a basket with offerings[29]. Another M.M. III/L.M. I rhyton, of the same material and showing the same kind of peak sanctuary, was discovered in Kato Zakro by Platon[30]. In addition to many examples of horns of consecration, this sanctuary is also associated with a sacred tree, Minoan type "portable" altars (with incurving sides)[31], and a number of wild goats, four of which are sitting on the roof of the central portion of the shrine.

These scenes are fairly explicit regarding this kind of sanctuary. Other representations of the subject are found on seals or their impressions. Therefore scenes from this source are much smaller in scale and in some instances, one suspects, they have come to be touched by a good deal of artistic imagination. Altogether there remains only one other pictorial representation which can with reasonable certainty be referred to mountain peak cult. That is the famous L.M. II seal impression from Knossos. On it we see a goddess, with staff or spear in her right hand, standing on the summit of a mountain which in turn is flanked by two lions. In front of her, on

---

[27] *K. Ch.* (1951) 154 ff.; (1959) 346 ff.; 364, Pl. 34; 35; M. S. F. Hood, Arch. Rep. *J. H. S.* 82 (1962) 27; 29.

[28] Faure, *op. cit.* 123.

[29] "Opferbrote", Schachermeyr, *min. Kult.* 159; "fruits", L. Press, "Mountain Cult Circles in the Aegean Iconography", *I Con. Myc.* 158.

[30] N. Platon, *Ergon* (1963) 173; A. H. S. Megaw, Arch. Rep. *J. H. S.* 84 (1964) 30 and fig. 39.

[31] Common on Minoan gems, like the one from the Idaean cave, Evans, *J. H. S.* 21 (1901) 142, fig. 25; cf. Nilsson, *Gesch.* I, 272.

the level ground, a male worshipper is shown, arms raised in adoration, while behind the goddess a two-storeyed cult building, with horns and pillars, is tucked away into the left corner of the picture[32]. The building, as has been correctly remarked[33], properly belongs on top of the mountain which here has been left uncluttered to allow for the epiphany of the goddess.

Other scenes adduced in this connection are of much more dubious value. They are, in fact, little more than useless as evidence, because the ritual scenes cannot be localised in any particular area. A good case in point is a M.M. III/L.M. I fragment of a steatite pyxis from Knossos depicting two men in a lively cultic performance in front of a sacred enclosure which perhaps surrounded a sacred tree[34]. The altar before the enclosure, in the centre of the picture, though also surmounted by a pair of horns, is isodomic in structure and therefore quite unlike the "portable" models we noticed on the Kato Zakro rhyton. This difference may well be of minor importance, but the fact remains that there is nothing to connect this scene with peak cult, despite what could be said about certain features of architectural resemblance to the temenos on mountain cult sites[35].

Basically the same objections hold true in the case of two other, occasionally cited, pieces of evidence. By far the more plausible of the two scenes occurs on an L.H. III gold ring from Pylos[36]. Despite the large presence of what is undoubtedly a goat, the epiphany of a deity (?), and the figure of a worshipper in front of some sort of sacred structure, the scene, it seems to me, is far from clear and cannot without reservations be identified with that occurring on a mountain peak[37]. This is not to say that we should reject such an identification out of hand, there is much to commend it, but the picture is too vague and involved to be disentangled with confidence[38]. We are, however, on very shaky ground with the last example, a gold ring from Knossos (L.M. I)[39], showing the epiphany of a small male

---

[32] *B. S. A.* 7 (1900/1) 29, fig. 9.
[33] Press, *op. cit.* 159 f.
[34] Evans, *J. H. S.* 21 (1901) fig. 2.
[35] See Press, *op. cit.* 162.
[36] C. W. Blegen, *A. J. A.* 58 (1954) Pl. 9, 13.
[37] This identification is made e.g. by Press, *op. cit.* 160, and by B. Rutkowski, "The Decline of the Minoan Peak Sanctuaries", *I Con. Myc.* 167 f.
[38] For some other views on this scene see Press, *op. cit.* 160 n. 18; Rutkowski, *op. cit.* 167 n. 20.
[39] Evans, *J. H. S.* 21 (1901) fig. 48.

figure to a female worshipper, this time in front of a tall pillar and a portion of a wall enclosing a sacred tree. Press again believes that this picture describes an instance of mountain cult[40]. So it might be, of course, but who can prove it? Closer to hand perhaps is the identification with a type of sanctuary depicted on many Minoan and Mycenaean gems[41], and referring to a form of rural tree cult[42]. One imagines that there existed many rural shrines in the plains of Crete and Greece in the Bronze Age, although all trace of them has vanished.

A survey of what might be called reasonably certain evidence regarding mountain peak sanctuaries, and the cult associated with them, produces no clear unified picture of the nature of such a cult. This does not surprise, however, in a period of Aegean religion whose scanty sources allow very little in the way of knowledge unclouded by conjecture. Nevertheless, the material there is does make some tentative deductions possible concerning the timing of cult observance in these localities and perhaps even about the form of cult. Most valuable is a consideration of the peak cult material in the light of what is known of Minoan religious ritual in other localities. We would already take a large step forward if we could with reasonable certainty either set aside this kind of cult from domestic and cave cult, or alternatively assert, on the strength of the evidence – and this is, I think, possible –, that in all likelihood there was no fundamental divergence in the type of worship obtaining on mountain summits and in other sanctuaries. In other words, can one integrate peak cult with other forms of cult?

There is no doubt that certain vital features of cave cult continued in domestic shrines from Middle Minoan[43]. The point of contact between domestic and peak sanctuaries, as far as one can see from the sparse monumental remains regarding the latter, really lies in the similarity of the design of the cultic structures. The rhyta scenes, discussed above, depict peak sanctuaries with the same type of tripartite façade with which we are familiar from e.g. the palace at Knossos, or the villa at Vathypetro[44]. Nilsson, too, in discussing the sanctuary of Petsophas in eastern Crete,

[40] *Op. cit.* 160. See H. Biesantz, *Kretisch-Mykenische Siegelbilder*, 86.
[41] To cite a few: see the examples in Nilsson, *Gesch.* I, Pl. 13, 1–3; 5–8.
[42] Cf. Nilsson, *Gesch.* I, 280 ff.
[43] Above p. 92.
[44] S. Marinatos, *Praktika* (1952/3) 607 f.; Press, *op. cit.* 159, who says that "these buildings (on the rhyta) with their tripartite façades, which are sometimes represented on paintings or on gold objects, are usually associated with some palace... or with a villa, as at Vathypetro."

comes to the conclusion that "the character of the building is the same as that of the houses at Palaikastro belonging to the Late Minoan period"[45]. It would seem that aspects of the divinity, or divinities, worshipped on mountain peaks might well have been equally at home in the domestic chapel. Of course, architectural similarity in cult buildings alone does not prove that[46]. But consider the case of the sanctuary at Karphi. When the villagers from the plain of Lasithi, perhaps under the stress of political events at the end of the Bronze Age, came to settle on "the Nail", the inhospitable saddle below the mountain peak which formerly had housed their mountain shrine, they would hardly have built their sanctuary on the same site previously occupied by an alien deity or cult.

The case for a connection between cave and peak cult in Crete, one would imagine, is proved with even greater facility. The physical proximity of these two kinds of site should point to a similarity of cult or at least deity revered. There are instances, for example, when one mountain possessed both a sacred cave and a peak sanctuary. The best known of these is, of course, Mt. Juktas which, in addition to the temenos on its summit, has a sacred grotto, Khosto Nero, containing the usual offerings of vase fragments and terracotta animals[47]. There are, however, certain features which, at face value, should separate the two cults. Unlike sacred caves, for instance, peak sanctuaries by their very nature could not originally have been used for human habitation. In general, their sacred precincts were more elaborately constructed than the occasional temenos within a cave. Again, the deities revered on these exposed sites need not primarily have been chthonic in character, as were the figures of cave cult. There is, for example, no evidence of burial on mountain tops in the Bronze Age[48].

---

[45] Nilsson, *M. M. R.* 69. The evidence has recently been questioned by Rutkowski, "Minoan Cults and History", *H.* 20 (1971) 6.

[46] An interesting note in this connection comes from Hutchinson, *Preh. Crete*, 219, who tells us that the peak sanctuary on Mt. Juktas was constructed according to "a plan somewhat resembling that of the more or less contemporary temple of Tell Ai in Palestine." Cf. M. V. Seton-Williams, *Iraq*, 1949, 81, fig. 4.

[47] Taramelli, *Mon. Ant.* 9, 356 ff.; Cook, *Zeus* I, 160; J. L. Myres, *B. S. A.* 9 (1903) 379; Faure, *Fonct.* 175 f.

[48] The tradition which places Zeus' tomb on Mt. Juktas is probably late, and only one of several which variously put it on Mt. Ida or Mt. Dikte. For sources see Cook, *Zeus* I, 158; Faure, *Fonct.* 128. Evans, *P. M.* I, 158, believes the Juktas legend to be ancient, but it may go back no further than the Middle Ages, cf. Nilsson, *M. M. R.* 461; Faure, *Fonct.* 176.

These last points show that cave and peak cult could not have been identical in every respect. But none of the objections appears to rule out a connection between the two, a type of continuity, one might suppose, in the Middle Bronze Age of religious ideas which earlier had found expression in cave sanctuaries from the beginning of the age and, in some cases, from the Neolithic period[49]. But here too, we have to be careful, since cave cult did not come to a stop at the end of E.M., but continued occasionally into historic times. A more immediately tangible point of contact is the sacred tree which played a part in both peak and cave cult. Beside the tree from the Zakro rhyton, for example, we might cite the representation of a sacred tree on the famous bronze votive plaque (L.M. I?) discovered in the Psychro cave[50], and showing in the centre a tree mounted on some sort of base. To the right is the figure of a worshipper, while the rest of the scene is made up of three pairs of horns, each with a bough growing from the centre, a fish, bird, the sun, moon and stars. The bird is shown as perching on one of the separate boughs within a pair of horns of consecration, and it most likely represents the epiphany of a deity[51]. A tree again, as well as individual boughs, one in the centre of a pair of horns of consecration, feature on an L.M. II gem from the Idaean cave with, in the left foreground, the figure of a goddess(?) blowing into a large shell[52]. The fact that a tree plays an important part in cave and peak sanctuary does not identify the two cults, for the tree was ubiquitous in the Minoan religious scene[53], but it brings them closer together and helps to indicate that peak cult shared some basic religious concepts with other cult localities.

Of more immediate value to the comparison of cave and peak cult is the point already mentioned above, that is the obvious physical proximity of the two types of locality. In some cases apparently archaeologists cannot be certain whether we are dealing with a true peak sanctuary or with a kind of rock shelter which, one supposes, would have possessed features

---

[49] This idea of continuity does not, of course, work in every instance, since some Cretan caves saw cult from a comparatively late date. The Psychro cave is a case in point, see above e.g. p. 82. For Faure's views against similarities between peak and cave cult see *Fonct.* 176. In *B. C. H.* (1967) 132, he believes that the differing height of sites, offerings etc., speak against the unity of peak cult.

[50] Evans, *P. M.* I, 632, fig. 470; above p. 83 f.

[51] Cf. R. F. Willetts, *Cretan Cults and Festivals*, 146.

[52] Evans, *J. H. S.* 21 (1901) 142, fig. 25.

[53] Above p. 91 and n. 112.

of cult more closely allied with the cave. Even the site of Petsophas[54], by its nature and situation, at first glance leaves room for doubt whether it was a rock shelter or peak sanctuary[55]. The Middle Minoan building there, of course, is evidence that Petsophas was an example of the latter. Nevertheless, the point needs to be made that, as at Petsophas, to modern eyes the line between peak and cave sanctuary appears to be thinly drawn at times with respect to physical proximity or juxtaposition[56]. Perhaps the practice of placing peak offerings in the cracks and natural rock fissures points to a chthonic ritual[57].

Votive offerings found on mountain peak sites can be artificially divided into the two groups, (a) those common to other cult sites, and (b) those not found elsewhere. There is no need here to give exhaustive inventories, these can be found in the respective excavation reports. But confining ourselves to general types of offering, we may say that under (a) fall the numerous examples of figurines of animals and humans, male and female, many of the latter in the usual cylindrical form, that is conical from the waist downward[58]. The animal figurines with which we are familiar from other cult sites, including cave sanctuaries, are especially birds and goats, which, of course, also occurred on the rhyta described above with scenes of peak sanctuaries. Finally, the sacred precincts on mountain tops contained examples of the ubiquitous horns of consecration.

Quite unique to peak sanctuaries, however, are offerings (our category [b]) of animal figurines which can only be described as field pests or vermin whose inclusion in cult seems strange. The Petsophas deposit, for example, contained models of tortoises, hedgehogs, and weasels[59]. Juktas

---

[54] *B.S.A.* 9 (1903) 356 ff.; cf. Evans, *P. M.* I, 151 ff.

[55] Cf. Nilsson, *M. M. R.* 68, who, however, on p. 76, decides in favour of a peak sanctuary. But see Faure, *Fonct.* 11 n. 4.

[56] At least one similar juxtaposition of peak sanctuary and rock shelter seems to have existed at Pyrgos, Faure, *B. C. H.* (1967) 125.

[57] Faure believes this practice was due to a desire to hide *ex votos* and thus prevent their being used a second time, *B. C. H.* (1967) 132.

[58] See e.g. Petsophas, Nilsson, *M. M. R.* 69. Note, too, the examples from the same site, of figures sitting down in chairs, of separate chairs, and compare the finds from the M. M. II B Dove Shrine at Knossos which include a separate carrying chair. See e.g. Hutchinson, *Preh. Cr.* 221 and 214, fig. 41. From Petsophas we need not specially mention the many examples of small terracotta vessels, jugs, pitchers etc., which are probably models of ritual vases whose presence need not be peculiar to any cult site. See Evans, *P. M.* I, 152, fig. 111.

[59] See above p. 292.

possessed figures of weasels modelled in clay[60]. This feature, together with the many terracotta figures of detached human heads and limbs, and of bodies cloven from crown to fork[61], set peak cult apart from that obtaining in other localities.

Let us briefly consider these two aspects and their possible significance. A close definition is obviously impossible, because our evidence does not permit any definite conclusions, so that whatever we may propose in explanation of these ritual features must in essence remain conjectural. To begin with, we should agree with Evans and Platon who rightly said that the buildings on mountain peaks, especially at Juktas, and Petsophas, were sanctuaries[62]. Sir John Myres had at one time proposed that the house at Petsophas was a private building[63]. In the light of the more recent discoveries described above, and particularly in view of the scene on the Kato Zakro rhyton[64], Myres' view is no longer tenable. The curious animals like weasels, hedgehogs, etc., can only have one explanation, and this was already divined by Evans. They belonged to apotropaeic cult, and the small models were a kind of prophylactic offering made to the deity invoked as a protection against the ravages of such pests, and possibly against the diseases they spread amongst men. Evans compares the golden emerods and mice offered by the Philistines, "themselves, in part at least, of Cretan origin"[65].

This type of apotropaeic ritual was not confined to the East, but was known well enough to the Mediterranean world and does not require any specific references. One point, however, which is of some importance in connection with Minoan peak cult and the deity revered on these sites, is that apotropaeic cult and the protection from animal plagues was not only the province of a Mistress of Animals. The many models, therefore, on the summit precincts of stoats, mice, and weasels do not inevitably betray the presence of a *Potnia Theron*, as we come to know her later in the figure of Artemis. Male divinities could be equally responsible for the

---

[60] Hutchinson, *Preh. Crete* 219.
[61] See above p. 292.
[62] *P. M.* I, 151 ff.; *K. Ch.* 5 (1951) 96 ff.
[63] *B. S. A.* 9 (1903) 356 ff.
[64] Above p. 294.
[65] *P. M.* I, 153. Evans' last point is debatable, of course. Willetts makes the interesting suggestion in a footnote, *Cults* 72 n. 82, that this type of offering was also meant to ensure protection against the plagues and diseases carried by mice and rats. Cf. Branigan, *Pal. Crete* 106.

protection against animal plagues and pestilence. We need only think of Zeus Apomyios in Olympia[66], or Apollo Parnopios, the protector against locusts, and Smintheus, the protector against mice. The reason for these titles and the nature of the cult are obvious from the description in Aelian and Clement of Alexandria[67]. If then, as seems reasonable, we have in these models of vermin examples of apotropaeic cult in mountain peak sanctuaries, these latter need not have been the home of a *Potnia Theron*.

This would mean that an important part of Nilsson's thesis, according to which peak cults exclusively belonged to a Mistress of Animals, falls away[68]. Nilsson puts forward his idea with some misgivings which appear to be allayed by his interpretation of the other type of problematical offering, the separate limbs etc. These, in his opinion, formed a part of a fire ritual known from the historic cult of the Mistress of Animals. It seems that at Petsophas Sir John Myres discovered traces of a similar rite[69] which, like the Greek example, may have consisted in the casting into a large bonfire of idols, animal statuettes and perhaps even slaughtered animals. The fragments of figures, and the remains of the fire, would from time to time be raked over or deposited in the rock fissures[70]. The apparent coincidence between later Greek and Minoan practice is important and makes Nilsson's theory an attractive one, for the Mistress of Animals played a significant part in Cretan and Greek belief, while the peak of a mountain might well have been her natural habitat. But does all the evidence agree with such an interpretation? Should we not rather look for

---

[66] Pausanias, V, 14, 1; Pliny, *N. H.* 10, 40.
[67] Aelian, N. A. 11, 5; Clem. Alex., *Protrept.* II, 34 P. This apotropaeic practice inevitably came to be mixed up with genuine animal cult in Greece, cf. Clem., *ibid.;* Nilsson, *Gesch.* I, 213, in historical times. Also a number of subsequently invented aetiological myths tends to obscure the early history of true animal cult. One would, for instance, like to know the age and original reasons for the Theban worship of weasels. By the time Aelian, *ibid.,* tells the story, it is already involved in the Galinthias and Heracles myth. Regarding Apollo's epithet of Smintheus, an interesting remark comes from the Schol. A on Homer, *Il.* 1. 39, where he says that *sminthos* is the Cretan word for *mus*, cf. Frazer's note on Paus. X, 12, 5.
[68] *M. M. R.* 75; *Gesch.* I, 264.
[69] *B. S. A.* 9 (1903) 358.
[70] Myres' own explanation of the human limbs and parts is that these were dedicated to a healing deity who had cured the affected parts, models of which were hung in the sanctuary in her honour. The difficulty of such an interpretation lies in the many other kinds of offerings found on the mountain, in addition to Nilsson's own objections, *M. M. R.* 74.

a figure, or figures, of more general import? The fire ritual at Petsophas is too thinly documented. Furthermore, one should not lightly associate the votive human heads, limbs etc. with a Mistress of Animals, simply because some artistic representations show her surrounded by parts of animals. Separate human limbs very occasionally appear in Cretan art on gems and sealings. Like the similar examples in Egyptian and the largely independent Hittite hieroglyphic scripts[71], such limbs, mostly legs, might conceivably have held some religious connotation beside their purely symbolic meaning. Thus a human leg occurs beside a double axe and a fish on an M.M. clay sealing from the Early Pillar Basement at Knossos[72]. Again, a leg is shown beside a cat (?), and other signs, on a fine three-sided prism seal from M.M. III[73], while another – four-sided prism seal – also from M.M. (Hagia Triada) has a leg, bent at the knee, between objects similar to vases[74]. Once, on a sealstone from the necropolis of Phaestos, a human head is engraved between two *agrimi* lying back to back[75].

The significance of these legs, or heads, is obscure: there is little reason to connect them with a goddess solely concerned with animals. But if, especially in view of the peak offerings, such representations do possess some religious value, they may well refer to a cult in honour of a deity of nature whose functions extended over a wider area. Perhaps, then, one must suppose these severed limbs to be remnants, as it were, of a savage worship performed for a great goddess, a worship which fell into disuse at a relatively early time. We may mention in this context the strange find of human bones scattered at random – unlike any burial – in a pit beneath the niche and bull head on the east wall of the Second Shrine at Çatal Hüyük[76]. Whatever the ritual, which involved such strange offerings, it must have been compatible with, and formed a part of, those larger cultic features that were not alien to cave and domestic worship.

In peak cult we appear to meet with certain features of apotropaeic cult, and with a deity in some ways closely related to animals, domestic and

---

[71] Cf. O. R. Gurney, *The Hittites*, 126 f.
[72] V. G. Kenna, *Cretan Seals*, Oxford 1960, fig. 44.
[73] Kenna, *ibid*. fig. 74.
[74] Kenna, *ibid*. fig. 90. Cf. a human leg and a lion on a gem from Mycenae, *Eph. Arch.* (1888) Pl. X, 9.
[75] *Mon. Ant.* 14, 622, fig. 96; Pl. XL, 9. Nilsson, *M. M. R.* 234, believes that the head in this instance may be no more than a decorative motif.
with Cretan cult see ch. II above.
[76] EVI, 10, *A. S.* 13 (1963) 70, Pl. XIV b. For a comparison of Çatal Hüyük shrines

wild, in a bond which recalls aspects of a Mistress of Animals. A great deal, therefore, of what we can say about peak cult hinges on the identity of the divinity concerned with the rites celebrated there. However, a survey of our relevant pictorial evidence produces only one certain example of an anthropomorphic divine figure associated with peak cult. This is the clay impression of an L.M. II gold ring from Knossos[77] showing a goddess, staff in hand, on the peak of a mountain which is flanked, heraldic fashion, by two lions. The male figure in front of her, with his arms thrown up in a gesture of adoration, is obviously a worshipper of the goddess who appeared to him. Here we come to the heart of our problem: this mountain peak scene is an epiphany, that is the goddess appears to her worshippers in the same way, we may imagine, as in other cult sanctuaries, in domestic cult, and presumably in caves. What we cannot quite so easily tell is whether this goddess functioned alone in the mountain sanctuaries, or whether she shared her cult with other figures.

One other figure which has suggested itself in this connection is the youthful male paredros who featured in other spheres of Cretan religion. As far as mountain peak cults are concerned we are, alas, on less certain ground. There exists only one piece of concrete pictorial evidence which shows a male figure in association with this kind of cult, and that is the L.M. I gold ring from Knossos with the epiphany scene of a young (?) god before a tree sanctuary. But we were forced to admit above that this scene cannot, with certainty, be connected with a mountain peak shrine[78]. The rest of the evidence consists of inferences from the Minoan cultic scene at other sites, and from later tradition which strongly connects a male deity with peak sanctuaries. The many features which peak cult shared with other cult localities might well have included the presence of the male figure who played a significant part in Minoan religion. Much more valuable in this connection is the stubborn association of the Zeus Kretagenes figure with the Mt. Juktas sanctuary – the tradition of his tomb there is late[79] –, an association which survived for many generations[80]. The last point in particular might offer some justification for supposing that in the precinct of the mountain peak the well-known figure of the male god,

---

[77] Above p. 294.
[78] Above p. 295; cf. Biesantz's reservations regarding the genuineness of the ring, Kr.-Myk. Siegelb. 86.
[79] See above n. 48.
[80] See e.g. Evans, P. M. I, 153 f.; cf. Cook, Zeus II, 939 f.

probably the assessor of the nature goddess, had his place, too, although we should hesitate to name him, with Hutchinson, the Master of Animals[81].

A male figure, then, in association with a goddess was a possible object of worship in mountain peak cult, although his presence cannot be proved beyond all doubt. Our proposal is not new, however, since Platon, in his examination of peak cults made some sixteen years ago, came to the same conclusion[82]. Where we differ from Platon is in the description of the goddess, whom he calls the Great Nature Goddess. Neither can we agree with his description of the nature of the cult as a magic ritual concerned with healing[83]. Nilsson in part agrees with Platon by seeing in the goddess a Mistress of Animals[84]. We already noticed above that the identification with a cult of healing will not easily stand up on the strength of the *ex votos* of limbs etc. Furthermore, we must be careful with our terminology when describing the goddess as a *Potnia Theron*, for this is an arbitrary term, devised on analogy with the later function of great classical goddesses like Artemis. It seems more important to recognize in this divinity, worshipped on mountain tops, a figure, or an aspect of a figure, at home both in cave and domestic cult.

The goddess, one might say, central to all Minoan cult was concerned with nature, the growth and decay of vegetation, human birth and death, all aspects which can be isolated from cave cult and which continued in some form when this cult was transferred to domestic shrines[85]. As a nature goddess she was also concerned with animals, and to that extent can be called a Mistress of Animals. But if we compare this Cretan goddess with the well-known figure of the Eastern Great Goddess and her paredros, and consequently speak of one Mother Goddess presiding over Bronze Age Minoan religion, we are oversimplifying matters, if we are to put any trust in the evidence of the Linear B tablets which know of a number of deities. And it does not really matter that the written evidence cannot be earlier than the middle of the fifteenth century B.C., for we are dealing with a religious subject which continued a tradition that must at the very least have gone back to Middle Minoan, but in fact came into being earlier.

---

[81] *Preh. Crete* 221. Nilsson's scepticism concerning the male figure, *Gesch.* I, 288, seems overdone.
[82] *K. Ch.* (1951) 96 ff.
[83] Cf. above n. 70.
[84] *M. M. R.* 75.
[85] Above p. 92.

Also, the relationship between goddess and animals, which existed in peak cult as well, was more than that of mistress and servant[86].

In the light of the picture we drew of the Cretan religious scene in chapter II, I advisedly spoke of the sealing from Knossos[87] as our only extant representation of an *anthropomorphic* divinity connected with peak cult. For who can now say to what extent the lions flanking the goddess on the seal, or the birds and goats on the rhyta discussed above, were not meant to express an epiphany of the deity on these cult sites[88]? The important point to recognize, however, is that here in mountain peak cult we are confronted with essentially the same goddess, known at other sites, who was intimately associated with her animals, and who in this cult locality, too, may have been thought of as together with a male companion. Her name we cannot know, but, like that of other Cretan divine figures[89], it most likely consisted of an invocatory title. Two such titles, Potnia and Wanassa, are supplied by the Linear B tablets[90], and we may well suppose that the goddess in the mountain shrine was called upon by her worshippers under the name of Lady, Mistress, or Queen, in the same way as in cave or palace. In fact, the goddess revered on Mt. Juktas and at Petsophas was an aspect of the nature goddess, at home in mountain peaks, and comparable, therefore, with other aspects receiving cult in other localities.

Such departmentalization of divine function was a feature of both Minoan and Mycenaean cult. It is another matter, however, whether we can, with Guthrie, dogmatically divide these aspects into three distinct types of goddess, namely 1) an Earth Mother, 2) a Mountain Mother, and 3) a Snake and House Goddess[91]. The evidence suggests that the separate figures were more numerous, whether we find them in the Linear tablets or amongst the deities destined to survive in Greek legend and religion, such as Eileithyia, Diktynna, Aphaea, Ariadne, and others.

The goddess, or one of her aspects, revered in mountain peak sanctuaries was essentially the same as the goddess who stood behind, as it were, the various aspects at the centre of cave and domestic cult. In this departmentalization obviously some special features of divine functions devel-

---

[86] Cf. Faure, *Fonct.* 194.
[87] See above p. 303.
[88] Cf. also Willetts, *Cults* 73.
[89] Cf. A. W. Persson, *Preh. Rel.* 125 ff.; 130 f.; cf. above p. 180.
[90] Cf. the discussion in ch. III, 181 ff.
[91] W. K. C. Guthrie, "Early Greek Religion in the Light of the Decipherment of Linear B", *BICS* 6 (1959) 35–46; cf. above p. 179.

oped in particular cult localities. In caves, as at Amnisos, the most likely features to predominate in ritual were those concerned with birth and death and the annually recurring cycle of vegetation[92]. The goddess, or her particular aspect, in the palace shrine would be called upon for her protecting qualities: she was a guardian of the palace which was her domain, and she stood in a particularly close relationship with the king[93]. Peak cult, too, enjoyed special features peculiar to itself, such as apotropaeic ritual and a religious concept whose true significance now escapes us[94].

In the present state of our knowledge it is not worth while looking for political or physical reasons for the decline of peak cult, for none of them can be proved and few are very convincing. Rutkowski, for example[95], blames the natural disasters at the end of M.M. and later in about 1500[96], for the abandonment of these exposed cult sites and for renewed activity in the building of underground "cryptas" and cave sanctuaries[97]. This information is not particularly helpful, however, because we do not know the extent of total damage during these destructions, nor can we do more than guess if a relationship did indeed exist between these disasters and the institution of fresh cave cults in Middle Minoan. Not all cult centres need have been affected. The perhaps natural catastrophes of c. 1700 B.C.[98] may not have put out of commission the Mallia palace, for example[99], which probably continued to flourish well into the fifteenth century. The same most likely applied to the "Herrenhäuser" at e.g. Tylissos, Gournia, and

[92] Above e.g. p. 88 f.
[93] Above e.g. p. 184.
[94] Branigan, *Pal. Cret.* 108, says of the deity revered in peak sanctuaries that she was "a more 'specialized' deity whose attributes and powers were well defined and demanded certain specific rituals."
[95] "Decl. of Min. Peak Sanct.", 165 f.; *H.* (1971) 11 ff.
[96] Cf. S. Marinatos, "The Volcanic Destruction of Minoan Crete", *Ant.* 13 (1939) 425. Marinatos further enlarged on this subject in a lecture to the *Second Congress of Cretan Studies* (1966), and in another lecture to the *First Intern. Congr. of Mycen. Studs.* in Rome (1967). Recently this subject was treated again in the *Northcliffe Lectures* delivered by Prof. D. Page at University College London in February 1970 (Hellenic Studies Supplementary Paper No. 12). M. S. F. Hood's succinct report on the findings of *The International Scientific Congress on the Volcano of Thera 15–23 Sept. 1969 K.* 9 (1970) (98–106) shows quite clearly the many difficulties of drawing final conclusions about the dating and effect on Cretan culture of the Thera eruption. See now Dietrich, "Minoan Peak Cult: A Reply", *H.* 20 (1971) 521 ff.
[97] "Decl. of Min. Peak Sanct.", 166 and n. 15; 16.
[98] Doro Levi's date, cited by Schachermeyr, *min. Kultur* 84.
[99] Schachermeyr, *op. cit.* 84; 89.

Palaikastro[100]. In any case, at least some parts of the island which, like Knossos, suffered from the different earthquakes, eruptions, and fires quickly recovered, late in M.M. and in L.M. I, without any lasting obvious ill effects[101]. The political scene in Crete, at the beginning of L.M., is too little known for any safe hypothesis to be made regarding contemporary religious culture.

The true state of affairs was probably much less dramatic. At a time when palace culture had reached its brightest lustre, in early Late Minoan, some parts of peak cult may have been moved to the new abode. Individual features of peak cult, however, undoubtedly survived, albeit in greatly diminished form. The archaeological picture in support of this belief is obviously vague. But some archaeological evidence remains to vouch for continued cult in sites like Kumasa (L.M. III B)[102]. Further arguments in favour of the enduring sacredness of peak sites are the long association of Zeus with these high places[103], and the continuation of an old mountain top site at Karphi. The refugees, who settled there in order to escape the cataclysmic events at the end of the Bronze Age, felt at home in their inaccessible stronghold which, from Middle Minoan, had been consecrated to one aspect of the nature goddess[104].

---

[100] *Op. cit.* 89.

[101] *Op. cit.* 85, "Aus den Grabungen ergibt sich..., daß sich Kreta von diesen Zerstörungen sehr rasch erholte...".

[102] See above p. 293 and n. 22. In these instances it seems safer to discover continuity of cult rather than speak of the power of heavenly divinities which, though "shaken in M.M. III to L.M. (III) B, never died out", so that new peak cults were instituted at the end of the Bronze Age. This is Rutkowski's thesis, *op. cit.* 166.

[103] Cf. Hutchinson, *Preh. Crete* 218 and n. l. Cf. the association of Apollo Hyacinthus with peak cult in classical times, Faure, *B. C. H.* (1967) 132 f.

[104] On the conservatism of Karphi see also C. G. Starr, *Origins*, 81-83.

Appendix II: APOLLO AT DELPHI.

How old was Apollo's cult at Delphi, and to what extent was the god involved in the Mycenaean type worship which may have preceded his presence there? Quite frankly, there is at present no convincing answer to these questions. On the contrary, the problem becomes yet more involved in view of Apollo's function at Delphi as god of the oracle. This function was known to Homer already and therefore dates back to the Greek Archaic Age'. Yet there was another well-known tradition in Greek literature which speaks of Apollo as an intruder at the oracular seat at Delphi. He was said to have displaced the earlier figures of Ge and Themis[2]. We cannot digress to examine the history of the Delphic oracle or the age of the tradition associating with it Ge and Themis[3]. The origin of the oracle is wrapped in mystery, but in some way it must be connected with the story, however varied in points of detail, which speaks of Ge and Themis as early oracular deities. Neither Ge nor Themis has ever been particularly concerned with oracular activity[4]. Their presence at Delphi seems to indicate that the early cult there was chthonic in nature[5].

The famous *omphalos*, too, was a direct descendant of the Minoan baetyl[6], and testifies to the antiquity of the Delphic cult which, most likely,

---

[1] *Od.* 8, 79 f.
[2] See e.g. Aeschylus, *Eumenides* 1ff.; Euripides, *Iph. in Taur.* 1259 ff. This tradition suffers from a measure of uncertainty. In the *Eumenides* Themis succeeds Ge to the mantic shrine before Apollo's arrival (cf. Paus. X, 5, 6, where Ge gives Themis her share of the shrine, while the latter surrenders it to Apollo as a present). In Euripides Ge becomes Themis' mother, while Apollo forcibly takes over the oracular seat. Again, in *Prom. Vinct.* 211 ff., Aeschylus calls Themis and Ge identical, both names of Earth. A startling version can be found in the schol. on Pindar's *Hypoth. to the Pyth. Odes*, where Night was the first oracular power at Delphi and predecessor of Themis. Ge's association with Delphi most likely gave rise to the belief held by the French excavators of Delphi that the cult there, from the beginning of the Bronze Age to its end, was devoted to a Mother Goddess. See the references in e.g. Nilsson, *M. M. R.* 467 f.
[3] See e.g. Nilsson, *Gesch.* I, 170 ff.; Dietrich, *Death, Fate, Gods* 169 f.
[4] Cf. Nilsson, *Gesch.* I, 172.
[5] For similar beginnings of oracles, of the type obtaining at Delphi, compare that of Trophonius at Lebadeia, and Ge's other oracle at Olympia, see Dietrich, *op. cit.* Append. VI.
[6] Cf. H. W. Parke – D. E. W. Wormell, *The Delphic Oracle*, Oxford 1956 I, 6 f.

was concerned with our Bronze Age goddess and with nature and vegetation. A later replica of the stone now stands in the modern museum. In classical times it was perhaps hidden within the temple's sanctuary: its sacred memory alive, while its original significance had long been forgotten[7]. Was Apollo an intruder in this chthonic nature cult? Did the tradition, which accuses him of usurping Ge's seat at Delphi, reflect historical events? And, if so, when should we suppose Apollo to have arrived on the scene? The issue really hinges on Apollo's original home, which, much speculation notwithstanding, still defies identification. Nilsson stresses Apollo's Eastern "Beziehungen"[8], and he therefore inclines to the belief that the god was a relatively late arrival at Delphi[9]. Despite the fact that Apollo's name cannot yet be read on the Linear tablets, we should not dismiss out of hand the possibility that he was known already to the Mycenaean Greeks.

We noticed[10] that, with Athena and Artemis, Apollo was most apt to enjoy cult at originally Mycenaean sacred localities, as at Amyclae and Epidaurus. Furthermore, the memory of his ties with Crete, especially with Knossos, survived into historic times, and is expressed, for example, in the Homeric Hymn in his honour[11]. Even if we were to label as a late invention the story (told in the Hymn) of his arrival at Delphi from Crete[12], we would still be left with a number of historic Apolline Cretan cults and epithets, including those of Delphinios and Pythios, which, as far as it is possible to tell, belonged to ancient tradition[13]. It seems wisest, therefore, to reserve judgment with regard to Apollo's Delphic history, for, with the possible exception of the oracle, all features of Delphic worship probably trace back to the Bronze Age, to a chthonic cult of nature and the principal goddess central to it.

---

[7] See also above p. 52 for the part played by the *omphalos* in genealogical mythology.
[8] *Gesch.* I, 559 ff.
[9] *M. M. R.* 467 f.; 576.
[10] See p. 154.
[11] *Hom. Hymn Apollo* 388 ff. Apollo is said to have come to Delphi from Crete. Cf. Picard, *Rel. Préh.* 207 f., for further sources.
[12] Nilsson, *M. M. R.* 577, rather unconvincingly explains this episode away by claiming that is was made up "as a recollection of the link between Delphi and the chief seats of Minoan religion."
[13] These are collected and discussed by Willetts, *Cretan Cults* 256 ff. On Apollo's connection with stone cult and with the Delphic *omphalos* in particular see Nilsson, *Gesch.* I, 203 ff. Perhaps it was by way of a common bond in stone and pillar cult that we should explain the puzzling juxtaposition at Delphi of Apollo and Dionysus.

Appendix III: GREEK MYTHOLOGY IN THE MYCENAEAN AGE

Scholars who oppose Nilsson's thesis that Greek mythology had been formed in Mycenaean times base their view on two main points. The first concerns the many names of Greek mythological personages which describe common people on the Linear B tablets and therefore could only subsequently have become associated with figures of legend. The second point consists of the virtual absence, or extreme scarcity, of identifiable mythological scenes in art from the Mycenaean to the Geometric Age[1].

Both arguments are rigorously conducted by L. Banti[2], who maintains that, since names like Achilles and Theseus are used for ordinary people on the tablets, they could not have been part of myth in the thirteenth century. The legends of Elysium and the Garden of the Hesperides, which Nilsson derived from Minoan myth, have, according to Banti, left no trace in Minoan or Mycenaean art. In fact, if Minoan and Mycenaean mythological scenes had been depicted in some form, they would have differed, for the former were a peaceful people while the mainlanders were warlike and fond of the hunt, both opposing attitudes which should have been reflected in their mythology.

One scene only Banti will admit as evidence of contemporary myth in art, that is the group of a woman (Europa) riding on the back of a bull, cut into the famous blue glass plaque from Dendra-Midea[3]. But the Europa story came from Syria, and the presence of this plaque in a fourteenth century grave is evidence only of the fact that that myth was known to the Mycenaean world. At best, therefore, according to Banti, Greek myth might have been in the process of formation at the end of the Bronze Age[4]. Indeed, in view of our poor evidence this might well be a generous guess, and it may be more reasonable to blame the Dorian invasion as a *terminus* after which the Greek myth-makers got to work[5].

---

[1] See the discussion in A. Sacconi, "Il Mito nel Mondo Miceneo", *P. d. P.* 15 (1960) 161 ff.
[2] "Myth in Pre-Classical Art", *A. J. A.* 58 (1954) 307 ff.
[3] Found in a tomb which is dated c. 1350 B.C., Persson, *Preh. Rel.* 133 and fig. 24.
[4] Cf. Pugliese-Carratelli, *P. d. P.* 9 (1954) 473 ff.; Ehrenberg, *H. Z.* 180 (1955) 1 ff.; R. Hampe, *Gym.* 63 (1956) 38.
[5] Cf. Vermeule, "Mythology in Mycenaean Art", *C. J.* 54 (1958) 106.

Neither argument is sufficient, however, to destroy Nilsson's contention that Greek mythology was a continuation of themes already formed in the Bronze Age. A great many names, which can be read on the Linear B tablets, survived in Greek myth and literature, notably Homeric epic[6]. Our knowledge of Mycenaean conditions and practices is too incomplete to allow the argument that mythological names then were tabu for ordinary mortals. Sacconi reasonably points to a similar habit of giving classical heroic names to common people in Hellenistic times[7], and the same practice survived, of course, into modern times[8]. Sacconi also argues along the well-known, but eminently valid, lines that heroic epithets in Homer, like Achilles *podarkes, podas okus*, or Patroclus *hippokeleuthe*, which refer to certain qualities not reflected in epic activity, must go back to Mycenaean times[9]. Whether or not the Mycenaeans possessed their own epic poetry, the occurrence of many heroic names on the Knossos and Pylos tablets, as well as Homeric memory, strongly suggests an acquaintance with some myths which endured in Greece into classical times and later.

How far we may look for support in artistic representations is another question which is subject to some considerable debate. There is enough material, however, to reach a positive finding. The difficulties involved in this quest are substantially increased above all by every scholar's commendable caution in interpreting particular scenes where, perhaps by virtue of the artist's lack of skill, the content and subject are not absolutely clear. There is also the danger of mistaking for parts of legends pictures which were merely designed to reproduce contemporary occupations, such as hunting and war on Mycenaean vases, or battle scenes and sea-fights, or shipwrecks, so popular on Late Geometric vessels[10]. Alternately battle, and similar, scenes on Geometric vases might well be drawn from epic tales and therefore prove valueless as evidence that a particular myth was known

---

[6] Ventris and Chadwick conservatively identify fifty-eight, *Docs.* 104 f. See also the discussion by D. H. F. Gray, "Mycenaean Names in Homer", *J. H. S.* 78 (1958) 43 ff.

[7] *P. d. P.* 15 (1960) 164 f.

[8] Examples of the use of mythological names in classical times are also cited by Webster, "On the Track of Mycenaean Poetry", *Cl. Med.* 17 (1956) 158 ff. *Myc. to Hom.* 114 ff.; 323 f. For another view, favourable to this argument, see C. M. Bowra, *Homer and his Forerunners*, 24. F. Cassola, *La Ionia nel Mondo Miceneo*, 62 ff., does not commit himself either way.

[9] *Op. cit.* 169; cf. Webster, *Myc. to Hom.* 119.

[10] G. M. A. Richter, *Bull. Met. Mus.* 29 (1934) 172; Homann-Wedeking, *Archaic Greece* 22; 149 ff.

at the time[11]. Mythological scenes of gods and of the war between the gods and giants became extremely popular subjects for vase painters of the sixth century. But these, too, are copied from Homer, they are contrived and have little religious or mythological significance[12]. Enough remains, however, to plead our case. If the extant material is not plentiful we should not grow discouraged, for even isolated instances will prove the point of contemporary acquaintance with at least some myths.

In addition to the Dendra-Midea glass plaque of Europa riding on the bull, Sacconi cites a few more instances of probable mythological scenes in Mycenaean art, and four certain examples belonging to the same group of the "riding goddess"[13]. These are 1) a terracotta statuette (13th/12th century) from a Mycenaean tomb at Spata[14]. This statuette shows a woman[15] riding side-saddle on a horse. To this we may add a similar group of a male figure on horseback from the same tomb[16], 2) a 13th cent. gem[17] of a goddess side-saddle on a mythical animal 3) an early L.M. 'cretula' from Hagia Triada showing a woman riding another strange animal[18], 4) a hematite cylinder (L.M. III) from Hagia Pelagia, near Candia, with a woman riding a similar animal[19]. All these scenes, like the story of Perseus' slaying of the Gorgon and the Bellerophon tale, represent imports from the East[20] which, and this is the important point, were familiar in the West at least by Late Helladic. To these few Bronze Age examples of the "riding goddess" we may add an interesting scene on a Late Mycenaean

---

[11] Webster, *B. S. A.* 50 (1955) 43 ff.; *Myc. to Hom.* 167 ff.

[12] Boardman, *Pre-Class.* 135 ff. Homann-Wedeking, *op. cit.* 149 f., maintains that mythological scenes were only used by Greek vase painters after "the inrush of oriental motifs".

[13] *Op. cit.* 180 ff., with further references.

[14] Doro Levi, "La Dea Micenea a Cavallo", *Studs. Rob.* I 108 ff., Pl. 4 a–b; Mylonas, *Mycenae* figs. 118 f.

[15] Typical Mycenaean goddess figure with raised arms.

[16] Levi, *op. cit.* Pl. 4 c.

[17] From Mycenae, Mylonas, *Mycenae* fig. 117, where the author calls the figure the Goddess of Blessing.

[18] Levi, *A. S. I.* 8/9 (1925/6) 136 f.; *A. J. A.* 49 (1945) 270. On p. 275 Levi claims that the animal in this representation was derived from the Babylonian dragon figure, and that the goddess riding it symbolically showed her domination over the forces of nature.

[19] Evans, *P. M.* IV, 497, fig. 436 (Evans calls the animal a fox); P. Demargne, *La Crète Dédalique*, Paris 1947, 82, fig. 2; Mylonas, "Seated and Multiple Mycenaean Figurines in the Aegean and Near East", *Studs. Gold.* 112.

[20] Cf. Sacconi, *ibid.*

vase (13th cent.) from Ialysos on Rhodes. The picture consists of five women, two of whom are standing in a horse-drawn chariot, dressed in long stiff cloaks[21] and armed with throwing spears. The scene may be identified with the five daughters of Danaus whom their father, on his flight from Egypt to Argos, left behind on the island of Rhodes in order to serve the goddess Athena Lindia[22].

Mythological scenes on Geometric vases are less confidently identified, precisely because of the reservations already mentioned. However, there is one particular story which quite frequently recurs on eighth century vases mostly from the Athenian Kerameikos. That is the fight between a hero and a pair of Siamese twins, a group which has plausibly been identified with the myth of Nestor's fight with the Molionides Twins. The story is told in *Iliad* 11, but antedates the composition of Homeric epic and, through the connection of the Molione with Poseidon (their father) and Nestor, probably fell within the ambit of Mycenaean Pylos[23]. There seems little doubt that these Molione scenes on eighth century Geometric kraters are mythological, and it does not matter whether such vases were "personal monuments" to members of the Neleid clan who were buried beneath them in the Athenian cemetery[24]. On the contrary, a firm connection between Nestor's Pylian family and this particular legend strengthens the belief in the latter's existence in Mycenaean times.

The Dark Age left us nothing in the way of literary or archaeological remains from which one might argue either for or against the survival of an earlier *corpus* of mythology. However, at both ends of this period, that is Late Mycenaean and Late Geometric, there is some indication of the existence and continuance of Greek legends. The reasons for the relative scarcity of myth in art, prior to the seventh century, are difficult to fathom, and this was said earlier on. Perhaps it was merely unfashionable to paint such subjects before the Orientalizing period. There are, however, two assumptions which one is entitled to make in this connection. Firstly Nilsson's arguments concerning the origin of Greek mythology in Mycenaean times are as valid now as they were thirty-five years ago. Secondly Eastern

---

[21] Like the contemporary Syrio-Egyptian linen-armour?
[22] Wiesner, *Olympos* 245 f. and text figure.
[23] Cf. on the myth and sources P. Grimal, *Dictionnaire de la Mythologie Grecque et Romaine*², Paris 1958, 301. The Cretan connection through Molos (their maternal grandfather) may well have been a later invention.
[24] Coldstream, *Geometric Pottery* 351.

motifs, which unquestionably came to the Greek world, did not make their first appearance in the seventh century B.C. when for a time they dominated the style of decoration of Orientalizing ware as well as plastic art forms. Such ideas had come West much earlier, in fact during the Bronze Age[25], and it was most probably then that they chiefly influenced Western myth which the classical Greeks inherited from their Mycenaean ancestors.

---

[25] Cf. above p. 278 ff.

SELECT BIBLIOGRAPHY

The following list includes only those books and articles that have been repeatedly used throughout the text. Full reference to other works will be found in the notes. A list of periodicals and works, with the abbreviations used for them, is given at the end of the biliography.

Alexiou, S., "The Goddess with Raised Hands", *K. K.* 12 (1958) 179.
Ålin, P., *Das Ende der mykenischen Fundstätten auf dem griechischen Festland (Studies in Mediterranean Archaeology, vol. i)*, Lund 1962.
Andrewes, A., *The Greeks*, London 1967.
Andronikos, M., "The 'Dorian Invasion' and Archaeology", *Hell.* 13 (1954) 221.
Astour, M. C., *Hellenosemitica*, Leiden 1965. Now in sec. ed.

Banti, L., "Myth in Pre-Classical Art", *A. J. A.* 58 (1954) 307.
Bennett, E. L., *The Olive Oil Tablets of Pylos*, Salamanca 1958.
Bianchi, U., *La Religione Greca, Storia delle Religione II*, Turin 1962.
Biesantz, H., *Kretisch-Mykenische Siegelbilder*, Marburg 1954.
Bittel, K., *Grundzüge der Vor- und Frühgeschichte Kleinasiens*^{2}, Tübingen 1950.
Boardman, J., *The Cretan Collection in Oxford, The Dictaean Cave and Iron Age Crete*, Oxford 1961.
    Pre-Classical. From Crete to Archaic Greece, Penguin Books 1967.
Bossert, H., *Altkreta*^{3}, Berlin 1937.
Bottero, J., *La Religion Babylonienne*, Paris 1952.
Bowra, C. M., *Homer and His Forerunners*, Edinburgh 1955.
Brandon, S. G. F., *Creation Legends of the Ancient Near East*, London 1963.
Branigan, K., *The Foundations of Palatial Crete*, London 1970, with bibliography.
Broneer, O., "Athens in the Late Bronze Age", *Ant.* 30 (1956) 9.
Buchholz, H. G., *Zur Herkunft der kretischen Doppelaxt*, Munich 1959.
Buck, R. J., "The Mycenaean Time of Troubles", *H.* 18 (1969) 276.

Cassola, F., *La Ionia nel Mondo Miceneo*, Naples 1967.
Chadwick, J., "Potnia", *M.* 5 (1957) 117.
Chadwick, J., *The Decipherment of Linear B*^{2}, Cambridge 1962.
    "The Prehistory of the Greek Language", *C. A. H.*^{2} II (1963).
    "The Greek Dialects and Greek Prehistory", *G. R.* 3 (1956) 38.
Cook, A. B., "The Bee in Greek Mythology", *J. H. S.* 15 (1895) 1.
Cook, J., "The Dorian Invasion", *P. C. P. S.* 1962, 16.
    "Greek Settlements in the Eastern Aegean and Asia Minor", *C. A. H.*^{2} II (1961).

Daniel, J., Broneer, O., Wade-Gery, H. T., "The Dorian Invasion", *A. J. A.* 52 (1948) 107.
Davaras, C., *B. C. H.* 93 (1969) 617.
Demargne, P., *Aegean Art*, London 1964.
Desborough, V. R. d'A., *The Last Mycenaeans and their Successors*, Oxford 1964.
& Hammond, H., "The End of Mycenaean Civilization and the Dark Ages", *C. A. H.*² II (1962).
Protogeometric Pottery, Oxford 1952.
"The Greek Mainland c. 1150–c. 1000 B. C.", *ProcPS* 31 (1965) 213.
Devoto, G., *Le Origine Indoeuropee*, Florence 1962.
Dhorme, E., *Les Religions de Babylonie et d'Assyrie*, Paris 1945.
Dietrich, B. C., *Death, Fate and the Gods*, sec. impr., London 1967.
"Prolegomena to the Study of Greek Cult Continuity", *A. C.* 11 (1968) 153.
"Some Evidence of Religious Continuity in the Greek Dark Age", *BICS* 17 (1970) 16.
Dirlmeier, F., "Homerisches Epos und Orient", *R. M.* 98 (1955) 18.
Dodds, E. R., *The Greeks and the Irrational*, Berkeley 1963.
Dornseiff, F., *Antike und Alter Orient* (Kleine Schriften), Leipzig 1956.
Dow, S., "The Greeks in the Bronze Age", *XIConScHist.* (1960) 1.
Driver, G. R., *Canaanite Myths and Legends*, Edinburgh 1956.
Dunbabin, T. J., *The Greeks and their Eastern Neighbours*, London 1957.
Dussaud, R., *Les Religions des Hittites et des Hourrites, des Phéniciens, et des Syriens*, Paris 1949.
Prélydiens, Hittites et Achéens, Paris 1953.

Eissfeldt, O., *Kanaänaisch-ugaritische Religion* (Handbuch der Orientalistik viii, i, i) Leiden 1964.
Engnell, I., *Studies in Divine Kingship in the Ancient Near East*, Uppsala 1945.
Erbse, H., "Orientalisches und Griechisches in Hesiods Theogonie", *Phil.* 108 (1964) 2.
Evans, A., *Mycenaean Tree and Pillar Cult*, London 1901.
The Earlier Religion of Greece in the Light of Cretan Discoveries, London 1931.
The Palace of Minos at Knossos, London 1925–36, vols. I–IV, Index.

Faure, P., *B. C. H.* 80 (1956) 95; 82 (1958) 495; 84 (1960) 189; 86 (1962) 36; 87 (1963) 493; 89 (1965) 27; 91 (1967) 114.
Fonctions des Cavernes Crétoises, Paris 1964.
Fimmen, D., *Die kretisch-mykenische Kultur*² (G. Karo, ed.), Leipzig–Berlin 1924.
Forsdyke, J., *Greece before Homer*, London 1956.
Frankfort, H., *Kingship and the Gods*, Chicago 1948.
The Birth of Civilization in the Near East, London 1954.
Furlani, G., *La Religione degli Hittiti*, Bologna 1936.
Furumark, A., *The Chronology of Mycenaean Pottery*, Stockholm 1941.
The Mycenaean Pottery; Analysis and Classification, Stockholm 1941.
"Gods of Ancient Crete", 4, X, Lund 1965, 85.

Gadd, C. J., *Ideas of Divine Rule in the Ancient East* (Schweich Lect.) 1945.
"The Cities of Babylon", *C. A. H.*² I, xiii, Cambridge 1962.
Gaster, T. H., *Thespis*², New York 1961.

SELECT BIBLIOGRAPHY

Glotz, G., *La Civilisation Égéenne* (C. Picard, P. Demargne [ed.]), Paris 1952.
Gordon, C. H., *Ugaritic Literature*, Rome 1949.
Graham, J. W., *The Palaces of Crete*, Princeton 1962.
Graziosi, P., *Palaeolithic Art*, London 1960.
Grumach, E., *Bibliographie der kretisch-mykenischen Epigraphik*, Munich 1963.
Güterbock, H. G., *Kumarbi*, Zürich-New York 1946.
"The Hittite Version of the Hurrian Kumarbi Myths: Oriental Forerunners of Hesiod", *A. J. A.* 52 (1948) 123.
Gurney, O. R., "Anatolia c. 1750–1600 B. C.", *C. A. H.*² II, iv, Cambridge 1962.
The Hittites, Penguin Book 1961.
Guthrie, W. K. C., "The Religion and Mythology of the Greeks", *C. A. H.*² II (1961).
"Early Greek Religion in the Light of the Decipherment of Linear B", *BICS* 6 (1959) 35.
The Greeks and their Gods, repr. London 1968.

Haag, H., *Homer, Ugarit und das Alte Testament*, Einsiedeln-Zurich-Cologne 1962.
Hammond, N. G. L., "Prehistoric Epirus and the Dorian Invasion", *B. S. A.* 32 (1931/2) 131.
Hampl, F., "Die Chronologie der Einwanderung der griechischen Stämme", *M. H.* 17 (1960) 57.
Harrison, J., *Prolegomena to the Study of Greek Religion*, repr. New York 1955.
Heitsch, E. (ed.), *Hesiod*, Darmstadt 1966 (contains important essays by Lesky and Heubeck).
Hemberg, B., *Die Kabiren*, Uppsala 1950.
Anax, Anassa und Anakes, Uppsala 1955.
Hempel, J., *Die alttestamentliche Religion* (Handbuch der Orientalistik), Leiden 1964.
Hermann, H. V., *Omphalos*, Münster 1959.
Herter, H., "Griechenland und Orient", *A. Soz. Eth.* 10 (1967/8) 49.
Heubeck, A., *Aus der Welt der frühgriechischen Lineartafeln*, Göttingen 1966.
Higgins, R. A., *Greek Terracottas*, London 1967.
Hittite Art and the Antiquities of Anatolia, The Arts Council, London 1964.
Homann-Wedeking, E., *Archaic Greece*, transl. by J. R. Foster, London 1968.
Hood, M. S. F., *The Home of the Heroes*, London 1967.
Hooke, S. H., *Babylonian and Assyrian Religion*, Oxford 1962.
Middle Eastern Mythology, Penguin Book 1963.
(ed.), *Myth, Ritual, and Kingship*, Oxford 1958.
Hope Simpson, R., *A Gazetteer of Mycenaean Sites*, BICS Suppl. No. 16 (1965).
Hutchinson, R. W., *Prehistoric Crete*, Penguin Book 1963.
Huxley, G., *Achaeans and Hittites*, Oxford 1960.
Crete and the Luwians, Oxford 1961.

Jacob, E., *Ras Shamra et l'Ancien Testament*, Neuchâtel 1960.
Jean, Ch.-F., *La Religion Sumérienne*, Paris 1931.

Karageorghis, V., "Myth and Epic in Mycenaean Vase Painting", *A. J. A.* 62 (1958) 383.
Karo, G., *Die Schlachtgräber von Mykenai*, Munich 1930–3.
"Mykenische Kultur", *P.-W.*, Suppl. VI (1935) 584.

Kirk, G., *The Songs of Homer*, Cambridge 1962.
— (ed.) *Language and Background of Homer*, Cambridge 1964.
Kramer, S. N., *History begins at Sumer*, London 1958.
— *Sumerian Mythology*, New York 1961.

Lämmli, F., *Vom Chaos zum Kosmos*, Basel 1962.
Landau, O., *Mykenisch-Griechische Personennamen*, Göteborg 1958.
Levi, D., "Gleanings from Crete", *A. J. A.* 49 (1945) 270.
— "Gli Scavi del 1954 sull'Acropoli di Gortina", *A. S. I.* 33/4 (N. S. 17/8) (1955/6) 207.
Levi, D., "Il Palladio di Gortina", *P. d. P.* 11 (1956) 285.
— "Per una nuova Classificazione della Civiltà Minoica", *P. d. P.* 15 (1960) 81. *A. S. I.* 39/40 (1961/2) 123.
— "Ricerca Scientifica e Polemica sull'Evoluzione della Civiltà Minoica", *P. d. P.* 84 (1962) 206.
Lorimer, H. L., *Homer and the Monuments*, London 1950.

McDonald, W. A., "Prehistoric Habitation in South-western Peloponnese", *A. J. A.* 65 (1961) 221.
Malten, L., "Der Stier im Kult und mythischem Bild", *Jahrb.* 43 (1928) 30.
Marinatos, S. N., Hirmer, M., *Crete and Mycenae*, London 1960.
Marinatos, S. N., "The Minoan and Mycenaean Civilization and its Influence on the Mediterranean and Europe", *VIConPre* (Rome 1962).
Matz, F., "Die Ägäis", *Handbuch der Archaeologie* 2, 1 (1950).
— *Kreta, Mykene, Troja*[4], Stuttgart 1957.
— *Göttererscheinung und Kultbild im minoischen Kreta*, Akademie der Wissenschaften und der Literatur, Wiesbaden 1958.
— "Die Katastrophe der Mykenischen Kultur im Lichte der neuesten Forschung", *VIIArcCon (I)* 197.
— *Crete and Early Greece*, London 1962.
— "Minoan Civilization, Maturity and Zenith", *C. A. H.*[2], II, iv (b) 1962.
Mellaart, J., "Excavations at Çatal Hüyük", *A. S.* 12 (1962) 41; 13 (1963) 43; 14 (1964) 39.
— *Earliest Civilizations of the Near East*, London 1965.
— *Excavations at Haçilar* (1971).
Mendelsohn, I., *Religions of the Ancient Near East*, New York 1955.
Milojčić, V., "Die dorische Wanderung im Lichte der vorgeschichtlichen Funde", *Anz.* 1948, 12.
Möllendorff, U. v. W., *Der Glaube der Hellenen*[3] (repr. Darmstadt 1959) vol. I.
Mylonas, G. E., "The Cult of the Dead", *StudsRob.* 64.
— *Ancient Mycenae: The Capital City of Agamemnon*, Princeton 1957.
— "Homeric and Mycenaean Burial Customs", *A. J. A.* 62 (1958) 56.
— "The Grave Circles of Mycenae", *Minoica*, Berlin 1958, 276.
— *Eleusis and the Eleusinian Mysteries*, Princeton 1961.
— *Mycenae and the Mycenaean Age*, Princeton 1966.
— *Mycenae's Last Century of Greatness*, Sydney 1968.
Myres, J. L., *Who were the Greeks?*, Berkeley 1930.

SELECT BIBLIOGRAPHY 319

Nicholls, R., "Greek Votive Statuettes and Religious Continuity, c. 1200–700 B.C.", *AuckClEss.*
Nilsson, M. P., *The Mycenaean Origin of Greek Mythology* (Sather Class. Lect.) Berkeley 1932.
    Homer and Mycenae, London 1933.
    "Mycenaean and Homeric Religion", *A. R. W.* 33 (1936) 84.
    *The Minoan-Mycenaean Religion and its Survival in Greek Religion*², Lund 1950.
    Cults, Myths, Oracles and Politics in Ancient Greece, Lund 1951.
    "Das frühe Griechenland", *H.* 3 (1955) 257.
    *Geschichte der griechischen Religion*³, Munich 1967.
Numazawa, F. K., *Die Weltanfänge in der japanischen Mythologie*, Lucerne 1946.

Otten, H., *Die Religionen des alten Kleinasien* (Handbuch der Orientalistik viii, i, i) Leiden 1964.
Otto, E., *Die Religion der alten Ägypter* (Handbuch der Orientalistik iii, i, i) Leiden 1964.

Page, D. L., *History and the Homeric Iliad*, Berkeley 1959.
Palmer, L. R., *Achaeans and Indo-Europeans*, Oxford 1955.
    "New Religious Texts from Pylos", *T. Ph. Soc.* 6 (1958) 1.
    The Interpretation of Mycenaean Greek Texts, Oxford 1963.
    *Mycenaeans and Minoans*², London 1965.
Pendlebury, J. D. S., *Aegyptiaca*, Cambridge 1930.
    The Archaeology of Crete, London 1939.
Persson, A. W., *The Royal Tombs at Dendra near Midea*, Lund 1931.
    The Religion of Greece in Prehistoric Times (Sather Lect.), Berkeley 1942.
Pettazzoni, R., "Les deux sources de la religion grecque", *Mnem.* 4 (1951) 1.
    La Religione nella Grecia antica fino ad Alessandro, Turin 1953.
    Essays on the History of Religions, Leiden 1954.
Picard, Ch., *Les Religions Préhelléniques (Crète et Mycènes)*, Paris 1948.
Piggot, S. (ed.), *The Dawn of Civilization*, London 1961.
Platon, N., *K. Ch.* 5 (1951) 96.
Porzig, W., "Sprachgeographische Untersuchungen zu den altgriechischen Dialekten", *Ind. F.* 61 (1954) 147.
Pugliese Carratelli, G., "Aspetti e Problemi della Monarchia Micenea", *P. d. P.* 15 (1960) 401.
Puhvel, J., "Helladic Kingship and the Gods", *Minoica* 327.

Riemschneider, M., *Die Welt der Hethiter*, Stuttgart 1954.
Risch, E., "Die Gliederung der griechischen Dialekte in neuer Sicht", *M. H.* 12 (1955) 61.
    "Frühgeschichte der griechischen Sprache", *M. H.* 16 (1959) 215.
Rizza, G., Sant. Maria Scrinari, V., *Il Santuario sull'Acropoli di Gortina*, Rome 1968, I.

Sacconi, A., "Il Mito nel Mondo Miceneo", *P. d. P.* 15 (1960) 161.
Saggs, H. W. F., *The Greatness that was Babylon*, London 1962.
Sakellariou, M., *La migration grecque en Ionie*, Athens 1958.
Santerre, Gallet de, *Délos Primitive et Archaïque*, Paris 1958.

Schachermeyr, F., "Welche geschichtlichen Ereignisse führten zur Erstehung der Mykenischen Kultur?", *A. Or.* 17 (1949) 331.
Schachermeyr, F., *Die ältesten Kulturen Griechenlands*, Stuttgart 1955.
"Prähistorische Kulturen Griechenlands", *P.-W.* 22, 2.
Die minoische Kultur des alten Kreta, Stuttgart 1964.
Ägäis und Orient, Vienna 1967.
Schliemann, H., *Mykenae*, repr. Darmstadt 1964.
Séchan, L.-Lévèque, P., *Les Grandes Divinités de la Grèce*, Paris 1966.
Severyns, A., *Grèce et Proche-Orient avant Homère*, Brussels 1960.
Skeat, T. C., *The Dorians in Archaeology*, London 1934.
Snodgrass, A. M., "Barbarian Europe and Early Iron Age Greece", *ProcPS* 31 (1965) 229.
Starr, C., *The Origins of Greek Civilization*, New York 1962.
Staudacher, W., *Die Trennung von Himmel und Erde*, Tübingen 1942.
Steiner, G., *Der Sukzessionsmythos in Hesiods 'Theogonie' und ihren orientalischen Parallelen*, Diss. Hamburg 1958 (hard to get).
Stella, L. A., *Il Poema di Ulisse*, Florence 1955.
"La Religione Greca nei Testi Micenei", *N.* 5 (1958) 18.
La Civiltà Micenea nei Documenti Contemporanei, Rome 1965.
Stoll, H. A., *Schliemann und die Ausgrabung von Knossos, MinH*, 51.
Stubbings, F. A., "The Rise of Mycenaean Civilization", *C. A. H.*² II (1963).
"The Expansion of Mycenaean Civilization", *C. A. H.*² II (1964).
"The Recession of Mycenaean Civilization", *C. A. H.*² II (1965).
Styrenius, C. G., *Submycenaean Studies*, Lund 1967.

Taylour, Lord W., *The Mycenaeans*, London 1964.
The Sacral Kingship, VIII ConHRel.
Thomson, G., *Studies in Ancient Greek Society, The Prehistoric Aegean*², repr. London 1961.

Ucko, P. J., *Anthropomorphic Figurines*, London 1968.

Ventris, M.-Chadwick, J., *Documents in Mycenaean Greek*, Cambridge 1956.
Vermeule, E., "The Fall of the Mycenaean Empire", *Arch.* 13 (1960) 66.
"The Mycenaeans in Achaea", *A. J. A.* 64 (1960) 1; 63 (1959) 203; *Gn.* 35 (1963) 495.
"Götterkult", *Arch.Hom.* (1964).
"Mythology in Mycenaean Art", *C. J.* 54 (1959) 97.
Greece in the Bronze Age, Chicago 1964.

Wace, A. J. B., *Chamber Tombs at Mycenae*, London 1932.
Mycenae: An Archaeological History and Guide, Princeton 1949.
"The Last Days of Mycenae", *Aeg. N. E.* (1956).
Stubbings, F. H. (ed.) *A Companion to Homer*, London 1962.
Walcot, P., *Hesiod and the Near East*, Cardiff 1966.
Webster, T. B. L., *From Mycenae to Homer*², London 1964.
West, M. L., *Hesiod Theogony*, Oxford 1966.
Whitman, C., *Homer and the Heroic Tradition*, Cambridge Mass. 1958.
Widengren, G., *Sakrales Königtum im Alten Testament und im Judentum*, Stuttgart 1955.

Wiesner, J., *Grab und Jenseits (RGVV XXVI)*, Berlin 1938.
Olympos, Darmstadt 1960.
Willetts, R. F., *Cretan Cults and Festivals*, London 1962.
Witzel, P. M., *Tammuz-Liturgien und Verwandtes*, Rome 1935.

Yavis, C., *Greek Altars, Origin and Typology, including the Minoan-Mycenaean Offertory Apparatus* (Saint Louis University Studies Monograph Series: Humanities No. 1) (1949).

Zervos, C., *L'art de la Crete neolithic et minoenne* (Cahiers d'art) 1956.

I. INDEX OF NAMES

A'ash 50
Acarnanes 258
Achaea 212
Achaeans 69, 194 f., 197, 198, 218, 221, 222 n. 194
Achilles 65, 264, 310, 311
Achniadae 250, 253 n. 336
Adonis 11, 29
Aegean, neolithic 123
Aegina 213, 225, 226, 228, 268
Aeolians 196 f., 250
Aeolis 216
Aeschylus 58, 67 n. 315, 316, 308 n. 2
Aetolians 196
Aetos 217
Agamemnon 65, 135, 184 n. 297, 209
Ahhiyawa 22
Aigimios 197 n. 28 a
Akkad, Dynasty of 63
Akkadian 26 f.
Alalash 50
Alalu 53, 55, 61
Alcinous 47, 254
Alcmaeonidae 250
Alea, see Athena
Alectrycon 260 n. 379
Alexander 66
Altis 223
Amaltheia 109 n. 230, 171 f. n. 217
Amnisos 70, 110, 124, 216
– cave at 78 f., 81, 87 f., 111, 177, 185 n. 305, 220, 226, 228, 306

Amorites 44
Amyclae 18 f., 138, 154 f., 174 n. 227, 194, 215, 222 and n. 194, 223, 224, 233, 247, 309
Amyklaieis 258
Amyklaion 222 n. 194
An, Anu 27, 30, 31, 32, 49, 51, 53 ff., 56, 61
Anath 3, 45
Anatolia 12, 23, 59 n. 276, 72 f., 75, 84, 123, 165, 261 f. n. 384
– archaeology of 94
– cave cult 75, 93, 94 ff., 112, 120, 122
– cult implements 20, 96
– culture of 19
– figurines 20, 113
– frescoes 20, 95, 101 n. 178, 104, 119 f., 122, 126
– goddess 102 ff., 113, 116, 119
– kingship 34
– religion 72, 94, 98, 101
– shrines 95–107, 109, 112 n. 255, 114, 117, 122, 123 f.
Anavlochos 218
Annunaki 44
Anshar 51
Anthesteria 12, 168 n. 201
Antoninus 88 n. 95
Anush 50
Apesokari 92 n. 118 a
Aphaea 35, 65, 179, 226, 228, 244, 305
Aphrodite 11, 53, 154 n. 124
– *Ephippus* 119 n. 303

INDEX OF NAMES

– *Epitragia* 119 n. 303
– *Ourania* 85
– riding 119 n. 303
Aplomata 217 f. and n. 153
Apollo 19, 44, 65, 138, 139, 154, 186, 217, 222, 223, 224, 228, 231, 233, 240, 241, 264, 268 n. 416, 276, 280, 286
– at Delphi 308 f.
– Cretan connection of 309
– *Delphinios* 309
– Eastern origin of 309
– *Epikourios* 270
– *Hebdomaeus* 253 n. 336
– *Hyacinthus* 222, 307 n. 103
– *Maleatas* 155, 222
– oracular 308 f.
– *Paean* 176 n. 245
– *Parnopios* 301
– *Parrhasius* 270
– *Pythias* 270
– *Pythios* 309
– *Smintheus* 301 and n. 67
– *Wanax* 16
Apollodorus 58 and n. 270
Apsu 31, 33 n. 155, 51
Aqat, epic of 35
Arcadia 87, 196, 177 f., 199, 212, 247, 257, 269 f., 277
Ares 176 n. 245
Argo 39
Argolid 128, 130 f., 137, 147, 170, 196, 201, 202 f., 213 f., 232, 263, 268
Argonauts 215
Argos 43, 147, 207, 213, 313
Ariadne 35, 65, 69, 179, 305
Aristaeus 121
Aristodemus 196
Aristotle 248, 250, 267, 274 n. 438, 440
Arkades 218
Arkalokhori 84 f., 86, 88 f., 91
Arkhanes 142
Artemis 35, 44, 65, 66, 125, 139, 146 f., 154 and n. 126, 156, 158, 176, 178 ff., 217, 218, 227, 228, 233, 235, 236, 238, 240, 244, 252, 260, 280, 286, 300, 304, 309
– *Aphaea* 154, 157, 226

– armed 84
– Brauronian 267, 268
– connected with birth 88
– *Hyakinthotrophos* 174 n. 227
– *Eileithyia* 87 f.
– Ephesian 96, 120
– in cave cult 86
– *Kallisto* 118
– *Lochia* 87 f.
– on Linear tablets 172 n. 218
– *Orthia* 220, 281 n. 469, 283
– *Potnia* 181 ff.
– temple of 139
– with animals 103
– zoomorphic 117
Ashur 27, 30, 43, 49, 61
Asine 133, 135, 137, 147 f., 149 ff., 170, 213 f.
Assyria 30, 45, 49
– art of 278 ff.
– epic 47
– history of 32
– kingship 34
Astarte 53
Athena 35, 38, 39, 43 n. 198, 44, 51, 66, 68, 76, 138, 146 f., 154, 155 f., 158, 171, 176, 178 ff., 187, 227 f., 230, 233, 235, 236, 238, 240, 246, 252, 260, 266, 280, 286, 309
– *Alea* 154, 157
– city goddess 43, 244, 247
– *Cydonia* 245
– fostered nature god 18
– guardian of palace 65, 188, 278
– *Gygnia* 245
– *Itonia* 157
– *Kranaia* 222
– *Lindia* 245, 313
– *Magarsia* 245
– Mother 179 n. 261
– *Oleria* 245
– *Polias* 244, 247, 267 f.
– *Potnia* 181 ff.
– protectress 175 n. 241, 188, 247
– *Samonia* 245
– warlike 151

INDEX OF NAMES

Athens 43, 90, 128, 174, 193, 194, 212 f., 227, 229, 230, 243, 246, 265, 267, 268, 270 f., 274, 276, 287 f. n. 513
- cult of nature god in 18
- goddess figurine at 210

Atherat 33
Atlas 52
Attica 130, 139, 177 n. 249, 196, 201, 205, 207, 210, 212 f., 227, 248, 251, 266 f., 274
Attis 11
Autochthon 52
Ayios Andreas 215
Ayios Elias 215

Baal 31, 44 f.
Babel 45
Babylon, Babylonia 26 f., 29, 30, 58 n. 273, 61, 312 n. 18
- art of 78 ff.
- city-state 34
- cults of 35
Babylon, Babylonia
- culture of 26
- epic 47, 56, 57 n. 258, 66
- First Dynasty of 27, 49
- history of 32
- gods of 176 n. 244
- king-list 29
- kingship 34
- mythology of 49, 60
- religion of 35, 54
Baitylos 52
Bassae 270
Battos 254, 264
Bel 61
Bellerophon 192, 279, 312
Berbati 147, 148, 203
Beruth 52
Beycesultan 100 n. 172
Boeotia 150, 210, 214, 250
Bogazhkeuy 46, 50
- palace 40
- tablets 34 n. 160, 46, 53, 60 n. 284, 65 n. 303
Boutadae 250
Brauron 267, 270, 275 n. 443

Britomartis 35, 65, 157, 179, 182 n. 281
Buzygae 257 n. 358, 266

Cadmus 22
Callimachus 16, 85 n. 72
Canaan 29, 31, 44
- pantheon 35
Candia 213, 312
Cassites 27
Castalia 223
Çatal Hüyük 9, 11, 19, 21 n. 106, 72, 93, 94–107, 109, 110, 112, 116, 119, 122, 123 f., 125 f., 165, 173, 302
- pantheon 102 f. n. 185
Chalandritsa 212
Chaos 50
Chimaira 279
Chios 216, 229
Chrysolakkos 120
Cilicia 58
Cleisthenes 248, 267, 272 n. 429
Clytidae 250
Codrus 196
Colonus Hippius 90
Corinth 150, 193, 214, 232, 268 and n. 416, 273, 276
Corinthia 214
Cresphontes 196
Crete 6, 8, 12, 16, 69 ff., 75, 131, 220 f., 290, 293, 296, 309
- contacts with East 9, 20, 47, 59, 61, 72, 74 f., 112, 124, 138, 150, 210, 228, 281
Crete
- Dorians in 194, 196, 250, 262 f.
- invasion of 203
- politics of 306 f.
Cybele 11
Cyclades 75, 113
Cyclopes 50
Cydonians 69
Cyprus 23, 131, 208, 210, 220, 245
- language 200
- jewellery 208 n. 84 a
Cyzicus 286

Daedalus 69
Dagon 52, 59, 63

INDEX OF NAMES

Daktyloi 186
Damateres 287
Danaus 22, 313
Danel, epic of 34
Daphnephoria 61
Dekeleies 251 n. 327
Delos 87, 139, 140, 142, 144, 160, 218, 225, 226, 233, 276, 287
Delphi 55, 102 n. 184, 120 n. 313, 138, 155 f., 215, 223 f., 226, 227 f., 233, 243, 275, 276, 308 f.
Demarus 52, 53, 55 f.
Demeter 11 f., 41, 120, 142 n. 52, 146, 189, 227, 235, 240, 252, 267, 269, 272, 273 ff., 277 f., 286 f.
– Arcadian 118
– at Athens 268
– at Eleusis 18, 141 f., 190, 274 ff., 287 and n. 513
– Boeotian 118
– etymology of 240
– in cave cult 86
– on Linear tablets 172 n. 218, 176 n. 245
– *Potnia* 181
– with animals 103
– zoomorphic 117
Demotionidae 253 n. 336
Dendra-Midea 119 n. 301, 213 f., 214 n. 120, 310, 312
Despoina 269
Despoinae 286
Deukalion 66, 194, 263
Dhimini 19
Dictaean Cave 218
Dictynna 35, 65, 157, 179, 182 n. 281, 305
Diktynnaion 78
Diomede 39, 192
Dionysus 14, 168 n. 201, 173 f., 175 n. 239, 176, 226, 235, 238, 272, 273, 275 f., 278, 286, 309 n. 13
– as bull 116 f., 238 n. 266
– *Eleuthereus* 274
– origin of 116 f.
Dioscuroi 17, 168 n. 201, 171 n. 215, 175 n. 241, 185 ff.
– as children 187 ff.

Dioscuroi
– as house gods 187 and n. 322, 188
– as saviours 187 f. and n. 324
– etymology of 187
Dipylon 220
Diwia 176 f. n. 246
Dodona 227, 263 and n. 394, 264 n. 399
Dorians 69, 193 f., 197, 202 ff., 209, 218, 222 n. 194, 228 f., 250, 258 n. 369, 261, 263 f., 282
– cult of 230, 277
– gods of 230
– invasion by 169 ff., 200, 204, 207, 229, 230, 246, 277, 310
– tribes of 69, 197, 246, 249 f., 251 n. 325, 259, 261 ff.
Dorus 263
Draco, Law of 251 n. 329, 270 f.
Dreros 145
Dyaus Pitar 241
Dymanes 249, 258 n. 369

Ea, Enki 30, 33 n. 155, 49, 50 f., 53 n. 238, 54, 177 n. 250
Egypt 72, 113, 123, 159 ff., 281, 313 and n. 21
– architecture of 232
– art of 276 f.
– scarabs 292 n. 15
– script 302
Eileithyia 87, 109, 110, 124, 141, 176, 178 ff., 228, 235, 236, 244, 305
– as goddess of birth 87 and n. 86, 88
– as goddess of healing 87 n. 88
– cave of 78, 81, 87, 111, 177, 185 n. 305, 220
– votives of 87 n. 89
El 47 n. 218, 51, 52 f., 55, 62 f., 64 n. 304
El Amarna 27
Elateia 222
Eleusinium 267
Eleusis 139, 140 ff., 149, 175, 206, 212, 213, 223, 224 f., 226, 231, 233, 247, 260, 267 and n. 414, 274 f., 287 f. and n. 513
– cult 18, 167

INDEX OF NAMES 325

– Mysteries 18, 41, 66 n. 311, 141 f., 167, 252, 267 f., 269 n. 419, 270, 274 f., 287 f. n. 513
Elis 117 n. 284, 196, 201, 215, 257
Eliun (Hypsistos) 52, 55
Ellilush 50
Elysium 66 n. 313, 160, 310, see also Isle of the Blest
Emporio 229
En 32
Enki, see Ea
Enkomi 217 n. 145
Enlil 28, 29, 32, 33 n. 155, 49, 63
Enuma Elish 33 n. 155, 44, 50 f., 55 f., 59 n. 279, 63, see also creation epic (Index II)
Enyalios 176 n. 245
Epano Zakro 292 f.
Ephesus 216, 127, 225, 228
Epidaurus 154, 222, 226, 309·
Epigeios 52
Epirus 263, 264 n. 399
Episkopi 116 n. 279
Era, epic of 57 n. 258
Erebos 50
Erech 32 and n. 152
– cult at 31
– gods of 30
– period 29
Erechtheus, Erichthonius 14, 18, 174, 230
Eridu 30
Erinys 62, 168, 176, 190
Eros 50, 58
Esagila 33 n. 155
Etana, epic of 31
Eteobutadae 247, 266
Eubouleus 287 f. n. 513
Eumenides 190
Eumolpidae 252
Eunomia 58 n. 273
Euripides 227, 308 n. 2
Europa 16, 119 n. 303, 310, 312
Eurystheus 135, 213
Eusebius 51, 53, 54 n. 245
Eutresis 2, 201

Fortetsa 280

Gaia 8, 14, 16, 18, 50 f., 57, 308 f. and n. 2
Galaxidi 215
Galinthias 301 n. 67
Gazi 144, 146, 150, 170
Ge, see Gaia
Gilgamesh 279
– epic of 32, 47, 48, 66 f.
Gla 201
Glaukos 120 n. 310, 186 n. 314, 192
Gortyn 70, 147, 152, 175 n. 241, 216, 218 ff., 222 n. 194, 226, 281 n. 469, 282–286
– coins of 116, 173
– goddess figurine 210, 218, 280, 282 ff.
– inscriptions 16
Gournia 143, 145, 173 n. 223, 306
– burial at 79
– temple of 76
Greece 12, 143, 150, 210, 221, 296
– cave cult in 93
– contact with East 20, 265, 278 ff.
– invasion of 193, 195 ff., 200, 202 ff., 261 f. n. 384
Greeks 2, 16, 66 f., 131
– art of 278 f.
– dialects of 197 ff.
– epic of 43, 45, 56 ff.
Greeks
– gods of 42, 44
– migration of 2, 198 ff.
– myth of 71, 81, 114, 116, 191, 305, 310–314
Grotta 217, 218 n. 153
Gudea 29
Gypsadhes 294

Hacilar 9, 11, 19, 21 n. 106, 72, 97 n. 157, 98, 113 n. 262, 123
Hadad 31, 44
Hades 90, 167 n. 198
Hagia Eirene 140, 142, 152, 210, 218, 221, 226
Hagia Kyriaki 154
Hagia Pelagia 312
Hagia Triada 15, 97 n. 154, 142 n. 56, 175 n. 236, 220, 280, 312

- figurines 218, 284
- sarcophagus 41, 97 n. 153, 100, 116 n. 279, 133, 158 f., 161, 164, 281, 284, 294
- sealings 119 n. 301
- temple 76, 233
Halikarnassos 217
Hammurabi 31
Hekate 181
Hekatoncheires 50
Helen 65, 175 n. 241, 186, 222
Helios 268
Hellanes 258
Hellen 263
Hellenospelio 78
Hephaestus 42, 44, 176 n. 245
Hera 43, 44, 55 n. 251, 59 n. 276, 64, 65, 66, 146, 175 n. 239, 176, 178 ff., 189, 225, 228, 235, 236, 238, 240 and n. 273, 278, 280, 286
- etymology of 179 n. 267
- *Polias* 267 f.
Heracleidae 193, 197, 199, 262 f.
Heracles 39, 135, 196, 197, 202, 209, 230, 249 n. 313, 262, 284, 301 n. 67
Heraion 223, 231, 232
Herakleion 70, 144
Hermes 65, 176, 177 f., 235, 238 and n. 268, 240 and n. 273
- *Anax* 178
- chthonic 178
- *Cyllenius* 178 n. 254
- in cave cult 87, 178
- *Kranaios* 80 and n. 50, 87, 111
- *Psychopompos* 178 n. 254
Hermione 196
Herodotus 55, 263, 277
Hesiod 14, 44, 47 n. 221, 48 n. 224, 67 n. 315, 88
- *Theogony* 48, 50 f., 52 f., 54, 56 f., 57 n. 258, 58, 61, 62 n. 290
Hesperides, Gardens of 310
Hestia 241
Hesychidae 252
Hesychius 52, 255 and n. 349
Hierapetra 79
Hippeia 182

Hippias 266
Hippos 176 n. 246
Hittites 4, 25, 27, 31, 46, 256
- culture of 34
- epic 46 f.
- gods of 176 n. 244
- legend of 54
- script 302
- texts of 50, 68, 195
- Weather-god of 45, 60 f., 120
Homer, Homeric epic 2, 7, 43, 45, 46 ff., 61, 66, 78, 89, 128, 135, 153, 160, 161, 166, 177, 182 n. 281, 184 n. 297, 185, 189, 195, 226, 229, 237, 238 n. 266, 245, 251, 253, 255 n. 346, 257 n. 357, 258, 260, 262 f., 264, 268, 274, 308, 311, 312, 313
- Catalogue 250, 262 f.
- divine genealogy in 7, 52 n. 233, 55
- Hymn 141 f., 309 and n. 11
Humbaba 279
Hurrians 25, 27, 46
- epic 47, 56 f., 61
- mythology of 49, 62
- texts of 55
- theogony of 52, 53 ff., 63
- Weather-god of 45
Hyacinthus 14, 18 f., 19 n. 96, 154, 174
Hylleis 249
Hyllus 197
Hyperborean Maidens 160

Ialysos 313
Iasos 217
Iliad 67, 185, 192, 259
Illuyanka 58 n. 270
Imbrasos river 225
Innin 29, 31
Iolkos 194, 201, 215
Ionians 196 ff., 225, 250
- communities of 250, 251 n. 325, 262
Iphimedeia 176 f. n. 246
Ishtar 11, 29
- associated with Hadad 31
- temples of 26
Isopata 284
Isthmia 214

INDEX OF NAMES

Itea 215
Ithaka 217, 254 and n. 342
Itonos 157

Jasion 12, 41
Jason 39

Kabiroi 185, 187 n. 317
Kalokhorio 151, 221
Kamares 81, 85 f.
Kaphirio 215
Karphi 135, 137, 144 n. 68, 145, 170, 216, 218, 219 n. 164, 232 n. 241, 285, 293, 297, 307 and n. 104
Kastellos 79, 112 n. 253
Kato Englianos 215
Kato Zakro 70, 100 n. 176, 294, 295, 300
Katsamba 144
Kavousi 218, 219
Kefala 143
Keos 36, 139, 140, 142, 152, 218, 221, 225, 226, 233
Kephallenia 217
Kerameikos 205 and n. 58, 206, 212 f., 234 n. 254, 313
Keret, epic of 33, 34, 35, 46, 47
Kerykes 257 n. 358
Khaniale Tekke 142
Khosto Nero 112 n. 253, 297
Kingu 31, 51, 52, 56
Klaros 217
Knossos 6, 16, 36, 38, 61, 69 ff., 89, 91 n. 112, 94, 110 and n. 240, 111, 130, 135, 142, 171 f. n. 217, 175 n. 238, 176, 182, 207, 291, 294, 295, 299 n. 58, 303, 305, 309
– Central Palace Sanctuary 118
– Double Axe Shrine 113, 143, 147, 148
– Little Palace 92, 110, 112, 113, 124
– Pillar Basement 302
– sacred cave 82
– Spring Chamber 137, 145, 170, 216, 280
– tablets 132, 135 n. 16, 176 n. 244, 177, 183, 192, 311
– Temple Repositories 119 n. 301
– Temple Tomb 158, 159 n. 157
– Throne Room 37, 40

Kokkinochomata 215
Kolonna 154 n. 124, 157 n. 152
Kolophon 216, 217
Kophinas 293
Kore 267, 269, 274
Korybantes 85, 186
Kos 216
Koutsochira 215
Krisa 201
Kronion 223
Kronos 14, 16, 50, 51, 52, 55, 56 ff., 62 ff.
– cult of 64 n. 304
Kumarbi 53, 55 ff., 62, 64
– epic 45, 50, 53 ff., 61 ff.
Kouretes 15, 85, 88 f., 186, 187 n. 317 f.
Kusor 53
Kyparissia 139

Labarna 34 n. 160
Labyadae 250
Laconia 215
Lagash 29, 30
Lasithi 78, 79, 297
Lato 87
Lebadeia 308 n. 5
Lefkandi 207
Lemnos 210
Lerna 203
Lesbos 216, 286
Leto 139 and n. 36, 253 n. 336
Leukas 207, 263
Lindos 287
Lychnospelaion 93, see also Parnes
Lycomidae 252
Lycosoura 269
Lyttos 70, 80

Magasa 79
Mallia 70, 120, 306
Malthi 147, 148, 215 and n. 127
Marathon 80 f. n. 52, 108 n. 226, 130, 213, 175 n. 443
Marduk 27, 30, 32, 33 n. 155, 35, 43, 44, 49, 51, 56, 59 n. 279, 61 f.
Marmaria 155 n. 135, 156, 224, 233
Mavro Spelio 110, 162 n. 174, 173 n. 223
– Sacred Spring 76

INDEX OF NAMES

Maza 293
Medeon 207, 215
Megalopolis 269 f.
Megara 273
Melidoni 87
Melos 196
Menelaion 201
Menelaus 41
Mesara 145, 162
Meskine 79
Mesopotamia 23, 25, 28 f., 31, 45, 96 n. 141
– art of 43 n. 198
– city in 64
– gods of 30, 36, 63
– kingship 33 and n. 155, 34, 41, 46
Messenia 139, 196, 215
Miamou 79
Miletus 216, 217, 228, 286
Minos 38, 61, 69, 89, 120 n. 310
– Ring of 91 n. 112
Mirabello, gulf of 145
Mitanni 27
Mitropolis 144
Mitylene 273
Mochlos 101 n. 178
Modhi 293
Moirae 178 n. 254, 190
Molione 313
Molionides Twins 313
Molos 313 n. 23
Mons Casius 45, 58
Mother Earth 88, 109, 305
Mouriatadha 139
Mt. Cyllene 87, 178
Mt. Cynthus 93
Mt. Dikte 16, 297 n. 48
Mt. Hazzi 45, 58
Mt. Ida 16, 70, 80, 81, 85 and n. 72, 297 n. 48
– cave 85, 86, 91 n. 111, 108 and n. 226, 111 n. 248, 112 n. 253, 298
Mt. Jouktas 16, 82, 112 n. 253, 290 ff., 294, 299 f., 303, 305
Mt. Lycaion 270
Mt. Saphon 45
Mursilis I 27

Mycenae 36, 110 n. 240, 130, 150, 151, 193, 201, 210, 213 f., 227
– Chamber Tomb 76
– Clytemnestra's Tomb 119 n. 301
– destruction of 194
– gems 138, 302 n. 74
– Lion Gate 40
– Lion Tomb 164
– Shaft Graves 22, 99, 120, 121, 136, 158 f., 161, 164, 165 n. 186, 166, 206
– tablets 132
– temples 37
Myrtos 36

Naram-Sin 34
Nauplion 213 f.
Naxos 87, 217
Nebuchadnezzar II 29
Neleus 196
Nemesis 181
Nestor 247, 251 n. 325 and n. 326, 262, 313
– Ring of 97 n. 153, 121 and n. 315
Nichoria 215
Night 308 n. 2
Ningirsu 30
Ninhursag 31
Nippur 28, 29, 31
Nonnus 58
Nyx 50

Oceanus 55 and n. 251
Odysseus 39, 47, 67, 69, 254 and n. 342
Odyssey 185, 263
Olympia 64, 223, 255 n. 346
– oracle 223, 227, 301, 308 n. 5
Olympus 45, 189, 239
Orchomenus 214
Oresteia 272
Orestes 196
Orthia 175 n. 239
Osiris 11, 15

Paean 176 n. 245
Paiania 275 n. 443
Pakija 258 f.
Pakijanes 138, 183 n. 289, 258

INDEX OF NAMES

Palaeocastro 212
Palaikastro 291, 297, 307
Palestine 283, 297 n. 46
Pamphyli 249
Pan 269
- cave of 80 n. 52, 86, 93, 130
- *Sinoeis* 269
- *Skoleitas* 269
Pankalokhori 144 n. 70
Parnes 93, 135
Paros 87 and n. 88
Patroclus 311
Patso 80, 87, 91 n. 110, 108 n. 226, 111, 112 n. 253, 115 n. 272, 171 n. 217, 219
Pediadha Plain 151, 221
Pegasus 279, 280
Peisistratus 64, 225, 140, 267, 273 f., 275 and n. 445, 276
Peloponnese 128 f., 131, 193 f., 196, 211
Perachora 220, 231
Pericles 272 n. 429
Peristeria 120 n. 313
Persephone 287 f. n. 513
Perseus 197, 279
Petsophas 290 ff., 296 f., 299, 301 f., 305
Phaistos 70, 88 n. 92, 101 n. 178, 116, 173, 216, 219, 221, 302
Phaneromeni 80, 82, 112 n. 253
Pharae 93
Philioremos 293
Philistines 300
Philo 50, 51 ff., 57 n. 261, 63
Philochorus, Law of 272
Phocis 201, 215
Phrygia 116 n. 283
Phytalidae 252
Phytalos 177 n. 249
Pindar 58, 67 n. 316
Plato 89
Plutarch 61
Pluto 167 n. 198
Pluton 287 f. n. 513
Plutos 287 f. n. 513
Plutus 14, 18
Poimenidae 252
Polis 217 and n. 150

Polycrates 273
Pontos 50, 52, 53
Poseidon 44, 65, 115 n. 271, 176 f., 228, 235, 236, 238, 246 f., 252, 259, 260, 266, 268
- as bull 238 n. 268
- chthonic 185 and n. 305
- *Enesidaon* 177, 185 n. 305, 220 f.
- etymology of 240
Pothos 58 n. 271
Potnia 34, 42, 142, 167, 169, 170, 172, 177, 180 ff., 189 f., 236, 238, 281, 287 f. n. 513, 300 f., 304, 305
Potniae 286 f.
Praesus 79, 218
Praxiergidae 266
Prinias 137, 145, 154 n. 126, 156, 219
Proitos 192
Prostovitsa 212
Psychro 80, 82 ff., 85 n. 69 and n. 72, 86, 89 n. 99, 90, 91, 108 n. 226, 109 n. 234, 111, 112 n. 253, 115 n. 272 f., 171 n. 216 f., 298
Pylos 36, 116 n. 283, 138, 150, 164, 176 n. 243, 177, 183 ff., 207, 236, 247, 253 ff., 257, 258, 268, 281, 313
- destruction of 194, 201
- ring 295 f.
- tablets 132, 135 and n. 16, 168 n. 201, 176 n. 244, 177, 182 f., 192, 253 ff., 258, 260, 281, 311
- throne 40
Pyrgos 77, 79 f., 90, 109 n. 232, 163, 299 n. 56
Pytho 264

Ras Shamra 23, 33, 34, 35, 48, 55
- texts 22, 29, 35, 44, 45, 51, 54 n. 245
- tombs 23
Resheph 31
Rhadamanthys 41
Rhea 14, 16, 50, 146
Rhodes 131, 144, 194, 207, 210, 216, 255, 262 f., 283, 284 f., 287, 313

Salamis 205, 206, 213, 214 n. 121
Samos 210, 216, 225, 228, 232, 273, 286

INDEX OF NAMES

Samothrace 286, 287
— Mysteries 187 n. 324
Sanchuniathon 50
Saphon 57 n. 262
Scheria 299, 254
Sea Peoples 282
Semele 117 n. 285, 120 n. 311
Semnae 90, 190, 252, 286
Sesklo 11, 19, 21 n. 106
Shamash 31
Siduri 66
Sin 31
Skaphidia 79
Skirophoria 96 n. 148
Skoteino 82
Solon 67 n. 315, 267 n. 414, 272 n. 429
Souvloto Mouri 293
Sparta 154, 188, 220, 222, 232, 258, 287
— goddess figurine 210, 283, 284 f.
— royal family of 196, 202
Spata 312
Sumeria 25, 48
— art of 48
— city-state 28
— culture of 25
— epic 47, 49, 58 n. 273
— gods of 25, 26 f., 43, 63
— king 32
— mythology of 28, 30, 49, 56, 60
— sculpture 26
— seals 26
— *temen* 41 n. 189
— temples of 26, 28 f.
— theogony 57 n. 258
— writing 26 f., 48
Syria 31, 34, 44 f., 58, 63, 72, 97 n. 153, 124, 283, 310, 313 n. 21
— king 41

Tammuz 11, 15, 29, 34
Tarsus 217 n. 145
Tartarus 50
Taurus 23
— Mountains 106, 108
Tegea 154, 156, 222
Teisamenos 196

Telemachus 39, 254 n. 342
Telepinu 60 and n. 284, 120
Temenos 196, 202
Tenos 87
Teshub 31, 45, 53 n. 241, 54, 56 ff.
Tethys 55
Theagenes 273
Thebes 214 and n. 121, 280
Themis 181, 308 and n. 2
Thera 196
Thermos 222, 231
Theseus 310
Thesmophoria 96 n. 148
Thespiae 117 n. 284, 173 n. 223
Thessalians 196, 250
Thessalus 197
Thessaly 131, 142 n. 52, 201 f., 215, 263
Thrace 142 n. 52
Tiamat 31, 51, 53 n. 238, 55 f., 59 n. 279, 62
Tilphossion 90
Tiryns 38, 193, 194, 213 f., 227
Titans 50, 51, 55 n. 251
Tlepolemus 197, 262
Tragana 215
Traostalos 293
Trapeza 79
Triptolemus 287 f. n. 513
Trophonius 120 n. 309, 308 n. 5
Troy 4, 6, 9, 26, 192, 195, 196 n. 18, 197, 201, 207, 209, 263
Tsoutsouros 87 n. 86
Tydeus 39
Tylissos 82, 144, 108 n. 226, 112 n. 253 and n. 254, 175 n. 238, 306
Typhon 51, 53, 56 ff., 58 n. 270
Tyrtaios 249

Udum 46
Ugarit see Ras Shamra
Ullikummi 45, 52, 53 ff., 56 ff.
Upelluri 54, 56
Ur 45
— Third Dynasty of 29, 31
Uranus 50, 51, 52, 53, 55 f., 58 f., 62 and n. 293, 64
Uruk see Erech
Utanapishtim 66

Vasilike 36
Vathypetro 296 and n. 44
Velchanos 15 f., 88 n. 92, 239 see also Zeus
Velchania 16
Vrokastro 218, 219

Yahweh 31
Yamm 52 n. 236, 53

Zeus 6, 14, 35, 43, 44, 50, 55 ff., 58 f., 61, 65, 67 n. 316, 68, 85, 135, 151, 175 n. 239, 176, 177, 187 n. 318, 188, 225, 235, 238, 241, 243 n. 291, 246, 252, 264, 265 n. 404, 266, 286, 307
– *Apomyios* 301
– *Arotrios* 63
– as bull 119 n. 303, 173
– as snake 189
– at Dodona 264 n. 399
– birth of in cave 14 f., 16 f., 85 and n. 72, 87, 88, 109, 120, 125, 178, 239

– cave of 61, 80 f., 81, 88 f., 108, 111 n. 248, 112 n. 253
– childhood of 85, 88
– chthonic 239
– cult of 86, 236
– death of 16 f., 88 n. 95, 239, 303
– *Dictaeus* 177
– *Karios* 266 n. 408
– *Kretagenes* 14, 17, 19, 59, 64, 66, 88 n. 92, 174, 186 n. 314, 239, 303
– *Ktesios* 171 n. 215, 188, 189 n. 334, 239
– *Lycaeus* 270
– *Meilichios* 189, 239
– Olympian 239
– oracle of 223
– *Philios* 188, 270
– *Polieus* 245 n. 299, 267 f.
– *Siton* 63
– Sky-god 239, 241
– *Velchanos* 15, 88 n. 92, 173, 239
Zygouries 201

II. SUBJECT INDEX

adelphos 250
aesymnetes 273
after-life 77, 122, 160 ff., 166, 275
agora 264
agrimi 302
altar 76, 81, 84, 91 n. 111, 136, 233, 266, 295
– portable 294
amphictyonies 243, 248
anak(t)es 186 ff., 236, 284, 287 f.
anassa 176
anax heros 177 n. 249
ancestor 259, 272
– clan 260
anchisteia 261 n. 383
aniconic symbols 74, 92
– cult 84
– figurines 92, 106, 107, 111 f., 113

animals 301 and n. 67, 302 f., 304
– cult of 301 n. 67
apotropaeic cult 300 f. and n. 67, 302 f., 306
apotropaeic sign 97 n. 157
aristocracy 229 f., 248, 249, 251 n. 326, 252, 259, 260, 264, 265, 271 ff., 277
Artemision 218

baityl 52, 55, 92, 308 f.
Bandkeramik 21 n. 106
basileus 32 n. 152, 38, 39 and n. 185, 65, 184 and n. 297, 229, 230, 248, 252, 258, 259, 260, 262, 264, 265 and n. 404, 266, 271, 278
– *archon* 266
bebek 106
bee 104 f., 109 n. 230, 119 ff.

SUBJECT INDEX

beetles 292 n. 15
bird 83, 91, 97 n. 153, 118 and n. 298, 144, 146, 235, 237, 285, 292, 298, 299, 305
- of death 105, 171 f., 178
birth 88, 102 ff., 107, 126, 143, 165, 171, 136, 244, 275, 285, 304, 306
bitch 109 n. 230
blood-guilt 251, 271
boar 96, 99, 104 f.
- Shrine 107
bone 96, 105, 302
- tools 108 n. 227
boopis 43 n. 198, 178 n. 257
bough 298
boule 264
breast 96, 104 f.
bucrania 81, 83, 100, 110, 111 n. 244, 114 n. 263, 171 n. 217, 182
bull 76, 101 and n. 178, 103, 114 ff., 117 and n. 288, 119 and n. 303, 165, 173, 235, 237, 302, 310, 312
- Anatolian 99, 104 f., 116
- as Divine Child 116, 125, 182
- chthonic 116
- connected with birth 117
- connected with death 117
- connected with double axe 114 and n. 267
- connected with nature goddess 76, 110, 116 f., 118, 124 f., 171 and n. 217, 175 n. 238, 182 f., 221
- connected with Poseidon 115 n. 271
- divine power of 100
- figurines 111, 115 n. 272, 148, 150, 154 f., 163, 210, 218 f., 220, 221
- games 74
- god 114 and n. 265, 178 n. 257
- in cave sanctuaries 111, 117, 182
- in palace 114
- sacrificial 116
- worship of 100
burial 104, 105 f., 109 n. 234, 124, 158 ff., 166
- in honey 120
- multiple 163 f., 205, 206
- on mountain peaks 297

- pithos 163 f.
- secondary 104, 165
- single 205, 206 f.
butterfly 104, 119 ff., 165 n. 187, 166

cat 302
cave 76 ff., 124, 297 ff., 305. see also topographical names of caves.
- burial in 77 ff., 89 f., 93, 163
- connected with birth 88, 109 f., 117
- connected with death 106 f., 109 f.
cult 75, 77 ff., 81, 84, 86 ff., 90 ff., 94 ff., 98 n. 161, 106, 108 f., 109 n. 234, 110, 111, 113, 114, 122, 124 f., 126 f., 135 f., 165, 167, 169, 171 n. 217, 173, 183, 237 n. 263, 287, 296 f., 298 f., 302, 303, 304, 305 f.
- divinities of 77, 81, 85, 86, 88, 90 f., 170 f., 182, 287
- entrance to underworld 90, 106, 167 n. 198
- habitation in 93, 108
- offerings in 77, 81, 82, 84 ff., 90 f., 221
- of Zeus 61, 81, 120, 177, 188
- sanctity of 81
- sanctuaries 76, 111, 113, 114, 135, 173, 237
- transference of cult from 92, 94, 105 ff., 110, 124, 125, 126, 165, 183, 304
- votives in 91, 218 f.
chamber tomb 164, 206 f.
charnel house 122
child-birth 31
chronology 2, 70, 131 f., 196
- of Linear tablets 169 n. 204
chrysalis 104 f., 119 ff., 166
cist graves 3, 205, 206 ff., 214 n. 121
city-state 28, 31, 32, 35, 36, 40, 41, 42, 60, 64, 65 f., 244, 268
- Babylonian 33
clan 242, 246, 248, 250, 251, 258, 260 f., 265 ff., 271
- Neleid 313
comes 259
community
- Bronze Age 253 ff., 261, 277

- cult of 252, 265
- Dark Age 231, 242–266
- gods 265 ff., 277
- king of 266
- land of 254 f.
- matrilineal 253
- names 258
- patrilineal 253
- Pylian 255
- religious structure of 247 f.
- sacral rights of 255
- totemistic 253

continuity of cult 80, 81, 146, 153 ff., 157, 174, 175 n. 241, 209, 210 f., 218 ff., 222 ff., 227 ff., 235, 260, 273, 278, 287, 304, 307 n. 102
- Amyclae 154, 222 f.
- Anatolian 96 n. 141
- Athens 227
- cave 86, 93, 298 and n. 49, 304
- community 245, 260
- Delos 139, 218, 226
- Delphi 155 f., 222 ff.
- Didyma 217
- Eileithyia 88
- Elateia 222
- Eleusis 141 and n. 46, 222, 224 f., 274 f., 287 f. n. 513
- Ephesus 217, 218
- Epidaurus 154 f., 222
- Gortyn 219, 282 ff.
- Karphi 145, 218
- Keos 140, 218, 226
- Klaros 217, 218
- Kumasa 307
- Mesopotamian 96 n. 141
- Mycenae 227
- Olympia 222
- Prinias 145
- Samos 225
- Tegea 222
- Therapnae 222
- Thermos 222
- Tiryns 227

continuity of settlement 212–219

Corinthian style 280
cow 109 n. 230, 148, 178
- goddess 178 n. 257
creation
- epic of 30
- myth of 31, 33 n. 155, 50 ff., 60 f., 63 f.
cremation 7, 207 f.
cult, see under religion, Mycenaean, Minoan, shrines, palace etc.
cuneiform script 26

daemon 97 n. 153, 118, 190, 277
- of Winds 176
damokoro 257
damos 41 n. 189, 255, 256, 257 ff.
Dark Age 66 n. 312, 192 ff.
dead 121
- cult of 75, 79, 90, 97 n. 153, 100, 102, 104, 116, 120, 121, 124, 158 ff., 281
- *eidolon* of 122
- offerings to 79, 158, 162
- soul of 121 f.
demarchos 229
demes 248, 251 n. 328
demos 248, 255, 258, 264
demotes 256
Dike 58 n. 273, 67 and n. 315
disk 285
divine
- functions, division of 22, 143, 152, 167 ff., 179, 181 f., 236 ff., 285 ff., 305 f.
- pair 286 f.
- society 36, 42, 44, 64, 66 n. 312
- trinity 30 f., 284 ff.
Divine Child 14 ff., 41, 88 f., 109, 116, 167 n. 198, 171 f. n. 217, 172 ff., 177, 188, 239
divine consort 32, 88, 109, 116, 118, 119 n. 303, 124 f., 172 ff., 182 ff., 287 f. n. 513, 304, 305. See also paredros
divine dynasty 21, 43, 48, 49 f., 54 ff., 58, 59 f., 61 f.
divine power 97
- of animals 102
- of bull 100, 114
dokana 188

SUBJECT INDEX

dospotai 261
double axe 37, 74, 81, 82, 83, 84, 85, 91, 101 n. 178, 114 and n. 267, 143, 148, 294, 302
– shrine 113
dove 102
dragon 312 n. 18
drepanon 50, 62
dress-pins 208 f.

ears 97
Earth 49, 117 n. 285, 177, 308 n. 2. see also Gaia (Index I), Heaven, Mother Earth (Index I)
earthquake 306 f. and n. 96
emasculation
– motif of 53, 56, 62 f.
ensi 32 n. 152
epic 36, 311
– composition 262. see also Mycenaean
epiphany 83, 91, 119 n. 303, 152, 171, 236, 237, 284 f., 295, 298, 303, 305
eqeta 259 f.
Erechtheum 266
eta 255 n. 343
etas 256, 257 and n. 357
etes 255 n. 343
etonijo 255 n. 346
eyes 97

family 252, 265 f., 271
fertility 4, 8, 11, 20, 96, 102, 271, 274
– chthonic cult of 22, 28, 32, 62, 90, 105 f.
– daemons of 89
fibulae 208 f.
fish 298, 302
Five Ages, myth of 58 and n. 273
Flood 53, 54, 55
flower 122
fox 312 n. 19
frescoes 37, 40, see also Anatolia (Index I)
– at Çatal Hüyük 95, 101 n. 178, 104
– Minoan 136

gennetai 251 n. 328, 272
genos 247, 248, 249, 250, 251, 252, 253, 257, 259, 261 f.

geometric 282 n. 473
– art 234, 278, 310 ff.
– vases 311 f., 313
giants 312
glaukopis 43 n. 198
goat 15, 99 and n. 169, 101, 109 n. 230, 110, 111 n. 241 and n. 242, 118, 124, 171 and n. 217, 182 and n. 286, 235, 291 f., 294, 295, 299, 305
– as foster mother 111
– mountain 59
goddess 73, 91, 113, 151, 165, 179, 187, 189 f., 203, 218, 227, 230, 235, 236 ff., 265, 279, 285, 294 f., 298, 302, 303
– Anatolian 102, 304
– anthropomorphic 111, 113, 152
– armed 280
– birth giving 102 f., 104, 105, 110, 112, 113, 116, 117, 124, 125, 171, 178 f., 183, 189, 236, 285
– city 219, 285 f.
– connected with animals 102 f., 110 f., 116, 117 ff., 124 f., 145 f., 156, 158, 163, 171 ff., 180 ff., 221, 235, 305
– connected with plural figures 186 ff.
– death giving 103 f., 112, 171, 183, 285
– Dove Goddess 176, 238
– figurines of 138, 141 ff., 148 ff., 154 ff., 163, 210, 216, 218 f., 221, 282 ff.
– Great Goddess 269, 270, 287 f. and n. 513, 304
– house 305
– invocatory names of 157, 167, 180, 189, 236, 238 ff., 285, 286, 305
– of Blessing 312 n. 17
– of healing 301 n. 70
– of nature 19, 39, 74, 84, 87, 103, 110, 114, 116, 117, 118, 124, 126, 141, 143, 145, 151 f., 156, 165 ff., 169 ff., 171 ff., 189, 225, 235, 239, 285, 287 f. and n. 513, 302, 304, 305, 307, 309
– of palace 126, 143, 157, 167, 170 ff., 178, 181, 184 n. 297, 187 f., 227, 229, 236, 247, 277 f., 306
– of wild life 125
– pregnant 104 n. 198

SUBJECT INDEX 335

- protecting 173, 175, 244, 265, 306
- riding 119 n. 301 and n. 303, 310, 312
- snake 305
- Twin Goddess 102 n. 181
- universal 10
gods 2, 33, 67, 90, 129, 132, 152, 235, 238, 277, 279
- anthropomorphic 43, 107
- baetylic 92
- chthonic 90, 109, 237, 271, 286
- epic 46
- family of 35, 42, 44, 66
- Homeric 43, 46, 65
- Horse God 238
- names of 35, 50, 241
- of caves 77, 86, 87
- of city 30, 31, 37, 38, 40, 154, 182, 193 f., 203, 219, 227, 237, 244, 268, 270 f., 272, 273 ff., 285 f.
- of community 244, 265
- of corn and harvest 52, 59, 62 f.
- of family 271
- of mountain 45
- of vegetation 28, 36, see also vegetation
- Olympian 7, 28, 42, 43, 44, 65, 128, 135, 168, 176, 179 f., 189, 243 n. 291, 244, 266, 274, 276 f., 278
- origin of 48, 55 and n. 251, 59 n. 279
- own temenos 41 n. 189
- servants of 31, 40, 66, 97 n. 153, 118
- tribal 252
- youthful 187, 189
- zoomorphic 43 and n. 198, 103, 235, 238
Gorgon 279, 312
Grey Minyan Ware 3
griffin 40, 97 n. 153, 147, 278 f.

hair 291
Halaf culture 25
hands 97, 104 f.
harpe 50, 51, 52, 62, see also *drepanon*
head 302 and n. 74 and n. 75, see also male figure
Heaven 119 n. 303
- god of 56

- separation of from Earth 28, 49, 51, 52 n. 237, 54, 56, 59 and n. 279, 62 f.
hedghogs 292, 299, 300
hepetes 259, 260
hero 160, 168, 179 n. 267, 190, 191, 260, 272, 284, 313
- cult 66 n. 311, 160 f., 191, 227, 272 n. 431
- epithets 311
hetaireiai 250
hetairoi 259 f.
hieros gamos 12, 16, 34, 39, 61, 103 n. 194, 225
hippokeleuthe 311
homogalaktes 251 n. 328, 253 and n. 337, 272
honey 120
honeycomb 104 f., 119 ff.
hoplites 271
horns of consecration 82, 83, 91 and n. 111, 92, 100 f., 101 n. 178, 110, 111, 114 n. 264, 115 n. 273, 136, 143, 148, 285, 292, 294, 295, 298, 299
horse 146, 154, 187 n. 321, 312
horse
- winged 278 f., 281 n. 469

idols 9, 10, 108 n. 226, 111, 138, 147, 149 ff., 162 and n. 174, 165, 170, 210, 218 f., 224, 301
- anthropomorphic 106 f., 111 ff., 125, 223, 292, 299, 301
- armed 283
- bell shaped 143, 144, 145, 148, 285
- Cretan 102, 108, 112 ff., 232 n. 241, 291, 292
- cylindrical 113, 150, 219, 220, 221, 299
- draped 155 n. 135, 283
- fragmented 291, 292, 300
- multiform 283 ff.
- nude 155 and n. 135, 282 f.
- of cult 112 and n. 256
- part-human 106 f., 107 n. 215, 113
- "Phi" 150, 155
- "Psi" 141, 150 f.
- seated 155 n. 135, 299 n. 58
- "Tau" 150
- votive 112 and n. 256, 159, 292

– zoomorphic 112, 150, 174, 223, 292, 297, 299, 301
Indo-Europeans 2, 3, 6 f., 123, 239 f., 261 f. n. 384
– arrival of in Greece 130
– cult of 5
– elements 4
– god of 4, 59, 188, 239, 241, 264, 287 f. n. 513
– invade Babylonia 27
– languages 4, 20, 130 f.
– myth of 50
– names 134, 262
Isle of the Blest 58 n. 273, 160, see also Elysium

jewellery 208 f.

kalathos 149, 163
kama 255 n. 343
kamaewes 255 n. 343
kasignetos 250
kekemena 254 f., 256, 260 n. 375
kernos 90, 141 and n. 49, 147, 149, 163, 175 n. 241
kilims 96
king 23, 25, 31, 32 and n. 152, 36, 37, 39, 40, 65, 89, 132, 135, 172 f., 188, 229, 230, 235, 245 n. 299, 252, 264 f., 278, 306
– dead 41, 61
– divine 33, 39, 40 ff., 44, 161, 170, 173, 229 n. 231
– military 64
– owns temenos 41 n. 189, 254, 264
kingship 7, 33 f., 38, 39, 42, 45, 48, 50, 66, 249
– Eastern 33
– Egyptian 33 n. 155
– in heaven 31 f., 53
– Mesopotamian 33 n. 155, 41, 46
– Minoan 42, 44, 61
– Mycenaean 42, 43, 44, 184 n. 297
kinship 242, 246, 247, 248, 250, 253, 255, 257 n. 357, 259, 261, 270
kitimena 254 f., 256
komai 243

korete 254 n. 338, 257
kotona 254 f.
kotoneta 255, 256
kotonewe 255 n. 344
kotonooko 255, 256
kouroi 187 n. 318
ktoina 255
ktoine(a)tes 255, 256
ktoinetai 255 and n. 346, 256

labrys 37, 114 f. n. 267, see also double axe
labyrinth 37 n. 170
ladle 291
Lady 167, 180, 236, 305
land (tenure) 251 f., 253 ff., 257, 258, 278
– common 254 f.
– *damos* 256
– leased 254
– private 254 f., 256
– public 254 f.
larnax 79, 116 n. 279, 158
Lausitz Culture 208 n. 84 a
lawagetas 39, 41 n. 189, 184 and n. 297, 230, 254, 278
lawgiver 273
legs 302
leopard 99, 101, 103, 110, 117 and n. 288, 118 and n. 297
– Shrine 103, 107
libation
– tables 81, 90, 93 n. 126
– vessels 81, 90, 148, 149, 155, 163
limbs 291, 292, 300, 301 and n. 70, 302, 304
Linear A 70, 72, 86
Linear B 6, 7, 36, 38, 39, 70, 74, 87 n. 87, 132, 134, 138, 142, 146, 150, 152, 167 ff., 174 ff., 192 f., 199, 221, 235, 236, 237, 241, 253 ff., 259 ff., 264, 278, 285, 304, 305, 309, 310 f.
– Semitic loanwords in 41 n. 189
linen armour 313 n. 21
lion, lioness 40, 102, 118, 146, 147, 294, 302 n. 74, 303, 305
– head of 155
Lord 180, 186, 188 f., 236
lugal 32 n. 152

male figure 11 ff., 14, 17 f., 44, 59, 73 f., 85, 117 n. 288, 120, 125, 150, 151, 172 ff., 236, 239 f., 295 f., 303 f.
– at Çatal Hüyük 107
– at Hagia Triada 12
– at Knossos 12
– at Petsofa 12
– at Psychro 12
– connected with goddess 13, 42, 116 f., 143, 151, 158, 172 ff., 180 ff., 189 f., 235, 236, 238 f., 303, 305
– cult of 14
– head of 147, 151, 221
– in myth 13
– of vegetation 86, 124
– on rings 12
– protecting 300 f.
– riding 312
– winged 280
Master 186
– of Animals 117 n. 288, 118 n. 299, 119 n. 303, 174, 236, 281 n. 469, 304
matriarchy 131, 176 n. 244
Megaloi Theoi 284, 287 and n. 513
megaron 3, 24, 38, 136, 138, 139, 140 f., 217, 225, 231, 232, 233, 241, 246, 274
Minoan, see also religion
– archaeology 123
– art 97 n. 153, 113, 118, 121, 126, 133 f., 280, 302, 310
– chronology 70
– cult 17, 71, 75, 85, 87, 94, 114, 116, 123, 126, 137, 145, 149, 151
– daemon 118
– goddess 84, 96, 110 n. 238, 114, 118, 150 f., 179
– king 34, 89
– myth 310
– society 23, 71 f., 101 n. 178, 123, 133
– temples 76
Mistress 167, 180, 183, 189, 236, 305
– of Animals 97 n. 153, 102, 114, 117 f., 119, 125, 126, 146 f., 172 n. 218, 300, 301 ff., 304 f.

monotheism 10
monsters 51, 54, 57, 278 ff.
moon 84, 119 n. 303, 298
Mother Goddess 4, 5, 7 ff., 20, 29, 31, 33, 59 n. 276, 102, 109, 117, 187 n. 324, 304, 308 n. 2
– Anatolian 117
– as bull 119 n. 303
– as Demeter 11, 12, 240
– Eastern 183
– idols of 8 f., 102
– Minoan 110 n. 238
– Potnia 181
mountain 50
– cult of 296
– holy 96 n. 151
– Mother of 118 n. 300, 305
– peaks 290 ff.
murder 251
Mycenaean 2, 5 ff., 128 ff., 197, 202, 216, 262, see also religion
– architecture 134, 137, 145, 170, 174
– army 259
– art 126, 133 f., 149, 150, 280, 310 ff.
– citadel 37
– city 252
– collapse 6, 48, 57 n. 258, 128 ff., 152, 193 ff., 200 ff., 245, 262, 264, 265
– communities 243, 264, 278
– continuity 209
– culture 2, 5, 48, 123, 130 ff., 204 f., 263 f.
– cult vessels 137, 149
– Eastern connection 23, 35, 65, 132, 159, 168, 172
– epic 48, 311
– hierarchy 132
– king 34, 41, 43, 64 f., 235
– language 169, 199
– migration 129, 130 f., 174
– mythology 310–314
– sanctuaries 137, 154 n. 124, 156
– scribes 167
– settlements in Anatolia 22
– society 23, 36, 64, 66, 130 ff., 167 ff.
– statuettes 110 n. 238, 148, 210, 312 n. 15

– tombs 24, 93, 99, 136, 160, 165, 310, 312
– unity 134 f.
– votives 137, 155
– world 131 ff.
– writing 192 f., 238
myth 1, 14, 16, 35, 41, 62, 46, 47 n. 221, 48, 49 ff., 56, 65, 71, 109, 114, 119, 123, 135, 153, 166, 171, 191, 196, 227, 235, 239, 243 n. 291, 244, 245, 268, 274, 279 f., 287 f. n. 513, 301 n. 67, 305
– cosmogonic 56 f.
– in Mycenaean Age 310–314
– names in 311

Neolithic
– idols 9
– Revolution 8
New Year Festival 27, 32, 35, 40, 44, 61
nymphs 15, 81, 93
– Melian 62

oikos 248, 251 n. 327, and n. 328, 252, 253, 261 and n. 383
omphalos 55, 92, 120 n. 313, 308 f.
oracle 227, 276, 308 f.
orgeones 251 n. 328, 253, 261, 272
orgeonikos 260 f.
orientalizing style 313, 314
Orphics 178 n. 254, 275 and n. 445
oushebti 10, 162 n. 174
oxen 291 f.

palace 23, 25, 32, 36, 39, 72, 76, 100, 132 f., 158, 183 n. 289, 209, see also religion, shrines.
– architecture 136
– as store house 24, 36, 99
– at Alalakh 24, 36
– at Athens 38
– at Beycesultan 24
– at Bogazhkeuy 40
– at Gournia 143
– at Hagia Triada 148, 173 n. 222
– at Iolkos 201, 215
– at Kato Zakro 70
– at Knossos 36, 70, 92, 114 n. 264, 143 and n. 58, 155, 291, 296
– at Mallia 306
– at Mari 36
– at Mycenae 36, 129, 136
– at Phaistos 216
– at Pylos 24, 36, 38, 129, 136, 138
– at Tiryns 24, 38, 136
– at Ugarit 24, 35, 36
– Baal's 45
– bull in 114
– central court of 24
– commercial function of 36 f.
– cult in 78
– destruction of 193 f., 216
– frescoes in 37, 72
– goddess of 126, 167, 181, 187, 227, 229, 236, 247, 277, 278, 306
– gods of 90, 99, 132
– guardian of 65
– Minoan 24, 28, 35, 69, 72, 133, 136
– Mycenaean 24, 28, 34, 35, 37, 38, 72, 132, 136, 138, 174, 183, 231
– religious function of 37, 136
paredros 11, 16, 167, 174 f., 176 n. 243, 177, 182, 235, 238 n. 268, 287 f. n. 513, 303, 304, see also male figure, divine consort
– in Crete 12
patra 251 n. 328
patria 251 n. 328
peak sanctuaries and cult 76, 100, 126 f., 152, 237 n. 263, 290–307
Phoenician
– alphabet 192
– creation myth 51 ff., 54, 63
– epic 56, 58 n. 273
– in Crete 73
phrater 250
phratry 247, 248, 249, 250 f., 252 f., 257 and n. 358, 258, 259, 261 f., 267, 270 f., 272
– gods of 252
phyle 248 ff., 257 and n. 358, 258, 261 ff., 267
phyletes 256
phylobasileus 252, 258, 262
phylon 250

pigs 292
pillar 84, 92, 111, 187 n. 322, 294, 295, 296
– cult 309 n. 13
pit graves 206
philosophy 275, 276, 289
plague 300 f.
Ploutonion 167 n. 198
podarkes 311
podas okus 311
Polias 267 f.
Polieus 267 f., 270
polis 2, 66, 209, 229, 230, 237, 242 ff., 246 f., 248, 258, 265–276, 277, 286, 287
polos 282
polytheism 244
pomegranate 285
Posidaion 138, 183 n. 289
pre-Artemision 139, 233
priest-king 23, 28, 31, 32 n. 152, 33 and n. 155, 36, 37, 38, 42, 65 f., 172 f.
– Relief 38
– renews power 39 f. n. 185
priests 38, 40, 252, 264 ff., 276, 278
– hierarchy of 35
property rights 251 f., 253, 260
prophets 276
psyche 122
psychostasia 121
pupae 122
Pythagoreans 275

Queen 180, 305

ram 99 and n. 169, 103, 105, 110, 111 n. 241, 118, 171, 292
raven 102
religion
– Aegean 74, 109, 127, 160, 239, 296
– comparative 47, 98, 109, 132
– conservatism of 123, 129, 169, 192, 218, 219, 221, 242, 265
– Cretan 35, 71 f., 74, 123 ff., 131, 303, 305
– Eastern 35, 65, 89, 94, 101, 123, 239, 241, 281
– Greek 117, 126, 128, 237 f., 245, 246, 265, 271 ff., 278, 289, 305

– Hebrew 33
– Homeric 66 n. 311
– Minoan 36, 39, 72, 74, 75 ff., 79 ff., 85, 89, 94, 98, 101, 104, 107 ff., 121, 127, 133 f., 137, 142 ff., 149, 151, 169 ff., 174 ff., 186, 189 f., 232, 239, 241, 274, 280, 287 f. n. 513, 296, 303, 304, 305
– Mycenaean 35, 39, 48, 65, 66 n. 311, 74, 121, 126, 133 f., 137, 139, 142 ff., 149, 151, 157, 166, 169 ff., 174 ff., 186, 189, 190, 232, 239, 241, 174, 280, 287 f. n. 513, 296, 305, 308
– of community 258, 260, 277
– of family 267
– of palace 37
– of state 2, 29, 46, 267, 268, 272, 286
– popular 186, 189, 273, 275 ff.
– transmission of 247, 251
– uniformity of 28, 44 f., 48, 50, 53, 55 f., 64 ff., 72, 74, 93 f., 96, 98, 133 f., 135 f., 137, 221, 237
rhyton 81, 83, 90, 100 n. 176, 111 n. 244, 149, 155 and n. 133, 163, 171 n. 217, 221, 224, 294, 295, 296, 298, 299, 300, 305
ritual 1, 119, 123, 129, 135, 137, 148, 159, 169, 239, 268, 274, 292, 295, 296, 300, 304, 306
– apotropaeic 306
– fire 301, 302
– funerary 162
– vases 299 n. 58
rock-shelters 77, 79, 290, 298 f.

sacral knot 114 f. n. 267
sacrifice 33, 224
– burnt 81, 83, 158, 162, 165, 291
scales 121, 126, 165 n. 186, 166
seiren 281
Semitic
– language 26
Semitic
– myth 50, 57 n. 258
– settlement in Greece 22, 73
– Western 63
– words 63
seremo 281

sex 284, 287 f. n. 513
sheep 111 n. 242
shipwreck 311
shrines 36, 37, 92, 94, 100, 123, 140, 145, 148, 155, 166, 203, 290
– at Asine 170
– at Beycesultan 100 n. 172
– at Çatal Hüyük 95 ff., 107, 124 f., 126
– at Delphi 224
– at Epano Zakro 293
– at Gazi 144, 170, 219, 285
– at Gournia 143
– at Hagia Triada 148, 220
– at Juktas 290 ff., 299 f., 303
– at Karphi 145, 285, 293, 297
– at Katsamba 144
– at Kefala 143
– at Kumasa 193
– at Olympia 223
– at Petsophas 291 f., 299 f., 301 f.
– at Sparta 283
– burial in 104, 105
– domestic 75, 76, 81, 86, 90, 99, 106, 107, 112 n. 225, 113, 114, 122, 123 f., 138, 143 f., 146 ff., 151, 170 f., 178, 182 f., 237 and n. 263, 296 f., 304
– Dove Shrines 136, 299 n. 58
– in cave 117, 178, 299, 304, 306
– in palace 76, 81, 86, 90, 99, 135, 136, 148 n. 99, 178, 231, 232, 233, 237, 293, 306
– models of 231 n. 238
– offerings in 108 n. 227
– of Potnia 182
– open air 135, 142 n. 56, 233, 290
– peak 290–307
– public 143
– rural 138, 290, 296
– tripartite 136, 175 n. 236, 285, 294, 296 and n. 44
sickle 62, 63 n. 300, see also *drepanon*, *harpe*
siege-poem 47, see also Keret epic (Index I)
siren 278 ff.
skulls 96
Sky-god 5, 17, 54, 62, 239, 241, see also Weather-god, Zeus (Index I)

slaves 278
sminthos 301 n. 67
snake 58 n. 270, 102, 118, 121, 149, 171 and n. 215, 172, 178, 187, 189, 235, 237
– goddess 305
– tubes 143 f., 145, 148, 162 f., 187
soul 121 f., 126, 166
sphinx 97 n. 153, 146, 278 ff.
stag 101
stalagmites, stalactites 81 f., 84, 87, 92 and n. 121, 106 f., 107 n. 223, 110 and n. 240, 111 and n. 243; 248, 112 and n. 255, 124 f., 292
stars 298
statues 140
stoats 292
stone cult 309 n. 13
Storm-god 62, see also Weather-god
sun 84, 114, 119 n. 303, 298
synoecism 252, 258, 265, 268, 269 f.

telesta 256
telestas 256, 257 and n. 358, 260
telester 256
telesterion 140, 225, 231, 233, 274
telestes 256
teletes 256
temenos 41 n. 189, 81, 83, 254, 264, 291 f., 295, 297
temple 23, 26, 28 f., 32, 33, 35, 36, 38, 41 n. 189, 45, 76, 138, 139, 140 ff. and n. 53, 146, 155 ff., 191, 218, 219, 222, 223 f., 226 f., 230, 233, 237
– administration of 35
– architecture of 230 ff., 278
– at Athens (Dionysus) 274
– at Bassae 270
– at Delphi 309
– at Mycenae 37
– models of 142 f., 231
tereta 254 n. 338, 255, 256
theocratic society 7, 24, 25, 35, 40, 41 n. 189, 46, 60, 65 f., 193, 268
theogony 7, 30, 45, 47, 48, 50, 58
theos, *theoi* 176 and n. 244, 180 n. 271, 235, 259 and n. 371, 287 f. n. 513

theoxenia 188 n. 326
tholos 90, 158 f., 162, 164, 206 f., 214 n. 120
titanomachy 51
Tonaia festival 225
tortoise 292
tradition, oral 193, 195 ff., 200
tree 74, 83 f., 115 n. 273, 171, 295, 298, 303
– cult of 91 and n. 112, 178, 186, 296
tribes 66, 69, 242, 246, 248, 251, 252 f., 257, 259, 260, 265, 266 f., 272
trisheros 175 f. n. 242, 260 f. and n. 380, 272 n. 431
tritopator 175 f. n. 242
tritopatreis 252, 260 f. n. 380
trittyes 248, 267
Trojan War 193, 195, 197, 209, 262, 263
tyrants 270, 273 ff.

Ubaid culture 25

vegetation
– annual cycle of 32, 60 f., 64, 74, 75, 110, 112, 114, 117, 119 f., 122, 124, 141, 158, 166, 179, 235, 237, 274, 304, 306
– cult of 5, 11, 15, 25, 35, 43, 75 ff., 77, 81, 85, 86 f., 89 f., 103, 104 ff., 134, 165 ff., 186, 275, 278, 309
– gods of 28, 30, 31, 36, 56, 59 ff., 88 f.,

103, 110, 165 ff., 169 ff., 225, 304, 309
– powers of 62
– symbol of 16, 88
vermin 292, 299, 300 f.
votive offerings 299, 301
vulture 96 f., 102, 104 n. 195, 105
– Shrine 107

wanasoi 175 f.
wanassa 180, 182, 189, 238, 305
wanax 34, 39, and n. 185, 42, 168 and n. 201, 169, 170, 172, 180 ff., 184 n. 297, 185 ff., 229, 230, 235, 236, 237, 238, 248, 254, 265 f., 287 f. n. 513
war, of gods and giants 312
Warrior-god 85, 188
wastu 138, 183 n. 289
weasel 292, 299, 300
– cult of 301 n. 67
Weather-god 4, 14, 22, 34 n. 160, 44 f., 50, 53 ff., 56, 59 n. 276, 60 n. 284, 241
– as Nerik 106 n. 211
– in theogonic myth 31, 43, 52 f.
– on mountain 45
winds, priestess of 176 n. 246
worokijonejo 260
writing 192 f.

ziggurat 29, 45

III. INDEX OF MODERN AUTHORS

Adcock, F. A. 249
Aistleitner, J. 41
Åkerström, A. 147
Alexiou, St. 11, 102, 144, 151
Ålin, P. 130 f., 147, 154, 156, 212 ff., 222, 223
Amandry, P. 224
Andrewes, A. 194, 226, 231, 240, 242, 248, 249, 250, 251, 259, 261, 272
Andronikos, M. 203
Astour, M. 24, 32, 41, 58, 73
Aström, P. 212

Barnett, R. 63
Banti, L. 142, 148, 233, 280, 310
Baumbach, L. 87, 116, 172, 175 f., 240, 254, 255, 258 f.
Bennett, E. L. 16 f.
Benton, S. 217
Bethe, E. 139
Bianchi, U. 48, 59, 227, 245
Biesantz, H. 13, 121, 296, 303
Blegen, C. W. 38, 159, 169, 295
Boardman, J. 22, 73, 82, 83, 115, 219, 225, 229, 232, 234, 267, 279, 283, 286, 312

INDEX OF MODERN AUTHORS

Borda, M. 280
Bossert, H. Th. 99
Bowra, C. M. 311
Boyd-Hawes, H. 143
Branigan, K. 90, 162, 292, 300, 306
Brown, W. E. 254, 255, 256, 260
Buchholz, H. G. 101
Buck, C. D. 198
Burkert, W. 16, 103, 116, 198
Buschor, E. 154
Busolt, G. 249

Calhoun, G. 184
Cary, M. 249, 259
Carpenter, R. 48, 202
Carratelli, C. P. 168, 176, 181, 258, 310
Caskey, J. L. V. 3, 140, 203, 218
Cassola, F. 311
Chadwick, J. 41, 87, 116, 167, 172, 175 f., 181, 192, 198, 240, 254, 255, 256, 258 f., 260 f., 311
Charbonneaux, J. 174
Chapouthier, F. 187, 284
Childe, V. G. 24
Coldstream, J. N. 234, 243, 282, 313
Condoleon, N. M. 217, 218
Cook, A. B. 16, 114, 116, 120, 173, 290, 297, 303
Cornford, F. M. 184

Dakaris, S. 263
Dawkins, R. M. 80, 210, 220
Deiters, P. 87
Demangel, R. 156
Demargne, P. 87, 208, 231, 312
Desborough, V. R. d'A. 131, 132, 134 ff., 139 ff., 144 ff., 153, 156, 163, 170, 194 f., 201, 202, 204 ff., 208, 210, 212 ff., 222 ff., 226, 280, 282
Deshayes, J. 204, 207, 209
Deubner, L. 184
Dhorme, E. 43
Diamant, S. 101
Dirlmeier, F. 46, 63
Dodds, E. R. 278
Dornseiff, F. 56

Dörpfeld, W. 188
Dow, S. 195
Drerup, H. 231
Dunbabin, T. J. 192
Dussaud, R. 45, 51, 55, 63

Effenterre, H. van 41, 158
Ehrenberg, V. 3, 222, 240, 271, 273, 276, 310
Eisfeldt, O. 41
Erbse, H. 47, 59
Evans, A. 37, 38, 41, 69 ff., 74, 76, 77, 80, 84, 88, 92, 100, 109, 110, 119, 121, 122, 130, 145 f., 151, 162, 170 f., 280, 290 ff., 297, 300, 312
Evans, J. D. 24, 73, 94, 123, 240

Faure, P. 15, 78, 80, 82, 84, 85, 86 f., 88, 89, 92, 93, 108, 109, 110, 111, 290 ff., 297, 298, 299, 305, 307
Ferguson, W. S. 249
Fontenrose, J. 57
Forrer, E. 48, 60
Forrest, W. G. 224
Forsdyke, E. J. 110
Fowler, O. H. N. 177
Frankfort, H. 26, 31, 32, 34, 43, 45, 60, 97
French, D. H. 3, 4, 23, 240
French, E. 151
Frisk, H. 257
Frödin, O. 147, 207
Fryer-Schauenburg, B. 225
Furtwängler, A. 157
Furumark, A. 17, 39, 131, 133, 150, 152 f.

Gadd, C. J. 32
Gardner, E. A. 249, 259
Gaster, T. H. 15, 60, 106
Georgiev, V. I. 20
Ginsberg, H. L. 51
Glotz, G. 10, 114, 249
Goldman, H. 203
Gordon, C. H. 22, 41, 46, 47
Götze, A. 34
Grace, F. R. 220
Gray, D. H. F. 311

INDEX OF MODERN AUTHORS

Gray, J. 22, 23, 33, 35, 40, 292
Graziosī, P. 94
Griffith, J. G. 62
Grimal, P. 313
Grumach, E. 169, 199
Guarducci, M. 249
Gurney, O. R. 40, 46, 60, 302
Güterbock, H. G. 30, 48, 49, 50, 52, 53, 54, 57, 58, 60, 63
Guthrie, W. K. C. 65, 114, 168, 176, 179, 181, 274, 275, 276, 305

Haag, H. 46
Hadzisteliou-Price, T. 283
Hägg, R. 212
Hainsworth, J. B. 265
Halbherr, F. 85
Hall, E. H. 219
Hammond, N. G. L. 195, 197, 198, 249, 262 f., 264
Hammond-Tooke, D. 253
Hampe, R. 310
Harrison, J. 120, 189, 228
Hausmann, W. 199
Hazzidakis, J. 78, 82, 84, 108
Heitsch, E. 47
Hemberg, B. 175, 177, 185, 186 f., 260 f., 272, 286 f., 288
Herter, H. 49
Heubeck, A. 46, 47, 48, 54, 58, 135, 154, 176
Higgins, R. A. 150, 155, 208, 218, 219, 221, 225
Hignett, C. 249
Hillis, W. B. 276
Hölscher, U. 49, 58, 63
Homann-Wedeking, E. 274, 311, 312
Hood, M. S. F. 3, 10, 24, 92, 143, 158, 240, 261, 306
Hooke, S. H. 29, 32, 35, 60
Hooker, J. T. 70
Howell, R. J. 240
Hutchinson, R. W. 14, 16, 24, 92, 143, 144, 158, 293, 297, 299, 300, 304, 307

Jacob, E. 55
Jawad, A. J. 31, 43

Karageorghis, V. 280
Karo, G. 134, 136, 159, 160, 280
Kenna, V. G. 302
Keramopoullos, A. 214
Kinch, K. F. 144
Kirk, G. S. 4
Klengel, H. 31
Körte, A. 167
Kraiker, W. 205
Kramer, S. N. 26, 30, 33, 49, 58
Kretschmer, P. 64, 117
Kübler, K. 205

Lacy, A. D. 204
Lämmli, F. 48
Lang, M. 265
Latte, K. 248, 249, 250, 251
Lejeune, M. 176, 181, 185, 281
Lenzen, H. 29
Leon, V. 215
Lerat, L. 138, 155, 156
Lesley, A. 46, 48, 63
Lévèque, P. 235, 240, 281
Levi, D. 144, 147, 175, 210, 216, 219, 220, 280, 283, 284 ff., 306, 312
Lorimer, H. L. 7, 207

Macqueen, J. G. 4, 22, 59
Maiuri, A. 178
Malten, L. 114, 185, 279
Marinatos, S. 3, 4, 78, 80, 84, 85, 120, 139, 144, 146, 160, 296, 306
Matz, F. 24, 77, 80, 90, 93, 111, 113, 118, 119, 120, 149, 171
Mavriyannaki, C. 208
McDonald, W. 215
Mellaart, J. 8, 9, 11, 22, 24, 25, 73, 94 ff., 109, 120, 171
Mollard-Besques, S. 150, 220
Morenz, S. 11
Mortgaat, A. 48
Mühlestein, H. 281
Müller, K. 231
Müller, M. 69
Murray, G. 278
Mylonas, G. E. 119, 130, 140 f., 146, 159,

160, 165, 166, 167, 194 f., 204, 225, 231, 233, 242, 266, 282, 284, 288, 312
Myres, J. L. 290, 297, 300, 301

Nicholls, R. 142, 143, 144, 150 f., 210, 219, 221, 233, 280
Nilsson, M. P. 5, 10, 11, 13, 14 f., 16, 17, 19, 37, 38, 41, 45, 58, 62, 65, 71, 74, 76, 79, 80, 83, 87, 89, 90, 91, 97, 108, 109, 110, 111, 112, 113, 114, 115, 116, 117, 118, 119, 121, 122, 138 f., 144, 146 f., 151, 153, 160, 162, 166, 170 f., 175, 186 f., 222, 224, 225, 226, 229, 240, 243, 262, 263, 266, 269, 270, 272, 279, 280, 287 f., 292, 296, 299, 301, 309, 310 f., 313
Nixon, J. G. 192, 263
Numazawa, F. K. 52, 59

Ohli, D. 225
Otten, H. 27, 58

Page, D. 306
Palmer, L. R. 138, 168, 175 f., 181, 254, 256, 257 ff., 260
Paris, P. 222
Parke, H. W. 223, 224, 263, 308
Papadimitriou, I. 155, 222
Pendlebury, J. D. S. 145, 216, 290, 291, 293
Perdrizet, P. 138, 155
Pernier, L. 148
Persson, A. W. 38, 75, 91, 99, 114, 119, 120, 144, 147, 151, 157, 160, 207, 214, 284, 305
Pestalozza, U. 178, 238, 287
Pettazzoni, R. 1, 7, 129, 237, 242, 277
Picard, C. 10, 13, 76, 85, 88, 92, 97, 108, 110, 112, 119, 120, 121, 160, 162, 173, 174, 187, 284, 310
Pini, I. 158, 159, 165
Plassart, A. 93, 144
Platon, N. 70, 76, 92, 290, 293, 294, 300, 304
Pohlenz, M. 64
Pollard, J. 280
Popham, M. 70, 143
Porzig, W. 57, 58, 198
Poulsen, F. 155

Preller, L. 15, 109
Press, L. 294, 295, 296
Pritchard, J. B. 48
Privitera, G. A. 238
Puhvel, J. 168, 169, 182, 184

Renfrew, C. 4, 20, 240
Richter, G. M. A. 220, 232, 311
Risch, E. 198
Rizza, G. 210, 218, 219, 279, 280, 282, 283, 284 f., 286, 288
Rohde, E. 276
Rose, H. J. 275
Rutkowski, B. 295, 297, 306 f.
Rutter, J. 101

Sacconi, A. 176, 310, 311, 312
Saggs, H. W. F. 27, 30 f., 32, 34, 45
Sakellariou, M. B. 195, 196
Santerre, G. de 139, 218
Schachermeyr, F. 2, 3, 19, 20 f., 24, 36, 72, 76, 88, 100, 101, 102, 110, 114, 115, 120, 123, 124, 131, 171, 177, 240, 241, 268, 280, 290, 306 f.
Schaeffer, C. F. A. 24
Scharff, A. 48
Schliemann, H. 69, 99, 121, 130, 160, 240
Schmidt, J. 57
Schmökel, H. 30
Schröder, F. R. 180
Schwabl, H. 48, 50, 51, 52, 53, 55, 56, 57, 61, 62, 63
Scrinari, F. S. M. 210, 279, 280, 288
Séchan, L. 235, 281
Severyns, A. 245
Simpson, R. H. 212, 215, 216, 222, 223, 282
Skeat, T. C. 201
Snodgrass, A. M. 262
Speiser, E. A. 51
Starr, C. G. 129, 131, 132, 159, 191, 203, 204, 213, 227, 231, 234, 240, 242, 264 f., 278, 280, 287, 307
Staudacher, W. 52, 59
Steiner, G. 53, 54
Stella, L. A. 39, 40, 46, 173, 176, 254, 261
Stubbings, F. H. 152, 193, 208

Studniczka, F. 117, 170
Styrenius, C. G. 199, 206, 207, 212, 213, 214, 215, 223, 224
Swoboda, H. 249

Taramelli, A. 79, 82, 297
Taylour, L. W. 2, 3, 37, 131, 138, 142, 164, 166, 210, 233
Thomson, G. 246, 249, 259
Travlos, J. 141
Tsountas, C. 99 f.

Ucko, P. J. 10, 113
Usener, H. 190

Valmin, N. 147
Vatin, C. 228
Ventris, M. 41, 172, 175 f., 254, 258 f., 260 f., 311
Vercouttes, J. 282
Verdelis, N. M. 214
Vermeule, E. T. 20, 23, 140, 164, 165, 166, 175, 207, 212, 213, 217, 223, 225, 230, 240, 282, 310
Vian, F. 57

Wace, A. J. B. 130, 159, 174, 192, 207
Wade-Gery, H. T. 249
Walcot, P. 48, 49, 57
Warren, P. 6, 9, 24, 36, 72, 73, 113, 128
Webster, T. B. L. 2, 33, 36, 37, 39, 40, 41, 46, 47, 52, 174, 192, 195, 208, 216, 217, 218, 225, 228, 229, 260, 266, 311, 312
West, M. L. 15, 16, 17, 48, 49, 50, 53, 57, 58, 61
Wide, S. 214
Wiesner, J. 161, 192, 194, 223, 225, 268, 284, 288, 313
Wilamowitz, U. 1, 49, 185
Willetts, R. F. 38, 41, 42, 61, 77, 80, 82, 87, 88, 91, 105, 109, 111, 112, 114, 119, 171, 298, 300, 305, 309
Winter, F. W. 283
Witzel, P. M. 29
Woolley, L. 24
Wormell, D. E. W. 308

Xanthoudides, S. 90, 162, 163

Yalouris, N. 215

Zafiropoulo, J. 120, 121
Zervos, C. 80